Virtual Holocaust Memory

Virtual Holocaust Memory

MATTHEW BOSWELL AND ANTONY ROWLAND

OXFORD
UNIVERSITY PRESS

Oxford University Press is a department of the University of Oxford. It furthers the University's objective of excellence in research, scholarship, and education by publishing worldwide. Oxford is a registered trade mark of Oxford University Press in the UK and certain other countries.

Published in the United States of America by Oxford University Press
198 Madison Avenue, New York, NY 10016, United States of America.

Library of Congress Cataloging-in-Publication Data
Names: Boswell, Matthew, 1979– author. | Rowland, Antony, author.
Title: Virtual Holocaust memory / Matthew Boswell and Antony Rowland.
Description: [New York] : Oxford University Press, [2023] |
Includes bibliographical references and index.
Identifiers: LCCN 2022035009 (print) | LCCN 2022035010 (ebook) |
ISBN 9780197645390 (hardback) | ISBN 9780197645406 (paperback) |
ISBN 9780197645420 (epub)
Subjects: LCSH: Holocaust, Jewish (1939–1945) in mass media. |
Holocaust, Jewish (1939–1945)—Electronic information resources. |
Holocaust memorials—Interpretive programs—Moral and ethical aspects. |
Memorialization—Moral and ethical aspects.
Classification: LCC D804.3.B675 2023 (print) | LCC D804.3 (ebook) |
DDC 940.53/18—dc23/eng/20220802
LC record available at https://lccn.loc.gov/2022035009
LC ebook record available at https://lccn.loc.gov/2022035010

DOI: 10.1093/oso/9780197645390.001.0001

1 3 5 7 9 8 6 4 2

Paperback printed by Marquis, Canada
Hardback printed by Bridgeport National Bindery, Inc., United States of America

I'm certainly no Luddite. The whole drift of my mind is pretty clearly stated in my work; basically, one has to immerse oneself in the threatening possibilities offered by modern science and technology, and try to swim to the other end of the pool.[1]

—J. G. Ballard

Today, I am not sure that what I wrote is true.
I am certain it is truthful.[2]

—Charlotte Delbo

Contents

Acknowledgments   ix

Introduction: Holocaust Memory Culture, 2001–2049   1

PART I: INTERACTIVE VIDEO TESTIMONY

1. Entering Dimensions in Testimony   35
2. Ghosting the Museum   61
3. Witness in the Light Stage   83

PART II: READING THE VIRTUAL

4. Virtual Landscapes   119
5. The Virtual Anne Frank   151
6. The Topography of Terror and Resistance to the Virtual   182

Conclusion   202

Notes   215
Bibliography   261
Index   271

Acknowledgments

We would like to thank the following individuals and organizations who generously engaged with us while we researched this book over many years. We are indebted to them for talking with such openness and passion about the projects and institutions that are shaping this new era of Holocaust memory culture. Sincere thanks to Stephen D. Smith, Kia Hays, and colleagues at the USC Shoah Foundation; Heather Smith at Conscience Display; the Museum of Jewish Heritage, New York; the United States Holocaust Memorial Museum; Stephanie Billib at the Bergen-Belsen Memorial; Iris Groschek at the Neuengamme Concentration Camp Memorial; Bas Kortholt at Camp Westerbork Memorial Centre; Tom Brink and Gerrit Netten at the Anne Frank House; Syste Wierenga and Paul Verschure at SPECS-Lab; Thomas Lutz at the Topography of Terror; Richard Freedman, Tali Nates, and colleagues at the South African Holocaust and Genocide Foundation; James Griffiths and colleagues at The National Holocaust Centre and Museum; and Chris Walker at Bright White.

We are also grateful to the following for conversations and insights that informed this book in a range of vital ways: Eva Schloss, Pinchas Gutter, Danny Abrahms, Robert Eaglestone, Tim Cole, Jay Prosser, John Whale, John McLeod, Lizzie Oliver, Matthew Whittle, Dale Townshend, Kara Critchell, Tom Jackson, Alberto Giordano, Barney Heywood, and Lucy Telling.

We gratefully acknowledge the support of the Arts and Humanities Research Council for two grants that facilitated research for this book at critical periods.

Finally, we would like to thank Norm Hirschy, Sean Decker, and their colleagues at Oxford University Press for supporting this project and expertly steering us through to publication.

Introduction

Holocaust Memory Culture, 2001–2049

As digital technologies transform all aspects of contemporary life at a speed approaching "the limits of the acceleration of reality," propelled by what Paul Virilio calls "turbo-capitalism," memories of the Holocaust that once seemed familiar, pervasive, and durable are being comprehensively refashioned.[1] The cultural memory of the Holocaust still incorporates images and narratives that originated in predigital media such as black-and-white film and photography, captured through devices such as the portable DeVry Standard cine cameras used by the British Army Film and Photographic Unit to record the liberation of Bergen-Belsen and other wartime events.[2] Yet newer technologies are continually modifying and repurposing the archive they created. For example, the evolution of the mass media in the late twentieth century turned Holocaust memory into an increasingly spectacular, Technicolor phenomenon. With Hollywood playing a particularly influential role in the uplift of Holocaust consciousness during the 1980s and 1990s, scholarly debates turned to topics such as the globalization, industrialization, commodification, and trivialization of Holocaust memory. The rapid expansion of digital culture and the internet at the turn of the millennium then provided the foundations for the next major transformation of the textures, trajectories, and structures of Holocaust memory that we explore in this book. What Zygmunt Bauman identifies as the "heavy," "solid," and hardware-focused era of modernity gave way to the "light," software-focused era of postmodernity.[3] As we moved into the twenty-first century, communication technologies such as social media became ubiquitous and "the linear media of the 1980s" were, as Wulf Kansteiner observes, "rapidly reframed and displaced by interactive digital networks."[4] Media such as film, television, and books still profoundly shape the cultural memory of the Holocaust. However, immersive technologies such as virtual reality (VR) and augmented reality (AR) are increasingly providing the public with their portals to the past. Participatory narratives are preferred to linear ones. Readers and

Virtual Holocaust Memory. Matthew Boswell and Antony Rowland, Oxford University Press. © Oxford University Press 2023. DOI: 10.1093/oso/9780197645390.003.0001

viewers have become users. The currency of the age is data. In Holocaust studies, these shifts were reflected in the focus of the edited collection *Probing the Ethics of Holocaust Culture* (2016), which revisited Saul Friedländer's seminal collection of essays, *Probing the Limits of Representation: Nazism and the "Final Solution"* (1992). Returning to themes and debates that had dominated Friedländer's collection a quarter of a century earlier, such as narrative theory, cultural representation, and the threat of relativization and revisionism, *Probing the Ethics of Holocaust Culture* also included essays on topics such as GIS mapping, digital archives, and algorithms that would have doubtlessly perplexed Friedländer and his contemporaries.[5]

With so many new communicative and archival possibilities emerging, the 2010s was a pivotal decade for institutions engaged in the safeguarding of Holocaust memory. Working in a highly challenging political, social, and ecological context, such institutions became increasingly willing to explore the ways in which emerging digital technologies might facilitate new forms of emotional and pedagogical engagement with events that were quickly receding in historical time. One of the most arresting examples, which serves as a central case study in this book, is Dimensions in Testimony, led by the University of Southern California (USC) Shoah Foundation, which uses 360-degree film recording and natural language processing to produce what the Foundation has variously described as "interactive video testimony" and "interactive biography." By the end of the decade, Dimensions in Testimony had already been installed in museums in the United States and China, allowing visitors to hold what a 2016 USC Shoah Foundation publicity leaflet calls a "virtual conversation" with recordings of survivors who are viewed through advanced display technologies in either a two-dimensional or three-dimensional form, with the latter constituting what would popularly be understood as a hologram.[6]

Often controversial, technologically sophisticated reimaginings of Holocaust memory culture such as Dimensions in Testimony have been invested with a sense of heightened urgency by the prospect of the period of living Holocaust memory coming to an end. Organizations working on Holocaust digital memory project in the 2010s were acutely aware that soon there would be no new Holocaust testimony and no living survivors (or perpetrators or bystanders) to share their experiences in person. The irreversible chronologies to which technological development and survivor mortality inevitably adhere meant that what we characterize as an age of connectivity was also, so far as Holocaust memory culture is concerned, very much an age of anxiety, not least because there was only a very limited window within which to engage survivors with these new memory projects. As Marianne Hirsch writes: "The Shoah Foundation's massive investment in creating slick, life-like projections for an interactive encounter is the most recent symptom of a long-standing anxiety: What happens to the story of the Holocaust when the last survivors die out? How will it be remembered?"[7]

Between 2008 and 2018—the specific period spanned by our case studies—the pace at which digital technologies transformed Holocaust memory culture was truly staggering. In the space of a decade, we witnessed the evolution from what we might now regard as the digital primitivism of online "virtual worlds" such as Second Life—we discuss the United States Holocaust Memorial Museum's (USHMM) Kristallnacht exhibition in the fourth chapter—to immersive, interactive projects such as Dimensions in Testimony and 360-degree VR experiences produced by influential institutions such as the Anne Frank House. Even as more traditional museum exhibitions continue to have a profound effect on the ways in which the Holocaust is remembered, immersive technologies and social media are making institutional engagement with that history increasingly interactive, embodied, and experiential. They are also helping to reconfigure the ways in which members of the public engage with the physical spaces of Holocaust memory. Many memorial sites, including Auschwitz-Birkenau, now offer "virtual tours" via their websites, making use of three-dimensional photography and similar technologies to guide people around their estates via their home computers and mobile devices. In our fourth chapter, we discuss how the Bergen-Belsen memorial site is even experimenting with AR apps for iPads to enhance the experience of on-site visitors.

Such uses of digital technology as a tool for Holocaust remembrance have proven to be highly contentious, with passionate advocates and dissenters on both sides of the debate. Those who take a more cynical view tend to feel that mobile technologies and social media apps allow people to transgress on the sacred ground of Holocaust memory rather too glibly. This view prevailed in the mainstream media coverage of the online controversy that erupted when an Alabamian teenager, Breanna Mitchell, tweeted a smiling selfie that she had taken at Auschwitz in 2014.[8] Satirizing this phenomenon, in 2017 the artist and comedian Shahak Shapira's online project Yolocaust invited those visiting his website to scroll over selfies taken by tourists at Berlin's Monument to the Murdered Jews of Europe, only to reveal graphic images of the dead Jews whom Shapira understood the monument's stelae to represent.[9] Similar concerns about the deleterious impact of technology on Holocaust memory were raised by the renowned scholar Geoffrey Hartman at the turn of the millennium. Reflecting on the future of oral histories of the Holocaust, Hartman worried about the "opening towards popular culture" being "as ominous as Pandora's Box," asking, "What if we can soon tap into thousands of such witness accounts through an access technology that allows video-on-demand?"[10]

Anxieties such as Hartman's owe much to traditions of skepticism about technology that have marked liberal schools of political philosophy and cultural theory since the 1960s. Sean F. Johnston cites texts such as Rachel Carson's critique of the chemical industry, *Silent Spring* (1962), and Herbert Marcuse's dissection of advanced consumer capitalism, *One-Dimensional Man* (1964), as contributing to a tradition of distrust of technologized modernity that drew on a wide variety of disciplinary perspectives: "What these diverse books shared was an increasingly critical vision of modern culture, identifying our faith in technologies and progress as a key failing."[11] Acclaimed works of science fiction added to the generally dystopian view of new technologies that emerged in the 1960s, none more so than Stanley Kubrick's iconic *2001: A Space Odyssey* (1968), with a screenplay by Kubrick and Arthur C. Clarke inspired by Clarke's short story "The Sentinel" (1951). In Kubrick's film, an artificial intelligence (AI) computer, HAL 9000, turns homicidal while operating a doomed mission to Jupiter. AI is represented as a threat to the basic category of the human, generating a crisis that warps the fabric of space and time. The film reflects the way that science fiction of this period also commonly associates technological progress with political conspiracies and corrupt capitalist companies. The mission to Jupiter follows the discovery of a strange monolith on the moon, which has been covered up by the United States National Council of Astronautics, and much has been made of the fact that the acronym HAL is displaced by just one letter from IBM. The company, who were consulted on the film, allegedly refused to let Kubrick use their logo when he described HAL in a letter as a "psychotic computer."[12]

Concerns about technological progress also informed dominant cultural theories of the late twentieth century, most notably postmodernism, with critics such as Jean Baudrillard arguing that technologized modernity was a "hyperreal" dystopia: one in which there is "more and more information, and less and less meaning," indeed an "immense process of the destruction of meaning."[13] But, as Johnston observes, as the twentieth century wore on, cultural articulations of the relationship between (post)modernity and technology increasingly presented visions of the future—and critiques of the present—in which dystopian and utopian elements combined. In the 2020s, growing comfort with technological innovation and a broadening consensus about the role it must play in safeguarding societies from existential threats such as the climate crisis contrast with the more pervasive cynicism of the late 1960s and films such as *2001* that captured the prevailing zeitgeist. Times are changing, and contemporary science fiction films and television programs rarely offer a view of technology through a wholly dystopian lens. For example, *Blade Runner 2049* (2017), the sequel to Ridley Scott's 1982 film *Blade Runner* (based on Dick's 1968 novel, *Do Androids Dream of Electric Sheep?*), embodies human virtue almost entirely in its nonhuman characters. The film features a hologram with AI, Joi, played by Ana de Armas, who at one point takes possession of the body of a human being so that she can make love to her bioengineered "replicant" boyfriend, Officer K, played by Ryan Gosling, who has been tasked with the destruction of an earlier generation of less sophisticated replicants. Also featuring a hologram of Elvis playing in the ruins of a Las Vegas auditorium—perhaps representing the ruin of the consumerist culture and also the *thinking* of the sixties and seventies—*Blade Runner 2049* charts a journey from the hyperreal to the real, with hologram and replicant alike being humanized through emotions and acts that are recognizably those of creatures with souls. As the 2010s progressed, films and television series from *Blade Runner* to *Westworld* (2016–)—a protracted, posthuman bloodbath in which android "hosts" face a Darwinian struggle for survival in a Wild West–themed amusement park—became increasingly sympathetic in their representations of the evolution of nonhuman consciousness; for example, by exploring the possibility of authentic emotional connections between human and nonhuman beings. Indeed, the ending of the first *Blade Runner* film could be regarded as a cultural turning point away from *2001* and toward its own sequel, with Harrison Ford's human character—the former policeman turned bounty hunter, Rick Deckard—driving into the sunset with his replicant lover, Rachael, played by Sean Young. This comes shortly after another replicant, Rutger Hauer's Roy Batty, saves Deckard's life and delivers a monologue about memory and the nonhuman witnessing of traumatic histories that Mark Rowlands describes as "perhaps the most moving death soliloquy in cinematic history":

> I've seen things you people wouldn't believe. Attack ships on fire off
> the shoulder of Orion. I watched C-beams glitter in the dark near the
> Tannhäuser Gate. All those moments will be lost in time, like tears in rain.
> Time to die.[14]

In these contemporary science fiction films and television series, advanced technological evolution is no longer simply "psychotic" and dysfunctional; rather, it is a human story in an altogether more sympathetic mode, where nonhuman beings such as androids have much to teach the humans they increasingly resemble.

Frequently characterized by the humanism of the *Blade Runner* films rather than the cynicism of *2001* and postmodernists such as Baudrillard, the digital Holocaust memory projects discussed in this book reflect cultural aspirations and anxieties that arise through the entanglement of diverse factors including the institutionalization of Holocaust memory culture, the approaching end of the period of living Holocaust memory, the development of technologies that draw together human and nonhuman agency, and the complex political and economic drivers of rapid technological innovation. In exploring this decisive cultural moment, our objective is to trace the general direction of travel of Holocaust memory culture as it undergoes a digitally powered paradigm shift, focusing on the period from 2008 to 2018 as a pivotal, transitional decade. Rather than making definitive judgments about the value of projects that form early case studies for an emergent virtual Holocaust memory culture that remains in its infancy, we propose new ways of thinking about how the value and integrity of such projects might be secured in the future as immersive technologies and digital culture mature.

Our first three chapters focus on the early years of Dimensions in Testimony, exploring how institutions such as the USC Shoah Foundation are refashioning Holocaust memory culture through the pioneering use of technologies such as holographic displays, natural language processing, and machine learning. This project forms a fitting in-depth point of departure for this study, as the Foundation has done more than any other to bring Holocaust memory into the digital age. Even in 2002, Hartman's concerns about "an access technology that allows video-on-demand" were in the process of being realized through the Visual History Archive (VHA), which was first established by the organization's founder, Steven Spielberg, in 1994, following the release of *Schindler's List* (1993). At the time of writing, the VHA contains over 55,000 video testimonies and is the largest such archive in the world.[15] Significantly, in recent years the archive has expanded to include testimonies relating to the Armenian Genocide, the Nanjing Massacre, the 1994 Genocide Against the Tutsi in Rwanda, and the Guatemalan Genocide.

As more testimonies have been added to the VHA, digital technology has enabled the Foundation to advance its educational mission. It has given access to the VHA to a global community of learners through online resources such as the IWitness platform. Through a major project that ran between 2008 and 2012, the Foundation honored its commitment to preserve the testimony of survivors in perpetuity by copying all the original VHA interviews from video tape (which has a life expectancy of around twenty years) onto a digital format.[16] The files are now constantly being recopied by robots to ensure their quality never degrades. The Foundation is also using digital technologies to restore badly damaged video testimonies, overcoming previously insoluble problems such as flickering, non-existent visuals, and poor audio quality.[17] Moreover, the demands of Holocaust memory have led them to develop their own cutting-edge technological innovations, with Chief Technology Officer Sam Gustman filing ten separate patents between 1996 and 2002 for the VHA information architecture.[18] These have subsequently been referenced by more than seventy other patents filed by companies including Xerox and Microsoft.[19]

Since the mid-2010s, the Foundation has also been developing a portfolio of immersive technology projects, such as Dimensions in Testimony, that sit alongside the VHA, allowing new generations to engage with testimony in increasingly sophisticated virtual environments. In 2016, the Foundation began filming survivor testimony in 360-degrees at locations such as the former Mauthausen concentration camp. Extending the scope of the screen-based VHA platform, testimonies filmed in 360-degrees have the potential to be used in a range of immersive environments in the future. The Foundation then launched its first VR film, *The Last Goodbye*, in 2017, in which the Holocaust survivor Pinchas Gutter (who also gave the first Dimensions in Testimony interview) takes viewers on an immersive tour of the Majdanek death camp, where he was imprisoned during the war and where his parents and sister were murdered.[20] The first room-scale VR film to include testimony by a Holocaust survivor, *The Last Goodbye* was premiered at the Tribeca Film Festival and subsequently screened at a number of festivals and museums, including the Illinois Holocaust Museum and Education Center and the Museum of Jewish Heritage in New York (see Chapter 2).

VR films such as *The Last Goodbye* and visualization tools such as the VR model used to assist with the prosecution of a former Auschwitz-Birkenau guard in a trial in Germany in 2016, making it possible to know what the defendant would have been able to see from his watchtower, have ensured that Holocaust memory has been at the forefront of what has widely been regarded as a watershed moment for the VR industry.[21] The arrival of affordable headsets on the mass market in the mid-2010s coincided with the release of a number of important VR documentary films tackling serious humanitarian and social issues. These included three films commissioned as part of the United Nations Virtual Reality (UNVR) series: *Clouds Over Sidra* (2015), which explores a Jordanian refugee camp during the Syrian refugee crisis in 2014; *Waves of Grace* (2015), which centers on the outbreak of Ebola in Liberia in 2015; and *My Mother's Wing* (2016), which recounts a young Palestinian mother's experience of coping with the loss of two of her children during the Israeli airstrikes on Gaza in 2014. Other notable humanitarian VR films released in 2016 tackled issues such as the UK's immigration detention centers (*Invisible*), the Calais "Jungle" refugee and migrant encampment (*Home: Aamir*), nuclear disaster (*Chernobyl VR Project*), and solitary confinement (*6x9*). The most famous icon of the Holocaust, Anne Frank, also features prominently in this evolving virtual landscape. As we outline in Chapter 5, Frank has been the subject of online applications, VR tours of the "secret annex" produced by the Anne Frank House, and a VR film in which the viewer can mingle with the annex's trapped inhabitants.

"The Ultimate Empathy Machine"

While researching this book, we have not found any evidence to suggest that those driving these diverse digital memory projects deploy technologies such as VR simply for technology's sake, as is sometimes assumed. However, more revealingly, we have frequently encountered the fervent commitment of the Holocaust museum and education sectors to a master narrative which holds that immersive technologies can transform the ways in which we understand contemporary and historical suffering by deepening our empathetic engagement with the victims of political violence.

In Dick's *Do Androids Dream of Electric Sheep?*, empathy is what makes us human. Deckard identifies androids by forcing them to take an empathy test: an eerie inability to be moved by accounts of distressing social situations is the only way that the bounty hunter can distinguish the new, sophisticated Nexus-6 replicants from real human beings. But Dick also satirizes the cult of empathy that has evolved around the Christ-like figure of Wilbur Mercer: an elderly pauper whom humans are encouraged to engage with through a "black empathy box."[22] Grasping the box's twin handles, users lose all sense of self and their surroundings, experiencing "mental and spiritual identification" with Mercer as he ascends a "drab hill" before being plunged into the "pit of corpses and dead bones" known as the "tomb world."[23] Characters such as the "subnormal chickenhead" John Isidore have become so consumed by their engagement with Mercer's rise and fall that Mercerism has "evolved into a full theology," with even the UN Secretary General desperately proclaiming: "Mankind needs more empathy."[24]

Dick's account of the experience derived through the "empathy box" uncannily portends the quasi-evangelical discourse that surrounds the contemporary VR sector. In the virtual landscape of the 2020s, something akin to Mercerism is alive and well. The sector's investment in the concept of empathy is usually traced back to a notorious claim made in a TED talk by Chris Milk, one of the VR sector's leading entrepreneurs and directors, which is that "virtual reality can create the ultimate empathy machine."[25] The mission statement of the VR company LightShed, who created *The Last Goodbye*, exemplifies how the sector has been quick to follow Milk's lead in claiming that these "empathy machines" can lead to humanitarian activism:

> LightShed uses the power of immersive storytelling, and cutting-edge technology, to create positive social change. We shed light on the lives of everyday people struggling to survive today's gravest humanitarian crises. Because we believe that immersive storytelling leads to empathy—and empathy leads to action.[26]

The homepage of the USC Shoah Foundation's website similarly states: "Our mission is to develop empathy, understanding and respect through testimony."[27] And the UNVR website describes how the project "uses the power of immersive storytelling to inspire viewers towards increased empathy, action and positive social change."[28]

In many ways, Holocaust memory projects such as Dimensions in Testimony sidestep some of the more contentious aspects of the VR sector's claims about empathy and humanitarianism, which hinge on VR's ability to offer immersive experiences of contemporary sites of suffering and disaster.

By interacting with VR films featuring those who live in places such as refugee camps, the sector argues that users gain a deeper understanding of other people's traumatic experiences. Most of the Holocaust projects that we discuss in this book, on the other hand, do not attempt to simulate historical spaces as they were for, say, a survivor such as Pinchas Gutter when he was incarcerated in Majdanek. While they offer performative, immersive experiences that engage us with Holocaust testimony, the user's interaction in the USC Shoah Foundation projects is always with *memories* of the past that are drawn out in contemporary spaces such as museums, heritage sites, or former camps.

The growing multidisciplinary literature on empathy and its mobilization in the discourse of the VR and humanitarian sectors nonetheless raises significant questions about the affective potentialities of virtual Holocaust memory. These include the basic phenomenological issue of whether immersive experiences allow us to comprehend highly traumatic experiences from the point of view of people whose culture and life experiences most likely bear very little relationship to our own. Do these embodied encounters create meaningful forms of identification across difference, allowing us to understand the experiences of victims of political violence in profound and galvanizing ways? Or, more cynically, as one *Guardian* headline put it, as "the cornerstone of the tech industry's masterplan for mainstreaming VR," is empathy simply "the latest gadget Silicon Valley wants to sell"?[29] A related debate concerns whether empathy is a limited or limitless resource. During a presentation at the United Nations in 2018, the USC Shoah Foundation's Executive Director, Stephen Smith, interestingly argued that empathy can be learned as a skill: one that entails both listening and critical thinking.[30] If this is the case, then empathy with the victims of historical and political oppression might be improved through practice, supported by projects such as Dimensions in Testimony or VR films. However, in *Evil Men* (2013) James Dawes represents a contrasting point of view when he worries that "empathy isn't so much like a muscle that can be trained as capital that can be overspent."[31] Rather than regarding empathy as a skill, critics such as Dawes argue that endless claims on our sympathies are more likely to result in "compassion fatigue" than meaningful political action.

A related set of questions concerns how users are positioned within VR. Some critics have found there to be something troubling about VR's tendency to adopt a bystander position. The problematic nature of this positionality is drawn out in Jordan Wolfson's Holocaust-inflected VR artwork *Real Violence* (2017), in which users bear witness to the artist appearing to beat a man with a baseball bat while a voice sings Hebrew blessings in the background. One reviewer notes a paralyzing effect: "It occurred to me, before the action began, that Wolfson was getting to the frustration at the heart of VR: you feel like you're present, but you have zero effect on the outcome of events."[32] Pursuing the logic of Wolfson's provocative installation, we might argue that projects such as Dimensions in Testimony do not allow us to modify the installation, or indeed make any imprint on the witnesses with whom we hold the virtual "conversation." Moreover, in Chapter 5 we note how the incitement to "explore a space" in the Secret Annex Online leads to actions that can feel uncomfortably furtive and voyeuristic—as when users are prompted to uncover intimate family objects such as photographs and clothing—or hopelessly belated, as when users witness the aftermath of the police raid on the annex. In what ways do such projects therefore confine users to the position of "new bystanders" who are powerless to change the virtual events they witness? To what degree might they even connect to the positionality of what Michael Rothberg terms the "implicated subject," whose "actions and inactions help produce and reproduce the positions of victims and perpetrators," with users ambiguously located between victims and perpetrators in an uncomfortable structural entanglement with historical events from which they might unwittingly benefit?[33]

Finally, while we recognize the sociopolitical rationale for the kind of politically engaged memory activism based on empathy advocated by institutions such as the USC Shoah Foundation and the USHMM, we remain mindful of the critique of "sentimental politics" that Dawes traces back to Jean-Jacques Rousseau and, in particular, Rousseau's claim that emotion expended on fictional stories allows us to satisfy "all the rights of humanity without having to give anything more of ourselves."[34] Sharing some of Rousseau's reservations about the political utility of the aesthetic manipulation of emotion, our study takes as an important reference point Carolyn Dean's assertion—drawing on Didier Fassin's work on "humanitarian reason"—that a human rights discourse grounded in empathy and digitally generated affect risks becoming an empty mode of "philanthropic condescension" when it "neglects the structural causes of oppression," such that it can only generate an enfeebled "politics that eschews resistance and strategy in favour of proclamations of injury."[35]

Virtual Holocaust Memory: Notes on Terminology

What, then, is virtual Holocaust memory?[36] And how might it help us move beyond the frequently bombastic yet epistemologically questionable rhetoric of empathy? The myriad connotations and frequently contested semantic resonances of our three key words—"virtual," "Holocaust," and "memory"—make them notoriously difficult to pin down. Before attempting to define the key characteristics of the immersive, interactive, technologized encounter with the past that interests us, we will therefore offer our pragmatic position in respect of each term.

To begin with the historical focus of our study, our broad understanding of the Holocaust as an event is largely shaped by our case studies and by our critical and cultural reference points. Many historians and institutions constrain their use of the term Holocaust to definitions such as that employed by the USHMM: "the systematic, state-sponsored persecution and murder of six million Jews by the Nazi regime and its allies and collaborators."[37] Recognizing that the Nazis also persecuted other groups on racial, political, ideological, and behavioral grounds, for organizations such as the USHMM, the genocide of the Jews is nonetheless a distinct crime. However, while all our case studies primarily focus on Jewish victimhood, adopting a definition such as that employed by the USHMM risks marginalizing non-Jewish victims. It also risks foreclosing productive forms of historical comparison by emphasizing the uniqueness of the genocide of the Jews. Moreover, some of our key reference points are drawn from the work of non-Jewish victims who we nonetheless consider to be Holocaust writers. Centrally, these include Charlotte Delbo, a non-Jewish French communist who was arrested in Paris on March 2, 1942 and sent to Auschwitz-Birkenau and Ravensbrück for her involvement in resistance activities. In addition, we do not limit our understanding of the timeframe of the Holocaust to the period after the Wannssee Conference in January 1942 when the "Final Solution" was implemented, primarily because our case studies involve events such as Kristallnacht in November 1938 and experiences such as hiding from the Nazis in occupied countries during the Anschluss and the early years of the war. Finally, while its connotations of a "burnt offering" make the Holocaust an uncomfortable term, its usage is widespread and alternatives such as "Shoah," the "Final Solution," or "the Nazi genocide" are arguably even more problematic by virtue of the religious and perpetrator perspectives they entail.

We take a similarly capacious approach to our use of the word "memory." In *Multidirectional Memory* (2009)—another important reference point for our study, and indeed for much work in memory studies in recent years— Rothberg adopts Richard Terdiman's "minimalist definition" of memory as "the past made present."[38] This useful formulation positions memory as, above all, a contemporary phenomenon, while the verb "made" underscores Rothberg's understanding of memory as "a form of work, working through, labor, or action."[39] Following Rothberg, our understanding of virtual Holocaust memory is very much that of a dynamic contemporary practice that generally involves those with personal memories of the Holocaust connecting with members of later generations, often drawn together as a result of the active efforts of educational institutions who serve as facilitators and custodians of these encounters. The word "memory" usefully conjoins the work of these diverse actors who mutually shape each other's present-day experiences of the past. Indeed, while the aim of projects such as Dimensions in Testimony is to ensure that survivor memories inform the historical understanding of later generations, the methodologies that are used to create these immersive experiences also affect and (re)shape the memories of survivors. Fritzie Fritzshall, for example, describes how the experience of giving her protracted Dimensions in Testimony interview triggered new memories: "It brought me back into the camp. It gave me the nightmares again. I was hungry again. I was cold again."[40]

Following Rothberg in adopting Terdiman's "minimalist definition" of memory also helps us to contribute to the ongoing study of memory as a form of work that involves "simultaneously the individual, embodied, and lived side *and* the collective, social, and constructed side of our relations to the past."[41] However, a concept of "virtual memory" expands the individual versus collective (or cultural) memory dyad that has dominated the field of memory studies ever since it was inaugurated by a resurgence of interest in scholars such as Maurice Halbwachs in the 1990s through the addition of a third mnemonic element: computer memory. With computer memory transforming the "how" of remembering at both an individual and collective level, developments brought about by advanced computing and new media technologies demand recognition in a vocabulary and conceptual framework that goes beyond that which has been employed for the study of mass media forms to date, such as Alison Landsberg's work on "prosthetic memory."[42] The rapidly evolving impact of computer memory on memory culture cannot be underestimated. Steve Goodman and Luciana Parisi even argue that our understanding of these increasingly interactive, dynamic memory spaces must move beyond cybernetics—which concerns how information storage systems communicate across humans and machines—to a "postcybernetic conception of memory" that ushers us toward the experiential "archive of the future": an intelligent, nonlinear archive that "anticipates change, anticipates the not yet experienced."[43]

Finally, while not synonymous with the word "digital," our formulation draws on the way in which contemporary usage now routinely connects the word "virtual" with digital technologies in a broad and imprecise sense. Rather than simply identifying a discrete group of technological platforms, then, our use of the word "virtual" aims to capture some of the defining characteristics of the qualitatively new form of Holocaust memory work that was instigated by the rapid evolution of digital technologies in the 2010s. "Virtual Holocaust memory" thus refers to an emerging cultural practice that is shaped by the diverse ideologies, beliefs, and discourses (such as the VR sector's mobilization of the rhetoric of empathy) that are being brought to bear on these new digital infrastructures. We are also drawn to the idea that as well as referencing immersive platforms such as VR that stimulate these "memories" of the past, the word "virtual" pertinently implies that the phenomenon we are studying is akin to an organic, personal memory of one's own past, but also categorically different and, to a degree, artificial. However, much as with the relationships between human beings and replicants in the *Blade Runner* films, we would argue that this does not mean to say that such phenomena are bereft of meaning. Indeed, quite the opposite.

The relationship between the virtual and the real has been the subject of long-standing philosophical reflection. For Michel Foucault, for example, the virtual offers a way of discussing experiences in which one encounters oneself in a displaced space, such as a mirror:

> In the mirror, I see myself there where I am not, in an unreal, virtual space that opens up behind the surface; I am over there, there where I am not, a sort of shadow that gives my own visibility to myself, that enables me to see myself there where I am absent: such is the utopia of the mirror.[44]

Foucault's sense of the interrelatedness of the real and the virtual in the mirror reflects the way in which memory has itself long been understood as a virtual phenomenon. A tradition of continental philosophy connecting Henri Bergson, Marcel Proust, and Gilles Deleuze explores the coexistence of perception and memory in an embodied temporal configuration in which the virtual is inseparable from the real. As Andreas Huyssen therefore observes:

> To insist on a radical separation between "real" and virtual memory strikes me as quixotic, if only because anything remembered—whether by lived or imagined memory—is itself virtual. Memory is always transitory, notoriously unreliable, and haunted by forgetting, in brief, human and social.[45]

More recently, Marc Redfield's formulation of "virtual trauma" in *The Rhetoric of Terror* (2009) denotes a similar understanding of the September 11 attacks, where " 'virtual' intends to suggest the trembling of an event on the edge of becoming present: one that is not fully or not properly 'actual.' "[46] Redfield's evocative, imagistic definition of the virtual characterizes the so-called "trauma" of ordinary Americans who watched the attacks on television. These viewers were not traumatized "in the technical, psychological sense."[47] Rather, Redfield argues that they were traumatized by the sense of "possible catastrophes to come" and the free-floating anxiety created by the aesthetic spectacle of the double strike on the World Trade Center that stood "at the symbolic center of technological, capitalist, and national power."[48] The ambiguous reverberations of this "haunting event" would go on to inform America's subsequent "War on Terror."[49] As such, Redfield insists that describing America's trauma as "virtual" "is not at all a synonym for insignificant or nonexistent."[50]

The virtual qualities that permeate the realities of mirrors, memory, and mediated terrorist attacks have much in common with the "pseudo-concepts" of "spectrality" and "hauntology" that Jacques Derrida introduces in *Specters of Marx* (1993): a study that offers perhaps the most provocative and influential reading of the virtual in contemporary cultural and political theory. Derrida's evocation of events, ideas, and other forces that exert a subtle pressure on the edge of consciousness forms an important reference point for Chapter 2, in which we argue that in the near future, as the Holocaust fades from living memory, holograms of survivors may constitute a new kind of haunting machine: what we term, following Alexander Etkind's formulation, "ghostware."[51] In the most literal sense, these technologically sophisticated, pedagogically direct, and phenomenologically present machines would appear to have little in common with Derrida's oblique and elusive concepts. Yet, we argue, Derrida's understanding of the spectral is highly pertinent to the way in which this ghostware connects memories across the human lifespan, making significant ethical demands on those who encounter it.

In summary, then, virtual Holocaust memory signals our interest in technologized "moments of encounter," to apply Landsberg's phrase, with the Holocaust, in which the past is made present—albeit in ways that might sometimes seem artificial or unreal.[52] Created through immersive digital environments such as, but not limited to, VR, these encounters tend to be highly performative, embodied, and interactive, offering the kind of "experiential mode of engagement" with the past that Landsberg identifies as a contemporary "cultural dominant."[53] Unlike traditional linear media such as films and television programs, users are actively able to determine the narrative journey they take through a body of content, meaning that each immersive experience is unique. Through our diverse selection of case studies, we identify some of the formal mechanisms that shape these encounters, including the "digital palimpsests" that enhance visitors' experiences of historical sites such as Bergen-Belsen (Chapter 4) and the frequently confounding syntax of conversations with what we term "virtual survivors" that are engendered through Dimensions in Testimony (Chapter 1). We then go on to argue that virtual Holocaust memory projects have the potential to reproduce the sensation that Foucault describes when looking in the mirror, displacing us from ourselves in order that we might inhabit ourselves differently. As such, they hold great promise for empathetic identification. However, the confidence of Milk's assertion that VR can "create the ultimate empathy machine" belies the fact that the ethical foundations for such displacements must involve some recognition of what we do not know, not just what we think (or feel) we know. Above all, the well-intentioned impulse to identify and empathize must not spill over into forms of overidentification that appropriate the experiences of historical victims to service the identity politics of the present. The more self-aware and ethically distanced form of identification that we value therefore has much in common with what Dominick LaCapra terms the "empathetic unsettlement" that emerges through the "virtual" experience of trauma. Here LaCapra's use of "virtual" again does not refer to technology, but rather to trauma "undergone in a secondary fashion by one who was not there." He writes:[54]

> In the virtual (in contrast to the vicarious) experience of trauma, one may imaginatively put oneself in the victim's position while respecting the difference between self and other and recognising that one cannot take the victim's place or speak in the victim's voice.[55]

Our contention is that the digital memory projects that we discuss in this book, including the virtual survivors created by Dimensions in Testimony, have the potential to engender productive forms of empathetic unsettlement that do not collapse into overidentification, but which rather generate new forms of affect, original ways of thinking, and considered engagement with the trauma suffered by Holocaust survivors. In this way, we hope that our study helps to recover some of the positive connotations of the word "virtual" contained in the Latin original *virtus*—meaning courage, potency, strength—thereby rejoining the virtual with the possibility of human virtue.

The Poetics of Virtual Holocaust Memory

This book is an interdisciplinary study that puts long-standing traditions of thinking about the cultural representation of the Holocaust into dialogue with a contemporary Holocaust memory culture that is becoming increasingly technologized. Our methodology is best understood as a poetics: a term commonly associated with the study of literary form, technique, and textual effects that can be traced back to Aristotle, whose systematic analysis of Greek drama continues to inform diverse branches of contemporary narrative theory. The aesthetic and ethical challenges of cultural representations of the Holocaust have frequently been theorized in terms of poetics, from Theodor Adorno's famous meditations on the "barbaric" condition of poetry after Auschwitz through to Antony Rowland's sense of the "awkward poetics" that characterize the self-reflexive, fragmented representational strategies employed by poets such as Sylvia Plath, Tony Harrison, and Geoffrey Hill.[56] However, in exploring virtual Holocaust memory through the prism of poetics, we do not intend to offer a totalizing theory of the ways in which these digital memory projects make meaning, or to suggest that our case studies coalesce around a single, coherent representational agenda. This is not a study of poetics in a structuralist sense. Rather, following the example of Linda Hutcheon in *A Poetics of Postmodernism* (1988), we offer a more flexible, provisional, and wide-ranging critical engagement with cultural practices beyond the literary sphere, identifying and exploring conceptual and creative innovations that are shaping an emerging and fluid mnemonic space. Recognizing that we are focusing on prototypes, pilots, and early adoptions of new technologies, our poetics is conceived as an "open, ever-changing theoretical structure by which to order both our cultural knowledge and our critical procedures," allowing us to interrogate themes that have long been concerns for theorists and practitioners with an interest in Holocaust memory, but which are taking on new meaning as memory culture becomes increasingly virtualized.[57] Four of these emerging, interconnected themes are particularly notable for the way in which they resonate across our case studies, forming key points of departure for virtual Holocaust memory both as a theoretical concept and a creative and curatorial practice.

1. Truth and Truthfulness

Our first chapter begins by drawing on Hartman's periodization of Holocaust testimony to describe how memory institutions with pedagogical missions supported by increasingly sophisticated technological infrastructures are shaping the parameters for a fifth and final period of Holocaust witnessing. Through each previous period of testimony identified by Hartman, in settings ranging from the courthouse to the living room, the central thing at stake has always been some conception of "truth." For historians such as Annette Wieviorka, who argued that "the era of the witness" valued sentiment and emotion over rational critique and rigorous historical analysis, the inclusion of survivor testimony in Nazi trials was controversial precisely because it was at best a distraction from, and at worst a threat to, the kinds of historical and legal truths that such trials ought legitimately to establish.[58] The truths that came to define Hartman's fourth era of witnessing—during which the grassroots oral history projects of the 1970s and 1980s scaled up into larger, internationally-renowned archives such as the VHA in the 1990s—were then increasingly influenced by psychoanalytic approaches to trauma. Noting that concerns about the factual accuracy of testimony had precipitated a "crisis of witnessing," studies such as Shoshana Felman and Dori Laub's *Testimony* (1991) argued that factual inaccuracies did not invalidate testimony's truth content or negate its historical value. Rather, they were symptomatic of deeper truths concerning the enduring impact of traumatic experience on the damaged psyches of survivors.

Focusing on what we identify as the fifth and final act of Holocaust witnessing, this study asks what forms of truth will be fostered and valued as testimony moves from legal, psychoanalytic, and cultural paradigms to more technologized, experiential, and pedagogic memory spaces. A key reference point will be the epigraph to Delbo's *None of Us Will Return* (1965) that was included in her *Auschwitz and After* trilogy (1985):

> *Today, I am not sure that what I wrote is true.*
> *I am certain it is truthful.*[59]

In making a distinction between truth (*vrai*) and truthfulness (*véridique*), Delbo suggests a separation between what might be thought of as the objective "facts" of history (or History) and another more ambiguous order of meaning, perhaps evoking the distinction that is often made between history and memory. As Hirsch and Leo Spitzer observe, this "truthfulness" seems to oscillate between representational profundity and mnemonic limitation, with Delbo's writing conveying either "a deeper truth about her camp experience, its essence, its deep memory" or the exact opposite, characterizing her own writing as a vague approximation to the things she actually experienced.[60] The virtualization of Holocaust memory culture demands that we continue to reflect on the complex interdependency of truth and truthfulness that is evoked by Delbo's testimony, as the case studies explored in this book suggest that an uncertain, equivocal truthfulness is set to become the dominant "truth" of the digital age.

This paradigm shift in part relates to the experiential, affective turn in global memory culture, and the way in which visitors to museums and heritage sites, for example, are arguably becoming less interested in what we might traditionally think of as objective historical truths (such as those that we encounter in the lengthy displays of museums such as the Topography of Terror, detailing facts, figures, dates, and the like) and more interested in immersive experiences that *feel truthful*. But as the quotation from Delbo illustrates, we must not lose sight of the fact that any such invocation of truthfulness is not antagonistic to the category of objective historical truth: indeed, it is completely bound up with it. As Bernard Williams writes in *Truth and Truthfulness* (2004):

> The subject of this book is truthfulness: various virtues and practices, and ideas that go with them, that express the concern to tell the truth—in the sense both of telling the truth to other people and, in the first place, telling the true from the false. My aim is to explain the basis of truthfulness as a value.[61]

This sense of truthfulness *as a value* is distinct from the kinds of truth that are the concerns of history books and courthouses, yet completely formed in the crucible of such truths. Neither privileging the objective truths of history nor the subjective truths of memory, but instead constantly invoking and interrogating both, a concept of truthfulness also moves us beyond postmodern paranoia about simulation as a force that, as Baudrillard puts it, "threatens the difference between the 'true' and the 'false', the 'real' and the 'imaginary'."[62] In proposing truthfulness as a value and virtue for the age of virtual Holocaust memory, we hope to find a more constructive "middle way" between the binaries on which Baudrillard's dismissal of the virtual depends.

Given the immersive, experiential nature of virtual Holocaust memory, it is also important to recognize that truthfulness is an aesthetic construct: one whose forms and textures are constantly changing. The Holocaust took place in an analog age and has long resided in the historical imaginary as such. The monochrome textures of films and photographs that traditionally mediated Holocaust memory have meant that the Holocaust has often seemed to exist at a significant imaginative remove from the present, recalling L. P. Hartley's famous opening line in *The Go-Between* (1953): "The past is a foreign country: they do things differently there."[63] As time passes, the world of gas chambers, cattle trucks, eugenics, and Nazi doctors may come to seem ever more remote and otherworldly, especially for the digital natives of the twenty-first century, playing out Primo Levi's apprehensions concerning the "gap that exists and grows wider each year between things as they were down there and things as they are represented by the current imagination fed by books, films and myths."[64] How will digital aesthetics navigate this widening gap, now that the current imagination is fed by VR films, apps, and holograms, as much as by books and films? On the one hand, there is a risk that the aesthetics of virtual Holocaust memory might alienate older generations unfamiliar with new technologies, or even younger ones, if Holocaust memory projects do not keep pace with the increasingly sophisticated aesthetics of commercial entertainment culture. In Chapter 4, we note how the blocky visuals of the USHMM exhibition in Second Life have dated rather badly—especially when compared to the high-definition cinematic experience provided by contemporary videogames and VR experiences—creating an uncanny, disorientating, dreamlike experience of Kristallnacht. Given that the new technologies of "turbo-capitalism" are notorious for becoming quickly obsolete, there is a risk that an overdependence on technological innovation might actually speed up the very process of historicization against which Holocaust memory culture is so desperately struggling.

Yet it is equally possible that new technologies might help future generations to encounter the past with a heightened sense of connection and proximity by employing innovative aesthetic strategies to *narrow* Levi's gap and create new forms of historical consciousness. We would argue that this possibility is movingly illustrated by the digitally recolored photographs of Auschwitz victims created by Marina Amaral for the *Faces of Auschwitz* project. Amaral's images include the haunting photograph of a fourteen-year-old Polish Catholic girl, Czesława Kwoka, taken just under four months before she was murdered with a phenol injection to the heart, that is reproduced on the back cover of this book. The image went viral on social media when the Auschwitz Memorial Museum posted it, along with details of Kwoka's life story, on the seventy-fifth anniversary of her death. In an interview, Amaral describes the impact of recoloring photographs of victims:

> I think it humanises them. . . . They are no longer just numbers or statistics, but are people like you and me. Colours make us feel more empathetic. They help us to connect with the subject in a deeper, meaningful way. . . . When we see the photos in colour, there's no longer an emotional barrier there. . . . These people are suddenly more relatable; more real, flesh and blood—literally.[65]

After Amaral completes her coloration work, each image is scrutinized by an expert for historical accuracy.[66] Viewers of these images do not encounter history "literally," as Amaral claims, and there can be no guarantee that they offer an exact reproduction of the colors of Kwoka's clothes, hair, or skin. However, in creating an affective experience of the past through a creative engagement with documentary material, these charged images epitomize our understanding of Delbo's notion of truthfulness as an aesthetically engineered value that is central to the ethos of the digital memory projects that we explore in this book.

2. The Limits of Connective Memory

Amaral's images also push back against a representational tradition forged by an earlier generation of survivors, philosophers, and artists who possessed an acute awareness of the limits of language, culture, and the imagination when confronted with the physical and psychological extremes of the Holocaust. From the 1960s to the early 2000s, there was broad critical consensus around the idea that an ethical approach to representing the Holocaust involved figuring the past as a potentially unknowable absence, caesura, or void. This position was encapsulated by Friedländer in *Probing the Limits of Representation*, in which he characterizes the Holocaust as an "event at the limits."[67] Concerned that the record of "the most radical form of genocide encountered in history" might be "distorted or banalized by grossly inadequate representations," Friedländer's collection explores "limits to representation *which should not be but can easily be transgressed*."[68] Centrally concerned with the kinds of "truth" that are at stake in such representations, Friedländer points to Ida Fink's short stories and Claude Lanzmann's documentary *Shoah* (1985) as examples of "literary and artistic works which give a feeling of relative 'adequacy' in bringing the reader and viewer to insights about the Shoah":

> A common denominator appears: the exclusion of straight, documentary realism, but the use of some sort of *allusive or distanced realism*. Reality is there, in its starkness, but perceived through a filter: that of memory (distance in time), that of spatial displacement, that of some sort of narrative margin which leaves the unsayable unsaid.[69]

Amaral's work, on the other hand, holds fast to the promise of "straight, documentary realism" as a mechanism for drawing the past closer to the present. Her contention that digital coloration helps viewers across an "emotional barrier" echoes discourses celebrating the empathetic potential of immersive technologies such as VR, following what Andrew Hoskins calls the "connective turn."[70] Reflecting her commitment to what we term "connective memory," Amaral's comments typify the approach of a new generation of creative practitioners who are highly invested in the aesthetic and emotional impact of digital technologies, deviating starkly from the self-consciously "distanced realism" that Friedländer identified in an earlier corpus of Holocaust literature and film that was primarily concerned with representational limits and restraint.

A critique of connective memory that completely rejects any attempt to engage with other people's suffering on an intimate, affective, empathetic level sits quite comfortably—and maybe, in our view, *too* comfortably—with approaches to Holocaust representation that hold that when it comes to extreme human suffering and trauma, the only ethical position is to accept that we will not and cannot know. Through this study, we hope to challenge such pieties. Equally, however, those critics and practitioners currently romanticizing affect and "empathy machines" would do well to consider why earlier artists and cultural critics, such as Friedländer, took questions of representational distance so seriously. Recognizing that there are always limits to what we can know of the past, and to how far experiential forms of historical encounter allow us to empathize with historical victims whose suffering will never be completely grasped by most people, we argue that these contrasting approaches to Holocaust memory and representation need not be mutually exclusive.

Strategies for entwining connective memory with distanced realism include digital instances of what we term "palimpsestic testimony." In Chapter 4, for example, we discuss future developments of the Bergen-Belsen iPad app that currently uses geolocalization and AR to allow visitors to visualize the position of former camp buildings at the same time as reading contemporaneous testimonies as they explore the present-day site. Specifically, we argue that the app could be developed to include creative responses to the site and a wider range of sensory data, including sound. It might also draw more boldly on footage of the camp's liberation in the manner of Alain Resnais's iconic film *Night and Fog* (1956) to disturb the peaceful tranquility of a historical site whose physical traces have been almost entirely erased. The sensitive curation of Anne Frank's diary by the Anne Frank House in the Secret Annex Online also illustrates the potential of palimpsestic testimony (see Chapter 5), with digitized documents, photographs, and newsreel footage presenting striking metatexts for online visitors to the annex. By presenting users with a layered experience that draws together different information and viewpoints, inviting empathetic identification while also stimulating critical thinking and historical analysis, palimpsestic testimony has the potential to create immersive experiences that fall under the sway of both connective and distanced approaches to Holocaust memory. The forms of interactivity and embodiment that we experience in projects such as Dimensions in Testimony afford further opportunity for developing self-reflexive connective memory practices that are more aware of their own limitations. In the second and third chapters, we draw on the work of Vivian M. Patraka to explore the way in which meaning is constructed performatively through interactive testimony, outlining how the survivor testimony is first recorded in 360-degrees in a high-tech, cinematic light stage, and then encountered by visitors in museum settings such as the USHMM. In describing virtual Holocaust memory in terms of its performativity, we highlight how connective encounters with the past are becoming increasingly haptic, working across interrelated physical and virtual spaces. Positioning such experiences in terms of disappearance, loss, and limitation, rather than rebirth and redemption, might render them even more powerful.

As discussed, another of the many notable claims being made for connective memory is the degree to which it can express political commitment, both at an individual and collective level. Throughout this study, we return to the contention made by Landsberg and others that the powerful affect of immersive experiences can form the bedrock for revitalized forms of political subjectivity based on empathy. For Landsberg, affect can act as "a catalyst to new thought or to action, pressing the individual to process a particular experience intellectually, to grapple with that which has previously been unthought."[71] As such, Landsberg argues that affective encounters with history can directly influence social behavior: "There can be a political dimension to feeling connected to history—to feeling that the past matters in an intimate individual way. . . . A personal stake in knowledge about the past can in turn catalyze one's desire to engage in politics, to work against injustices in the present."[72] As noted, this logic shapes the educational missions and memory activism of institutions such as the USC Shoah Foundation and the USHMM, and also the VR-based humanitarianism advocated by a range of organizations, from technology companies through to the UN. But it remains to be seen whether virtual Holocaust memory will resolve so neatly into transformative political action. Might it not just as easily lead to moral complacency? Rigorous third-party evaluations of projects such as Dimensions in Testimony and the UNVR film series might ultimately provide the most robust evidence to support or rebuff such claims.

At the collective level, connective memory also promises to shape new relationships between different histories and different generations. Increasingly oriented toward young people, projects such as Dimensions in Testimony move critical debates about transgenerational transmission beyond influential concepts such as Hirsch's "postmemory." Rather than passing between two generations, the memories circulating through such projects connect the living and the dead with those not yet born, spanning three generations or more. The study of transgenerational memory will therefore need to account for more remote family dynamics. What might it mean for a grandchild to have a virtual conversation with a survivor grandparent once they are dead? What might it mean for a great-grandchild to have a virtual conversation with a survivor relative whom they never met in person?

Finally, given the forms of political solidarity that Rothberg finds in multidirectional memory and sensitive, nuanced forms of historical comparison, we would argue that future virtual Holocaust memory projects might mobilize the transnational and transcultural potentialities of connective memory to greater effect by presenting the Holocaust not as an isolated case study, but rather as an event that is situated in relation to its colonial prehistory and more recent genocides and human rights abuses. This will, however, involve overcoming the somewhat entrenched historical, cultural, and political forces that lead influential institutions such as the USHMM and the Topography of Terror (see Chapter 6), operating in quite different contexts, to characterize the Holocaust as unique and exceptional. There are also more technical difficulties to overcome. How can testimonial projects such as Dimensions in Testimony make meaningful multidirectional gestures, given that a recorded testimony presented in the form of an interactive hologram can know nothing of the crises of the present? Are such projects inevitably insulated from contemporary life, such that they cannot offer meaningful lessons for the present? Or will virtual Holocaust memory evolve within dynamic immersive environments that allow users to create connections between diverse, global histories, prompting future generations to ask important questions of their world and themselves, the past and the present, thereby securing the ongoing relevance of Holocaust memory as we wade deeper into the digital age?

3. The Institutionalization of Holocaust Memory Culture

As some of these questions indicate, in its current early incarnation, virtual Holocaust memory is a highly institutionalized phenomenon. Drawing on studies such as Noah Shenker's *Reframing Holocaust Testimony* (2015), the question of the institutionalization of Holocaust memory therefore informs our analyses of projects led by high profile educational organizations and memorial sites such as the USHMM, the USC Shoah Foundation, the Anne Frank House, and the Bergen-Belsen Memorial.

The prominent role that these institutions have played in the early years of virtual Holocaust memory can partly be ascribed to the fact that immersive technology projects are generally expensive to produce. In an interview at the Sheffield Doc/Fest, Smith revealed with refreshing candor that the first twelve Dimensions in Testimony interviews cost $6 million to record, noting that the cost is set to lower in the future now that the software and technical infrastructure have been developed.[73] Holocaust educational organizations and museums are not, however, particularly wealthy organizations. Some are, of course, wealthier than others; yet all depend on significant grants and private donations to fund digital projects on this scale. This economic land-scape raises the possibility of private companies developing a larger stake in Holocaust memory culture in the future, much as they do in sectors such as film and television. In Chapter 5, we draw on our interview with Danny Abrahms, director of a forthcoming VR film about Anne Frank's experience of hiding in the secret annex, who predicts that the influence of independent technology companies on Holocaust memory will quickly "balloon."[74] The market for Abrahms's film is the education sector, but if immersive experiences are increasingly led by companies with backgrounds in cinema and videogames, to what degree will commercial objectives and the imper-ative to entertain replace the pedagogic and social missions that drive the institutions that are currently at the vanguard of virtual Holocaust memory?

While these educational institutions have taken significant risks to ensure that future generations will engage with Holocaust memory through digital platforms that older generations might have more reservations about, various forms of cultural conservatism are often entrenched in their representational practices. These include an almost unanimous aversion to the simulation and fictionalization of historical events, with immersive technologies yet to be granted the permissiveness that has long been afforded to more traditional screen-based media. Such conservatism has implications for the growing opposition that Wulf Kansteiner identifies between "official" Holocaust memory culture and unofficial forms of memory work being forged by dig-ital natives through new media practices:

> Official Holocaust memory is professionally managed for the purpose of safeguarding the mission and long-term interests of the respective memory institution. In its current format, official Holocaust culture therefore represents an antithesis to the nimble, decentralized exchanges of opinions driving social media communication.[75]

Kansteiner argues that social media and changing cultural preferences will increasingly exert a more bottom-up influence on Holocaust memory culture. How, then, will established Holocaust memory institutions—with their preference for neat, distilled, controlled, messages—engage with the ungoverned, user-led spaces of the new digital media landscape? Will control of Holocaust memory culture be relinquished to groups, organizations, and platforms that invite forms of engagement with the past that are more playful, irreverent, or disruptive?

Such developments will, in turn, influence the kinds of lessons that we derive from Holocaust memory: long a source of controversy, these are now more than ever in a state of contestation and flux.[76] At the time of writing, the world is negotiating what the economist Mariana Mazzucato terms "capitalism's triple crisis": a compound disaster involving the Covid-19 pandemic, the attendant global economic downturn, and the ongoing climate crisis.[77] How will the precarious social and economic conditions that characterize this crisis affect the Holocaust's place in the global memory landscape of the future? Will the comprehensive transnational frameworks of the pre-digital, pre-pandemic age that helped to forge broad consensus in areas such as the nature of good and evil and respect for human rights endure? Proponents of "cosmopolitan memory," such as Daniel Levy and Natan Sznaider, point to the formation of international bodies such as the United Nations, documents such as the Universal Declaration of Human Rights, and legislation such as the Genocide Convention, to explain how Holocaust memory provided the foundations for the global human rights regimes that were established in the latter decades of the twentieth century. The Holocaust was the subject of education programs around the world and countless museums and memorials. But, even as people continue to visit Holocaust museums and memorial sites in record numbers, the foundations of cosmopolitan memory seem to be eroding. We are told that Holocaust knowledge is at an all-time low, with 2018 surveys commissioned by the Claims Conference and CNN pointing to a pervasive lack of knowledge about basic facts of the Holocaust in the United States and Europe.[78] Moreover, the contemporary relevance of Holocaust memory is a question on which expert opinion is divided. For example, in an article on the emergence of "illiberal democracy" in the United States midway through the presidency of Donald Trump, the historian Christopher Browning observed, "The Nazi dictatorship, war, and genocide following the collapse of Weimar democracy are not proving very useful for understanding the direction in which we are moving today" as "current trends reflect a significant divergence from the dictatorships of the 1930s."[79] For Browning, the Holocaust no longer provided the insights needed to address present day political regimes or global challenges. However, historians such as Timothy Snyder have continually found urgent contemporary relevance in the study of the Holocaust. In *Black Earth* (2015), for example, Snyder argues that the genocide needs to be understood as the consequence of an ecological panic that continues to this day.[80] And in an article reflecting on the invasion of the Capitol by Trump supporters in January 2021, Snyder draws parallels between Trump's attacks on truth and the rise of fascist regimes.[81] Dubbing Trump the "high priest of the big lie," he observes that "like Adolf Hitler, he came to power at a moment when the conventional press had taken a beating."[82] Noting Trump's references to reporters as "enemies of the people" and comparing his fondness for slogans such as "fake news" with the Nazi smear Lügenpresse ("lying press"), Snyder argues that "post-truth is pre-fascism."[83] Will more commercial virtual Holocaust memory projects follow Snyder's lead in probing the relationship between past and present in order to uncover historical patterns and anticipate "future possibilities"?[84] Or will they take the view that the social and economic conditions that gave rise to the Nazi genocide are unique, rendering comparison taboo and perhaps reducing the lessons of the Holocaust to well-worn platitudes such as "never again"? Or will they simply not care, seeking simply to excite, entertain, and stimulate the senses, but having little interest in the social activism and political commitment that were the motivating forces behind the early virtual Holocaust memory projects designed and hosted by "official" institutions such as the USC Shoah Foundation and the USHMM?

4. Perpetrators and Impiety

The projects that we discuss in the first five chapters of this book primarily center on Holocaust victimhood. But we are intrigued by the prospect of virtual Holocaust memory soon undergoing the kind of "perpetrator turn" noted in Holocaust literature and film in the early 2010s.[85] Other than Wolfson's allusions to the Holocaust in *Real Violence*, we are not aware of any VR films that incite us to think about Nazi perpetrators. While the disconcertingly depopulated landscapes that we encounter in digital applications such as the Bergen-Belsen iPad app and the USHMM Kristallnacht exhibition in

Second Life unwittingly risk presenting visitors with a perpetrator ideal, explicit engagement with perpetrator perspectives seems to be a new taboo in digital memory culture, echoing previous taboos surrounding the representation of perpetrator consciousness in literature. In addition, the virtual is off limits for memory institutions concerned with perpetrators, such as the Topography of Terror in Berlin, which we discuss in Chapter 6. Curatorial nervousness inevitably surrounds the intertwining of the virtual with perpetrator memory in such museums: an interactive hologram of a perpetrator would clearly risk a kitsch vulgarity, as if to confirm what Lanzmann identifies as the "absolute obscenity in the project of understanding."[86] Yet, given that there are many videogames themed around the Second World War that involve gamers assuming a perpetrator perspective, might a more permissive approach to the gamification of Holocaust memory at least allow us to probe the problematics of perpetration and implication in more compelling and challenging ways?

As things stand, somewhat predictably, videogames such as *Call of Duty: World War II* (2017) and the *Wolfenstein* (2014–) series developed by MachineGames invest the perpetrator position with a sense of righteousness. The victims are always Nazis, making them legitimate targets within the moral universes of these games. But does the popularity of such videogames, alongside the rise of "serious games," offer fertile ground for digital memory projects wishing to explore topics such as the psychology of the "ordinary men" who became the perpetrators of genocide? In his preface to *Ordinary Men* (1992), Browning reflects on the risks inherent in his project of trying to understand how middle-aged, middle-class police reservists came actively to participate in mass murder. Notably, empathy is a key term:

> The policemen in the battalion who carried out the massacres and deportations, like the much smaller number who refused or evaded, were human beings. I must recognize that in the same situation, I could have been either a killer or an evader—both were human—if I want to understand and explain the behaviour of both as best I can. This recognition does indeed mean an attempt to empathize. What I do not accept, however, are the old clichés that to explain is to excuse, to understand is to forgive. Explaining is not excusing; understanding is not forgiving. Not trying to understand the perpetrators in human terms would make impossible not only this study but any history of Holocaust perpetrators that sought to go beyond one-dimensional caricature.[87]

Might it one day be possible to *play* a complex historical text such as *Ordinary Men* through interactive narratives that seek to provoke the unflinching self-scrutiny called for by historians such as Browning? When considering such a project, we are reminded of Gillian Rose's similar thought experiment in *Mourning Becomes the Law* (1996), where she imagines a *bildungsroman* in which the reader would experience the "crisis of identity" of the ordinary Nazi "in their own breast."[88] Acknowledging that the performative, heuristic logic of such a text would be stymied by the foreshadowing that would inevitably inflect our reading of a novel about a Nazi perpetrator—if we know we are reading a book about a Nazi, then we know where the narrative is heading—Rose instead offers the Merchant Ivory adaptation of Kazuo Ishiguro's *The Remains of the Day* (1989) as an example of the kind of film that draws us into a more empathetic relationship with somebody who turns out, ultimately, to be a Nazi sympathizer. Rejecting the emotional safety of sentimentality, Rose argues that *The Remains of the Day* "induces a crisis of identification in the viewer" who emerges shedding "the dry tears of deep grief" that belong "to the recognition of our ineluctable grounding in the norms of the emotional and political culture represented."[89] Injecting virtual Holocaust memory with a bolder streak of what Matthew Boswell terms "Holocaust impiety" (a sensibility that would almost certainly could not be cultivated within official Holocaust memory culture) might result in more troubling acts of representation that induce users to engage with serious, difficult questions about perpetration, complicity, and implication, rather than leaving them stranded in the new bystander position that they occupy in *Real Violence* and the Secret Annex Online.[90]

Such a game might also meaningfully interrogate the complex relationship that exists between digital technology and mass violence. Technology has always shaped the perpetration of violence as well as the memory of violence. Historians have frequently pointed to the "scientific" methods and industrial mechanisms deployed by the Nazis, characterizing the genocide as an identifiably modern event. What Bauman terms the "machinery of destruction," made up of steam engines, gas chambers, medical equipment and the like, depended on large companies such as Krupp for materials, IG Farben for chemicals, and IBM for data processing.[91] Indeed, the technologized violence of the Second World War—which also included the atomic bombs and firebombs dropped by the Allies—played a huge role in shaping the cultural mistrust of technology that developed in the 1960s. However, following Bauman, the "machinery of destruction" that underpins contemporary warfare is becoming increasingly "light"; as such, it has much in common with the machinery of memory discussed in this book. Warfare, like memory culture, is becoming increasingly dependent on technologies that have emerged from the computer games industry, with bullets fired by drones rather than handheld guns. To what degree does such violence nonetheless conform to the earlier logic that led to the creation of gas chambers, wherein victims were first dehumanized, so that perpetrators did not see them, philosophically, as human beings, and executioners were distanced from their victims so that they did not see them, physically, at all?

Interactive digital memory projects involving immersive technologies are uniquely positioned to address such questions. Given the close connection that has long existed between the US military and Silicon Valley, the Californian location of projects such as Dimensions in Testimony is also particularly pertinent. Indeed, while researching Dimensions in Testimony, we noted that the same USC Institute for Creative Technologies studio that was being used to film interactive testimonies with Holocaust survivors also housed simulation machines that had been developed for the US military. These included a project called Bravemind: Virtual Reality Exposure Therapy, which enables soldiers returning from Iraq and Afghanistan to confront traumatic memories through "virtual reality exposure therapy." The project website explains:

Exposure therapy, in which a patient—guided by a trained therapist—confronts their trauma memories through a retelling of the experience, is now endorsed as an "evidence-based" treatment for PTS. ICT researchers added to this therapy by leveraging virtual art assets that were originally built for the commercially successful X-Box game and combat tactical simulation scenario, *Full Spectrum Warrior*. The current applications consist of a series of virtual scenarios specifically designed to represent relevant contexts for VR exposure therapy, including Middle Eastern themed city and desert road environments. In addition to the visual stimuli presented in the VR head mounted display, directional 3D audio, vibrations and smells can be delivered into the simulation. Now rather than relying exclusively on imagining a particular scenario, a patient can experience it again in a virtual world under very safe and controlled conditions. Young military personnel, having grown up with digital gaming technology, may actually be more attracted to and comfortable with a VR treatment approach as an alternative to traditional "talk therapy."[92]

Notwithstanding the potential therapeutic benefits of such technologies, the suggestive proximity of Bravemind and Dimensions in Testimony in a Californian studio illustrates how virtual environments are now integral to the perpetration and perpetuation of political violence. It could even be argued that a virtualized killing cycle is evolving: one that moves through gaming, training, and warfare (for example, through drone strikes by unmanned combat aerial vehicles) to therapy and testimony, helping states such as the United States work through the consequences of war in ways that render it tolerable. Does this problematize the prevailing view of immersive digital memory projects as a straightforward source of moral edification, instruction, and empathy? How might future projects engage with the ideologies, identities, technologies, and complex geopolitical and technological structures that conjoin to produce the virtual and physical spaces of contemporary conflict? Could virtual Holocaust memory projects even address the literal and imaginative separation of perpetrators and victims in contemporary warfare, showing how this trend has its origins in the industrial killing of the Holocaust, thereby offering a form of resistance to a logic that risks giving rise to more and more eyewitnesses, more and more testimony, more and more victims?

PART I

INTERACTIVE VIDEO TESTIMONY

1

Entering Dimensions in Testimony

The Last Act of Holocaust Witnessing

It is a bright Monday morning in Los Angeles in December 2015. In a warehouse on an industrial estate in the suburb of Playa Vista, a few blocks inland from Venice Beach and the Marina Del Rey, photographers, reporters, and a team of technicians and production staff gather in a narrow corridor that runs around the perimeter of a large, dome-shaped light stage. The imposing metal framework is laced with wires and high-definition cameras that point toward a red armchair mounted on a raised platform in the center of the stage. A message printed on A4 paper and taped to the outside of the rigging reads:

HOT SET

DO NOT TOUCH

An expectant hush envelops the studio as an eighty-six-year-old Holocaust survivor, Eva Schloss, is led into the stage, accompanied by her granddaughter.[1] Wearing matching gray top and trousers, Schloss takes a seat in the red armchair, confessing to feeling "a little nervous" as the crew runs through a final series of lighting and sound checks (see Fig. 1.1). At one point, Schloss is asked to sit with her hands raised above her head, as you would for an airport security check, while the studio lights flicker rapidly on and off. Before filming begins, Schloss poses with her granddaughter and members of the production team for some publicity photographs. Then she is left on her own.

Over the five-day interview that follows, Schloss is filmed against a vivid green screen. Her testimony is recorded through a slim microphone that dangles above her head on a blue lead. With her soft gray shoes carefully fixed to place markers outlined on the floor, Schloss remains composed and largely undemonstrative as she answers the interviewers' questions in a thick central European accent, her pearl necklace and rings glinting whenever they catch the clusters of stage lights that shine all around her like stars in a

Virtual Holocaust Memory. Matthew Boswell and Antony Rowland, Oxford University Press. © Oxford University Press 2023. DOI: 10.1093/oso/9780197645390.003.0002

Figure 1.1 Eva Schloss's Dimensions in Testimony interview at the USC
Institute for Creative Technologies
USC Shoah Foundation—The Institute for Visual History and Education

digitally powered night sky. Occasionally, she moves her hands for emphasis
or closes her eyes when visualizing a specific place or incident. This happens
most often when she is describing painful physical sensations, like hunger or
itchy wounds caused by lice. After each question, Schloss returns to what is
known as the "resting pose," with her right hand propped on her thigh and
her left on the arm of the chair.

The interviewers, who rotate on a regular basis, take it in turns to sit on
a chair just outside the light stage. They speak into a microphone and their
questions are amplified through speakers inside the stage. To ensure that
Schloss's gaze is always directed toward the main camera—a formidable
piece of equipment known as a Red Dragon—the interviewer is covered by
a black screen and only visible to Schloss via a tilted mirror to the side of
the camera. Over the five days of filming, she works her way through some-
where in the region of one thousand questions, including many about her
stepfather, Otto Frank, and the legacy of his daughter and Schloss's posthumous stepsister, Anne Frank. Schloss recounts how an oversized coat and
hat helped her to fake her way through one of Joseph Mengele's infamous
selections on the ramp at Auschwitz-Birkenau, and how she gained special

privileges by working in the Kanada block where inmates sorted through the confiscated clothing and possessions of new arrivals. Schloss discusses the death of her father and brother before the camp's liberation and the chain of events that led to her own survival, while also reflecting on the lessons of the Holocaust and their continuing relevance for the world in which we live today. Some questions are asked by local schoolchildren who have helped the project team to identify topics that future generations are likely to be interested in. These include: "How did the Holocaust affect your childhood?" and "If there was one thing you could say to the Nazis, what would it be?" During these sessions, Schloss's responses are considered yet concise; her tone intimate, warm, and engaging. One senses that Schloss modulates her answers to account not only for the knowledge base and sensibilities of the schoolchildren leading the present day interviews, but also for those whom she will address in the future when her answers will be accessed through a simulated conversation made possible through a form of speech recognition technology known as natural language processing, with Schloss assuming the form of a three-dimensional, interactive video recording; which is to say, what is popularly known as a hologram.

The Dimensions in Testimony project is the result of a collaboration between the USC Shoah Foundation, the USC Institute for Creative Technologies, and the exhibition design and digital storytelling company Conscience Display, who first came up with the interactive video testimony concept.[2] The first phase of the project had resulted in sixteen testimonies being recorded by early 2019: fifteen with Holocaust survivors, including one in Hebrew, and one with a victim of the 1938 Nanjing massacre filmed in Mandarin.[3] The following three chapters consider Dimensions in Testimony in its formative years, drawing, in particular, on Schloss's 2015 interview in Los Angeles and the subsequent pilot of her interactive testimony at the Museum of Jewish Heritage in New York in 2018. Through the discussion that follows, it is important to remember that this innovative, experimental form of Holocaust witnessing is only just beginning to take shape, with museums, educational organizations, members of the public, survivors, and their families exploring how the cutting-edge technologies of Silicon Valley might be used to ensure that conversations with survivors remain a primary vehicle for the transmission of Holocaust knowledge long into the future.

Schloss is one of the few Holocaust survivors to have given extensive testimony in written, oral, and interactive forms. Studying her interview therefore allows us to consider the relationship between the mode of witnessing that takes place through Dimensions in Testimony and more traditional forms of written and oral testimony. It also affords a unique opportunity to consider how testimony evolves over time and how it is shaped by different media and institutions. Alongside Schloss, our other case study will be Pinchas Gutter, who was the first survivor to be interviewed for Dimensions in Testimony and the first to have had his virtual namesake piloted in public settings (we will use "the virtual Pinchas Gutter" and "the virtual Eva Schloss" to differentiate between the interactive recordings that are activated through speech recognition technology and the real-life survivors who gave the original interviews). These included temporary exhibitions at the United States Holocaust Memorial Museum (USHMM) in 2016 and the Museum of Jewish Heritage in 2018, where the virtual Gutter appeared alongside the virtual Schloss, as well as a shorter exhibition at the Sheffield Doc/Fest in 2016. In each of these pilots, the interactive testimonies were installed on two-dimensional plasma screens, so had not properly taken the form of "holograms" (a term to which we will return). However, these opening chapters also draw on media coverage of the first three-dimensional versions of Dimensions in Testimony, which were made available to the public through the multimillion-dollar Survivor Stories Experience at the Illinois Holocaust Museum and Education Center in 2017, with four rotating testimonies placed on permanent display in a purpose-built auditorium (see Fig. 1.2).[4]

Writing in 1996, Geoffrey Hartman argued that at that point in time there had been four distinct periods of Holocaust testimony:

> The first was immediately after the war, when the camps were disclosed. That period did not last: a devastated Europe had to be rebuilt, and the dis-belief or guilt that cruel memories aroused isolated rather than integrated the survivor. What has aptly been called a "latency period" intervened. A second opening was created by the Eichmann trial in 1960, and a third came after the release of the TV series *Holocaust* in 1978.[5]

Hartman goes on to note that a fourth period of witnessing was inaugurated when a number of grassroots oral history projects began to spring up in the USA and Europe, pointing to the opening of the Video Archive for Holocaust Testimonies at Yale in 1982 as a key date.[6] That period continued into the 1990s and 2000s, expanding significantly through large-scale oral history projects such as the USC Shoah Foundation's Visual History

Figure 1.2 The virtual Sam Harris at the Illinois Holocaust Museum and Education Center
Ron Gould Studios

Archive (VHA), established in 1994 by the organization's founder, Steven Spielberg, following the release of *Schindler's List* (1993). The archive now contains over 55,000 oral testimonies relating to histories such as the 1994 Rwandan genocide against the Tutsi, the 1937–1938 Nanjing massacre, and the Armenian genocide, as well as the Holocaust, and is the largest such collection in the world.

There are of course numerous initiatives that bleed across these periods of witnessing—all manner of precedents, anachronisms, overlaps, and countertraditions—yet Hartman's schematization offers a useful overview of shifts in the testimonial landscape that help us to understand how, in the early 2010s, pedagogical imperatives combined with technological innovation and an acute awareness of the fact that we are coming to the end of the period of living memory to form the parameters for a fifth period of Holocaust witnessing: one that finds unique educational value in the experience of listening to, and speaking with, Holocaust survivors. Recognizing that opportunities to have such experiences were becoming increasingly limited, Holocaust museums and educational organizations turned to digital technology to ensure that they were not lost altogether. At the forefront of this emergent period of virtual Holocaust testimony were two ambitious interactive video testimony projects: Dimensions in Testimony and a parallel initiative led by the National Holocaust Centre and Museum in the United Kingdom, in partnership with the creative design consultancy Bright White, called the Forever Project.[7] The first phases of these projects will cumulatively give rise to a corpus of twenty-six interactive testimonies—with more in the pipeline—bringing eyewitness accounts into the digital age in ways that will doubtless impress, baffle, and provoke experts and public alike.

It should be emphasized from the outset that if these projects imagine an exciting, technologically enabled "new dimension" in testimony, as the original title of the USC Shoah Foundation project put it, then they also entail, just as importantly, the sense of an ending. This is almost certain to be the most technologically advanced medium in which eyewitness accounts of the Holocaust are captured. Indeed, it is the last time that many of the Dimensions in Testimony and Forever Project survivors will testify in any kind of recorded format. By reflecting on the wider historical and cultural significance of elderly survivors such as Schloss and Gutter sitting in a light stage for five days recounting their Holocaust experiences, knowing that in the future the transmission of their testimonies will rely not on their own presence in real time but instead on high-definition recordings of their interviews and questions posed by people who are perhaps not yet even born, these first three chapters seek to open out key debates that will surround this pioneering last act in the long-running drama of Holocaust witnessing.

The Traumatic Syntax of Virtual Conversations

The first major pilot of the virtual Pinchas Gutter installation took place at the USHMM in 2016, when it was made available to the public for a limited time each day over a four-month period, with museum staff on hand to support visitors when required. Located in a small, sealed-off space at the entrance to the Wexner Center on the first floor of the museum, a panel on the wall and an accompanying leaflet provided basic background information about the project and Gutter's biography. During our observations, the exhibit generated a certain amount of passing curiosity. Of the visitors who stopped, however, many did not speak to the virtual Gutter directly. Instead, they were happy simply to watch while others interacted with the system. The virtual conversation worked best when the number of nonactive spectators was either very small or else so large that many visitors were not paying close attention to the interaction. Having a smaller, more intimate group seems to ensure that visitors' attention is more directed at the interaction with the virtual survivor and their testimony, rather than the surrounding audience. As we shall see, much of the connective power of the virtual conversation derives from a sense of personal contact with the recording. This means that, ironically, once a group grows to more than a handful of people, social etiquette, and positive personal behaviors such as politeness work *against* visitors having a deep engagement with testimony, with people happy to ask one or two token questions to trial the technology before moving aside to let others have a go.

The exhibition at the Museum of Jewish Heritage marked a notable progression from the USHMM pilot. Over a period running from September 2017 to February 2019, the virtual Gutter and Schloss were displayed side-by-side in the spacious Rotunda Gallery on the top floor of the museum in a far more developed version of what a permanent exhibition space might look like (see Fig. 1.3). At the entrance to the exhibition, a panel and short film provided extensive background information about the project—at that point still known as New Dimensions in Testimony—with the film offering a useful insight into the recording process that we discuss in Chapter 3. Panels inside the gallery offered brief biographies of Gutter and Schloss. Visitors sat on eight benches in a hexagonal-shaped room, with natural light flowing into the space through a white-framed skylight. Two large plasma screens were mounted against the gray museum walls, with the sitting figures of the virtual

Figure 1.3 Dimensions in Testimony pilot at the Museum of Jewish Heritage
Antony Rowland

Gutter and Schloss set against black backgrounds. Separate microphones in front of each installation allowed the testimonies to be used simultaneously (although this rarely happened in practice) and for visitors to move between the two installations. This meant that visitors could, in theory, ask the same question to both virtual survivors. They could also choose which one they would prefer to answer any given question, based on their knowledge of the survivors' biographies. Rather than attracting groups of curious passers-by, visitors who entered the exhibition space had usually made a deliberate effort to come and see the installations. These included school groups accompanied by docents. At the time of our visit, however, the exhibition had not been incorporated into a formal educational program. The objective of these short visits therefore seemed to be more about showcasing the technology than deeply engaging with testimony, with the docents urging their often rather shy students to pose questions that they knew would generate interesting answers, such as asking the virtual Gutter to sing or asking the virtual Schloss about Anne Frank. Visitors who were not part of school groups interacted with the testimonies with little introduction or instruction. It was common for them to begin by asking simple questions such as

"How old are you?," "How old were you during the Holocaust?," "Where were you born?," "Did you have any brothers or sisters?," and "Did your family survive?" Most visitors moved on from the installation after asking a small number of questions, or else after watching others use the system, having got a feel for how it worked but without probing the testimony too deeply.

A certain novelty value is always going to inflect a user's initial experience of engaging with an unfamiliar communication system such as interactive testimony, which functions by creating a spoken exchange with a recording of a survivor interview using natural language processing. Yet, for all its innovativeness, this voice-activated search, which interrogates a database of answers created through bespoke interviews, is not overly complex or intimidating. Indeed, it has much in common with the way that we already engage with oral testimony through online interfaces. Anyone faced with the corpus of more than 55,000 testimonies held in the VHA, for example, will generally use a typed search to access the content they are looking for, rather than watching any single testimony from start to finish. Natural language processing simply allows such a search to take place through a verbal rather than a typed command, and in the form of a question rather than a series of keywords. In doing so, it aligns with wider advances in digital technology, which increasingly enables us to interact with electronic devices through speech.

While the answers to users' questions all derive from the bespoke interviews with the real-life survivors (and not the VHA interviews, as is sometimes mistakenly assumed), the selection of the most appropriate answer is automated. As David Traum, the Director for Natural Language Research at the USC Institute for Creative Technologies, explains, in relation to the virtual Gutter prototype, "We have to distinguish two concepts of response. Everything that is said comes directly from Pinchas. However, the decision of which recording to present as a response to a specific question is made by the technology, based on its training data of how Pinchas and other people have answered questions."[8] One of the aims of the museum pilots was to increase the volume of this training data because, as USC Shoah Foundation Executive Director Stephen Smith observes, "as time goes by and many more users use the content, machine learning will enhance its intelligence—it will understand a wider range of questions as each interaction helps train the system."[9] The outcomes of machine learning were in evidence at the Museum of Jewish Heritage, with the more extensively used installation of the virtual Gutter seeming to provide more accurately matched answers than the virtual Schloss.

As the natural language processing software learns to select the most relevant answers to specific questions, evolving through each new interaction, there seems, however, to be a potential risk, which is that a small group of answers will become foregrounded at the expense of those that are triggered less frequently. During both pilots, the installations repeatedly returned to a small subset from the vast archive of available answers. This could, of course, be because some questions are more common than others. But machine learning also seems to echo an aspect of survivor memory observed by Primo Levi, whereby "a memory evoked too often, and expressed in the form of a story, tends to become fixed in a stereotype, in a form tested by experience."[10] If the process of defaulting to "stock answers" therefore seems human enough, the "stereotyped memory" used by Holocaust survivors crystallizes around moments of emotional, personal, or historical significance. However, the second concept of response identified by Traum is incognizant of such considerations. Machine learning trains the system to source answers that provide the best linguistic fit to particular questions. While this is obviously desirable from a technical point of view, it may ultimately mean that the system ends up foregrounding answers that are not particularly interesting from either a personal or historical point of view. Certain pedagogical practices could counteract this: educators may learn how to frame questions that trigger some of the more interesting answers, as we already saw happening at the Museum of Jewish Heritage. These may then come to assume heightened prominence in the automated hierarchies created by machine learning. But the real-life survivors would have had no say in the elevation of particular responses over others, and the risk is that the richness of the archive of answers elicited through the five-day interviews is reduced to a more limited number of overdetermined highlights.

During the pilots, the user experience was clearly affected by the fact that the voice recognition aspect of the installation was performing inconsistently, with machine learning still at an early stage. While well-matched answers offered a kind of dialogic pleasure, suggestive of the type of immersive experience that might one day be possible, the installations often gave repeated answers or ones that did not match the question. In such situations, users either cut short the interaction by immediately reframing the question, or else they listened politely to the answer, presumably finding the testimony interesting enough in its own right, notwithstanding its lack of relevance to their question. As a rule, most users quickly grasped how the underpinning technology worked, framing their questions in ways that increased the likelihood of getting an accurately matched answer, while speaking slowly and clearly and emphasizing keywords. As with early pilots held with high school students as part of an independent evaluation, during the museum pilots, badly matched answers tended to prompt users to modify their language, asking "more broad and general questions that they thought could be answered by the survivor through the . . . technology."[11]

Through a well-matched answer, Dimensions in Testimony successfully simulates certain aspects of an everyday conversation. Yet there are of course many aspects of conversations that cannot be simulated through this technology, meaning that the project does not live up to the USC Shoah Foundation's claim that the project "delivers a learning environment in which a survivor answers questions as if he or she were in the room."[12] Above all, while the interaction allows a questioner to talk *to* a virtual survivor, it does not allow them to converse *with* them. There are none of the digressions, interruptions, interrogations, or two-way flows of information that mark most real-life conversations. Neither can the system deal with complex, multifaceted questions, or questions that are asked in an unclear way. In such situations, the virtual survivors fall back on a stock set of brief answers, such as "Sorry, I don't know what that is," "Can you say again please?," or "I can't answer that, but I can talk to you about something else if you like?"

Another drawback is that the installations lack any memory of the questions they have been asked during any given encounter with a unique user, leaving the "conversation-like experience" feeling stunted and fragmented. The project aspires to allow users to shape their own narrative journey through testimony, yet the current interaction only offers a series of discrete, self-contained answers to individual questions. As such, there is no sense of a conversation developing through time. You cannot ask a follow-up question, such as "Then what happened?," and it would take detailed knowledge of the installation's possible answers to get two or three questions and answers to fit together in such a way as to piece together a chronological sequence of events from the survivor's life. As a result, even tracing the steps in a survivor's journey from, say, a ghetto to a camp, is currently almost impossible, meaning that the Foundation's recent preference for describing the system as an "interactive biography" is somewhat misleading.

Splicing up emotional trajectories that developed over a significant timeframe during the real-time interview (see Chapter 3), the system's lack of narrative coherence can, on the one hand, be understood as a fundamental failing of an interactive experience that only very loosely approximates to a real-life conversation. However, there is something moving and affecting about the frailty and fallibility of an interaction in which virtual survivors mishear questions, get things wrong, and repeat themselves. The system's quirks also very often contain their own dark humor. In New York, when asked if she had met Steven Spielberg, the virtual Schloss replied that she had not met Elie Wiesel. The virtual Gutter confused a death march with the March of the Living. Asked if he was a ghost, the virtual Gutter responded by telling his favorite Yiddish joke. In a live demonstration of Dimensions in Testimony at the United Nations, during an event to mark the seventieth anniversary of the adoption of the Genocide Convention, the virtual Schloss twice replied to the question, "Did you know Anne Frank?" with the same answer: "I never met Hitler."[13] Investing the recordings with a quirky, posthuman personality, such errors will be rectified as more test data helps to improve the system's functionality. Yet, in this early phase, they give interactive testimony an unpredictable quality whose effects range from the poignant to the comic. Such effects might even be understood to speak to the complexities and challenges of Holocaust memory in a bold and subversive way, exploring the experiences of elderly, damaged survivors through an impious poetics of fragmentation, dislocation, and dissonance.

Some of the more disturbing aspects of this admittedly rather mischievous reading of Dimensions in Testimony were illustrated by an unsettling moment that we witnessed toward the end of our observation of the virtual Gutter pilot at the USHMM. A young user had asked the virtual Gutter whether he had any pets, but the system misinterpreted the question as pertaining to whether he had any regrets. Subsequent investigations found that the installation contains numerous different answers to the latter question. One involves the virtual Gutter saying, rather perfunctorily, "I don't think so. I can't think of any." In another, he responds by recalling a time he was put on food distribution duty in Majdanek. As inmates were pushing to get served, Gutter threw a ladle of food in their faces. He confesses that he has always regretted that moment because he felt like he had behaved like a Nazi. However, when the young user asked the virtual Gutter the question about pets in Washington, the incorrectly matched answer began in an altogether different register. In this response, the virtual Gutter has red eyes from the very beginning, having clearly been moved to tears by a previous answer during the real-time interview. Choked with emotion and shaking his head, he says: "I regret my family, my surroundings, my life." He wipes

Figure 1.4 The virtual Pinchas Gutter at the Museum of Jewish Heritage
Matthew Boswell

a tear from his eye, and there is then a long, disconcerting pause, during which he remains perfectly still (see Fig. 1.4). For a moment, it seems that the installation might have stopped working, with the virtual Gutter's static, seated posture, occasional blinks, and short intakes of breath suggesting a possible return to the resting pose that begins each question. But, after gathering his thoughts through a pause that lasts for over half a minute, the virtual Gutter resumes:

> I regret the fact that I am not . . . that life that existed in Poland before the war doesn't exist. I regret the fact that I am not part of that life and that a life that I was born into being and that I had to, you know, go through all these, you know, tortures and sufferings. And mostly, I regret not being able to remember my sister. That when I think of my sister, Sabina, I can only remember her braid, her golden braid, nothing else. And I think that is something that is so deeply hurting that I would say that's the thing that I most regret: that I cannot remember her more than I cannot be with her, my twin sister.

As can be imagined, this answer came as a shock to the young visitor who had asked the virtual Gutter about his pets. It was sharply out of kilter both with their expectations and the overall atmosphere in the room, where a small group of people had watched amiably as the student gamely sought to engage with the technology. Something like the opposite of dialogic pleasure was achieved (dialogic terror?) through an answer that would have been compelling for some and profoundly disturbing for others.

As well as highlighting the unpredictability of a system in its infancy, the variations in the virtual Gutter's answers reflect the diversity of responses that were captured through the original interviews and the wide emotional register of a database in which deeply personal reflections sit alongside "stereotyped" memory (which we discuss in Chapter 3) and answers to more mundane questions, such as "What is your favorite color?," "Did you ever meet Hitler?," and, indeed, "Did you have any pets?" While the Dimensions in Testimony team and their museum partners would most likely regard this incident as nothing more than a teething problem that will be ironed out by machine learning and improvements to the natural language processing system, the qualities of fragmentation, awkwardness, and uncomfortableness that emerge in such encounters might be read as powerful, individuating characteristics of the virtual interaction. The virtual Gutter's highly emotional "wrong" answer, coming when users least expected it, was unsettling in a way that Holocaust testimony has every right to be. Moreover, survivors rarely express such raw emotions during conversations in public settings. One might argue that in such moments Dimensions in Testimony effectively conveys an enduring trauma. With the system breaking from its own realistic form and operating more in the manner of a surreal, modernist artwork than naturalistic oral history, the virtual Gutter's answer is suggestive of the transient, embodied form of "truthfulness" that we develop in the next chapter. Perhaps we should accept this apparent dysfunctionality as a valuable quality of virtual interactions—one that is equally a product of the vicissitudes of modern technology and the traumatic experiences being recounted by survivors— unsettling museum visitors through a syntax of Holocaust memory that confounds our expectations, refusing to make sense in the ways we might have predicted.

The Cultural Life of Holocaust Holograms

Initial responses to Dimensions in Testimony in the media have been largely positive. In 2017, *Smithsonian Magazine* listed the exhibition in Illinois as one of twelve "must-see fall exhibits around the world" and the project has been the subject of enthusiastic reports by a diverse set of outlets, including National Public Radio, *The Washington Post*, and Fox News.[14] The public response has also been generally enthusiastic. In a publicity leaflet, the USC Shoah Foundation notes that "a survey of the Illinois pilot found that more than 95 percent of the visitors agreed that the technology enhanced their ability to connect with Pinchas's story."[15]

Academic responses, on the other hand, have been more mixed. The philosopher Berel Lang waxes lyrical on the Foundation's website: "I found the interview to be amazing! I felt like someone who'd never seen a plane, but now watched one land and a human being step out of it."[16] Other eminent scholars have, however, been more skeptical. In an article in *The Forward*, Lawrence Langer suggests that interactive testimony is an artificial and inappropriate form for Holocaust memory. The literary critic does not hold back, stating: "this is the craziest thing I have ever seen . . . I don't want to call it a gimmick, but I believe it is."[17] In the same article, Joanne Rudof, the archivist at the Fortunoff Video Archive at Yale University, questions the ultimate goal of the project and likens the technology to a videogame.[18] The article closes with Langer ominously observing, "I don't think I have to tell you how technology is taking over our lives."[19]

While Rudof's comments suggest that she has little personal experience of either Dimensions in Testimony or videogames, in an article in the *Los Angeles Review of Books* Marianne Hirsch reflects on her personal interactions with Dimensions in Testimony in a more considered fashion. Hirsch notes that the "*liveness*" she experiences watching "film or video testimony" was missing from her "encounter with the disembodied life-like projection of Eva Kor and the algorithm that selected her responses."[20] Notwithstanding the fact that Kor's Dimensions in Testimony interview is itself an example of "film or video testimony," Hirsch suggests that the technological interface that gives the virtual Kor's testimony enhanced interactivity *detracts* from the way in which viewers of conventional filmed testimony already participate in "the spontaneous and embodied co-creation of testimonial narratives."[21] Hirsch recognizes that her reservations could be ascribed to a number of factors:

As much as I value the voice of the survivor witness as a carrier and vehicle of memory for the future, I also know that living memory is subject to the passage of time. Is my response a generational one, I wonder? Or could it be that the desire to interact with survivors well beyond their lifespan is driven by the technology that makes its simulation possible?[22]

While it is of course entirely reasonable to question displays of technological prowess that threaten to overwhelm the Holocaust narratives being mediated, there is also a sense in which such comments betray a "technologic fatality," to borrow Hartman's phrase, that has much to do with what Hirsch concedes might be broad, generational fears rather than the specifics of Dimensions in Testimony.[23] We would further observe that in our extensive discussions with the creators of Dimensions in Testimony and the Forever Project, the practitioners consistently emphasized that their choice of technology was driven by pedagogical and curatorial questions and objectives rather than technical ones. There was strong resistance to any suggestion that these projects were using technology merely for technology's sake.

Without wishing to place undue emphasis on Hirsch's book review or Langer and Rudof's online magazine interview, we would argue that being too quick to dismiss new technologies can sometimes blind us to their potential benefits, not least for those who may never watch the Fortunoff and *Shoah* (1985) interviews that Hirsch, Langer, and Rudof understandably value. The mediation of historical memory depends, by definition, on the evolution of new media forms and technological innovation. What we know of the Holocaust already rests on revolutionary advances in media such as print technology, photography, and the capture of the moving image. As Andreas Huyssen writes, suspicions about the uses and abuses of new technologies are not only a feature of the present:

> New technologies of transportation and communication have always transformed the human perception of time and space in modernity. This was as true for the railroad and the telephone, the radio and the airplane as it will be true for cyberspace and cyber-time. New technologies and new media are also always met by anxieties and fear that later prove to have been unwarranted or even ridiculous. Our age will be no exception.[24]

As we wade deeper into the digital age, we might therefore do better to heed the example of J. G. Ballard who, as we note in one of the epigraphs to this book, saw it as his duty as a writer to immerse himself "in the threatening possibilities offered by modern science and technology" and do his best "to swim to the other end of the pool."[25]

One counterproductive consequence of responses such as those of Hirsch, Langer, and Rudof is that they appear to have led the USC Shoah Foundation consistently to downplay the role of technology in digital memory projects such as Dimensions in Testimony, and to adopt somewhat perplexing and even paranoid positions in respect of the terminology they deploy to describe these projects. The current project title, for example, is a puzzling contraction of the original title, New Dimensions in Testimony. Presumably seeking to sidestep the issue of the project's novelty, the shorter title no longer reflects the genuine innovation the project makes in respect of the "spatiotemporalities" of testimony that we discuss in the next chapter. The Foundation has also repeatedly sought to distance itself from the negative connotations of the word "hologram." Stressing that the originality of Dimensions in Testimony lies in a "virtual conversation" that is "authentic and spontaneous," while downplaying the innovative visual potential of the system, a 2016 publicity leaflet sternly warns that "words such as "hologram" and "avatar" fail to accurately describe" the project.[26] A subsequent National Public Radio broadcast about the Illinois exhibition prompted the Foundation to publish a rather exasperated news story on their website offering "a few clarifications [that] will help fill out the story."[27] The piece begins:

> Dimensions in Testimony is not displayed as a hologram, which is a 3-D display technology that does not yet exist, though many institutions world-wide are developing this technology, including teams at the University of Southern California. The current Dimensions in Testimony display uses a 2-D technology, including the Pepper's ghost installation at Illinois Holocaust Museum and Education Center.[28]

It would clearly be inaccurate to describe the pilots in New York and Washington as "holograms," as the recordings were displayed on two-dimensional screens.[29] Yet the "Pepper's ghost" installations at Illinois are designed to create the impression of three-dimensional images that would popularly be understood as holograms, and the museum's own website and publicity material consistently describes them as such.[30]

From initial academic misgivings through to excitable media reports that begin by citing scenes from *Superman* (1978), Dimensions in Testimony has already begun to take shape in a cultural imaginary that will be impossible for the Foundation to regulate or demystify.[31] Sean F. Johnston notes the simultaneous semantic imprecision and cultural power of the "h" word in his study, *Holograms: A Cultural History* (2015):

> Stretched by popular anticipations, promoters have always lamented the difficulty of explaining holograms to wider publics and bemoaned the misidentification of other technologies as holograms. A half-century after that futile dialogue began, the term *hologram* in pop culture has evolved from optical tricks to security patches to virtual entertainment in live settings.
>
> But…the borders of technological jargon can never be policed effectively. Current usage is imprecise and all-encompassing: the label may be applied to any ephemeral imagery associated with three-dimensionality, hanging in space and having an aura of mystery or spectacle. The term labels a cultural construct that has much greater potency than the scientific product itself.[32]

A further problem with the word "hologram" is that its potency as a cultural construction relates not so much to the fact that it sounds uncomfortably futuristic, than that to some it might sound uncomfortably dated. Contemporary holography has its origins in pioneering experiments undertaken by the Hungarian-British physicist Dennis Gabor in the 1940s, and the technology has long-standing associations of ghostliness, trickery, and spectacle as a result of the "visual trick most often misidentified with holograms" called "Pepper's ghost," referred to by the Foundation above, which was "a spectacular stage effect first seen by Victorian theatre audiences."[33] This eerie illusion was created when an offstage actor draped in a white sheet was illuminated by a lamp. Light was then reflected via an unseen pane of glass onto the stage, where it hung in front of the audience as a "three-dimensional and startling" image.[34]

In more recent decades, cultural conceptions of holograms have been largely shaped by the mass entertainment industries. Given the close connections that exist between Dimensions in Testimony and Hollywood on both an institutional and a methodological level (as we explore in Chapter 3), it is perhaps unsurprising to note similarities between Dimensions in Testimony and the holograms that feature in science fiction films such as *Minority Report* (2002), that was directed by the Foundation's founder, Steven Spielberg, and loosely based on another short story by Philip K. Dick. In the film, the lead character, John Anderton, played by Tom Cruise, feigns a two-way conversation with his son, whom he presumes to be dead, by speaking to a home video recording that is projected from a domestic wall in a ghostly holographic form (see Fig. 1.5).

One of the earliest and most notable cinematic representations of a hologram can be found in the first *Star Wars* film, *Episode IV: A New Hope* (1977), when Luke Skywalker discovers Princess Leia's holographic appeal for help hidden inside the memory of his recently acquired droid, R2-D2 (see Fig. 1.6). Leia is a leader of the Rebel Alliance, fighting a civil war against a totalitarian Empire with strong echoes of the Nazi regime, not least through its

Figure 1.5 Steven Spielberg, *Minority Report* (2002)

Figure 1.6 George Lucas, *Star Wars: Episode IV—A New Hope* (1977)

army of foot soldiers, known as storm troopers.[35] Beamed out of the droid from a single source and "evocative of a badly-tuned black-and-white television set," Leia's message marks an important moment in the cultural life of holograms, with cinematic holograms thereafter largely coming to adopt the convention of being "stuttering, run-down and imperfect."[36] Initially locked in a loop in which the captured leader repeats her famous line, "Help me, Obi-Wan Kenobi, you're my only hope," the future of the Alliance hangs on Leia's enigmatic hologram, not least as R2-D2 is also carrying stolen plans that highlight a weakness in the Death Star: the Empire's genocidal weapon that has the capacity to annihilate entire planets.

The *Star Wars* films will doubtless inflect the reception of the Dimensions in Testimony because of their flickering, blue holograms: an iconic aesthetic convention that famously returned in the final scene of *Star Wars: Episode VI—Return of the Jedi* (1983), in which the ghosts of three "force-sensitive" characters appear in a bluish, translucent form that strongly resembles Leia's hologram. Having originally been visited by these Jedi spirits, or "beings of light," in *Return of the Jedi*, Luke Skywalker becomes one himself in *Star Wars: Episode IX—The Rise of Skywalker* (2019), providing guidance to the film's protagonist Rey as she experiences a moment of crisis and self-doubt (see Fig. 1.7).[37] In a reference to the ending of *Return of the Jedi*, Luke and his sister Leia then appear to Rey in spirit form at the end of the film, thus concluding the trilogy of trilogies that form the "Skywalker Saga" with a final nostalgic holographic scene.

These *Star Wars* holograms lend the Dimensions in Testimony an uncanny familiarity, while drawing them into a cultural imaginary in which holograms of dead Jedi and missing members of the Rebel Alliance are dated

Figure 1.7 J. J. Abrams, *Star Wars: Episode IX—The Rise of Skywalker* (2019)

yet far from dystopian: indeed, these ghostly apparitions consistently offer solace, protection, and hope. As we shall see from the various discourses and metatexts that surround the project, the Dimensions in Testimony holograms also embody the hope that has been invested in them by a range of stakeholders who see the potential role that technological innovation can play in connecting past and future, the living, and the dead. Indeed, the hope that formed one of the original sources of inspiration for the project emerged from Gutter's missing memory of his twin sister, Sabina, who was mentioned in Gutter's "wrong" answer about his regrets that we discussed earlier. Sabina was murdered in Majdanek. Having been unable to remember what she looked like for much of his adult life, and with no photographs to remember her by, Gutter hoped that the extended Dimensions in Testimony interview would trigger memories and help him to visualize her face. Without in any way wishing to trivialize Dimensions in Testimony by pressing such comparisons, when Leia records her holographic message in the original *Star Wars* film before being captured by Darth Vader, the hope that she invests in a future that is both threatened and potentially safeguarded by technology resonates with that of stoical Holocaust survivors such as Gutter recording their interviews in the light stage in Los Angeles, precisely so they can reach out to past and future generations, placing their faith in holograms that are bound to powerful redemptive narratives concerning the recuperation of things past, the improvement of civil society, and genocide prevention.[38] If technology is not their *only* hope, then it is a strong and poignant one, all the same.

The redemptive narratives that surround the Dimensions in Testimony holograms thus draw on and actively reshape some of the more positive cultural understandings of holograms that have emerged through influential science fiction films such as *Star Wars*. As Johnston writes:

> It is intriguing . . . that the greatest impact of holograms has been in our minds. Holograms have had their most enduring influence—from their public revelation in 1964 and over the following fifty years—as a metaphor for the future. . . . Represented as a technology that will eventually and inevitably appear, holograms continue to channel cultural dreams.[39]

While digital natives and fans of science fiction films such as *Star Wars* might be broadly sympathetic to, or even excited about, educational projects that seek to harness holographic technology to transformative political agendas, many of the more negative responses to Dimension in Testimony's holograms, such as Langer's, rest on the presumption that their seemingly fantastical form threatens the integrity of historical knowledge and, as such, ought to remain the preserve of science fiction. While we would like to see a project such as Dimensions in Testimony take confident ownership of the term "hologram," instilling it with renewed relevance rather than disavowing it, we recognize that responses to the project range from extreme enthusiasm to extreme caution, with the "cultural dreams" of more optimistic individuals and institutions running up against "technologic fatality" and anxieties about the status of historical truth in a postmodern world. In order better to understand what is at stake in such debates, and what standards of veracity and verisimilitude we might reasonably expect from our encounters with Holocaust testimony in a virtual form, we will therefore close this chapter by turning to the question of the relationship between testimony and truth.

Performing Truthfulness

During a period spanning roughly twenty years, from the early 1980s to the early 2000s, as holograms were becoming culturally-encoded by the mass entertainment industries, postmodern theorists argued that digital culture in general—and holograms, in particular—represented a new order of reality that was characterless, depthless, and meaningless. Influential thinkers such as Jean Baudrillard repeatedly took holograms to exemplify the way in which the digital world was divesting reality of thought, imagination, morality, and critical distance.[40] Baudrillard warned: "holographic reproduction, like all fantasies of the exact synthesis or resurrection of the real . . . is already no longer real, is already *hyperreal*."[41] For Baudrillard, the fantastical simulations of the hyperreal were "much more destructive of the order of truth than its pure negation," which is, presumably, to say even more deadly than more outright forms of historical falsehood, such as Holocaust denial.[42]

Baudrillard's fear of holograms emerges from the pervasive poststructuralist questioning of history, truth, and representation that took place in the last decades of the twentieth century. Exploring the implications of these intellectual developments in a political context that required clear rebuttals to Holocaust denial, Saul Friedländer's landmark collection, *Probing the Limits of Representation: Nazism and the "Final Solution"* (1992) reflected the anxieties of the period. As Claudio Fogu, Wulf Kansteiner, and Todd Presner note in their follow-up collection, *Probing the Ethics of Holocaust Culture* (2016), "the debates in the late 1980s and early 1990s that gave rise to the first *Probing* book might be considered as a referendum on postmodernism and the alleged pitfalls of historical revisionism."[43] Central to this "referendum" was a concern with the status of historical truth in survivor testimony.

Coinciding with the rise of the fourth major period of Holocaust witnessing—that of oral history—during the late 1980s and early 1990s scholars increasingly accepted, as Hartman acknowledges, that "survivor testimonies recorded long after the event do not excel in providing *vérités de fait* or positivistic history."[44] However, theorists working in fields such as psychoanalysis located deeper truths in the very inaccessibility of the past to those who had suffered its worst excesses. This founding insight of trauma studies is famously encapsulated in Dori Laub's account of an eyewitness who, like Schloss, had worked in Kanada in Auschwitz-Birkenau. While the survivor described seeing four chimneys explode during the revolt on October 7, 1944 led by the Sonderkommando at Crematorium IV, historians agree that only one chimney was blown up during the uprising. During a conference discussion, some historians used this "error" to demonstrate the fallibility of testimony and to caution against historiographies that were overly dependent on subjective accounts. Laub, however, dissented, interpreting this "crisis of witnessing" as being symptomatic of a deeper truth:

> The woman was testifying . . . not to the number of chimneys blown up, but to something else, more radical, more crucial: the reality of an unimaginable occurrence. One chimney blown up in Auschwitz was as incredible as four. The number mattered less than the fact of the occurrence. The event itself was almost inconceivable. The woman testified to an event that broke the all compelling frame of Auschwitz, where Jewish armed revolts just did not happen, and had no place. She testified to the breakage of a framework. That was historical truth.[45]

Psychoanalysis thus provided a framework for the liberation of historical truth from the straitjacket of positivistic history; yet the possibility of wrestling "more radical, more crucial" forms of truth from devastating, traumatic experiences had long been a concern of Holocaust victims themselves. These include the Auschwitz and Ravensbrück survivor Charlotte Delbo, who, as discussed in the introduction, makes a much-cited distinction between "truth" and "truthfulness" in the epigraph to *None of Us Will Return* (1965) that begins her *Auschwitz and After* (1985) trilogy:

> *Today, I am not sure that what I wrote is true.*
> *I am certain it is truthful.*[46]

Seemingly conceding that traumatized memory is fallible, Delbo urges her readers to locate the value of her testimonial writing in its "truthfulness," which seems more related to its sincerity and what Nietzsche terms the "will to truth."[47] By separating truth and truthfulness—and, importantly, foregrounding her "certainties" concerning the latter—Delbo makes a distinction between, as Robert Eaglestone puts it, a conception of "truth as explanation, corresponding to evidence and states of affairs, and truth as in some way revealing of ourselves, of 'who and how we are.'"[48] Delbo's use of the present tense, which dramatizes the moment of writerly self-reflection, and Eaglestone's use of the language of revelation to describe the form of truth whose importance lies in what it tell us about the identity of survivors—of who they are and how they remember—are also each suggestive of the performative nature of testimony's truthfulness. Free from any intent to deceive, Delbo describes a form of representation that is made in good faith, setting out what one knows of the past but also conceding that there are some things one may never know. Understood in such terms, truthfulness provides the bedrock for Delbo's writing.

This sense of truthfulness as a dramatic, ethical, and self-reflective representational practice offers a valuable resource for the study of virtual Holocaust memory and projects such as Dimensions in Testimony. Such a practice centrally involves the creation of meaning through the kind of unfolding performative moment that Delbo transcribes in her epigraph and that Vivian M. Patraka, following Judith Butler, characterizes as "live, embodied, disappearing," driven by a "will to truth" that is authentic and sincere.[49] The truthfulness of virtual Holocaust memory as played out, for example, through a virtual conversation with a hologram of a virtual survivor in a Holocaust museum, is therefore not, as critics such as Baudrillard argue, reducible to a simulation value whose nefariousness lies in its confounding, destructive proximity to the real. The truthfulness of a virtual conversation is not a matter of similitude, nor what Baudrillard terms the "exact synthesis or resurrection of the real." Neither is it simply a matter of digitally reproducing historical sites and experiences. By the same token, it is not located in the "authenticity" or "spontaneity" of the virtual conversation, as the USC Shoah Foundation claims. By such standards, interactive testimony would at best be judged a well-intentioned failure. Rather, the embodied truthfulness of interactive testimony lies in the discovery of the user's responsibility for, and interpolation in, a performative encounter that leads to the co-production of historical meaning. This is an active, not a passive, form of embodied memory work, involving movement, touch, and speech. The museumgoer who simply observes the simulated conversation with the Dimensions in Testimony installations has an experience that is altogether different from that of the person using the system, merely paddling in the shallows of virtual Holocaust memory, rather than immersing themselves in its full ambiance.

As Patraka notes more broadly of spaces such as the USHMM, the dynamics of embodied performance already characterize the experiential logic of many modern museums: "It is the museum-goers (along with the guards) who constitute the live, performing bodies in museums. They are the focus of a variety of performance strategies deployed by museums for the sake of 'the production of knowledge taken in and taken home.'"[50] However, the truthfulness of virtual Holocaust memory, and the value of projects such as Dimensions in Testimony, lies not so much in the production and retention of prepackaged forms of knowledge that can be accumulated and "taken home" like objects from the gift shop (facts, interpretations, stories, and the like), than in the discovery of forms of self-knowledge and responsibility that will be understood in unique ways by each individual visitor.

Patraka's approach to the performative nature of Holocaust memory largely predates the virtualization of Holocaust memory culture. In *Spectacular Suffering* (1999), she develops a nuanced theory of the performativity of Holocaust memory that involves a negotiation between a doing and a "thing done," where the thing done stands for the "goneness of the Holocaust" and the "absoluteness of the thing done weighs heavily on any doing."[51] As such, Patraka argues, performances of Holocaust memory can constitute powerfully embodied metaphors for historical disappearance. It is possible that such a sense of overwhelming loss might be felt more acutely when visitors engage with Dimensions in Testimony in the post-survivor age, when the lack of living survivors might heighten the emotional impact generated by the installations and amplify the eeriness of the holographic "ghostware" that we discuss in the next chapter. A sense of "goneness" might also productively inflect the experience of conversations conducted through a "traumatic syntax," wherein the imperfect technological interface renders meaning in ways that are occasionally unintended or bewildering. However, the sense of rupture, goneness, and loss evoked by Patraka could easily be overlooked by future generations who do not already feel that history *as* loss. Indeed, Patraka's sense of a Holocaust performative has much more in common with the "distanced realism" advocated by Friedländer in the 1990s than with the more contemporary practice of connective memory characterized by affect and the desire to stimulate empathetic engagement with the victims of traumatic histories.[52] In all likelihood, the performative aspects of virtual Holocaust memory will therefore continue to be shaped as much by the dominant discourses and ideologies of the digital age as by the historical absences that "weighed heavily" on earlier performances and artworks. They will also be influenced by the ideologies and agendas that are inscribed in the physical spaces and buildings within which virtual Holocaust memory is enacted, not least the frequently evocative exhibition spaces in the museums that host installations such as Dimensions in Testimony. In such institutional spaces we also note, *pace Patraka*, a growing tendency to abjure mourning and melancholia in favor of a more energized ethos of political engagement and a philosophical commitment to the concept of redemption, as can be seen in the way that major Holocaust museums commonly position historical knowledge as a springboard for a form of social activism that has an almost sacred quality. Nowhere is this more powerfully illustrated than at the USHMM, to which we turn in the next chapter, in which we draw out some of the dominant ideologies and discourses currently shaping the reception of projects such as Dimensions in Testimony in the USA as we approach the end of the era of living Holocaust memory, before offering a more speculative and theoretically-informed discussion of the ways in which these interactive installations might be encountered in the future, once the real-life survivors are no longer with us and their virtual namesakes have transformed into the idiosyncratic haunting machines that we refer to as ghostware.

2

Ghosting the Museum

Powers of the Metatext: America, Virtual Mythologies, and the Eternity Narrative

Standing near the national monuments that line the Mall, the United States Holocaust Memorial Museum (USHMM) sits in the symbolic center of the nation's capital. Alongside films such as *Schindler's List*—released in 1993, the year that the museum opened—the USHMM represents the apotheosis of the upsurge in Holocaust consciousness that took place in the USA as the twentieth century drew to a close. In *The Holocaust in American Life* (1999), Peter Novick argues that during this period, Holocaust memory became a kind of "civil religion" that was central to American Jewry's "self-understanding and self-representation" and also to that of American society at large."[1] Edward T. Linenthal credits Michael Berenbaum, a former USHMM project director and research institute director, with coining the phrase "the Americanization of the Holocaust" to describe a desirable process whose ultimate aim was to make this episode in European and Jewish history relevant to a wider American audience.[2] What was initially a point of controversy soon became central to the museum's ethos.[3] In a letter to *The Washington Post* in 1990, the museum's current Director, Sara Bloomfield, expressed her wish for the museum to exemplify American values, serving as the "moral compass" of a nation that was the "standard-bearer of freedom and human rights."[4] Such an agenda is exemplified in the identification cards that visitors are given before they enter the main exhibition, which bear the Great Seal of the United States. Personalizing the experience for American schoolchildren and echoing the identity papers that Jews were required to carry during the war, the cards ask visitors not only to identify with Holocaust victims but also with American ideals, such as liberty and democracy, that are celebrated across the Mall. With the seal headed by the imperative, "For the dead <u>and</u> the living we must bear witness," the identity cards suggest that Holocaust memory lies at the heart of what it means to be a socially engaged member of American civil society. More cynically, as Novick observes, the identity cards might also be

Virtual Holocaust Memory. Matthew Boswell and Antony Rowland, Oxford University Press. © Oxford University Press 2023. DOI: 10.1093/oso/9780197645390.003.0003

symptomatic of a culture in which "Americans of all sorts came to see themselves as victims—oppressed by various aspects of modern life."[5]

With its main exhibition introduced by a large photograph of Dachau being liberated by American forces, the museum has been criticized by those who object to the "fiction of nationhood" that is created by the conflation of America's role as the liberator of a small number of concentration camps with the "story of American democracy," in order to reinforce the politically laudable but historically contestable assertion that "a democratic state comes to the aid of those peoples outside its borders subjected to genocide."[6] The many Presidential quotations and plaques that adorn the main building and its surrounding estate reinforce such sentiments. However, while the USHMM consistently looks to the Holocaust to affirm American values in sometimes contentious ways, the organization is, at the same time, much like the USC Shoah Foundation, genuinely committed to championing social justice and engendering memory activism. Ubiquitous slogans daubed in capitals on branded black, white, and orange banners, posters, and gift shop memorabilia emphasize the importance of taking personal responsibility for putting the lessons of the Holocaust into practice and translating words into action: "What you do matters," "Never again begins with you," and "This museum is not an answer. It is a question." As Linenthal writes of museums with this kind of socially engaged ethos: "Visitors, ideally, do not come merely to consume them as cultural commodities but to enter them as civic pilgrims, to be transformed by the lessons that emerge from imaginative narrative engagement."[7] While the USHMM has little to say about the mass killing and violence that marked the foundation of the American nation-state, it does confront sensitive historical topics such as complicity and collaboration during the Second World War. At the time of the Dimensions in Testimony pilot, for example, it was running a compelling special exhibition on what Americans knew about the Holocaust during the war, which provided a good deal of evidence to suggest that it was more than is commonly imagined. Neither does the museum shy away from confronting more recent crises, including the foreign conflicts with which the USA has been controversially engaged in Afghanistan, Syria, and Iraq. It also acknowledges the failure of the "never again" slogan (and, implicitly, American foreign policy) through special exhibitions on genocides that have taken place in countries such as Cambodia. Vivian M. Patraka notes that the tomb-like architecture of the main museum building further complicates the redemptive narratives that are foregrounded in the museum's exhibitions and merchandise.[8]

Through a long and complex genesis, the USHMM's ideology and discursive practices bear the influence of Jewish culture and the Christian values that are traditionally held to be embodied in the American presidency. The idea of building the museum first took shape when Jimmy Carter established the President's Commission on the Holocaust in 1978, in order to scope the creation of a national Holocaust memorial.[9] The commission was chaired by "the most influential American interpreter of the Holocaust," the Jewish survivor and writer Elie Wiesel, who viewed the Holocaust as "equal to the revelation at Sinai" in its religious significance, with any attempt to "desanctify" or "demystify" it constituting a form of anti-Semitism.[10] Rabbi Arthur Hertzberg's description of the USHMM as a place of modern pilgrimage is therefore apt in its conjoining of Jewish and Christian traditions:

> Historians . . . will no doubt see the unparalleled effort and passion which created the greatest of the Holocaust memorials in the United States on the Mall in Washington as the contemporary version of the building of a "national Jewish cathedral." It enshrines the Holocaust as the via dolorosa and crucifixion of the Jewish people. Those who come to remember are transformed in this shrine into participants in the great sacrifice. They are confirmed in their Jewishness, leaving with "never again" on their lips.[11]

Central to the museum's blurred Judeo-Christian philosophy is the idea that memory sanctifies history. A quotation from Bill Clinton displayed prominently on an inner wall near the main entrance modernizes this ethos for a generation of memory activists: "If this museum can mobilize morality, then those who have perished will thereby gain a measure of immortality."

Such lofty rhetoric has the potential to become doubly potent when conjoined with that which surrounds Dimensions in Testimony, which consistently flirts with the idea that the system immortalizes Holocaust survivors. For example, a leaflet produced by the USC Shoah Foundation for the USHMM pilot claims: "Through Dimensions in Testimony, survivor Pinchas Gutter can answer questions about his life before, during and after the Holocaust **as if he were in the room**."[12] Presenting interactive testimony as a miraculous interaction with the living consciousness of a Holocaust survivor, as opposed to a recording of an interview that took place in Los Angeles in 2015, requires a contradictory logic that holds that the technology both is and is not important. This is reflected in the way that, on the one hand, the Dimensions in Testimony team repeatedly claim that its technology is insignificant and unobtrusive. In an interview with the *Guardian* given at around the same time as the USHMM pilot in 2016, Heather Maio, Director of Conscience Display, commented:

> We wanted the visitor to experience the discussion and what that means to them. Not the technology that goes around it and makes it work. In fact, we didn't want them to think there was technology around them at all.[13]

At other times, however, the technology is explicitly brought to the fore. One of the gimmickier elements of Dimensions in Testimony comes when the virtual survivors respond to the question "How old are you?" by asking the questioner to calculate the answer for themselves, based on the date when they are asking the question and the survivor's date of birth. While users are supposed to arrive at an age that will ultimately end up being much greater than that of an ordinary human lifespan, the unresolved contradictions that mark the Foundation's approach to its technology are underscored by one of the virtual Schloss's stock answers for a question that has no direct match in the database, which is, quite correctly, "I'm actually a recording. I can't answer that question." Here the virtual Schloss's pragmatic and accurate answer gives the lie to the intimations of immortality contained in the response to the "How old are you?" question.

Critics such as Wulf Kansteiner read the inability to shed "small, yet pervasive, markers of historical non-simultaneity" as a limitation of a project that can never be "continuously brought up to date" and "embedded in the present-day social context of the observer."[14] However, we would argue that this is an unrealistic aspiration for a digital testimony project. Any attempt to elide historical non-simultaneity can only produce unhelpful mythologies, as with these perplexing attempts to obfuscate the question of the survivor's age. Kansteiner's fear is that the antiquation of media forms might make them less interesting for younger generations. Yet antiquation can equally produce powerful aesthetic effects, as Jeffrey Shandler observes in relation to the video testimony gathered in the VHA:

> Rather than constituting a loss in effectiveness, the aging of video may well endow the medium with the aura of a historical artefact [*sic*], much as has happened with black-and-white film footage of the World War II era. This added value may also facilitate greater awareness among viewers that the

videos are mediations of memory, rooted in the past by their form as well as their content.[15]

By attempting to conceal the fact that interactive video testimony involves a recording of a real survivor made on a particular day in the past, Dimensions in Testimony risks creating an illusion that cannot be sustained through the wider interaction, detracting from the potency of the testimony itself and what it reveals about the "struggle for survival" that endures right to the end of a survivor's life.[16] Knowing the real survivor's actual age at the time they were interviewed shapes the way that we respond to their testimony. By obscuring the question of their mortality, Dimensions in Testimony further risks overlooking the sense in which children, in particular, might be more moved by the virtual interaction if they are to see it as having much in common with the kind of conversation they might have (or have had) with an elderly relative, rather than seeing the survivors as immortal cyborgs. Talking to the virtual Schloss may become even more moving for it being a knowingly posthumous encounter, as we discuss in the "Ghostware" section below.

In some ways, the UK-based Forever Project has a more truthful approach to the temporal non-simultaneity that is such a source of confusion for Dimensions in Testimony. The interviews for the Forever Project foreground the fact that they took place on a particular date in the past, with the project team allowing survivors to refer to contemporary events in their interviews, thereby embedding them in a specific historical juncture that is clearly that of the survivor rather than their interlocutor. Moreover, the testimonies from the Forever Project can currently only be accessed when people visit the National Holocaust Centre and Museum and view them through three-dimensional glasses (if they choose to do so) on a special projection screen in the Memorial Hall as part of events and education programs led by the Centre. While limiting the uses to which the recordings can be put, this means that visitors' encounters with interactive testimony take place in conditions that closely match those of visitors attending talks by living Holocaust survivors. This also allows the Centre to explain exactly what the technology is and how it functions. In addition, the integration of interactive testimony into formal pedagogical frameworks and institutional settings shapes the questions that visitors ask and the answers that survivors give, with the latter able to assume a certain level of pre-existing knowledge (about the Holocaust and their own personal stories) that Dimensions in Testimony survivors cannot.

Yet the Forever Project is by no means devoid of the metaphysical schemata that characterize the metatexts used to describe Dimensions in Testimony in institutions such as the USHMM. The Memorial Hall at the National Holocaust Centre and Museum has been designed as a sacred space, with arched entrances, stained glass windows, and high brick walls inscribed with the Talmudic quotation used as the tagline for *Schindler's List*: "He who saves a single life saves the world entire." Such features combine to create a religious mood that lends a particular "aura," to use Walter Benjamin's term, to the encounter with interactive testimony.[17] The very title of the Forever Project also suggests a conformity with what we term the "eternity narrative," implying that interactive testimony confers on survivors a form of immortality that exceeds that which is possible through more traditional testimonial forms, such as literature or oral testimony, whose cultural longevity seems, ironically, far more certain.

The promotional film used to launch the funding campaign for the Forever Project shows how the eternity narrative is not only shaped by Judeo-Christian religious traditions, but also by the contemporary entertainment industries.[18] Attributing superhuman strengths and powers to survivors, while imitating the melodramatic aesthetics of a trailer for a Hollywood blockbuster, the film begins with an epic aerial shot of Canary Wharf in London. A voiceover then intones that "for the best part of a century" the mysterious elderly people who we see sitting on sofas and walking through parks, cities, and train stations, "lived quietly among us, sharing their powers" (see Fig. 2.1). As choral voices chant in the background, the voiceover continues:

Figure 2.1 The Forever Project promotional film
Property of the National Holocaust Centre and Museum.

Ordinary men and women with extraordinary strengths. If only they also had the power of immortality. Now, through the power of 3D technology, they can all keep their stories alive. Because these are the men and women who know the truth about mankind. A truth that needs to live forever.

While the script makes it clear that it is words, stories, and truth that will be immortalized through the project, the strategy of presenting Holocaust survivors as superheroes suggests that they are transcendent beings who are both mortal—the survivors talk explicitly about aging and the feeling of energy draining from them—and yet, at the same time, not (see Figs. 2.2 and 2.3).

The sacralization of survivor-witnesses — what Novick terms "the cult of the survivor as secular saint" — is not itself a new phenomenon.[19] Carolyn J. Dean traces it back to the landmark event of the Eichmann Trial which, she

Figure 2.2 The Forever Project publicity material
Property of the National Holocaust Centre and Museum.

Figure 2.3 The Forever Project publicity material
Property of the National Holocaust Centre and Museum.

argues, played an important role in restoring dignity to Holocaust victims by rebuffing a prevailing stigma of the postwar period, which regarded survival as shameful evidence of the Jews' failure to resist:

> The trial thus transformed the victim's powerlessness into a newly discovered source of inner strength: of honour, of glory, and of wisdom. It transformed the inconceivable dimension of survivors' experience into a source of supra-human wisdom and universal truths about life and death in the twentieth century.[20]

Dean goes on to note that survivors thereafter became a "source of special moral clarity."[21] In lifting the stigma and shame of victimization, this newly heroic and quasi-mystical conception of the survivor-witness served an important social function—as well as an important psychological function for the survivors themselves—which was subsequently made "culturally legible and symbolically powerful" in films such as *Schindler's List*.[22] Survivor sacralization also has much in common with what Zygmunt Bauman terms the "life strategies" that help societies deal with the terrifying prospect of death and dying.[23] Bauman writes: "Immortality is not a mere absence of death; it is *defiance* and denial of death."[24] Interactive testimony's sacred survivors and eternity narrative might therefore provide a cultural rejoinder to mass death, expressing a moral sentiment, rather than a realistic identity or temporality, that holds that survivor memory will always resist and outlive genocidal horror.

It is understandable, then, that such sentiments should have a powerful hold over projects led by institutions that are deeply invested in the memories of survivors with whom they have developed close personal relationships over long periods of time. Yet these discourses risk transforming into what (in a different context) Dominic LaCapra terms a "negative sacralization" when they spill over into uncritical forms of veneration that position survivors as the ultimate source not only of knowledge about the Holocaust but also of human virtue.[25] Rather than connecting users with survivors who are fallible, cantankerous, damaged, *human*, extreme veneration can serve, as Laub warns, to keep them "at a distance, to avoid the intimacy entailed in knowing."[26] And in the case of interactive testimony, survivor sacralization may even lead users to be more cautious about the virtual interaction, such that one of the most frequently cited advantages of interactive testimony over a "real" interaction is missed: namely, that an interaction with a video recording might embolden young people to ask questions that they might hesitate to ask a living survivor for fear of being indelicate.

There can be no doubting the benign intentions that motivate the institutional commitment to the eternity narrative, and its symbolism may, following Dean and Bauman, serve an important social function. Nonetheless, such inflated, melodramatic rhetoric risks transforming virtual spaces of memory into fantastical ones in which Holocaust memory is divorced from the passing of time. Moreover, the mythological structure of the eternity narrative contrasts sharply with the testimonial truthfulness valued by Delbo, whose virtue involves a "will to truth" and a sincere striving for accuracy. As Bernard Williams writes: "Truthfulness implies a respect for truth."[27] Viewing Dimensions in Testimony more soberly as an interactive encounter with a historical recording perhaps lacks the gravitas and paradigm-shifting promise of the eternity narrative. There may well also be some stigma attached to a conceptualization of Holocaust memory that emphasizes its performativity, even playfulness. But such a conception of interactive video testimony is based on a truthful assessment of what the technology is and what it does, attempting to lay bare the device rather than to conceal it.

Given the influential role that specific institutions, ideologies, and metatexts play in reinforcing the eternity narrative, we will pause here briefly to clarify the spatiotemporal relationships that come into play in Dimensions in Testimony and the Forever Project by comparing them to those that characterize more traditional forms of testimonial interaction.

Testimony's Spatiotemporalities

At the risk of some simplification, our engagement with culturally mediated testimony usually plays out across three spatiotemporal coordinates. These three spaces of memory are anchored in different moments of historical time, and it is the act of connecting them that brings testimony into being.[28] First, we have the periods and places associated with the survivors' historical experiences that they recall in their testimony, such as Gutter's childhood imprisonment in Majdanek. Second, we have the time and place in which the survivor testifies: for example, the light stage in Los Angeles in 2015. Finally, there is the moment of reception, when another person reads, sees, hears, or interacts with the survivor's testimony, such as our encounter with Dimensions in Testimony at the Museum of Jewish Heritage in 2018. In most forms of recorded testimony, such as written accounts and filmed interviews, each of these three spatiotemporal points is distinct, with the historical memory, the moment of testifying, and the moment of reception all subtly interacting but never completely collapsing into one another. The innovation or illusion that individuates interactive video testimony lies in the suggestion that the moment of testifying (the real time interview) and the moment of reception (the interaction with the virtual survivor) are synchronous, which both is and is not true, in that the real time interview took place at a spatiotemporal remove from its reception, but it is only triggered through a user's present-day interaction.

Written and filmed testimonies can, of course, play with the temporal divide that separates testimony from its reception: for example, by personalizing their address to give a heightened sense of authorial proximity. A notable literary example is Levi's poem "Shemà" that serves as an epigraph to *If This Is a Man* (1959), which begins: "You who live safe / In your warm houses."[29] However, oral testimonies rarely address viewers so directly; instead, the survivors' accounts are more usually addressed to a real time interviewer who may or may not be in shot. Interactive video testimony, on the other hand, allows users to feel as though the testimony emerges entirely because of their inquisitiveness, masking cultural mediation through a simulation of interpersonal communication. Indeed, the user's agency in cocreating the testimonial encounter might have been exploited even further in both the Forever Project and Dimensions in Testimony: for example, by getting the virtual survivors to ask their interlocutors questions, as they might do in a real time conversation, such as "What is your name?," "What do you know about the Holocaust?" or "Have we learned the lessons of history"? Of course, careful thought would need to have been given to how such interactions were structured, in order to offset (or exploit) the fact that the virtual survivor would not be able to hear or respond to the user's answers. Nonetheless, the survivor-writer's unresponsiveness does not weaken the power of direct address in literary testimony, and developing a two-way discussion, drawing users into a more introspective and personal mode of engagement with the system, would not have been altogether impossible.

A further distinguishing trait of interactive video testimony is that decisions about how to frame and mobilize the three spatiotemporal coordinates are to a large degree made by the institutions who create and host the testimony, rather than the survivors themselves. While survivors clearly have a say in what memories they choose to share or conceal when they answer their interviewer's questions, the focus of the interviews is to a large extent determined by the questions asked by the interviewer. As we discuss in the following chapter, the survivors do not have total freedom to talk about whatever they wish, as they broadly do with written testimony, or even when giving the more open form of oral testimony favored in the interviews for the Fortunoff Archive. Indeed, during the Dimensions in Testimony interviews, some answers were revisited and rerecorded if they were not sufficiently concise, relevant, or on topic. The degree to which the survivor interview is foregrounded, minimized, or—most problematically—eclipsed altogether is also entirely in the hands of the institution, rather than the survivor. While a survivor-writer can decide to foreground the moment of mediation, as in Delbo's "*Today, I am not sure that what I wrote is true*," in interactive video testimony, such meta-testimonial reflections are governed by the institution overseeing the project. And, as noted, the metatexts used by the USC Shoah Foundation frequently seek to propound the fiction that the spatiotemporal moment of the survivor interview and the spatiotemporal moment of its reception are one and the same, thereby significantly diminishing any claim to testimonial truthfulness.

But ought we to be so censorious about a testimonial form that operates through fabrication and formal playfulness? As noted, the temporalities and spaces of memory that are connected through interactive video testimony are essentially the same as those that we find in literature and filmed testimonies. And the way interactive testimony dramatizes the relationship between the narration of testimony and its reception could be compared to the way that a documentary film such as Claude Lanzmann's *Shoah* (1985) dramatizes the relationship between the past and the contemporary remembrance and recounting of that past. Lanzmann famously interviewed survivors in landscapes and settings associated with their Holocaust memories to create what he termed a *"fiction du réel"* (a fiction rooted in reality).[30] He does this precisely because he is in search of a different, more performative order of truth that transcends the purely historic. In their commentary on *Shoah*, Shoshana Felman and Dori Laub describe how, through these pertinently located interviews, the documentary brings two distinct spaces of Holocaust memory—the "inside" and "outside" of the event—into an unlikely, even impossible, dialogue with one another:

It is not really possible to *tell the truth*, to testify, from the outside. Neither is it possible, as we have seen, to testify from the inside. I would suggest that the impossible position and the testimonial effort of the film as a whole is to be, precisely, neither simply inside nor simply outside, but paradoxically, *both inside and outside*: to create a *connection* that did not exist during the war and does not exist today *between the inside and the outside*—to set them both in motion and in dialogue with one another.[31]

Through the dynamics of simulation, interactive video testimony occupies a similarly "impossible position," with the virtual conversation taking place across the borders of the light stage between interlocutors whose lifespans may never overlap. In doing so, future generations will have the opportunity to draw closer to the *inside of memory*—exploring and interacting with survivor memory as a seemingly living, contemporary phenomenon—if not to the inside of history itself.

In her essay "Theatres of Justice," Felman further argues that the Eichmann Trial returned the possibility of speech to the victims by creating "a *new space*, a language that is not yet in existence."[32] Felman's sense of the law as a structure that creates a "bridge to the future" also suggests an approach to the spatiotemporalities of interactive video testimony, wherein simulated bridges in time connect users not so much to the history of the Holocaust, as to *the memory of conversations with survivors about their memories of that history*.[33] By prolonging the possibility of a dialogue that is rapidly fading from existence, interactive video testimony aspires, as Kansteiner notes, "to stem the tide of history and decelerate the historicization of Holocaust memory."[34] While virtual interactions cannot defy temporality altogether by enabling survivors to live forever, they can construct imaginative bridges to cross, performative processes to enact, that have the potential to make Holocaust testimony feel more personal and proximate than it might in more traditional written and oral forms.[35] Exemplifying the innovative aesthetic strategies employed by proponents of connective memory, a strange, almost supernatural form of address that seems to emerge from beyond the borders of death places the inside and outside of memory into a striking new configuration.

Having focused on what the emergence of the interactive video testimony pilots tells us about Holocaust memory during the fifth and final era of Holocaust witnessing, then, we will close this chapter by turning to the possibility of encountering such testimony through three-dimensional interactive holograms in what may come to seem like a ghostly sixth era of Holocaust witnessing in the post-survivor age, once we have left the period of living memory altogether, asking what forms of truthfulness these simulated encounters might engender.

Ghostware

A common response to the Dimensions in Testimony pilot installations, even when presented as two-dimensional, screen-based interactions, is to find them disarming, strange, and even slightly creepy. In the article on Dimensions in Testimony in *The Forward* that featured interviews with Langer and Rudof, Dan Leopard, a digital media and education researcher, uses the theory of the "uncanny valley" to explain such responses. A popular reference point for those trying to get to grips with the visceral impact of interactive testimony, the theory describes how we respond to technologies that resemble human bodies, such as robots or prosthetic limbs, positing that we grow increasingly comfortable with such simulations as they become more lifelike, up until we reach a point where we are drawn into a sudden awareness of the object's artificiality and our comfort levels dip sharply, leading to sensations of revulsion. These feelings become most pronounced when the lifelike object moves. Drawing on Freud's use of the *unheimlich* to denote that which is familiar but strange, and therefore a source of anxiety, Leopard notes of the virtual Gutter prototype: "It's not really alive, but we expect it to be alive. That's a problem. It's sort of off-putting."[36] Such applications of the theory of the uncanny valley to interactive testimony are to a degree misplaced, given that this is an audio-visual recording of a real Holocaust survivor, not a humanoid robot, a stuffed animal, a zombie, or a corpse (other examples that are commonly used to illustrate the theory). Yet we recall Hirsch's observation concerning the "*liveness*" she experiences watching "film or video testimony," and how this was missing from her "encounter with the disembodied life-like projection of Eva Kor and the algorithm that selected her responses."[37] For Leopard and Hirsch, a sense of uncanniness clearly derives from the technological machinations that facilitate a user's interactions with these video recordings.

With screen-based versions of Dimensions in Testimony resembling interactions through online video calls, which quickly became a feature of daily life for many during the Covid-19 pandemic, it should perhaps not be surprising that many people should find these interactions slightly spooky or unpleasant on an instinctual level. Platforms such as Zoom and Skype, with which Dimensions in Testimony is often compared, are associated

Figure 2.4 The virtual Aaron Elster at the Illinois Holocaust Museum and Education Center
Jennifer Billock

with communication between living beings. Moreover, as noted, institutional metatexts flirt with the idea that the holograms are emerging into our world from a parallel universe. In this section, we therefore make some conjectures about the future of Holocaust memory as it moves from being a living memory to one that feels "life-like." We imagine a world in which three-dimensional interactive testimony (see Fig. 2.4) has become culturally significant, arguing that these posthumous virtual encounters will call for a substantial refashioning of received understandings of haunting, while at the same time underscoring the continuing relevance of Jacques Derrida's poststructuralist approach to the topic. Should the afterlife of Holocaust memory become radically reconstituted in newly virtualized, lifelike forms, the question of the embodiment of historical knowledge in all its aspects—as knowledge mediated through the intangible, digitized bodies of virtual Holocaust survivors, as knowledge experienced through the real bodies of future generations engaging in virtual conversations, as knowledge about bodies that were subjected to extreme forms of degradation and violence—will be integral to the evolving theory and practice of connective memory.

Over the last two decades, extensive critical interest in ghosts and haunting has developed largely in response to the "pseudo-concepts" of "spectrality" and "hauntology" outlined by Derrida in *Specters of Marx* (1993), in which he builds a "great problematic constellation" of digressions and interventions that thematizes the ways in which the past haunts literature, theory, and politics.[38] Taking inspiration from the opening sentence of *The Communist Manifesto* (1848)—"a specter is haunting Europe—the specter of communism"—Derrida argues that the trope of spectrality describes and performs the elusive, oblique, and non-governable nature of our relationship with the past and, above all, the relationship between the living and the dead. As we move deeper into the post-survivor age, the contemporary coordinate in the triangulation of spatiotemporal realms that are connected through recorded testimony—that is to say, that of the present-day virtual conversation—will become increasingly distanced from the other two spatiotemporal points (namely, that of the Holocaust and that of the moment when the survivor bore witness). Novick argues that such historical distancing is taking place at an accelerating pace, with the rapidly changing circumstances of contemporary life meaning that "the life expectancy of [collective] memories in today's society appears greatly diminished."[39] Novick further notes that the USA is the "most 'now' and amnesiac of nations."[40] In line with this process of cultural forgetting, one might expect the affect of any form of culturally mediated testimony to weaken over time: as the historical referent recedes from individual and collective memory, it seems reasonable to suppose that its cultural after-effects will be felt less forcefully. However, interactive testimony offers a unique formation whereby the *frisson* of a performative experience of the past may strengthen or intensify once the real-life survivors pass away and we engage in a posthumous interaction that seemingly traverses the limits of the human lifespan. While interactive testimony might therefore be understood in terms of specters and the spectral, its mode of historical return will be anything but furtive and oblique. Strongly evoking the idea of the return of the dead, with the installations of virtual Holocaust survivors seeming to speak to us from beyond the borders of death, societies of the future may increasingly feel themselves to be haunted—or, rather, they may feel the need to actively haunt themselves—in a direct and ostensibly non-spectral (in Derrida's sense) fashion by using what we will term, following Alexander Etkind, "ghostware."[41] While, for Etkind, ghostware describes the uncanny "ghosts, spirits, vampires, dolls and other man-made and man-imagined simulacra that carry the memory of the dead" through the "hardware" of monuments and the "software" of texts, the emergence of interactive testimony means that ghostware might be reimagined as a digitally-mediated form of haunting that sits alongside monuments and texts as a material actuality.[42]

The ghost that introduces Derrida's argument in *Specters of Marx* is that of Hamlet's father: a figure whose emergence on the ramparts of Elsinore poses dilemmas for Shakespeare's characters that remain almost implausibly pertinent to the experience of encountering the interactive testimony of virtual Holocaust survivors. First, there is the same initial ontological uncertainty. Derrida describes how the ghost disappears and reappears on the battlements, a "thing" that "concerns us" but which "remains difficult to name: neither soul nor body, and both one and the other."[43] Second, there is the question of what to do when confronted with this "thing." Derrida focusses on the dilemma faced by the incredulous scholar Horatio, who has been urged by his friend Marcellus to join them on the castle walls, "That, if again this apparition come, / He may approve our eyes and speak to it" (1.2.27–28). This leads Derrida to reflect on the impossibility of speaking to and of the ghost:

> As theoreticians or witnesses, spectators, observers, and intellectuals, scholars believe that looking is sufficient. Therefore, they are not always in the most competent position to do what is necessary: speak to the specter. Herein lies perhaps, among so many others, an indelible lesson of Marxism. There is no longer, there has never been a scholar capable of speaking of anything and everything while addressing himself to everyone and anyone, and especially to ghosts. There has never been a scholar who really, and as scholar, deals with ghosts. A traditional scholar does not believe in ghosts—nor in all that could be called the virtual space of spectrality. There has never been a scholar who, as such, does not believe in the sharp distinction between the real and the unreal, the actual and the inactual, the living and the non-living, being and non-being ("to be or not to be," in the conventional reading), in the opposition between what is present and what is not, for example in the form of objectivity.[44]

Here, Derrida's ironic conceptualization of the scholar's responsibilities toward Hamlet's father's ghost is suggestive of the challenges faced by users seeking to navigate three-dimensional interactive video testimony that can, much like the ramparts of Elsinore, be thought of as a "virtual space of spectrality." Following the lead of Marcellus and Horatio, it is not enough simply to look, to bear witness to the ghosts who inhabit such spaces, or even to wait for them to address us. When we encounter holograms of virtual Holocaust survivors in the resting pose, with their heads tilted toward us, waiting, listening, we understand that we must also speak to them.

For Derrida, this is not simply a function of the ghost's supposed humanity; nor is the ensuing speech act the same as speaking or conversing *with* a real person. Derrida argues that the ghost does not possess the self-consciousness of a real person: "How do you recognize a ghost? By the fact that it does not recognize itself in a mirror."[45] Much as Shakespeare's characters encounter a form of ghostly consciousness that is not fully human but, just as importantly, not fully nonhuman either, when confronted by interactive video testimony we know that we are not speaking directly *with* a human being. Yet we are also aware that we are not speaking to an *it*. Even if we understand that we are verbally interrogating a database through natural language processing, this does not offset our sense that we are also interacting with the testimony of a real human being. As Derrida acknowledges, the effect of this liminal space of memory is to undercut much of what we think we know:

> *It is* something that one does not know, precisely, and one does not know if precisely it *is*, if it exists, if it corresponds to a name and corresponds to an essence. One does not know: not out of ignorance, but because this non-object, this non-present present, this being-there of an absent or departed one no longer belongs to knowledge. At least no longer to that which one thinks one knows by the name of knowledge. One does not know if it is living or if it is dead.[46]

Such a confusion between the living and the dead often marks the experience of those encountering Dimensions in Testimony for the first time. Even in the pilots that we observed between 2016 and 2018, when the virtual survivors were displayed in two dimensions, many elderly users, especially, interacted with the technology in emotive terms that suggested an investment in the interaction that surpassed a simple "suspension of disbelief." For example, we watched one user at the Sheffield Doc/Fest in 2016 thank the Gutter installation very sincerely for the conversation, wishing him all the best for the future in a way that they would not do to a machine, a book, a video recording, or, indeed, a character in a Shakespeare play. Similarly, a visitor at the Museum of Jewish Heritage in 2018 was visibly put out when Gutter did not respond to their account of their own family's Holocaust history. In an interview for *The Guardian*, Smith recounts a similar moment:

> Smith says audience members have applauded the virtual Gutter, thanked him, argued with him. "One woman apologised to him for the negligence of the world, telling him she would have willingly traded places with him had she been alive then."[47]

As we have argued, the form of authenticity at stake in such interactions is not so much that of historical truth or simulation truth, but rather that of the *truthfulness* of interactions that are ambiguously situated between the human and the nonhuman, but which are no less "real" for being so. Through this chapter, we have built a sense of truthfulness as a performative moment, involving the fleeting, embodied, coming-into-being of a virtual interaction with a Holocaust survivor across long temporal distances, wherein the simulation of the survivor's presence allows for an overspill of posthumous meaning and sentiment into the present. This performance is, at heart, the performance of memory, that is to say a mode of relationship to the past, grounded in the idea that it is still possible to capture something of the essence of a conversation with a Holocaust survivor through immersive technology. The performative and emotional basis of this testimonial encounter is so strong as to suggest that what the installations tell us about history (or even what they fail to tell us about history) does not really matter all that much. Rather, what matters is what they tell us about how we *relate* to this history, and to the dead, through digital interfaces that personalize and humanize the mass suffering of the Holocaust. However kitschy or sentimental this might seem—and however virtual the framework—the sense of interpersonal connection will prove, for many, to feel very real.

Jewish tradition is full of revenants, from the dybbuks and ibbur of Jewish mythology to the spirits of the dead summoned by golems. Holocaust literature also frequently imagines the return of the dead in fearful, vengeful guises, with Levi's "Song of Those Who Died in Vain" being a notable example.[48] Should interactive testimony become pervasive in everyday life, it seems possible that the new potentialities of the virtual will refashion how future generations think about the return of the dead, and in ways that extend beyond the cultural memory of the Holocaust. Rather than fearing malicious spirits seeking to take possession of their bodies, or ghosts returning to right historical wrongs, societies of the future may welcome these "electronic phantoms" as they step out from the darkened confines of the historical unconscious and into the bright digital light of twenty-first century consciousness, not least because the technology gives future societies a significant degree of control and agency over the machinations of their own haunting.[49] This ghostware will produce the kind of haunting described by survivor Ruth Kluger in her poem "Halloween and a Ghost": "Unlike real people, ghosts are obvious, / Thinly disguised and come when most expected."[50] This very non-spectral aspect of interactive video testimony therefore ushers us into a period that feels very different to the one originally scrutinized by Derrida in *Specters of Marx*, when haunting centrally related to the return of repressed histories of violence that late twentieth century capitalist society had failed to mourn. Symptomatic of unmastered trauma, the fear of ghosts compelled such societies to do all that they could to ensure "that the dead will not come back: quick, do whatever is needed to keep the cadaver localized, in a safe place, decomposing wherever it was inhumed."[51] Conversely, in the newly virtualized post-survivor age, organizations such as the USC Shoah Foundation imagine digital revenants being installed in museums and schools that become safely haunted spaces, where the ghosts of the past are made available for our instruction and edification. We can choose the time, place, and duration of visitations by ghosts who have become pedagogical and technological, introduced into our present at the touch of a button. The only element of their diaphanous, three-dimensional, digital bodies that might possibly decompose is their bytes; yet the Foundation possesses technology that will ensure that the integrity of the data gathered during the original interviews can never be compromised.

If the emergence of interactive video testimony suggests that Holocaust memory culture is moving beyond the traumatic frameworks that shaped our understanding of earlier periods of witnessing, Derrida's sense of our *responsibility* toward the ghosts of the past continues to be relevant to this new era of connective memory. As we have intimated previously, our responsibility toward the real survivors who partook in Dimensions in Testimony is visually rendered through the dynamics of the resting pose (see Fig. 2.5). As they wait to be asked a question with their hands on their laps and, in the case of the virtual Gutter, his neck craned slightly forward, the virtual survivors assume a posture that expresses their readiness to respond to our questions. Importantly, they do not sit still. The recordings are not paused. Instead, they make fidgety movements: blinking, tapping their fingers, moving their heads. Left in this state of limbo, they seem jittery and agitated. At times, the virtual Schloss looks up to her right, as if disorientated, confused, or trapped. Rather than inertia,

Figure 2.5 Dimensions in Testimony pilot at the Museum of Jewish Heritage
Matthew Boswell

these movements ensure that the installations display signs of life. However, the virtual survivors remain locked in this mute state until they receive some form of verbal trigger. In this way, the resting pose communicates the system's functional dependency on users, as Gutter recognized when he first saw his own virtual pilot: "I saw myself sitting there, moving my hands and legs, being a presence and speaking to people . . . Not just speaking but answering. In other words, I'm listening. I'm not just speaking, I'm listening."[52]

The high-definition recordings of the survivors' eyes further humanize the interaction, conveying a sense of the user's responsibility toward the survivor whose testimony is captured in the system and almost imploring us to empathize with their experiences. In the two-dimensional version, the virtual survivors seem to strain to make us out across the plasma screen separating our world from theirs. One can imagine that with a hologram, this poignant effect will be even more pronounced, with the three-dimensional image being suggestive of a real human being trying to make out their interlocutors across a semi-transparent, digital veil. As Thomas McMullan observes:

My personal experience with the project hinged on eye contact. Having Gutter staring at me as he answered my question on the Warsaw uprising, or about whether he still believed in God, was affecting on an instinctive level.[53]

The strong impression made by the virtual survivors' eyes helps to shape the central illusion of the virtual conversation, which is that the real-life survivors are listening out for us in some parallel dimension to the present. This compelling visual articulation of the idea of looking and speaking across a spatiotemporal divide is effective on the "instinctual level" noted by McMullan. It also recalls the philosophical writings of Emmanuel Levinas, whose work on face-to-face encounters with "the other" underpinned much of the "ethical turn" in literary and cultural studies in the 1990s. As James Dawes explains, face-to-face encounters form a metaphor that sits at the heart of Levinas's philosophy:

> We come into being as particular persons in relation to others who, in the immediate face-to-face relationship, strike us both as infinitely foreign and irresistibly intimate—foreign because the other can never be assimilated or reduced to sameness; intimate because identity is, finally, intersubjective. In a sense, there is no self before and apart from its response to the other.[54]

For Levinas, communication involves opening oneself up to the other, becoming "complete not in the opening to the spectacle of or the recognition of the other, but in becoming a responsibility for him."[55] Lévinas's ethical system, grounded in looking, pertains to a highly spectral aspect of the connective dynamics of interactive testimony—far more spectral, in a philosophical sense, than the basic idea of being haunted by a ghostly incursion into our present— which involves, paradoxically, a complete reversal of the way in which Derrida conceptualizes the dynamics of looking as they pertain to Hamlet's ghost. For Derrida, the fleeting, insubstantial visuality of ghosts causes the living to feel observed from elsewhere: "We will call this the *visor effect*: we do not see who looks at us."[56] While the technological apparatus of interactive testimony gives users a sense of being watched by the virtual survivors, having a realistic, historicized, and truthful sense of the interview with which we are engaging allows us to read the uncanny eyes, performative posture, and visual dynamics of interactive testimony in terms of the fact that the survivors *cannot see their future interlocutors* while they are talking to them. To paraphrase Derrida, *they* do not see who looks at *them*, and it is therefore the real-life survivors, as much as their interlocutors, who are placed under a furtive form of surveillance by the machinery of virtual haunting. Much as, in the future, Holocaust survivors will seem to be addressing us from beyond the borders of death, we recognize that these survivors were themselves addressing those who were not yet born during their interviews, meaning that *their future interlocutors are productive of the specter's haunting,* casting a ghostly shadow in the light stage: one that arguably shapes the testimony just as much as the ghosts of the survivors' personal pasts.

"The time is out of joint" (1.5.188), as Hamlet puts it, in a phrase frequently quoted by Derrida. An acknowledgment of this inversion, whereby, in the post-survivor age, the living will come to understand how they once haunted the dead, as much as the dead now haunt the living, helps to clarify the ethical challenge and form of responsibility faced by those who find themselves implicated in this reverse "visor effect." How can we respond to our strange interpolation inside this moment when the survivor in the light stage speaks? Can we imagine forms of justice that are outside the purview of the law, but which engage our ethical responsibility to these specters as they listen out for us, impossibly, from the spatiotemporal remove of Los Angeles in the mid-2010s? For Derrida, ideas about justice form the foundations of spectrality. In the opening "exordium" to *Specters of Marx,* he writes:

> If I am getting ready to speak at length about ghosts, inheritance, and generations, generations of ghosts, which is to say about certain *others* who are not present, nor presently living, either to us, in us, or outside us, it is in the name of *justice* . . . No justice—let us say no law and once again we are not speaking here of laws—seems possible or thinkable without the principle of some *responsibility,* beyond all living present, within that which disjoins the living present, before the ghosts of those who are not yet born or who are already dead, be they victims of wars, political or other kinds of violence, nationalist, racist, colonialist, sexist, or other kinds of exterminations, victims of the oppressions of capitalist imperialism or any of the forms of totalitarianism.[57]

Demanding that we bestow our hospitability on the ghostly other, Derrida's sense of the ethical demands of the spectral highlights the responsibility that future generations will bear toward these recordings of fidgety, agitated Holocaust survivors waiting inside the featureless rooms of the electronic archive. It is down to future generations to assume responsibility for the co-production of these new testimonial conversations; whether they do so or not may ultimately depend on whether they are able to see themselves as the specters reflected in the virtual survivors' uncanny, electronic eyes.

3

Witness in the Light Stage

Performative Methodologies

As we have seen, interactive video testimony uses digital technology to generate simulated conversations with virtual Holocaust survivors in a highly innovative and original fashion, suggesting that the reception of Holocaust knowledge seems set to become an increasingly performative and interactive phenomenon. In this chapter, we consider the role that the real-life survivors play in shaping the performative logic of virtual Holocaust memory, recognizing that the characterization of testimony as a form of performance is not in itself a new insight. Indeed, Geoffrey Hartman's periodization of Holocaust testimony, which we outlined in Chapter 1, points to the diverse yet often overlapping performative contexts that have defined testimony's conditions of possibility and wider social significance from the very beginning, highlighting the ways in which Holocaust memory has been mobilized for distinct audiences and purposes. Hartman's schema can be understood as a framework through which to understand the rules and horizons of expectation that shaped performances of testimony at specific historical moments, with these changing contexts inflecting the type of information—factual or emotional, personal or impersonal—that survivors were able to share. Witnessing was arguably more limited in the immediate postwar period, for example, not only because traumatized survivors would not or could not speak about their experiences so soon after the event, but also because those eyewitness accounts that were produced during the years of reconstruction and incipient Cold War politics—very often originally in Yiddish—did not meet the kind of global audience that would become established by the 1990s.[1] The second, more receptive performative context for Holocaust testimony, following the so-called "latency period" of the 1950s, came about through a shift in the emphasis and objectives of legal trials. As Hartman notes, eyewitness accounts formed the centerpiece of the Eichmann Trial in 1961, which was conceived as a global exposé of Nazi brutality. Hannah Arendt's *Eichmann in Jerusalem: A Report on the Banality of*

Virtual Holocaust Memory. Matthew Boswell and Antony Rowland, Oxford University Press. © Oxford University Press 2023. DOI: 10.1093/oso/9780197645390.003.0004

Evil (1963) famously begins by drawing attention to the theatricality of the trial, describing a prosecutor indulging his "love of showmanship" in an auditorium that had been designed with "a theater in mind, complete with orchestra and galley, with proscenium and stage, and with side doors for the actors' entrance."[2] Continuing the analogy, for Arendt, this "spectacle as sensational as the Nuremberg Trials" had been carefully orchestrated by an "invisible stage manager": the Israeli Prime Minister David Ben-Gurion.[3] In a later article, Shoshana Felman uses the term "theaters of justice" to refer to the same trial.[4] While the theatrics of the prosecutor, Gideon Hausner, may have irked Arendt, the depositions of the survivors were integral to the trial's function *as spectacle*, with over one hundred eyewitnesses giving evidence, leading to notorious moments of courtroom drama, such as the collapse of Yehiel De-Nur on the witness stand, and the testimony of Rivka Yoselewska, given just one session after Hausner had announced that she had suffered a heart attack. Speaking at length about her escape from a mass grave, Yoselewska's testimony epitomized the way in which the trial, according to Carolyn J. Dean, transformed Holocaust survivors "into powerful icons of sacred knowledge about suffering, and their experience became a universal paradigm of evil, especially if not exclusively in the United States."[5]

At this same historical juncture, in the early 1960s, testimonial performances started to be significantly shaped by the impact of mass culture, with the televising of the Eichmann Trial proving to be as significant as its legal function. Forming a third performative context that significantly overlapped with the second, the incorporation of testimony into the mass entertainment industries continued through the screening of the popular television series *Holocaust* in the USA in 1978 and a proliferation of television documentaries and films in the 1980s and 1990s. Alongside these mass media performances of Holocaust memory, more intimate versions of testimony were being enacted within psychoanalytic and therapeutic frameworks; above all, through grassroots oral history projects. Beginning in the late-1970s and continuing into the early twentieth century, these projects saw testimony as a way of trying to restore survivors' emotional and psychological wellbeing. Early oral history initiatives such as the Holocaust Survivors Film Project, that would come to be housed in the Fortunoff Video Archive at Yale, sought to construct a "listening community" or "affective community" that opened the possibility of address for survivors still suffering from traumatic memories.[6] Led by practitioners including Hartman and Dori Laub, such projects gave rise to a fourth era of testimony that was designed to be as psychologically authentic as possible. During this period, many survivors were speaking about their experiences for the first time—or at least for the first time outside family or community settings—and Laub regarded the interviewer's role as that of a "listener and a companion" who had to be "*unobtrusively present*" and "nondirective," leaving the eyewitness space for periods of reflective silence whenever the situation demanded.[7] Interviewers were instructed to ask "a minimum of questions" in the hope that memories would "emerge from a deeper, more spontaneous level," while being discouraged from drawing too heavily on their pre-existing knowledge of events, which "should not hinder or obstruct the listening with foregone conclusions and preconceived dismissals, should not be an obstacle or a foreclosure to new, diverging, unexpected information."[8] While still ultimately placing testimony into the public realm, these interviews remain closely protected, with most only viewable by those given express permission to watch them in person at the Yale archives or their partner sites.

The testimonial performances elicited by Dimensions in Testimony emerge through a performative methodology that is about as far removed from the unobtrusive and nondirective Yale interviews as it is possible to imagine. Unshackled from the influence of psychoanalysis, Dimensions in Testimony engenders a completely new Holocaust performative that is shaped by a combination of the radically obtrusive technological capture system, the bespoke interview methodology, and transformational educational agendas. These combine to form the techno-pedagogical context for the fifth period of Holocaust witnessing.

Dimensions in Testimony is very much a big budget, Hollywood form of testimony, with each interview beginning with a series of shouted instructions and responses from the director and crew—"Quiet on set!," "Sound!," "Roll Panasonics!," "Checking all Panasonics!," "Roll Red!," and "Slate!"—that are immediately followed by the sharp smack of a clapperboard (as demonstrated by Pinchas Gutter while posing for publicity photographs in Fig. 3.1). Survivors accustomed to speaking in classrooms and lecture halls then find themselves alone in a futuristic light stage addressing a camera lens and the tiny reflection of their interviewer in a mirror next to the camera. The experience of giving testimony in this setting must feel highly impersonal, even as the survivors may be conscious of addressing an audience that is a complex composite of the real interviewer, imagined interlocutors in the future, and the small group of relatives, project team members, and visitors

Figure 3.1 Pinchas Gutter's Dimensions in Testimony interview at the USC Institute for Creative Technologies
USC Shoah Foundation—The Institute for Visual History and Education

who remain invisible, if occasionally audible, around the perimeter of the light stage.

Claude Lanzmann suggested that the survivors whom he interviewed for his epic documentary *Shoah* (1985) were "actors" who did not simply describe their history; rather, they "had to act it out, that is, they had to give themselves over to it . . . so that their speech can suddenly communicate, become charged with an extra dimension."[9] The survivors interviewed for Dimensions in Testimony are asked to give themselves over to an interview methodology that will literally allow their testimony to be accessed in a new virtual dimension. The aim of the recording sessions is therefore for the survivors to give relatively concise answers to a large volume of questions, often with only very small, nuanced variations in focus and emphasis, so that the team can build up a huge database of responses that capture, in the fullest possible way, an epic question-and-answer version of a life story that has been told and retold many times. As a result, the survivors' answers are highly directed, even micro-managed. More experienced interviewers proactively mold the survivor's responses by using hand signals that the survivors usually, though not always, notice in the mirror. "Wrap it up" motions are

Figure 3.2 Eva Schloss's Dimensions in Testimony interview at the USC
Institute for Creative Technologies
USC Shoah Foundation—The Institute for Visual History and Education

used to draw answers to a close when they are in danger of becoming overly
lengthy or off topic, and a thumbs-up gives positive reinforcement for model
responses that should now be drawn to an end. When Eva Schloss was being
interviewed (see Fig. 3.2), if she made a digression that seemed to stray too
far from the original question she would occasionally be interrupted and
asked to start again. Such interruptions did not, however, seem to deter her
or break her flow. Rather, she welcomed the opportunity to record another
take so that she could give a more focused answer. Indeed, Schloss seemed
highly conscious of the performative nature of the task in hand. She was
visibly pleased when she gave what the project team would consider to be
the best type of answer: one with the right level of detail and not too many
digressions. Even when recounting memories of highly distressing incidents,
Schloss remained focused on the practical task of delivering the optimal
answers for a virtual conversation.

As with *Shoah*, which opens with the Chełmno survivor Simon Srebnik
sailing down a river on a small wooden boat singing a Prussian military song
that he had been taught to sing by his SS guards when he was a teenage prisoner, Dimensions in Testimony includes actual performances of songs and

rituals. Pinchas Gutter, a cantor, puts on a yarmulke and sings a prayer. He also tells his favorite Jewish joke. Schloss reads out a poem that was written by her older brother, Heinz, who was murdered, along with her father, Erich, in Auschwitz-Birkenau. If, for Lanzmann, the objective of transforming survivors into actors is to produce an "incarnation of the truth" of their experiences, Schloss's reading of Heinz's poem is, as we discuss in more detail below, equally revelatory about the experience of survival.[10] There is no sense that giving these performances will help survivors deal with their trauma; if anything, there is a risk that deep, long-standing hurts may resurface through the protracted interviews in what Schloss dubbed the "cage" (see "Cracks in the Light Stage" below). The overwhelming objective here—one shared and respected by all who participated in the project—is for the survivors to re-count their experiences in a concise and engaging fashion and, perhaps even more importantly, to elucidate lessons that will be relevant to future gener-ations. And in our experience, the hardy, stoical survivors involved in the project were willing to do whatever it took to ensure that their stories will continue to be heard, taking a leap of faith with an untested testimonial format that may be physically and emotionally demanding, but which also has the potential to appeal to audiences of the future in ways that more tradi-tional written and recorded forms may not.

The Literary Origins of Eva Schloss's Dimensions in Testimony Interview

Since speaking about her Holocaust experiences in public for the first time at the opening of an Anne Frank exhibition in London in 1985, Schloss has become an experienced orator who gradually, as she put it, "found [her] voice and learned to tell [her] own story."[11] As well as giving public talks to a range of audiences, from schoolchildren to prisoners, she regularly appears on the television and radio. The five-hour-long interview filmed for the USC Shoah Foundation's Visual History Archive (VHA) in 1996 shows a survivor who had, by that time, become accustomed to discussing her life story at length. Having also produced three written memoirs, Schloss's extensive experience of testifying across di-verse forms inflects her Dimensions in Testimony interview in numerous ways. These include the skilled way in which she directs her testimony toward young learners who might be encountering the Holocaust at a significant historical remove, and who might not be familiar with even the most notorious features of the genocide or its historical context. Before exploring the performative dynamics of Schloss's Dimensions in Testimony interview in more detail, then, we will pause to survey three autobiographical texts that illustrate how Schloss's voice and story have evolved over the course of more than three decades, allowing different forms of truth and truthfulness to emerge.

One of the most striking aspects of Schloss's literary career has been how she has chosen to orientate her testimony towards different readerships, assisted through her recruitment of different coauthors. All of her memoirs are examples of what Matthew Boswell terms "hybrid testimony": a genre of literary witnessing that involves a survivor and a writer coming together to create a form of ghost-written testimony in which the "ghost" author reveals themselves to a greater or lesser degree.[12] In Schloss's memoirs, the professional writers generally remain hidden, contrasting with more postmodern forms of hybrid testimony in which the writer draws attention to their role in shaping the narrative.[13] Schloss's first memoir, *Eva's Story* (1988), was co-written with her friend Evelyn Julia Kent who, at the time, was an unknown and unpublished author. It is the rawest account of Schloss's experience of the Holocaust, as might be expected. Across three distinct geographies—"From Vienna to Amsterdam," "Auschwitz-Birkenau," and "Journey Through Russia"—the narrative focuses almost exclusively on the wartime period, with little attention being paid to Schloss's early childhood or postwar life. The book is particularly remarkable for its detailed, evocative description of the liberation of a snow-covered Auschwitz-Birkenau in January 1945. It also offers a moving insight into the physical and psychological state of Schloss, her mother, and Otto Frank as they returned to the Netherlands and started to confront the devastating loss of their families. Schloss's next book, *The Promise: The True Story of a Family in the Holocaust* (2006), was co-written nearly twenty years later with an American school curriculum coordinator, Barbara Powers, and published in Penguin's Puffin series. *The Promise* is written for children and young adults and primarily focuses on Schloss's relationships with her family. In particular, it celebrates the close bond she had with her brother, Heinz. Well over half the book is devoted to Schloss's childhood experiences before the family were captured by the Nazis, including the period they spent in hiding in Amsterdam. Schloss's final, most comprehensive, and commercially oriented account is *After Auschwitz* (2013), co-written with Karen Bartlett, an established writer and journalist. The first half of the book covers much the same ground as *Eva's Story*, but the second half offers a full and extremely candid account of the difficulties

Schloss faced as a survivor after the war, while also documenting her work to preserve the legacy of her posthumous stepsister, Anne Frank.

Of all her written accounts, Schloss's Dimensions in Testimony interview most closely resembles *The Promise*, both because of the anticipated age of the readers and listeners to whom she directs these accounts, and perhaps also in no small part because *The Promise* was being turned into a traveling exhibition by the South African Holocaust and Genocide Foundation at the time of Schloss's interview in Los Angeles. The book would therefore have been very much on her mind. Both book and exhibition reproduce some of the poems and paintings that Schloss discovered under the floorboards of Heinz's attic hiding place in Amsterdam after the war. During the Dimensions in Testimony interview, Schloss discusses her brother at length, reflecting on these same poignant artworks, including a painting depicting a young boy in a despairing posture, leaning on a desk with his head buried in his folded arms, and a poem called "Don't Cry, Mama." As with *The Promise*, Schloss's Dimensions in Testimony interview is pitched at schoolchildren and young adults, and pivotal events are recounted in almost verbatim fashion. The Dimensions in Testimony researchers were even thrown into ethical quandaries when mistaken or distorted memories from *The Promise* were repeated in her interview, such as her impression that Auschwitz was solely a men's camp and Birkenau solely a women's camp.[14] The researchers understandably sought to rectify this error by showing Schloss maps of the camp during breaks from filming. However, such mistakes reveal a great deal about traumatic experience, as Laub insisted in his reflections on the Auschwitz-Birkenau survivor who misremembered the number of chimneys that had been destroyed in the uprising. In Schloss's case, her historically inaccurate memory would appear to stem from the experience of being a young girl incarcerated in a camp that divided families along the lines of biological sex, separating Schloss and her mother from her father and brother in a way that would ultimately lead to the deaths of both men.

The coauthor of *The Promise* is credited on the front cover, albeit with her name in a smaller typeface than Schloss's. A short concluding section, "A Note from Barbara Powers," reflects on the coauthor's friendship with Schloss, whilst also briefly outlining her own biography. As such, this "Note" constitutes a clear authorial signature. However, the testimony is written in the first person and adopts the conversational tone of Schloss's speaking voice, suggesting that in *The Promise*, Schloss and Powers sought to translate

Schloss's talks to schoolchildren into a written form. The chapter titles register simple, easy to grasp experiences and emotions, such as "Born into a Loving Family" and "Confused by an Upside-Down World." Along with the book's tone, its short length and paratextual features such as the cover design—which uses a childish font and positions a real photograph of a teenage Schloss inside an illustration of a locket—these chapter titles emphasize that the book is both *for* teenagers and *about* one. Illustrations by a ten-year-old called Sophie Yaron further underscore the link between Schloss's age at the time of the Holocaust and that of the book's intended readership. Born in 1929, Schloss had only just turned fifteen when she arrived in Birkenau in May 1944. This proved to be just old enough to allow her to deceive Josef Mengele into believing that she was an adult in a selection that took place immediately on the family's arrival at the camp, during which Schloss wore an oversize hat and coat that her mother had recovered from their cattle truck. Schloss recalls that she was "the youngest person by far" in their transport line, hence also the youngest of this group of deportees to survive.[15]

Almost as much a reflection on the meaning of childhood as the meaning of the Holocaust, *The Promise* highlights the positive aspects of family relationships, with an extended prewar section giving details of Heinz's youthful creativity and the closeness of their sibling bond that were not included in *Eva's Story*. As such, *The Promise* is an overtly pedagogic text that aims to impart clear moral messages to its young readers. The short introduction and concluding chapters, titled "Uplifted by the Gift of Hope" and "Called to a New Horizon," echo some of the most well-known quotations from Anne Frank's *The Diary of a Young Girl* (1947) in their optimistic tone. The introduction ends with a direct readerly address:

> I hope through this book you will be moved to share kindness and tolerance with others; appreciate your parents, brothers, sisters and extended family, realizing that your time together is precious; develop your talents to make the world a better place; appreciate the freedom that was won for you through great sacrifice; and value each day.[16]

The concluding "Note" from Powers also emphasizes that Schloss "enjoys life to the full" and that she "has chosen not to harbour anger or bitterness."[17] *Eva's Story* begins with a Preface that similarly notes Schloss's disavowal of bitterness. However, in this earlier work aimed at an adult readership, Schloss overtly sets out to counter Anne Frank's optimism, writing: "I do not believe in the goodness of man."[18] She continues:

> My posthumous step-sister, Anne Frank, wrote in her diary: "I still believe that deep down human beings are good at heart." I cannot help remembering that she wrote this before she experienced Auschwitz and Belsen.[19]

The Promise is thus, in many ways, the text that puts the least distance between itself and its most important intertext, *The Diary of a Young Girl*. It is interesting to note, however, that it is also the only one of Schloss's three written accounts that does not advertise her family connection to Anne Frank through its cover or subtitle.

As well as softening the tone of Schloss's earlier memoir and favoring uplifting messages aimed at children, *The Promise* abridges and occludes some of the more traumatic and taboo aspects of Schloss's life story. Most notably, it omits incidents of a sexual nature that are discussed in *Eva's Story* and her most recent book for adults, *After Auschwitz*. For example, *The Promise* makes no mention of the period when Schloss was molested by a pedophile called Mr. Dubois in a boarding house in Brussels in 1938. Indeed, Schloss only finally writes about this episode in *After Auschwitz*, seventy-five years after its occurrence.[20] A stateless refugee, Schloss had just turned nine years old when she was first abused by the middle-aged Belgian. In *After Auschwitz*, Schloss recalls that Mr. Dubois was not evicted from the boarding house once he had been discovered, with the fact that he was a permanent boarder, and Schloss and her mother only temporary residents, leading the landlady to overlook his crimes.[21] In her Dimensions in Testimony interview, Schloss seems to have decided not to discuss these events. During the pilot installation at the Museum of Jewish Heritage in 2018, when we asked the question, "Were you sexually abused?" the virtual Schloss replied: "No, I never experienced sexual abuse." The phrasing suggests that this answer had been correctly mapped onto the question by the natural language processing software and hence was the intended response of the real-life survivor, rather than a mistake made by the system. One hesitates to call it a falsehood, yet clearly here Schloss's testimony is shaped by values and concerns that are quite different to the truthfulness that motivated the writing of Charlotte Delbo, as discussed in the Introduction.

There are of course many reasons why Schloss might have answered in this way during her Dimensions in Testimony interview, illustrating why the more distanced approach to Holocaust representation and concepts such as the unsayable, advocated by critics such as Saul Friedländer, continue to remain highly pertinent in the age of connective memory. First and foremost, Schloss may have been uncomfortable with talking about such traumatic material in the cold and impersonal setting of the light stage, which is so far removed from the welcoming, supportive, homely settings that were used for earlier forms of filmed oral testimony. Discussing her molestation might have been made even more difficult given the lingering sense of shame that she describes in *After Auschwitz*:

> Until now my memory of being sexually abused was so deeply shameful and painful that I have never discussed it, even though I've often spoken about far worse experiences that we were to go through as a family.[22]

Another reason why Schloss chose not to speak about some of the more personal topics that she addresses more frankly in her written accounts might relate to her wish to spare young listeners from the most distressing aspects of her life story. Indeed, having formed the clear impression that interactive testimony is primarily for schoolchildren, Schloss seemed broadly unwilling to discuss any topics of a sexual nature in her Dimensions in Testimony interview. For example, in *Eva's Story*, she describes the times she spent in bed with Heinz while in hiding in Amsterdam. In a tender account of an intimacy that offered her emotional and spiritual refuge from the abuse she had experienced four years earlier, Schloss describes how their "suppressed energy and budding sexuality" began to arouse them, with their kissing, cuddling, and petting leading to "blissful surges of adolescent love."[23] This incident, as far as we can ascertain, is not discussed in Dimensions in Testimony. When the family were then transported to Auschwitz-Birkenau, separated from her father and brother following their initial selection, Schloss repeatedly found herself subjected to more unwanted sexual attention. In *Eva's Story*, she describes arriving at Birkenau and being led to a room where the women were stripped naked so that their hair, including pubic hair, could be shaved:

> From time to time SS men came in and strolled around to look and leer at our bodies. It was a sport for them to pinch the bottoms of younger,

attractive women and I felt really degraded when one of the men walked near to me and then pinched my bottom.[24]

In *Eva's Story* and *After Auschwitz*, as well as in her VHA and Dimensions in Testimony interviews, Schloss further recalls the attention she received from a young guard while working in Kanada.[25] In *After Auschwitz*, she writes: "I saw him watching me in the showers and I noticed him in other parts of the camp too—keeping an eye on where I was and what I was doing."[26] Things came to a head when, one day in the summer of 1944, the guard followed her into a warehouse carrying a rifle over his shoulder. In *Eva's Story*, Schloss describes how she "prayed fervently, half-running, half-walking to keep in front of him"; fortunately, she was able to hide under a large pile of clothes.[27] As Schloss goes on to observe in the same account, "the threat was very real" and at the time she had feared for her life, facing the prospect of being assaulted or killed if she resisted.[28] This incident is one of the few times that Schloss discusses episodes of a sexual nature in her Dimensions in Testimony interview. Yet it is described in more light-hearted terms, with Schloss downplaying the element of danger even as she uses the episode to illustrate the specific threats posed to women in the camps. During the Museum of Jewish Heritage pilot, to the question "Were you molested" the virtual Schloss replied:

> That was the only . . . it was of course strictly forbidden to have any sexual intercourse or attraction with [unclear] the SS and the Jewish people. But in Kanada there were many quite young SS people who were supervising it and obviously they wanted, I don't know, they just wanted to play with us sometimes, do something with us, just be naughty, and I had some trouble. There was one SS boy, quite a young, quite a sweet boy actually, but he pursued me all the time. And if he would be caught or I would be caught, we would certainly, well he would've been heavily punished, and I would certainly have been killed, and of course, didn't want to have to do anything with him. So, had trouble to evade, to hide, when he was around.

Schloss may of course expand on this incident in other answers, but a weakness of the system is that it is very difficult to know what questions will trigger a response in which the virtual survivor elaborates on a specific event.

In her written accounts aimed at adults, Schloss also discusses her sexual development following her liberation from Auschwitz-Birkenau. Indeed,

Germans in his writing, and whether this means he has forgiven them, he offers a moral rationale for what is often perceived to be his unemotional tone:

> I believe in reason and in discussion as supreme instruments of progress, and therefore I repress hatred even within myself: I prefer justice. Precisely for this reason, when describing the tragic world of Auschwitz, I have deliberately assumed the calm, sober language of the witness, neither the lamenting tones of the victim nor the irate voice of someone who seeks revenge. I thought that my account would be all the more credible and useful the more it appeared objective and the less it sounded overly emotional; only in this way does a witness in matters of justice perform his task, which is that of preparing the ground for the judge. The judges are my readers.[37]

Levi's desire to "repress hatred" and avoid an overly plaintive or irate tone point to emotions that threaten to overwhelm his "calm, sober language": far from being absent, these turbulent emotions must be studiously avoided if the claims of justice are to be met. Schloss's tone in her Dimensions in Testimony interview is similarly that of a witness who does not wish to sound "overly emotional"; rather, reason and logic underpin the delivery of testimony through which future generations will come to form judgments about the past. Adopting the calm, poised persona so often assumed by elderly survivors, Schloss's responses generally operate at the level of "common memory" rather than "anguished" or "deep memory," to use Lawrence Langer's terms—by way of Delbo—for the contrast between everyday remembering and the more sensory, embodied recollection of events that have not been subject to repeated retelling: a phenomenon that was more common in earlier oral history interviews, such as those in the Yale archive.[38] However, the unique challenges of the Dimensions in Testimony interview format mean that survivors rarely maintain this front for the duration of their interviews, and painful memories that would typically be repressed in public settings are revealed, disturbing the outward placidity of "stereotyped" or "common" memory.

Cracks in the Light Stage

If the survivor must maintain a calm, consistent tone for a virtual conversation to function in an emotionally coherent way, a paradox of the Dimensions in Testimony interview methodology is that it makes such a tone almost impossible to maintain. During their week-long interviews, members of the Dimensions in Testimony team noted that survivors who were used to telling their stories in public were often visibly moved by recollections that would not normally disturb them. We have seen how Gutter was upset when asked to talk about his regrets, for example. Fritzshall also describes how she was shaken by the recording process: "It washed me out totally. It brought me back into the camp. It gave me the nightmares again. I was hungry again. I was cold again."[39] Such confrontations with deep memory are perhaps inevitable over the course of an extended interview in an impersonal and rather daunting light stage with no other human beings in direct sight, including the interviewer. The duration of the interview ensures that the survivor cannot simply default to stock answers and stereotyped memory in response to every single question. They will inevitably be asked new questions—or old ones with a different nuance—that address less-often discussed aspects of their personal histories, and their responses thereby regain a certain freshness. Indeed, if *The Promise* abridges Schloss's life story for a younger audience, reducing and toning down some of the more traumatic historical content, then her Dimensions in Testimony interview significantly expands the total volume of testimony that is available for the same audience. During her interview, the well-informed Dimensions in Testimony team were often surprised to learn new information they had never encountered in her talks or books.[40] Flying to Los Angeles to be filmed by a professional crew in an expensive studio also creates unique demands and expectations. One senses that these survivors placed a great deal of pressure on themselves to get these interviews right. Mindful of the fact that very few survivors will get the chance to create interactive testimony, they were keen not to waste the opportunity to tell their story in a unique manner in order to reach future generations.

When Schloss entered the core of her Holocaust story, spending hour after hour answering questions about her experiences in Auschwitz-Birkenau, it was also noticeable that she clearly visualized—or tried to visualize—specific scenes and moments. Her narrative was permeated by the refrain, "I see it how it was," suggesting that she was visually inhabiting the historical moment, envisaging the past in her mind's eye, leading to what Lanzmann refers to as an "incarnation" of the Holocaust as old wounds were opened and something of the true "nature of the offence" was exposed.[41] The strong visual dimension of Schloss's memory is also a salient feature of her written accounts. *The Promise* begins: "As I look back more than sixty years to the early part of my life, the pictures in my memory are crystal clear."[42] While a survivor visualizing the past in short bursts might remain in the relatively safe enclosures of stereotyped memory, doing so for five days must create unique psychological pressures.

As with *The Promise,* much of the emotion in Schloss's Dimensions in Testimony interview derives from her close relationship with her brother, Heinz. One of the most moving moments in her testimony came when she took a printed piece of paper out of her back pocket and read a poem Heinz had written in hiding. Entitled "Don't Cry, Mama," the poem is reprinted in full in *The Promise.* Based on the refrain, "Please, Mama, please don't cry," in the poem Heinz accepts that they will both soon die, yet urges his mother to find solace in the hope that they will be reunited in heaven.[43] It closes with the line: "Mama, just one more thing, Mama, / Please kiss me goodbye."[44] After finishing the reading, Schloss said: "He was just sixteen-years-old when he wrote that, and a year later he was killed." There was then a long pause, with Schloss's words left hanging as she placed the sheet of paper back into her pocket and waited for the next question. What those holding a virtual conversation with Schloss will never see is that, during the real-time interview, the next question did not arrive—or at least not immediately. Instead, the interviewer conferred on Heinz a traditional Jewish honorific: "May his memory be forever blessed." Clearly very moved, like the small group of spectators watching the interview, he then broke from the strict question-and-answer format and said: "Thank you for sharing that. I certainly will never forget it."

Drawing on Emmanuel Levinas's definition of ethics as "a relation of seeing and being for the other," Hartman describes how the "optics" of video testimony produce an "affective community" that bears witness to the witnesses.[45] In contrast to video testimony, the survivors being interviewed for Dimensions in Testimony have very limited visual contact with any kind of affective community: as noted, all they can see is the reflection of their interviewer in a small mirror above the main camera lens. To an unprecedented extent, the survivors' sense of their listeners is imaginary. Following the reading of Heinz's poem, the interviewer's decision to break from the question-and-answer format to offer words of thanks and consolation was even more moving for the way that it powerfully served to remind Schloss of the presence of the affective community sitting around the border of the light stage, which included her granddaughter and members of the

Dimensions in Testimony team. The moment also illustrated another paradox of Dimensions in Testimony, which is that, while the project aims to obtain the best possible capture of a story that has been told many times before, creating a vast database of answers that can map onto thousands of potential questions, the five-day interview has an emotional ebb and flow all of its own. Schloss may often read this poem to public audiences. Yet reading the poem in a light stage after speaking at length about Heinz clearly created a unique emotional intensity for survivor and interviewer alike. In such moments, the Dimensions in Testimony interviews convey something like the sense of "complex immediacy" noted by Langer in video testimony, when deep memory emerges, and the survivor's voice reaches us "simultaneously from the secure present and the devastating past."[46]

It is also important to recognize that the present, just as much as the "devastating past," shapes the emotional tenor of the Dimensions in Testimony interviews, not least because the present is not always so "secure" as Langer holds. The Dimensions in Testimony survivors often become more emotional in the later stages of their interviews when they are asked about their current life and family relationships. Recent disagreements or bereavements are often just as, if not more, affecting for survivors than tragic losses that occurred over seventy years earlier. An octogenarian grandmother, such as Schloss, is just as emotionally invested in the continuing impact of the Holocaust on her current family as she is in her own childhood trauma. Sadly, her husband Zvi, himself a refugee from Nazi Germany, died shortly after her interview, and his health must have been a huge concern to Schloss during her time in Los Angeles. While traumatic episodes from her past, such as sexual assault, were glossed over, Schloss became most animated when discussing more recent traumas, such as the death of her mother, which she described as "very, very tragic." A little over five minutes in length, her description of this bereavement leads to one of her longest and most detailed answers. As something that she had not, in all likelihood, discussed in public before, this answer is completely free from the conventions of stereotyped memory. Schloss begins by describing her mother's dementia and the pressures this placed on their relationship, before recalling that her mother's condition had significantly declined when she broke her leg after a trip to the cinema to see *Titanic* (1997). Upset and unable to sleep, despite having taken some sleeping pills, her mother got up during the night. Dizzy and confused, she fell and broke her femur. Schloss describes how they waited for "a few hours" for the ambulance with her mother in "horrific pain," before she was eventually taken to hospital. After a successful operation, her mother then experienced a "mini stroke." Having recovered from this, she suffered three more strokes. At this point, the doctors suggested to Schloss that there was no realistic prospect of her mother making a full recovery and that it would be best if they discontinued feeding her. But Schloss's reply was emphatic: "No way will you starve my mother. My mother must get food and you must treat her. And she's a strong woman, she will recover." Her mother lived for a further six months. Closing her eyes and shaking her head, Schloss recalls that her mother's immobile condition was "agony to see" and that perhaps the doctor had been right. With her decision clearly still haunting her, Schloss reflects:

> I just couldn't face the idea of especially starving, after we had gone through the camp's starvation. But I very often think perhaps it wouldn't have been necessary to have to go another six months of suffering, not being able to move, not being able to speak. It must have been horrible for her.

Highlighting how the memory of the Holocaust affects survivors right to the ends of their lives, Schloss's answer shows how testimony's "real strength," following Hartman, "lies in recording the psychological and emotional milieu of the struggle for survival, not only then but also now."[47]

Often traveling large distances to undertake an emotionally and physically grueling interview, while embracing daunting and unfamiliar technologies, the elderly survivors involved in Dimensions in Testimony also affirm Laub's observation about the existential significance of the act of witnessing: "The survivors did not only need to survive so that they could tell their story; they also needed to tell their story in order to survive."[48] Offering complex portraits of survival into old age, the Dimensions in Testimony interviews derive much of their poignancy and emotional texture—as well as unique historical significance—from the fact that they were made toward the end of the survivors' lives. One interviewee, Aaron Elster, passed away in 2018 at the age of eighty-five, underscoring the limited time that is available for this kind of project, and the way in which these testimonies often bookend many years of interviews and talks.[49] The testimonies convey a sense of the immeasurable losses that these elderly survivors have experienced throughout their lives, with many having outlived all the friends and family members who are the central characters in their Holocaust stories. Isolated first in the light stage, the interviews are then presented in a digital form whose aesthetics strangely underscore this solitude, be it through a two-dimensional plasma screen with a black background and impenetrable borders or through the three-dimensional aesthetics of the hologram. As such, these interactive testimonies starkly contrast with the video testimonies recorded for the VHA from the mid-1990s onwards that conclude with survivors such as Schloss in their homes, surrounded by family members who often span three generations. In their dignified, solitary way, the Dimensions in Testimony interviewees seem to stand very much alone, the last representatives of those who were cast adrift on what Levi calls an "ocean of pain."[50] While the phenomenon of stereotyped memory might convey an impression of surface calm, as the interviews develop it is as though what Schloss refers to as the "cage" is gradually lowered into that ocean. And the cracks that subsequently splinter across the light stage as it succumbs to the pressures of deep memory show how this ocean still has dark and turbulent depths. For all the virtual survivors' solitude, however, we recall that Dimensions in Testimony functions as an encounter that conforms to the logic of connective memory, with strangers interacting with survivors across innovative bridges in space and time. Following the insights of Jacques Derrida and Emmanuel Levinas discussed in the previous chapter, the ethical challenge for future generations will be to recognize their own spectral presence *inside* the light stage, and to understand that they formed part of an affective community in an impossible temporality, playing some small part in ensuring that these elderly survivors were not navigating this ocean of pain alone.

The Enduring Influence of *Schindler's List*

In the year following the release of *Schindler's List* in 1993, Steven Spielberg established the Survivors of the Shoah Visual History Foundation to record and preserve eyewitness accounts of the Holocaust. Originally an independent not-for-profit organization, what would become the USC Shoah Foundation — The Institute for Visual History and Education moved to its permanent home at USC in 2006. While Spielberg continues to serve as the Honorary Chair of the Foundation's Board of Councillors, he had little direct involvement in the development of Dimensions in Testimony. The project, however, seems to bear the founder's imprint as a kind of *Schindler's List* for Generation Alpha and beyond, with the original film and subsequent institutionalization of its ethos informing the development of interactive testimony in a number of ways. Noah Shenker makes much the same point in respect of the first survivor testimonies gathered for the VHA:

> *Schindler's List* embodies Spielberg's immersive, experiential, "you have been there approach" to representation and reflects his consistent interest in fostering participatory forms of reception. These points are essential, as Spielberg's film serves as a source narrative for the VHA, linking the archival project with its own narrative stakes in fostering hope and tolerance.[51]

Through its immersive aesthetic and redemptory schemas, Dimensions in Testimony is thus marked by what Walter Reich, a former director of the USHMM, terms the "Schindlerization of Holocaust testimony," thereby renewing long-standing debates about the Americanization of the Holocaust for the digital age.[52]

In the wake of Spielberg's film in the late 1990s, critics primarily worried about the use of the Holocaust as a means for generating commercial profit, with the slogan "there's no business like Shoah business" coming to embody the deep mistrust many felt toward what Norman Finkelstein terms the "Holocaust industry."[53] The high cost of producing interactive testimony (as noted, the first twelve recordings cost $6 million in total) mean that Dimensions in Testimony is of necessity a highly commercial enterprise that requires an institutional setting that is geared toward fundraising, philanthropy, and marketing, and which, as such, is far removed from the grassroots origins of the early oral history projects.[54] Yet a limited market consisting mostly of specialist Holocaust museums and educational organizations means that, so far as Shoah business goes, Dimensions in Testimony is hardly likely to be particularly lucrative. The project, embedded in an educational framework and financed through private donors and foundations, is clearly not primarily driven by consideration of likely profit.[55] Moreover, even if recording and interacting with this testimony is overtly performative and cinematic, it does not constitute entertainment in the same way that cinema does. Indeed, to focus debates about the Americanization of virtual Holocaust memory on the long-standing question of commodification would be to fail to account for the pedagogical turn that has characterized the fifth and final era of Holocaust witnessing. Rather than popcorn-eating filmgoers, Dimensions in Testimony imagines an audience of engaged learners whose involvement with Holocaust testimony takes place within struc-tured educational programs.

With young learners increasingly becoming the primary focus of Holocaust memory initiatives in the USA, Eric Tribunella argues that the "Americanization of the Holocaust is first and foremost an American *childization* of the Holocaust."[56] Here, the USA is again driving a global trend. While films and museums of the mid-1990s, such as *Schindler's List* and the USHMM, appealed to viewers and visitors of all ages, in the twenty-first century the Holocaust has increasingly come to feature in prominent books and films that are aimed at children and young adults, including pop-ular novels by non-American authors and their film adaptations, such as *The Boy in the Striped Pyjamas* (2006, 2008) and *The Book Thief* (2005, 2013). Similarly, Holocaust education seems to have increasingly abandoned adult audiences, with programs offered by organizations such as the National Holocaust Centre and Museum in the UK now targeting learners as young as eight years old. Dimensions in Testimony is clearly aimed at slightly older age groups. Underpinned by the USC Shoah Foundation's "Theory of Change," the project's formal learning outcomes state that Dimensions in Testimony will help students "foster empathy," "develop a more complex world view," "develop their capacity to recognize and value responsible participation in civil society," and "better understand genocide, its causes, global context, and continued ramifications."[57] An early evaluation of middle and high school experiences of the Dimensions in Testimony pilot finds evidence of positive outcomes against all these objectives.[58]

This target audience, and the pedagogical demands of the "Theory of Change," mean that users of Dimensions in Testimony can also expect to en-counter optimistic philosophies of history and positive, redemptive messages that very much align with the ethos of *Schindler's List*. Shenker argues that the USC Shoah Foundation's selection of interviews from the VHA for edu-cational purposes betrays a preference for "testimonies that favour lessons of healing and forgiveness rather than those that portray the darker, more trau-matic aftershocks of the Holocaust."[59] While the huge size of the VHA means that it contains a rich diversity of experiences, worldviews, and insights, its interview methodologies also steer survivors toward statements that re-inforce and authenticate a particular institutional worldview, serving to "Schindlerize" the testimonial content in ways that can seem formulaic. This is particularly evident in the conclusions that the survivors are asked to draw:

The prescribed final question of each interview—usually some variation of "What would you like to tell future generations?"—suggests a dialogue about postmemory, but tends instead to project a redemptive, didactic role onto testimonies.[60]

While complicity and moral ambiguity form central concerns of a film that is all about a shady wartime industrialist struggling with his conscience, we would argue that the complexities of collaboration are rather too neatly resolved in the redemptive ending of *Schindler's List* itself. The Jewish accountant, Itzhak Stern, played by Ben Kingsley, presents Schindler, played by Liam Neeson, with a gold ring bearing the Hebrew inscription from the Talmud that also served as the film's tagline, "Whoever saves one life saves the world entire." This prompts Schindler to fall to his knees and express remorse for the additional lives he might have saved.[61] A black and white shot of a long line of singing, liberated survivors walking across the empty fields of Czechoslovakia then transforms into a color shot of the real-life Schindler Jews walking across a field in present-day Israel to lay stones on Schindler's grave. This narrative trajectory, through which life-affirming meaning is drawn from Europe's tragic, monochrome history, thereby redeeming future societies in distant lands, continues to shape the USC Shoah Foundation's mission-driven projects.

Much as the VHA interviews close by asking the survivors if they have a message for future generations, the Dimensions in Testimony survivors are asked at length about their messages, hopes, and beliefs. As such, they confirm Henry Greenspan's observation: "When allowed, survivors' accounts are . . . as much 'oral psychology,' 'oral philosophy,' 'oral theology,' or 'oral narratology' as they are 'oral history.'"[62] Yet it might be argued that the interview methodology demanded for Dimensions in Testimony tends to favor what Greenspan terms "testimonial product" over more profound forms of reflection and introspection. For the most part, the survivors' messages consist of platitudes that might make Dimensions in Testimony seem rather banal, predictable, and alienating for many adult users. For example, Schloss's messages include:

I think the most important message which I can give you about this terrible event is that it will be you and your generation who have to try to keep that story alive so that future generation will be able to learn from it. And one says you can only learn from history if you know history and I think this is very important, that this terrible event will never ever be forgotten.

In a similar vein, Gutter offers:

My message to youth of today is to be as tolerant and as accepting of all different human beings, whatever religion, whatever colour, whatever culture, whatever their mode of living is, and try and make this world a better place. And that is my message, that is why I tell my stories, that is what I hope the youths, the leaders of the future, will achieve.

Such messages service the ideology of personal growth that underpins the USC Shoah Foundation's "Theory of Change." In many ways, this is of course a completely benign agenda, with the virtual survivors imparting messages that are wholly appropriate to their intended audience. Yet the risk is that redemptive, "Schindlerized" messages combine with virtual aesthetics to conceal the structural and political causes of genocide and mass violence, meaning that learners do not develop the intellectual resources to develop meaningful resistance to injustice, discrimination, and intolerance in the present. As "childization" increasingly shapes Holocaust memory culture in the digital age, both in the USA and globally, it will be important to ensure that piety, cliché, and sentimentality do not mean that people of all ages are left without the critical resources required to interpret the complex operations of structural violence, and that history is not totally whitewashed out of concern for what will be palatable for young learners.

It would be wrong, however, to suggest that the Dimensions in Testimony interviews consist solely of uplifting, institutionally approved messages lifted straight from the press pack of *Schindler's List*. As with the video testimonies in the VHA, the sheer length of the interviews ensures that the survivors are still able to express more negative emotions and what Jean Améry describes as the victims' "resentments."[63] For example, when asked if she believes in God, the virtual Schloss recalls that after liberation she was deeply depressed:

I didn't believe in anything. Not in human beings, in goodness of human beings, not in existence of a God. It sounds hopeless, and that's what it was really. I was really in a hopeless situation and I was damaged mentally and physically.

To a question about whether he forgives the Nazis, the virtual Gutter, a deeply religious man, says that he does not believe in the death penalty, but adds: "There is no way you can forgive. They should burn in hell forever." The main factor determining the type of messages imparted by Dimensions in Testimony is of course the personalities, views, and experiences of the survivors themselves, and the degree to which they decide to modulate their answers to specific implied audiences. However, while it is clearly down to the survivors to decide how to answer the questions that are put to them, they are nonetheless chosen to take part in the project precisely because the team anticipate that they will give responses that reflect the upbeat and socially committed ethos of the USC Shoah Foundation and its core belief that survivor testimony contains universal "lessons for humanity."

Shenker describes how the Foundation employs formal mechanisms and standardized methodologies, such as numerical rating systems, to make decisions about which testimonies to foreground and circulate from the VHA when it needs material for a website, education program, film project, or similar.[64] The selection of survivors for Dimensions in Testimony was not based on anything so formal, but the small number of testimonies means that a sense of an "exemplary witness" for interactive testimony emerges. Through conversations with Heather Maio, Director of Conscience Display, we learned that several factors shaped the selection of the first group of participants. A primary consideration was, understandably, whether the elderly witnesses were physically and psychologically able to withstand the demanding interview process. In addition, interviewees needed to be articulate and able to express themselves clearly. The project team were also concerned to be as representative as possible in respect of factors such as biological sex and nationality, while ensuring that they included testimony about a range of Holocaust locations and experiences. The chosen survivors were all well-known to the Foundation, with many of them having achieved a significant public profile following lengthy "careers" speaking about the Holocaust to audiences around the world. Maio stated her preference for survivors who had reflected deeply on their experiences and who had an inspirational message for future generations. The stories told by Dimensions in Testimony survivors also tend to have a distinctive "hook": a dramatic or emotional core that individuates their narratives. Schloss's familial connection to Anne Frank, for example, makes her a person of wider interest: her recollections of Otto Frank and her sometimes irreverent views on Anne's *Diary of a Young Girl* are of significant socio-historic value, while also being rather entertaining. In one answer, the virtual Schloss mischievously concedes that while it is "quite a nice book," she does not think it deserves all the "fuss" that has been made about it. Gutter's involvement stems from his long-standing friendship with Stephen Smith, who had previously accompanied him on a return journey to Poland, again hoping it would help Gutter to remember what his sister looked like. As noted in the first chapter, they now hoped that the Dimensions in Testimony interview might trigger Gutter's memory, leading to the recuperative act of visualization that he longed for.[65]

Even as the project seeks to be as representative as possible, insofar as factors such as sex, nationality, and type of Holocaust experience are concerned, there is inevitably a degree of group conformity in the survivors interviewed for Dimensions in Testimony and the Forever Project. Most obviously, the very fact that they survived makes these interviewees anomalous, recalling Levi's statement that "we the survivors are not the true witnesses."[66] Much like the academics and artists who pass as "essential workers" in Schindler's List, they tend to come from educated central European families. As a result, they experienced the ghettos and camps in Germany and Poland that have come to define Holocaust knowledge in the Anglophone world, rather than representing, say, the poorer rural regions of Eastern Europe and nation-states that fell under Soviet rule during and after the war (although this is set to change as a result of the plan to film two interviews with Russian-speaking Jews from the former Soviet Union).[67] As children or young adults during the Holocaust, the survivors interviewed to date generally avoided the devastating forms of moral compromise that befell those who occupied the more nefarious regions of what Levi calls the "grey zone," such as the Kapos, Sonderkommando members, and others who were directly involved in the persecution and killing. The Dimensions in Testimony survivors generally emigrated to countries such as the USA, Canada, Australia, and the United Kingdom after the war, meaning that they speak and act in ways that are familiar to people from those nation-states. As such, they will presumably prove easier for Western schoolchildren to empathize with, yet their worldviews and "messages" have been formed at a geographic and economic remove from the contemporary humanitarian disasters they are often asked about.

The upshot is that this first set of interactive testimonies are not a representative sample of Holocaust victims, and their messages are fairly uniform: pedagogically useful, perhaps, but currently quite homogenous. Of course, numerous factors mean that interviewing a much broader range of survivors would be almost impossible. Certain groups are inaccessible because of their age, health, country of residence, or their inability to speak English (although the latter point is again being addressed, with interactive testimonies now being developed in various languages, including German, Spanish, Russian, and Hebrew). Victims with intense resentments, morally compromised pasts, and cynical worldviews are unlikely to volunteer to sit in a light stage in Los Angeles for five days in order to be grilled about humiliating experiences, with the ultimate aim of being transformed into a hologram that will provide moral and spiritual uplift for future generations. Yet the risk is that the Dimensions in Testimony and Forever Project virtual survivors are presented as emblematic Holocaust victims who are then subsumed within powerful institutional narratives that tend toward the sanctification of all survivors. This means that a small subset of child survival narratives may seem to stand for *the* story of the Holocaust, thereby reanimating the reservations that some critics had about the influence of *Schindler's List* and its transformation of a highly anomalous historical episode into the Holocaust's master narrative.[68]

Remembering "the Drowned"

We have argued that the experience of interacting with Dimensions in Testimony goes far beyond mining the database for uplifting messages and that, even in the resting pose, the visual experience of ghostware makes complex demands on its users. Illustrating the intertwined aesthetic and ethical dimensions of connective memory, these holograms draw us into a deeper understanding of testimony's truthfulness by asking us to recognize *our responsibility for the coming-into-being of that testimony* as custodians and cocreators of an effective and affecting archive. Moreover, the system has the capacity to jolt and disturb through its functional dysfunction. While some of the virtual survivors' messages echo the piety of *Schindler's List*, this testimonial form still has plenty of space for the victim's resentments and offers poignant insights into deep memory and the experience of survival into old age. Significantly, Dimensions in Testimony is also being expanded to include interviews with Russian-speaking survivors and fighters. We will nonetheless conclude by reflecting on content that is *missing* from this archive: omissions that arise not so much because of economic or linguistic factors than because of the inherent difficulty of engaging with certain kinds of bodies through virtual aesthetics.

Critics such as Giorgio Agamben have long argued that written and oral testimonies contain much that is unsayable, thereby aligning with Friedländer's approach to Holocaust representation that we contrasted to the more recent turn to connective memory in the Introduction. Agamben observes:

> At a certain point, it became clear that testimony contained at its core an essential lacuna; in other words, the survivors bore witness to something it is impossible to bear witness to. As a consequence, commenting on survivors' testimony necessarily means interrogating this lacuna or, more precisely, attempting to listen to it.[69]

Following Agamben, listening to the lacunae in Dimensions in Testimony must involve listening for specific silences, such as those that surround taboo topics such as sexual abuse which, as noted, Schloss discusses more candidly in her written testimony, and asking ourselves how they impact on our understanding of this testimony's truthfulness. It also involves "deep listening" to the wider archive and thinking about the limitations and silences of a testimonial genre that will only ever include a small number of case studies due to its high cost. The thirty or so interactive video testimonies recorded to date through Dimensions in Testimony and the Forever Project cover limited ground when set against the tens of thousands of written and oral testimonies that have been produced over a period of more than seventy years for archives such as the VHA. For all the investment that Holocaust education organizations have in the historical and human knowledge that we might gain by interacting with survivor testimony, we must therefore be wary of prevailing narratives that risk giving the impression that all stories of survival are somehow edifying, because they do not give us the full story of the Holocaust. Far from it, in fact.

Rejecting the idea that some survived so they could tell their story, Levi presents us with a more troubling contention:

> The "saved" of the Lager were not the best, those predestined to do good; the bearers of a message. What I had seen and lived through proved the exact contrary. Preferably the worst survived, the selfish, the violent, the insensitive, the collaborators of the "grey zone," the spies. It was not a certain

rule (there were none, nor are there certain rules in human matters), but it was, nevertheless, a rule. I felt innocent, yes, but enrolled among the saved and therefore in permanent search of a justification in my own eyes and those of others. The worst survived—that is, the fittest; the best all died.[70]

As a result of this shattering assessment, Levi draws his powerful conclusion: "we, the survivors, are not the true witnesses."[71] Levi concedes that this is not a "certain rule," and the survivors interviewed for the interactive testimony projects discussed in this book, much like Levi himself, are all thoughtful, principled people, part of the "anomalous minority . . . who by their prevarications or abilities or good luck did not touch the bottom."[72] Yet this does not offset the fact that, for Levi, the "true witnesses" are "those who saw the Gorgon" and who "have not returned to tell about it or have returned mute," which is to say "the "Muslims," the submerged, the complete witnesses, the ones whose deposition would have a general significance."[73]

If future generations do indeed feel themselves to be haunted by Holocaust victims when they encounter the ghostware of interactive video testimony, it will therefore be important to recognize that they are not being haunted by the figure of the Muselmann, or "Muslim," which is to say the broken camp inmate on the edge of death, described by Jean Améry as "a staggering corpse, a bundle of physical functions in its last convulsions," or by those "true witnesses" who were killed before such extreme dehumanization had taken place.[74] Rather, they will be being haunted by a small number of child victims who survived in highly unlikely circumstances and lived into old age. As testimony undergoes its virtual turn, rather than encountering the bodies of those whom Levi calls "an anonymous mass, continually renewed and always identical, of non-men who march and labour in silence, the divine spark dead within them, already too empty to really suffer," we will be presented with elderly, humane survivors who have become temporarily reanimated in virtual spaces of memory.[75] Rather than suffering bodies on the edge of death, we will encounter bodies of light that seem to have emerged as much from science fiction films as from a fecal episode in history. Through aesthetic and historical transformations that present virtual survivors as archetypal witnesses, digital Holocaust memory projects such as interactive video testimony divert our attention away from the wounded, fragile bodies of Muselmänner and onto the intangible, miraculous, digitized bodies of elderly survivors as the primary sites of historical knowledge. Writing in the 1990s, Agamben followed Levi's lead in arguing that the Muselmann represented the paradigmatic Holocaust victim, barely existing on the border between life and death, the human and the nonhuman: "the being whose life is not truly life" and "whose death cannot be called death, but only the production of a corpse."[76] In the post-survivor age, when the survivor has become a simulated presence, explorations of the border between the living and the dead seem set to shift from the biopolitical to the virtual, from contemplations of human finitude (biological, philosophical) to fantasies of infinity and the eternal applicability of particular forms of truth and knowledge. Any conceptualization of Holocaust memory that, following Derrida, seeks to align itself with the claims of justice must remain continually vigilant about the ramifications of such a shift.

This is not to say that we must situate the suffering body of the Muselmänner into the immersive spaces of the virtual. Here, again, we run up against the limits of the form. Indeed, the idea of future Holocaust museums ever coming to terms with the biological bodies of victims is satirized in Jáchym Topol's *The Devil's Workshop* (2009), which offers an unsparing critique of the social and political formations that gave rise to virtual Holocaust memory culture in the 2010s. The novel opens by depicting the Americanization of a memorial museum at the Terezín ghetto, where an unnamed narrator helps to peddle "ghetto pizza" and Kafka T-shirts in the gift shops. In the latter sections of the novel, the narrator is enticed to Belarus by a cynical memory entrepreneur called Alex who is developing an even more ghoulish form of Holocaust museum: a bunker where dead survivors, including the narrator's friend, Lebo, are being revivified so they can continue to tell their stories. Presciently parodying the rhetoric of virtual Holocaust memory, Alex is portrayed as a kind of deranged Victor Frankenstein: "From now on he shall live in eternity, as our conscience, our strength, our weapon, Alex declaims, tugging on the wires poking out from Lebo's jacket."[77] Much like the digital revenants of interactive testimony, Alex's witnesses are uncanny: "Lebo moves. Tips his head—the current has kicked in. It's Lebo and it's not."[78] Christine Goelz argues that the novel's interest in immersion is suggestive of the narrative strategies used in first-person shooter videogames, thereby critiquing the gamification of Holocaust memory.[79] However, unlike interactive testimony and videogames, Alex's corpses are repulsive in their physicality. His bunker "reeks of chemicals, human bodies, death" and the reanimation procedure is grotesque:

There are six of them in this room, six old heads on six wrinkly necks, mechanically opening and closing their mouths, and always telling the same story—soldiers come into the village and kill, houses and people burn—repeating it over and over, and it will just go on like that, the soldiers will keep coming back, as long as Alex holds the wires that carry the electricity that runs the stories stuffed inside the people's innards.[80]

The strange, traumatized Czech narrator becomes the novel's voice of conscience—"I don't want to hear his voice coming out of a corpse," he says of Lebo—as Topol's novel takes a clear position on the ethics of Holocaust memory culture in the post-survivor age.[81] Whether Americanized or what we might term, following Adriana Cavarero, "horrorized," it remains ripe for satire precisely because of a misguided belief that the deaths of the last living Holocaust survivors can ever be prevented or deferred through technology.[82]

While Topol's gory atrocity exhibition exposes the ideologies and fantasies that lie behind projects such as interactive video testimony, the museum in Belarus is nonetheless contrasted with a Holocaust memory culture in the West that tends toward the sanitization, rather than the reanimation, of bodily horror. Indeed, figures such as the Muselmänner are largely absent from the immersive museums of the twenty-first century, their broken bodies and silent stories slipping further from view in part because of the possibilities that arise from the confidently digitalized turn to connective memory. Given the physical, embodied, performative nature of the virtual Holocaust memory projects that we discuss in this book, it therefore remains important to ask what place extreme physical and psychological suffering can hold within a rapidly transforming memory culture. How can interactive testimony work across diametrically opposed forms of bodily experience? How can we contemplate painful forms of bodily degradation as we immerse ourselves in the wondrous imaginaries of the virtual? Earlier, more cautious traditions of Holocaust representation always required us to think about the unthinkable, contemplate the unsayable, and to "probe the limits of representation," in Friedländer's terms.[83] But what forms of forgetfulness are being built into the seductive aesthetics of digital interaction and connective memory? As we fall under the sway of the immediacy of the virtual, asking such questions will allow us to retain a critical self-awareness about the limits of the form, helping us to gauge not whether what the survivors are saying is true, but whether our engagement with interactive testimony still *feels truthful.* In the absence of such questions, factors such as the eternity narrative, survivor sacralization, the childization of Holocaust memory, and the pious approach to history that we find in films such as *Schindler's List*, buffered by technological innovation and powerful metatexts, risk blinding future generations to the fate of the "true witnesses" of the genocide.

And if this happens, the unthinkable may become even more unthinkable, until it ceases to be thought altogether.

PART II
READING THE VIRTUAL

4

Virtual Landscapes

When we first visited the Bergen-Belsen memorial and museum in 2016, the iPads stopped working. After collecting our tablets from the visitor center in preparation for a digital tour of the site, a storm broke out over the expansive admixture of greenery, serendipitous memorials, and mass graves. We sheltered under a tree as the geolocalization technology began to fail, positioning us firmly in unknown woods way outside the *Gedenkstätte*, despite our position next to the site of the former tent camp. Determined to make use of our preliminary visit, we braved the increasingly inclement weather to test the juxtaposition of digital photographs, maps, and excerpted testimony against the rain-drenched site of the main road through the camp in 1945. As the augmented reality application began to fail too, the overriding impression was of an overwhelming swathe of trees and grass in which digital applications were patently unwelcome, despite their importance to the fifth stage of Holocaust memory that we have outlined throughout this book. When we revisited the camp in 2017, the vista could not have been more different: *Goldammer* ("yellowhammer") birds sang distinctively on gravestones in a sun-soaked landscape that gave the visitor the impression that they were walking through a nature reserve rather than a site of mass graves. This deceptive appearance is reflected in the concealed position of the original camp: as our journeys from Winsen, Celle, and Hamburg in 2016–2018 made clear, the camp is buried deep in the woodland of the Lüneberg heath. Compared to Auschwitz-Birkenau, that Benjamin Meed attacks as "a tourist mecca, with souvenir stands, shops, refreshment stands . . . and vendors walking among the crowds selling postcards and snacks," Bergen-Belsen has fewer visitors due to its location.[1] Around 300,000 people arrive at the museum and memorial each year, compared to over 1 million at the Topography of Terror, a tourist site in central Berlin that we discuss in the final chapter. Many of these visitors experience the "dialectic of normalcy" that we experienced during our second visit, in which familiar technology and *heimlich* conceptions of the pastoral vie with the mass graves.[2] These conflicted encounters resonate particularly in terms of national memory in Germany. As Caroline Pearce

Virtual Holocaust Memory. Matthew Boswell and Antony Rowland, Oxford University Press. © Oxford University Press 2023. DOI: 10.1093/oso/9780197645390.003.0005

describes, a "dialectic of normalcy" indicates how difficult it is for Germans to "process" past atrocities that are "so alien to the democratic, tolerant and anti-extremist profile of the country today."[3] The landscape and history collide in Bergen-Belsen in a way that can both "repel and fascinate."

These digital landscapes representing former camps such as those we encountered in Bergen-Belsen have not yet yielded sustained critical reflection.[4] As opposed to the postmodern museum's "site of spectacular mise-en-scène and operatic exuberance," such as Daniel Libeskind's extension to the Jewish museum in Berlin in 2001, these landscapes are increasingly figured through smaller-scale technologies and transportable installations such as the iPad application and digital reconstructions of the Bergen-Belsen concentration camp.[5] Digital products are now an integral part of what Andreas Huyssen terms our "hybrid memorial-media culture": some critics bemoan the incorporation of digital sceneries into the museum experience as pandering to the "childization" of the Holocaust that we discussed in the Introduction, and "expectations of an audience driven by a diet of the ubiquitous screen in public culture and memory."[6] On the other hand, such technology serves a "wider function [. . .] in forging new memory of the Holocaust today," as Andrew Hoskins proposes in relation to electronic media in the traditional museum.[7] As we have argued throughout this book, the "truthfulness" of virtual Holocaust memory lies in the user's responsibility for and implication in a digital encounter that relies on their active participation in the production of historical meaning. However, despite this key aspect of the fifth era of Holocaust witnessing, traditional museums cannot be opposed to virtual Holocaust memory in a binary that privileges conventional exhibitions' access to historical "truth." Both must grapple with *Nachträglichkeit*: in different formats, they are—as Huyssen argues in relation to both traditional and postmodern museums—"belated, reconstructive, at best approximating what was held to have been the real and often quite deliberately severed from its context."[8] Following Daniel Levy and Natan Sznaider's praise for "memoryscapes" that can "become the cultural foundation for global human-rights politics" in the twenty-first century, Alison Landsberg contends that representations of the Holocaust in mass media and developing technologies can now respond positively to "belatedness" by initiating "new vision and social change."[9] In *Aesthetic Theory*, Theodor Adorno criticizes Bertholt Brecht's political commitment, but praises the art forms in which it is expressed; similarly, it is not the utopian politics of Levy,

Sznaider, and Landsberg that are of primary importance in this chapter, but the *forms* of the "memoryscapes" that engage with these politics.[10]

All the digital landscapes we analyze in this chapter, from "3D" reconstructions of Bergen-Belsen to the Kristallnacht exhibition in Second Life, indicate latent possibilities in technological forms that could lead to complex representations of the Holocaust in the future, and an incorporation of awkward poetics. Digital palimpsests in the current iPad application at Bergen-Belsen already enhance visitors' experience of empty vistas, resisting the simplistic liberation narratives that surround the camp. The Second Life exhibition that we discuss later in this chapter also presents an uncanny landscape in an attempt to undercut viewers' potential complacency. However, as we argue throughout this book, these technologies do not yet adequately challenge the forms of their representation, as in the vexed aesthetics that we discussed in the introduction. Indeed, the digital technology introduced at Bergen-Belsen confronts some of the central problems for memory studies over the last twenty years, including anxieties over representation and issues surrounding connectivity that the USC Shoah Foundation summarizes in relation to Dimensions in Testimony as a need to "develop empathy, understanding and respect." Accordingly, the iPad application in Bergen-Belsen emphasizes the requirement for "identification," "understanding" the past and "assigning meaning" to primary witnesses' experience.[11] These statements indicate that the discourse surrounding testimony has changed radically over the last twenty years. Rather than adhering to Shoshana Felman's insistence—drawing on Charlotte Delbo's work—that we *cannot* understand survivors' experience, and Cathy Caruth's focus on the aporias of trauma, we are now encouraged to embrace, process, and respond to Holocaust witnessing as a form of prosthetic memory.[12] As we shall demonstrate in this chapter, the digital technologies of the 2010s and 2020s are transforming the meaning and forms of Holocaust remembrance.

iPads and the Extermination of Memory

In 2014–2015, a team investigating "Synthetic Perceptive, Emotive and Cognitive Systems" (SPECS) were working with the museum at Bergen-Belsen on a mobile tablet application alongside the "immersive interactive presentation," which we discuss later in this chapter.[13] SPECS describes the former as a "state of the art" application in the area of digital heritage that uses geolocalization and augmented reality in order to visualize the former camp for visitors.[14] Geolocalization technology allowed visitors from May 2014 to navigate through the memorial space outside the museum buildings—unless they encounter the inclement weather we describe earlier in the chapter—and view the entire route through the former camp, record sites, and note missed locations. One of the motivations of the tablet application designers was to "move away from mostly sequential 'tours' as prepared by guides or the memorial, and toward 'explorations' that are more directed by the interest of the users, and the expertise of guides, educators and researchers."[15] Visitors can choose from a variety of digital representations of the former camp that the iPad superimposes on the present-day landscape: the tour lasts over an hour, and contains palimpsests of documents, photographs, and excerpts from testimony (see Fig. 4.1). Ultimately, the museum team wish to embed two hundred files in what Stephanie Billib termed the "nonlinear" process of learning through the application.[16] Surveys of students and visiting soldiers indicate that "compared to traditional guided tours, the application enhances the

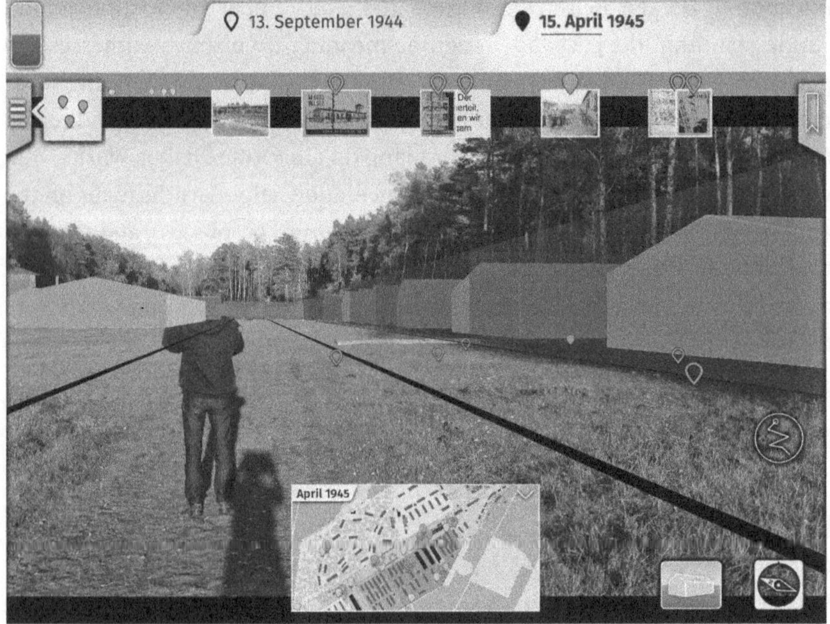

Figure 4.1 The iPad app
© Gedenkstätte Bergen-Belsen

exploration of the landscape, introducing users to more locations associated with the site's history."[17] Hence the augmented reality of the iPad application constitutes an intriguing attempt to marry Hoskins' sense of the "ubiquitous screen" with Landsberg's vision of "Contemporary modes of historical representation" that can "change the way ordinary people understand history and acquire historical knowledge in our distracted age."[18] Like Dimensions in Testimony, the user can choose their own digital route through the stored information, focusing on topics of their choice. Whereas Dimensions in Testimony relies on the visitor piecing together fragments of disparate testimony, however, the more palimpsestic approach in the iPad app allows the user to amass interlinked information about specific buildings in the form of official documents, images, and literature. As we discussed in relation to the USC Shoah Foundation project, this onus on the visitor provides the freedom of a user-driven experience, but also the potential drawback of missing key information that, in the context of Bergen-Belsen, a museum tour or audio guide can provide.

Huyssen considers the success of the postmodern museum to be beholden, paradoxically, to the "material quality of the object": if this is the case, then the iPad application might be expected to flounder, since it relies on what Hoskins refers to as "new memory" in the form of "presentist media."[19] On the contrary, the application is particularly effective around the open vistas surrounding the former main road through the camp (see Fig. 4.1): graphics of the digital barracks open out into sound files, poetry, and photographs of, for example, the former hospital. This digital technology allows schoolchildren, students, and other visitors to confront the Holocaust not as a "vast sea of footnotes and rationalistic analyses," but as an intense encounter with the present site and a palimpsestic trove of information about the history of the camp.[20] By directing the visitor's attention to the historical details surrounding this road, the augmented reality draws attention away from the burial grounds, and, by proxy, the footage taken of the bodies in the process of being bulldozed into mass graves that Alain Resnais controversially included at the end of *Night and Fog* (1955). The application thus subtly attempts to avoid what Tony Kushner refers to as "the use of Belsen as part of the British war story," inextricable from the liberation in April 1945.[21] When James Young visited Bergen-Belsen in the late 1980s, he noted that "little of what transpired specifically . . . is reflected in the outdoor memorial space. Instead, as if harking back to the grisly film footage by which Bergen-Belsen is most commonly recalled, the principal motif is the prisoners' 'deaths and mass graves.'"[22] The iPad application is thereby a successful attempt to convey precisely "what transpired" in the context of the current topography, and to open out the historical significance of the whole site beyond the sites of the mass graves; in effect, to turn users away from postwar memorialization and toward preliberation history.

Of course, there are also conceptual dangers inherent in this augmented reality (see Fig. 4.1): it might, for example, present history through the digitized buildings as a puzzle to be solved rather than Yehuda Bauer's conception of the Holocaust as an "abyss." At the beginning of Claude Lanzmann's film *Shoah* (1985), Simon Srebnik wanders around the remains of the Chelmno camp, a "void that compels engagement," and begins to "fill in" missing details as his diegetic testimony overlays the images of former barracks.[23] In contrast, there is a danger in the tablet application that such testimony is replaced with technology, so that augmented reality stands in for absent Belsen huts in Baudrillard's sense of the extermination of memory. As we noted in the Introduction to this book, Marianne Hirsch worries similarly in relation to Dimensions in Testimony that displays of technological prowess might threaten to overwhelm the Holocaust narratives being mediated.[24] However, the unreal "blocky" graphics in the augmented reality application indicate that the digitized space is clearly not presented as "real" or a replacement for the past, but precisely as enhanced ("augmented") reality. Akin to the absent barracks at Chelmno, many of the digital buildings have not accrued much testimonial or historical information: as in *Shoah*, they remain signs of what has been lost, and of an inaccessible historicity, rather than indices of Baudrillard's anxiety about the destruction of the referent. As we argued in the introduction, this "augmented" form of memory appears in one sense to parody Jacques Derrida's notion of the trace, in that the iPad application figures the unmistakable presence of the absence to which it attests.[25] In the ambiguous space between the digital representation and the absent original, virtual memory becomes a primary route for the transmission of historical knowledge. However, this potentially revolutionary grammar of Holocaust memory must be rigorously examined if it is to engage successfully—as we now go on to argue—with existing critical thinking in memory studies.

"This is a high tech tool," the SPECS website announces, "with invaluable informative and educational applications since it allows users to see what once was Bergen Belsen and in general to understand the importance of the holocaust [*sic*], to identify with its victims and to assign meaning to their experience."[26] As we argued in the introduction to this chapter, "understanding," identification, and "assigning meaning" are clearly loaded terms that are inextricable from the ramifications of connectivity. In relation to the Secret Annex Online, we pointed out that one of the defining aspects of Holocaust testimony for Robert Eaglestone in 2004 is that it *resists* identification: does the tablet application therefore court the "childization" of the Holocaust by encouraging students to simply "identify with [the site's] victims" in order to claim pedagogical success?[27] In *Auschwitz and After*, Delbo writes about the dangers of colonizing the victim's experience when she describes how Pierre, the husband of a former inmate, takes over his wife's experiences to the extent that he thinks he understands them better than she does (286–288).[28] This fraught process of identification is particularly problematic in the context of national memory in Germany, and the "difficulty [for Germans in] identifying with this period of national history."[29] Does the iPad application risk the colonization of victims' experiences in order to "assign meaning" for pedagogical discussion? Readers of Delbo's second book in her *Auschwitz and After* trilogy might also ask what business the secondary witness has in "assigning meaning" to a victim's experience, when Delbo describes her own survivor's understanding of Birkenau and Ravensbrück as "useless knowledge." Users of the tablet application will undoubtedly designate "meaning," but in relation to what and whom? The project website refers to the visitor's "responsibility to commemorate," but how this process might manifest itself is left open to interpretation.[30]

These issues in memory studies about assigning meaning through connectivity are addressed by Levy, Sznaider, and Landsberg. According to their work, empathetic responses to an inmate's experience can be a fulcrum for future activism in order to deploy—but not necessarily "understand"— the Holocaust as an example of violated human rights. As we have argued throughout this book, the user has a responsibility for the coming-into-being of testimony and memory through an effective and affecting archive. Nevertheless, if Levy, Sznaider, and Landsberg's proposed activism is the ultimate goal of Holocaust education through interactive testimony or the augmented reality of the tablet application in Bergen-Belsen, then Slavoj Žižek's guarded response to commitment still needs to be considered. In *Violence* (2009), Žižek proposes that critical reflection is required in order to "assign meaning" to atrocity, as well as the alternative activist responses.[31] In the context of the iPad application, schoolchildren and university students have been meeting in the museum's main building to discuss their experience of the digital technology and "captured" information with an experienced tutor precisely to encourage this kind of critical thinking about their pedagogical encounters. However, what does it mean to "understand" the Holocaust in the context of Lanzmann's famous remark about an "obscenity of understanding" in relation to the perpetrators' actions?[32] Following Lanzmann's logic, the recreation of the camp could be said to follow an obscene perpetrator logic in its attempt to "understand" Bergen-Belsen through the architectural specters of augmented reality.

Of course, Lanzmann's statement has to be understood in the context of discussion about the singularity of the Holocaust in the 1980s and early 1990s, which has now, for the most part, given way—as in Levy, Sznaider, and Landsberg's work—to critical arguments about the transnational and transcultural nature of Holocaust memory. Nevertheless, on a site that resists references to multidirectional memory like the Secret Annex Online and Topography of Terror, should students necessarily "assign meaning" by linking the digitized documents to other sites of persecution? And is there something inherent in the *form* of the iPad application that renders any "understanding" of these documents difficult in the first place, before this historical knowledge can be reassigned elsewhere? Currently, the application's floating guard towers juxtaposed with the surrounding fauna near to the former tent camp complement the information on the conventional site stations (see Fig. 4.2) and the documentation center, but do not lead to a more rigorous appreciation of the camp's history.[33] Landsberg's "ordinary people" have much to learn in the center's extensive exhibitions, whereas they must confront the confusing graphics of the unlabeled gray walls of former barracks in the augmented reality of the *Gedenkstätte*.

In comparison, the former Neuengamme camp registers the former landscape with steel poles for the guard towers and fence embedded in the actual landscape (see Fig. 4.3) that are reminiscent of the Berlin Wall memorial, and which provide material equivalents of the augmented reality in Bergen-Belsen. These analog examples of memorialization are arguably more effective than the digital technology in revealing the contours of the past, although the visitor's imagination must still work hard to connect the poles to the contemporaneous landscape.[34] In an attempt to "profoundly disturb," the tablet application could perhaps in the future shift between the different landscapes and media, such as the footage of the liberation in 1945. At present, such impious interaction might be regarded as insensitive when the museum staff are still welcoming survivors of the camp whose relatives or fellow inmates could be featured in

Figure 4.2 The iPad app and site station
Antony Rowland

the footage. As Victoria Walden notes, there has been a laudable shift in recent years from an emphasis on the disturbing footage as evidence of atrocities to an attempt to focus on the murdered inmates and survivors as individuals.[35] Yet a future synchronization of the film footage from 1945 with the accompanying digital material could disturb the "flatness" of viewing the augmented reality on a sunny day, when locals are walking their dogs in the grounds, and yellowhammers sing undisturbed on memorials and gravestones.

Figure 4.3 The perimeter fence in the former Neuengamme camp
Antony Rowland

In the future, digital palimpsests could also coalesce around individuals' testimonies, so an application could navigate through a particular survivor's "understanding" of their own experience in the camp. This possibility could create a more digitally enriched approach to the oral testimony than the Dimensions in Testimony project: as in the Secret Annex Online, witness statements could then interact with supporting metatextual evidence. This particularity could emphasize the "truthfulness" contained in testimony, such as Delbo's concerns that her writing may refer to historical events, but is not "true" in the sense that she can accurately portray the entirety of her experience in Birkenau and Ravensbrück.[36] In 2018, the tablet application focused on conveying the metanarrative of Bergen-Belsen through snippets of testimony, whereas applications that followed singular narratives of testimony could focus more on flawed human memory: as Delbo demonstrates in *Auschwitz and After*, the gaps created by traumatic dissociation result in an artistic condensation of her experiences. Walden argues that a focus on individual testimony might encourage the user to "empathize" simplistically with victims, but this particular response is not guaranteed in a form that, as Eaglestone suggested, has a tendency to alienate rather than embrace the listener or reader.[37] Understandably, the current technology focuses instead on historical information rather than awkward poetics. Yet Landsberg herself argues that film and digital media cannot produce "real" historical knowledge unless "the affective engagements that draw the viewer in [are] coupled with other modes that assert the alien nature of the past and the viewer's fundamental distance from it."[38] At present, the augmented reality in the iPad application at Bergen-Belsen does not work against its own form in order to specify this "fundamental distance."

The application would also benefit from its integration into mobile technology: it is inevitably unwieldy to carry an iPad with a protective case around fifty-five hectares, particularly during the inclement weather we experienced on our first visit. As with other sites of persecution such as the Topography of Terror in Berlin, the site stations at Bergen-Belsen (see Fig. 4.2) provide a variety of information about the former camp and allow the visitor to shift effortlessly between the text, photographs, testimony, and the present-day vista. In contrast, the iPad application offers access to letters and diaries, but can be distracting when the user's grappling with technology begins to occlude an appreciation of the actual site.[39] Yet when the technology works seamlessly, the augmented reality presents, as with the Secret Annex Online, an informative and intriguing sense of how the camp *might* have looked. The graphics of, for example, guard towers without supporting data indicate the aporias in existing historical narratives about Bergen-Belsen. In this sense, the palimpsestic information points to unknown stories surrounding the fragments of testimony as much as the details within the testimonial narratives themselves. As with the Kristallnacht exhibition that we discuss later in this chapter, the form of the iPad application is not just attempting to encourage empathy, identification, and understanding. These digital landscapes also point to the limitations of connectivity and users' potential difficulties in assembling coherent narratives out of their experiences of digital memoryscapes.

Digital Installations and the Reconstruction of Bergen-Belsen

Collaboration between staff at the Bergen-Belsen Memorial and SPECS resulted in the first digital installation at the Bergen-Belsen *Gedenkstätte* in summer 2012, a year before work began on the iPad application. Entitled "Here—Bergen-Belsen, Space of Memory," the installation opened on Anne-Frank-Platz near the entrance to the museum: this audiovisual installation formed part of activities marking the sixtieth anniversary of the memorial's inauguration on November 30, 1952.[40] Soon referred to as "the box," the installation introduced the site through an immersive presentation of "the words of surviving prisoners, images from then and now, and a 3D reconstruction of the former concentration camp."[41] One aim was "to make the visitor aware of her/his position in-between past and present," and to avoid a state in which, with "so little evidence of its past, the memorial threatens to float atemporally above its own history."[42] Though not yet interactive in 2012, the "box" installation integrated key project elements of the collaboration, such as "the 3D reconstruction . . . as well as its narrative interaction with archive material and interviews" (see Fig. 4.4).[43] In addition, it gave the collaborators an opportunity to interweave different technological and pedagogical expertise required for the project, including archaeological research and 3D animation. Feedback proved to be very positive: for many visitors, "including the children of former prisoners, the three-dimensional view of the reconstructed camp was the first time they were offered a clear, integrated view of the entire historical site."[44] The video loop lasted for twelve minutes: after a brief introduction to the history of the camp, the installation glided through a virtual reconstruction of the camp accompanied, as Walden notes, by Richard Dimbleby's famous BBC report on Bergen-Belsen, recorded on April 19, 1945.[45] As we discussed in relation to the Secret Annex

Figure 4.4 The original "box" installation at Bergen-Belsen
© Specs-Lab

Online and iPad application, palimpsestic testimony has the ability to enrich the users' experience: in this case, virtual "stops" revealed photographs and text on the sidewall screens; one noted that former prisoners were surprised that the camp has transformed "into a beautiful nature park."[46] Planned as a temporary exhibition, the box installation proved so popular that it remained in situ until spring 2014. It was then closed due to the problems of hoisting an electric cable through the air to support the installation from another building: in this instance, the electronification of memory had yet to supersede the twentieth-century technology that led to Huyssen's "cabling of the metropolis."[47] Subsequent problems also arose in obtaining planning permission for a new building at the front of the *Gedenkstätte* to house a permanent installation.

Inaugurated to mark the seventieth anniversary of the liberation of the Nazi concentration camps, the second version of the installation was displayed at the Wiener Library in London in 2015 (see Fig. 4.5). As with the "box," the display was described as a "3D reconstruction of the Bergen-Belsen concentration camp as it stood on 15 April 1945, when it was liberated by the British Army"; in 2019, the installation was renamed as the "Virtual Panorama."[48] The website promises the viewer that they will be able to "physically visit the former campsite" and "perceive and experience the historical spacial [sic] structures and details of fences, buildings and camp sections as part of the

Figure 4.5 Image of the 2015 "virtual panorama" at the Wiener Library
© Specs-Lab

landscape." As with the holograms we discussed in the first three chapters, this discussion of physicality and direct experience indicates a danger that such digital installations may attempt to function as overdetermined sources of supposed historical authenticity. Following on from their work on the first installation, SPECS nevertheless "took on the challenge to develop and implement applications that optimize [the Holocaust's] archaeological, social, cultural, psychological [and] medical aspects." Professor Paul Verschure, director of the Catalan Institution for Research and Advanced Studies (ICREA), worked closely with members of staff at the Bergen-Belsen memorial in order to complete the second version, particularly with Habbo Knoch, who was director of the memorial site foundation until 2014. In the initial stages of the collaboration, the team drew support from the European project CEEDS on "Future and Emerging Technologies." CEEDS, the Collective Experience of Empathic Data Systems, develops integrated technologies to support the analysis and understanding of large data sets. The ensuing, "impressive, semi-circular panorama" at the Wiener Library (see Fig. 4.5) included a "flight through the reconstruction" underscored with Dimbleby's report, and shared exhibition space with the library's section on the Jewish Relief unit, that "played an important role in the enormous humanitarian operation" organized after the liberation of Bergen-Belsen.[49]

This "virtual panorama" is more interactive than the box installation: the visitor can navigate through different areas of the camp, but the required four projectors still present—as with the original—a two-dimensional film on three walls that creates the illusion of a 3D experience in a similar way to Dimensions in Testimony (see Fig. 4.5). Despite the integration of touchscreen technology into the second version—and due partly to the slowness of the moving cursor—it is more cumbersome to "drill" down into the palimpsestic testimony of the digitized documents and photographs than in the portable iPad application. The two-dimensional "flatness" of the original installation is particularly evident when visitors have to swivel their heads in order to view the digitized material on the side screens. As such, this palimpsestic digital technology has not entirely superseded the power of introductory films such as the Soviet footage of the liberation of Auschwitz-Birkenau in January 1945. Nevertheless, the technological possibility can be anticipated of a complex layering of digitized material from the archives of the Bergen-Belsen Memorial and other museums and memorials that SPECS are now collaborating with in Falstad (Norway), Lety (the Czech Republic), and Jasenovac (Croatia).[50] The Wiener Library website explains that "Visitors will be given the opportunity to learn about the camp through exploring a virtual environment," and to view areas within the camp's reconstruction, "learning about the camp's history through digitised documents and photographs." Concurring with Susan Gubar's sense that the Holocaust is "dying" at the end of the "age of the witness," SPECS argues that existing memorial sites "or museums continue to offer a sound traditional historiographical approach. What is missing however is the integration of pertinent historical sources (e.g. images, maps, construction plans) and personal descriptions (e.g. from testimonies and diaries)."[51] As with the digital applications and virtual reality (VR) films arising out of the Anne Frank House, this palimpsestic approach to the museum experience promises an enriching encounter with the memorial site and attendant testimony. However, SPECS' distinction between the digital age and the historiographical is not entirely pertinent: many Holocaust and war museums already contain extracts from testimony, images, and maps to support their overarching historical narratives, such as USHMM and the Imperial War Museum. Indeed, the permanent exhibition at the Bergen-Belsen *Gedenkstätte* screens numerous video interviews with survivors as a "special focus" of the museum and documentation center.[52]

However, virtual and digital technology does contain the possibility of *intensifying* such sources within these palimpsestic narratives. For example, Tadeusz Hołuj's poetry is easily lost or ignored in the overwhelming exhibition spaces of Auschwitz I, whereas the digitization of Bergen-Belsen allows for the integration of similar poems as text or sound files. The interactions of history and testimony are more integrated in the Secret Annex Online that we discuss in our chapter on the virtual Anne Frank, but this interplay is certainly one of the benefits of the digital installations at Bergen-Belsen. This "layering" of the digital artifacts also forms a potentially instructive way of learning about the process of historical reconstruction akin to displays in Huyssen's "old" museums that, for example, emphasize the traces of the arson attack on the reconstructed barracks in Sachsenhausen. Application users might wish, for example, to learn more about the postwar history of the Polish cross at Bergen-Belsen, which is not an authentic relic: it has been replaced several times, due primarily to rotting wood. When and why, visitors might ask, was it installed? Why has it endured as a sign of Christian remembrance just by the former tent camp—where Anne and Margot Frank were interned—in contrast with the controversies over the crucifixes and eight-meter high cross at Auschwitz-Birkenau in 1984, 1989, and 1998?[53] The Bergen-Belsen website's description of "the camp's history" refers to the early 1940s rather than its postwar development as a DP camp, which only closed in summer 1950 when the remaining inhabitants were transferred to Upjever: such histories are not deemed relevant to the digital installation in its current form.[54] The museum contains a wealth of material in its Research and Documentation department about the "History of the Memorial since 1945" that could also be integrated into the palimpsestic applications in the future. Many of the staff at the Bergen-Belsen Memorial and SPECS are committed to the long-term project of experimenting with such different ways in which the virtual might complement the actual contours of the former camp and are sanguine about overcoming the current limitations in digital technology. However, "virtual panorama" at Bergen-Belsen represents a time mostly "untouched by post-Holocaust memory," unlike the questions about the postwar period encompassed in Dimensions in Testimony and the Forever Project.[55] Given its innovative medium, the installation paradoxically appears to "search for an authentic historical memory as the antithesis of a debased and mediated relation to the past."[56]

Following the utopian politics of Levy, Sznaider, and Landsberg, The Wiener Library presented the second version of the installation as demonstrating "how the use of virtual and augmented reality techniques can help to maintain and anchor historical facts to collective memory and enhance education."[57] Yet there are *formal* aspects of the digital representations that must impact on the "historical knowledge," which Landsberg is so confident users will gain from such technology. Visitors to Holocaust museums and exhibitions are used to viewing recreations of the camps, as with the detailed model of the Birkenau ramp in the Imperial War Museum. In contrast, the digital installations of Bergen-Belsen successfully draw attention to the overwhelming blank space (see Fig. 4.6). Analog as well as digital versions of the camps are partly fictions in the sense that the historian cannot know every detail of the original space. Historians are professionally disinclined to guess at or approximate the gaps in knowledge: Stephanie Billib, who works in the *Öffentlichkeitsarbeit* section of the museum, expressed an understandable reluctance to respond to visitors' requests for more detail in the digital landscapes, such as barrack windows, colors of buildings, and indications of texture. Her explanation was that historians are not sure, in some cases, where the windows were situated, or what constituted the exact colors of the brick and wooden barracks.

As the SPECS website comments, the resulting "modest, desaturated style" of the installations is deliberate: the company refrains from

Figure 4.6 Image of the 2015 "virtual panorama" at Bergen-Belsen
© Specs-Lab

"providing realistic details" because such historical details are, to a large extent, "simply unknown from current research." Billib noted that Richard Dimbleby identified the barracks' color as brown in his BBC recording on the liberation of Belsen, whereas a survivor described them as gray. What, she ruminated, was the historical truth in relation to these conflicting reports, and which color should the project team then choose for the installation? It may be that Dimbleby and the inmate were referring to different buildings (maybe wooden and brick barracks), or that both accounts are "true" in the sense that the buildings appeared to be a different color at different times. Such ruminations can easily be expressed in a discursive format, but the installation cannot effortlessly shift between opposing versions of color, and different timescales: hence the installation deploys a uniform gray to depict the different buildings (see Fig. 4.6). The second installation encompasses three different versions of the camp, in September 1944, mid-April 1945, and summer 2013, but the camp would of course appear very different on April 15, 1945, or on a date in 1965, compared to its current state. Rather than convey the "truthfulness" of the camp as it *might* have been—as with the digitized photographs in the Secret Annex Online—the virtual panorama at Bergen-Belsen strives to be as historically accurate as possible.

"Truthfulness," however, is often a direct product of the forms of digital technology that, like the VR films about the annex, cannot possibly present history "as it was." Accordingly, the digital installations at Bergen-Belsen are partial fictions in terms of certain oddities of their form. Dark circles under the uniform trees in the first installation are more of an aesthetic addition to the blank space than an accurate reflection of the past. SPECS was clearly keen to develop the digitization of the trees: the second version contains different shapes connoting a variety of trees that one viewer referred to during our visit as reminiscent of "dog shit." Trees were clearly not representative of real trees in the original installation, so it is unclear why SPECS felt the need to develop the arboreal graphics to appear more "real"; the answer probably lies in the grammar of the digital program, and a desire to improve on the uniformity of trees in the original. In contrast, the analog model at the former Neuengamme camp—constructed in 1947–1948 and now on display in the House of Remembrance—contains trees that (like the rest of the model's figures) are akin to those of a children's farmyard (see Fig. 4.7). Yet this reconstruction still allows for a better understanding of a camp's layout than the virtual installations in Bergen-Belsen, and a clearer, "integrated view of the entire historical site" that connects it to the "landscape of the present."[58] The "farmyard" model in the House of Remembrance has been updated with a new model opposite the 1947–1948 construction. Digital "grammar" has impacted on the updated model in that the trees in this model are reminiscent

Figure 4.7 Model of the Neuengamme camp (1947–1948)
Antony Rowland

of those in the first installation at Bergen-Belsen, yet the "farmyard" version still conveys a better sense of the camp's layout compared to the white space and distracting wooden trees in the updated version.[59]

Despite the potentialities of the technology that we are keen to stress throughout this chapter, such as the palimpsestic testimony in the iPad application and virtual panorama, the different versions of camp landscapes at Bergen-Belsen and Neuengamme indicate that digital technologies do not necessarily lead to enhanced historical knowledge. However, this does not mean that digital technology attempts to "exterminate" the past, as Jean Baudrillard argues in relation to televisual representations of the Holocaust.[60] These "3D" films do not form the characterless, depthless, and meaningless representations that we discussed in the introduction in relation to Baudrillard's critiques of early digital culture. Baudrillard presents simulacra as a kind of forgetting, in which

> the artificial memory will be the restaging of extermination—but late, much too late for it to make real waves and profoundly disturb something, and especially through a medium that is itself cold, radiating forgetfulness, deterrence, and extermination in a still more systematic way, if that is possible, than the camps themselves.[61]

His warnings in the 1980s about the ramifications of visual technology could be dismissed as outdated histrionics in the face of the digital. After all, the digital installations are not, despite their "truthful" fictional elements, "models of a real without origin or reality," inaugurated by "a liquidation of all referentials," but genuine attempts by historians and SPECS to connect the reality of the current memorial site with the historical "truths" of the camp's previous existence.[62] Yet Baudrillard's point that the simulacra cannot "profoundly disturb" deserves further consideration here in the context of the digital "cleanliness" of the second installation, and we shall return to his charge about "cold" media later in this chapter in relation to the Kristallnacht exhibition in Second Life.

Inevitably, a disjuncture persists between the "modest, desaturated style" of the installations, and the iconic footage of mounds of corpses at Bergen-Belsen that Alain Resnais includes to such devastating effect in his film *Night and Fog*.[63] As Walden notes, the digital films and iPad application keep "violence and death" outside their frames (207). "[D]esaturated" indicates that the virtual installations have to be concise, and "plain" in Walden's description, but the word is also uncomfortably close to connoting "sanitized." The insertion of palimpsestic testimony cannot alleviate a discomforting gap between the Speer-like monumentality and "clean" lines of the virtual reconstructions on the one hand, and, on the other, the film footage of the "most gruesome of all images relating to Nazi atrocities."[64] As we noted earlier, this "desaturated" style is primarily a response to worries over historical accuracies, such as the exact color of the huts. Yet the "truthfulness" of the depicted annex in the Secret Annex Online that must, due to its form, inevitably include some fiction such as the exact placement of objects, is more successful in drawing the user into empathic unsettlement than the "sanitized" second installation at Bergen-Belsen. In contrast to the latter, testimonies included at the closure of, for example, *Belsen in History and Memory* (1997) are far from "desaturated." Esther Brunstein admits that she fails to express and transmit "the trauma, fear and despair which were the norm of our existence"; Hugh Le Druillenec defers to Dante when he enters his first hut in Belsen in late 1944 and has to "splash and wade through excrement."[65]

Baudrillard's conception of simulacra remains pertinent in the context of this testimony: the digital installations' concerns are primarily pedagogical, and understandably about connectivity, accessibility, and transferability, rather than attempting to "profoundly disturb." Again, this issue with a formal aspect of the digital appertains not only to this technological medium: Delbo's "truthful" prose still worries about the "idyllic clarity of narrative" in her own testimony, and the problem—as she puts it—of making readers "see" what actually happened.[66] Nevertheless, questions remain as to what visitors are actually "seeing" in the second installation when they gaze at the cursor roving slowly through the graphics that are reminiscent of contemporaneous games such as Roblox and Minecraft. Are the formal aspects of the digital so distracting that some visitors think only about these "block" graphics rather than the memorial landscape? This was certainly their impact on us during our first visit in 2016. Do the palimpsestic documents and photographs make the user "see" history, or are they formally incapable of recreating the profoundly disturbing aspects of written testimony; when, for example, Delbo describes the agonizing death of a Birkenau inmate over six pages of *Auschwitz and After* (1965)?[67] Whereas awkward poetics in this passage are able to hold the "moment of rupture" open between the past and present, the installations form part of a wider, postmillennial focus on the transferability of knowledge about the Holocaust, of which Landsberg's work is illustrative. Like the gaps in Eva Schloss's recording for Dimensions in Testimony in relation to her sexual abuse, connectivity sometimes has to embrace censorship in order to shield young children from the more disturbing aspects of Holocaust testimony. This is not evidence of a simplistic "childization" of the Holocaust, but a measured and necessary approach to conveying testimony to a younger audience during the fifth era of Holocaust witnessing. Other elisions as a result of connectivity include necessary selections from witness statements. Delbo's *Convoy to Auschwitz* (1997) is an exhaustive attempt to capture information about all those inmates who were deported with her from Drancy to Birkenau.[68] In contrast, the Bergen-Belsen installations necessarily have to skip over the wealth of testimony available in order to function as short introductions to the camp.[69] However, despite the extracts of testimony in the second installation, the dominating graphics remain uncomfortably devoid of humans. Walden argues that this design allows the visitor to appreciate the "radical difference" between their current situation, and that of the victims.[70] The graphics actually suggest that visitors are witnessing the virtual perfection of a perpetrator ideal, in which all of the camps' inmates have vanished, leaving only the ghostly structure of Bergen-Belsen to float unimpeded through the digital landscape.[71]

Kristallnacht and Virtual Memory

Similar issues of perpetrator perspectives arise in the final example of virtual Holocaust memory that we shall discuss in this chapter. However, whereas the installations and tablet application are examples of digital technology that defers to the signified referent of the former camp, the Kristallnacht exhibition in Second Life creates a digital space whose contours do not directly map onto one particular site of persecution, even if the user still encounters a "ghostly structure" akin to "Here, Space of Memory." As Alison Landsberg recounts in *Engaging the Past* (2015), the United States Holocaust Memorial Museum (USHMM) worked with the organization Global Kids in 2008 to consider how Kristallnacht could be figured on a teen grid in Second Life.[72] Developed by the internet company Linden Lab, Second Life is an online virtual world: launched in June 2003, it had approximately 1 million regular users by 2013. After USHMM realized the potential of the teen grid in terms of pedagogical development and its sheer popularity, they then employed a design company to construct the Kristallnacht exhibition on the main grid of Second Life. David Klevan, an Education Manager in the Division of Outreach Technology at USHMM, conducted nine new interviews of Kristallnacht survivors for the site, and used extracts of around six minutes from each for the website.[73]

This deployment of fresh testimonial material indicates that the ensuing digital landscape is not akin to Baudrillard's simulacrum, and devoid of memory: it arises out of a palimpsest of different aspects of Kristallnacht, including—like the Bergen-Belsen examples—palimpsests of photographs, documents, and extracts of testimony. As with the installations and iPad application, the exhibition's attention to mediation does not result in the "fantasy of seizing reality live," and yet it might still, for some, come across as what Baudrillard termed a "cold" medium, potentially "radiating forgetfulness."[74] Members of Second Life can utilize a portal in order to visit the virtual site of Kristallnacht: after taking in a newsroom on the event, the visitor guides their avatar around the digital collage of deserted streets and a burning synagogue (see Fig. 4.8). Baudrillard penned his attack on televisual representations of the Holocaust in the late 1970s and early 1980s at the same time as Saul Friedländer's book on the "new discourse": both were responding to the controversial film *The Night Porter* (1974) and the mini-series *Holocaust* (1978), and what they perceived to be an increasingly popular enthrallment with Nazism and the Holocaust.[75] For Baudrillard and Friedländer, such films and the television series considered Nazism as "fascinating in its filtered cruelty": some critics might also regard the digital depiction of the aftermaths of

Figure 4.8 The burning synagogue in the Kristallnacht exhibition
© Linden Lab

violence in the Kristallnacht exhibition as a complicit and "realistic hallucination."[76] However, we argue in this section that the exhibition's "coldness" arises from the positive fact that it is not—as in the German definition of *heimlich*—"zum Hause gehörig" (literally, "belonging to the house"). Rather than adhere to Baudrillard's sense of a "cold" representation exterminating the referent, we propose that the formal characteristics of the exhibition result in a productive disturbance of the viewer's reception of history that, as with Dimensions in Testimony and the Secret Annex Online, is inextricable from the *unheimlich*. As opposed to the digital technology's inducement of mild discombobulation at Bergen-Belsen, the Second Life project has the potential to disconcert, if maybe not—following Baudrillard's lamentations on the televisual—"profoundly disturb."[77]

Whereas the first installation at Bergen-Belsen is unsettling only in terms of the extradiegetic music—reminiscent of a Max Richter soundtrack—the Kristallnacht exhibition is uncanny in its "particularly intense experience of strangeness."[78] Something would need to be added to the "novel and unfamiliar" media of the Bergen-Belsen films for them to be truly *unheimlich*: Sigmund Freud defines the "uncanny effect" as encompassing "silence, solitude and darkness," accompanied by an undefined threat that figures in this exhibition as the absent perpetrators.[79] In contrast, in the Kristallnacht exhibition, "The sim," as one visitor posted on the site, "is a grim": dimly lit streets littered with shattered glass, piles of furniture and antisemitic graffiti contribute to the disconcerting effect. Threats persist in the residue of perpetrator voices and actions throughout this detritus of violence: "IST IN DACHAU" painted on one wall follows extracts from an antisemitic children's primer, a Eugenics poster ("Nuremberg Law for the Protection of Blood and German Honour"), and sample pages from *Der Stürmer*; glass shatters as the avatar passes the Strauss shop window (see Fig. 4.9). However, the form of the fictional landscape—as with the interactive testimony we discussed earlier in this book—is just as central to the uncanny effect as the content, in this instance, of the signified absence of perpetrators. The viewer is initially lost in a digital space that "tricks us" by promising the depiction of history, "and then goes beyond it" with its digital collage.[80] For the new user, the limits of the digital space and the unwieldiness of the avatar add to the uncanny effect of what Freud referred to as "the helplessness we experience in certain dream-states."[81] For Ernst Jentsch, an early exponent of the uncanny, the *unheimlich* "would always be an area in which a person was unsure of his way around."[82] The avatar is key to "the realm of the frightening"

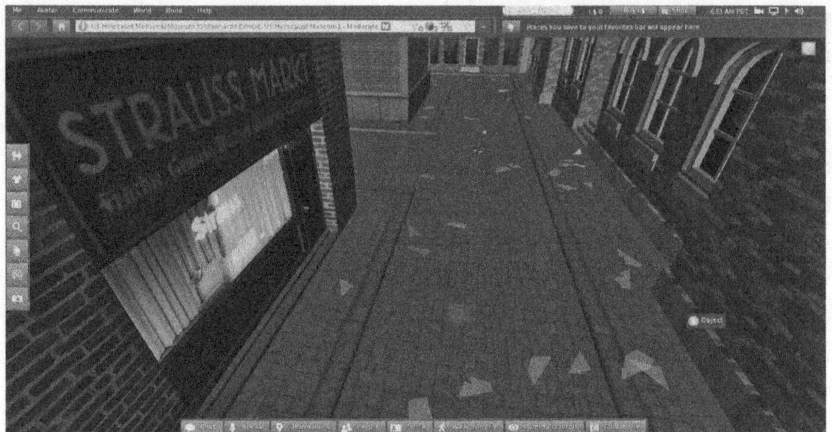

Figure 4.9 Smashed glass outside the Strauss shop window
© Linden Lab

in Second Life in that it potentially alienates the user, rather than figuring as a productive site of postmodern "becoming."[83] In 2016, if the unsettled user tried to break out of the limits of the exhibition in the form of buildings that are not "phantoms" (as are the desks and chairs), the avatar's teeth and eyes were revealed as belonging to an alien "other" akin to the disintegrating robot in *Terminator* (1984).

Such liminality is central to Freud's conception of the uncanny: in his eponymous essay, he explores, for example, the threshold between verisimilitude and fiction in E. T. A. Hoffman's "The Sand Man."[84] As a condensation of various aspects of Kristallnacht, the digital exhibition does not quash the signified referent, yet it still discombobulates in its attempt to code "beyond" history. The Second Life project is not VR in a technical sense, but it does create a space for virtual memory, in which memories of the event blend into a new digital realm that—unlike the installations mapped onto the landscape at Bergen-Belsen—has no equivalent in the analog world. In this context, we disagree with Phylis Johnson's assertion in *Second Life, Media and the Other Society* (2010) that "Second Life is real life, with a better graphics card."[85] As Landsberg puts it in *Engaging the Past*, in the digital exhibition the viewer is "having a real experience in the virtual arena, but it is not an experience of Kristallnacht."[86] Landsberg comments shrewdly on liminality in relation to the disembodied testimonies: there is "friction between the stylised graphics and the realness and authenticity of the survivors' accented voices."[87] Moreover, the combination of "the actual voices and the artificial, highly stylized graphics creates a kind of dissonance—it suggests that the real experience is out of reach, but that a trace . . . remains," which she reads as an important act of "imaginative translation."[88] The term "virtual reality" itself similarly indicates such paradoxical liminality, a state of digital progress that is neither purely one aspect of the term or the other. As with the *un/heimlich*, the two words wrestle in a dialectic of the familiar and the strange.

A state of anxious solitude is equally as important to the uncanny effect as this liminality. Second Life may have been devised as a social medium, but the Kristallnacht exhibition is disconcertingly depopulated, as if we are witnessing the virtual perfection of the perpetrator ideal that we discussed in relation to the Bergen-Belsen installations. Johnson's comment that Second Life is "generally [an] attempt to reinvent real life or *perfect* it" can only be read as darkly ironic in this context.[89] In this instance, the visitor confronts a scenario akin to a postapocalyptic landscape in which the avatar can fly above the empty streets toward a burning synagogue that periodically erupts into flame (see Fig. 4.8).[90] Hence the avatar shuttles between taking on the roles of secondary witness, bystander, and perpetrator: exploring the synagogue leads to the testimony of contemporaneous witnesses, yet this movement also triggers the flying glass and synagogue's flames. Similarly, when the avatar passes a shop named "Strauss Markt," the window shatters, as if the user is, or could have been, directly responsible for such vandalism. In this sense, the avatar's discovery of history is bound up with the reenactment of perpetration: indeed, the title of the exhibition encompasses a perpetrator perspective, since *Kristallnacht*, "night of the broken glass" was chosen "deliberately to mock and belittle."[91] As the user contemplates the shattered shop windows, we are clearly experiencing something markedly different to Dimensions in Testimony, in which the emphasis is on the visitor's empathetic response to the carefully edited testimony. In this uncanny space in Second Life, the user confronts the disturbing possibility that they might have been complicit in the violence that led to the content of the interactive testimonies.

Even in the newsroom, before the avatar has had a chance to encounter the *unheimlich* landscape, the viewer is forced to confront and potentially identify with an uncomfortable bystander perspective. When the visitor comes across a wall-sized photograph of "the broken shop window of a Jewish-owned business that was destroyed during Kristallnacht" (see Fig. 4.10), the avatar, aligned with the passing Germans, views the image from a complicit

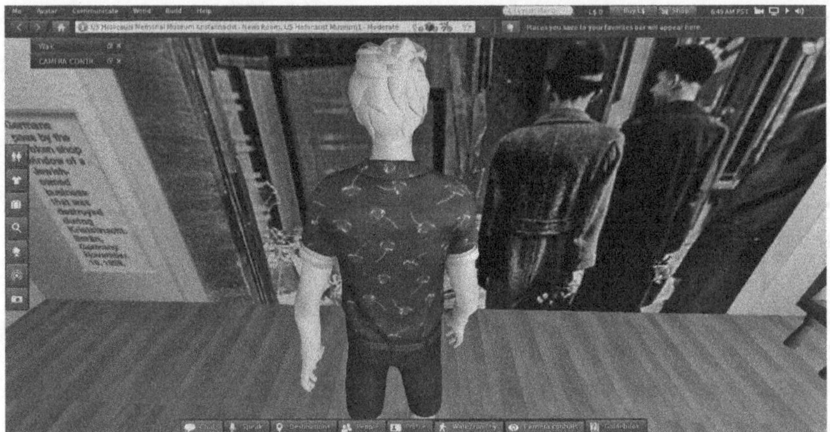

Figure 4.10 The Kristallnacht photograph
© Linden Lab

perspective. The removal of the frame as a doorway to the digital reenactment of Kristallnacht then implicitly refuses to allow us to merely "pass by." However, it is not entirely clear what we are looking at when the avatar views the photograph. Given that the shattered window is the focal point, the image prompts us to question how the camera is implicated in this aftermath of violence. We are not party to any information about who took the photograph, which leaves open the possibility that it was taken by a perpetrator who is celebrating rather than lamenting the broken window. Does this mean that a perpetrator perspective merges uncomfortably with that of the journalist in the opening rooms of the Kristallnacht exhibition? Should we resist the viewpoint of the photograph entirely, and, as in Dimensions in Testimony, attempt to identify only with survivors of violence through the testimonial extracts? After all, in *The Generation of Postmemory*, Marianne Hirsch argues that the camera itself, "however obliquely," connotes a weapon, so that "the postmemorial act of looking performs [an] unwanted and discomforting mutual implication" in the Kristallnacht photographs.[92] Yet the figures on the right-hand side of the frame in this wall-size photograph might not have been complicit in the sense of ignoring the event; this is only an assumption that the particular framing of the "passers-by" encourages. They may have been outraged, and perhaps even Jewish themselves, rather than hurrying by as complicit citizens. The user's discombobulation is compounded in this context, as they do not know at any given moment in the exhibition whether they are meant to be experiencing the digital collage as a figured bystander, perpetrator, or victim.

The plethora of survivor testimony throughout the site may convince the "noobie" that they are meant to identify specifically with the victims of Kristallnacht, and yet the return of the repressed as "our culture's disowned past that haunts us" takes the form of a disquieting recreation of perpetration and bystanders in the exhibition, as well as an engagement with forgotten history.[93] As opposed to the "familiar and comfortable" discourse of narrative history in Dimensions in Testimony, which is only punctured at certain moments—as when Pinchas Gutter begins to discuss his regrets—the Kristallnacht exhibition disconcerts the viewer with "what is concealed and hidden" in the guise of an event that is covertly deployed as synonymous with all incidents of antisemitic violence.[94] Persisting as a lonely outpost of Second Life's digital worlds, the exhibition with its absence of fellow avatars is symbolic of the cultural suppression of violent histories such as Kristallnacht. Avatar posts on the "Memory and Reporting Wall" at the end of the exhibition embody this inability to "understand" or "identify" with such atrocious events even when visitors are confronted with their digital reenactment. Landsberg begins her chapter "Virtual History Exhibits" in *Engaging the Past* with one of the few posts that focuses on contemplation: "Curiosity brought me. I entered skeptical, thinking this exhibit couldn't add much to what I had already learned about these horrible times. But after my visit, I had to log off and sit quietly. I came back to leave this message."[95] In contrast, another visitor posts that "it wasn't the Jews that scared America, it was the Martains [*sic*]. Some fool named Orson Welles put on a broadcast about a Martian invasion, and this sent panicked Yanks into the streets": this "extermination" of memory aligns Nazis with Americans and fails even to mention Kristallnacht. Confusingly, another user reads Kristallnacht as a purely heroic narrative, and eulogizes: "To those brave to keep their fave [*sic*] and culture, you truly are an inspiration." This visitor then adds a post that avoids reference to Nazi ideology in favor of an analysis of the general mood of international politics in 1938, and All Saints' Eve: "Perhaps the fact that it was Halloween was not obvious to some people because of the international tensions going on. But people were frightened easily at the time. No doubt that fear erupted during the Kristallnacht pogroms as well." (In fact, the events took place on November 9 and 10, not October 31.) In terms of these visitor responses at least, Baudrillard's concern that the digitization of memory might end up "radiating forgetfulness" would seem to be prescient.[96] If Levi, Snaider, and Landsberg's utopian vision is of memoryscapes producing "ordinary" viewers committed to defending human rights and initiating social change, then we still need to emphasize that these inspiring politics can still be drawn from instances of historical "forgetting."

All these posts above work against the journalistic narrative based on historical facts that the site designers hoped the visitor would be able to compile. In a comparable way to the iPad user at Bergen-Belsen bookmarking files for future reference, the viewer is encouraged to construct historical knowledge through a nonlinear encounter with the three-dimensional world. When we first enter the newsroom that looks like a contemporaneous crime desk (see Fig. 4.11), the curator invites us to "take the role of a journalist, recalling the testimony of eyewitnesses as you investigate what happened during the November 1938 pogroms"; an information tag also invites us to "reconstruct the events of Kristallnacht" through testimonial accounts. Following Landsberg's account of prosthetic memory, the designers wished that the tour might transfer "memory from the body of [the witnesses] to a person," the digital tourist, who "has no 'authentic' link to this particular historical past."[97] Yet the *unheimlich* experience of wandering through the homes of Jewish families and hiding places, momentarily catching snippets of testimony that are sometimes difficult to hear, undercuts the "idyllic clarity of narrative" that might ensue from the desired journalistic account.[98] Moreover, after leaving the virtual recreation of the event, the avatar is never required to produce their journalistic narrative.[99] As in the other examples of

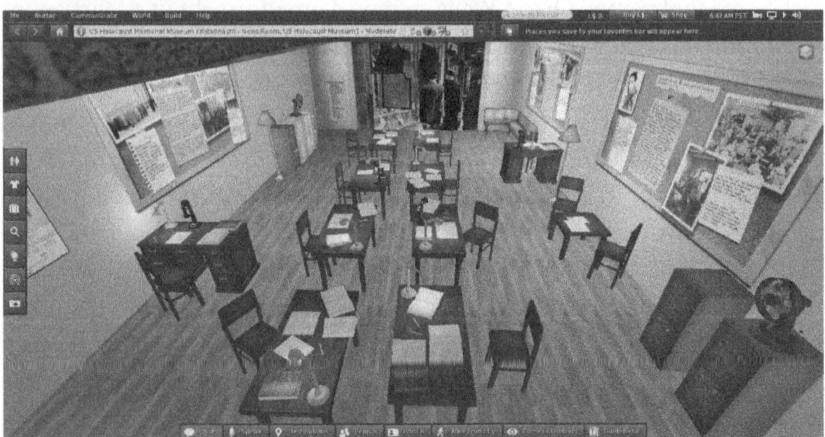

Figure 4.11 The crime desk
© Linden Lab

virtual Holocaust memory we have analyzed throughout this book, the user has implicitly to appreciate their responsibility for, and implication in, a digital encounter that relies on them for the coproduction of historical meaning. Despite the success of the exhibition in inducing an *unheimlich* experience, through the graphics and its refusal to let the user settle into a pattern of identification, the posts above suggest that this process of collaborative meaning can sometimes fall back into the user's untroubled idioculture.

After returning from the reenactment of Kristallnacht through the journalists' newsroom, visitors can then proceed to a memorial space akin to the Hall of Remembrance in the United States Holocaust Memorial Museum: as Landsberg notes, the former is "evocative of the brick and mortar museum" rather than identical to it.[100] The latter contains an eternal flame as well as buried soil from Holocaust sites and US military cemeteries: the architect James Freed hoped that the room would allow visitors to linger and meditate before "returning, albeit in altered condition, to the Mall."[101] In the digital exhibition, the United States Holocaust Memorial Museum's quotations from Deuteronomy and Genesis are eschewed in favor of the deceptively simple, "You are my witnesses" (Isaiah 43:10). Moving toward the exit, visitors are then encouraged to reflect on extracts from Pastor Martin Niemoller's "First they came for the Socialists," and Elie Wiesel's Nobel Peace Prize acceptance speech in 1986.[102] Proceeding through the exit, a sign then encourages the visitor to accept a free T-shirt and "Remember What You Saw"; the avatar can then contemplate the ocean expanses in a messianic pose at the edges of the Kristallnacht exhibition (see Fig. 4.12).[103] No one could doubt that the designers have genuinely attempted to make the user reflect on their experience of the digital reenactment of Kristallnacht and engage in the coproduction of historical meaning. However, given the posts listed above, viewers' meditations and remembrances may not bear much relation to the digital collage; the "idyllic clarity" of a journalistic narrative appears unlikely. In the next chapter, we note that users spend, on average, seven minutes in the Secret Annex Online, which—as Tom Brink claims— is an "eternity" for internet applications: in contrast, it would take at least forty-five minutes for visitors to the Kristallnacht exhibition to peruse the various rooms and listen to the testimony, in order to create the desired news report.[104] The exhibition often does not attribute these testimonial extracts clearly to a distinct speaker (as in "Hiding Places"), so even attentive visitors to the digital Hall of Remembrance would be more likely to reflect instead on the *unheimlich* experience of fragmented narratives, and the unnerving

Figure 4.12 The edges of Kristallnacht
© Linden Lab

experience of flying around the repeatedly burning synagogue, rather than produce a "familiar and comfortable" narrative of history.[105]

This elusive journalistic account is intended to arise out of a process of connectivity and identification as at the Bergen-Belsen installations, in which visitors are meant to "understand the importance of [Kristallnacht], to identify with its victims and to assign meaning to their experience."[106] In contrast with the aporias of the iPad application, there is no sense in the digital Hall of Remembrance that, as Landsberg puts it, "the past is foreign and cannot be definitively or conclusively grasped or understood," as in the sometimes bemusing experiences in the Kristallnacht exhibition.[107] A supposedly "objective" response to historical trauma might risk a numbed incapacity to "work through" the event, positing an easy closure in the form of a journalistic narrative. This desire for the news story actually grates against the *unheimlich* experience within the Kristallnacht exhibition, as the trapped avatar encounters the smashed glass, abandoned Torah scroll, and burning synagogue. In other words, the possibility of connectivity leading to empathic unsettlement in the uncanny landscape is undercut by the newsroom's desire for the "idyllic clarity" of narrative.[108] A text box that appears when the avatar enters the virtual German town expects the visitor to "touch everything," including the desecrated and discarded Torah in the synagogue. This idiopathic process of identification, which seeks (contra Delbo) to interiorize the experience of others, and then "coldly" reproduce them in an assimilation of testimony, is then subverted by the digital landscape, and the avatar's blurring of the line between victims and perpetrators.[109] In the same way as the other examples of virtual Holocaust memory we have outlined throughout this book, the exhibition does not self-consciously register the difficulties of understanding and "assigning meaning." Nor does it comply with Kaja Silverman's sense of heteropathic identification, in which "a recognition of the irreconcilable distance between the experience of self and other is maintained, even as forms of imaginative investment seek connection."[110] Nevertheless, the *form* of the Kristallnacht exhibition implicitly suggests this reflexivity, as the user senses an "irreconcilable distance" between the *unheimlich* landscape and ostensible requirement for a pithy news story.

Ending with a plea to defend others' rights and "always take sides," the exhibition adheres to the "committed" politics of Levy, Sznaider, and Landsberg, which we discussed at the beginning of this chapter. Kristallnacht becomes a sign for wider histories of oppression that visitors must henceforth attempt to curtail. However, as some of the avatar posts indicate, the possibility remains that viewers' failures to engage in heteropathic identification will only reinforce their own concerns and misreadings of history, rather than endowing them as "civic pilgrims, to be transformed by the lessons that emerge from imaginative narrative engagement."[111] Yet these caveats arise from users' lack of attention to the formal aspects of the digital technology, rather than inherent faults in the applications. As Phyllis Johnson argues in relation to Second Life more generally, the platform has the ability to "draw attention to the physical and social elements of culture that we often ignore in real life; the intensity of concentrated immersion into this virtual world allows for a greater introspection behind who we are and who we would like to be in real and second life."[112] The uncanny landscape in the Kristallnacht exhibition indicates the potential of virtual Holocaust memory to complicate issues of identification, connectivity, and the journalistic narration of atrocity.[113] Through the iPad application, the visitor is able to appreciate the disjuncture between the augmented reality and the present campsite, inclement weather or not, in which they are not just finding out about the camp's history, but potentially appreciating that there are past events that cannot simply be "learned," or—in Delbo's caveat about truthfulness—simply "understood." Instead, the iPad application stresses the requirement to approach the camp's history from a variety of perspectives through the juxtaposition of palimpsestic testimony, photographs, and sound files with the current landscape.[114] Inevitably, there are dangers in these digital forms of secondary witnessing: as we pointed out in relation to the Bergen-Belsen installations, a "sanitized" graphic space devoid of humans presents an uncomfortable perpetrator vision of a camp emptied of all inmates. Nevertheless, such exhibitions and applications will continue to marry digital memoryscapes with visitors' experiences of the actual sites in increasingly more complex ways. Emphasizing their "mediated status" and "artificiality," digital technologies will engage in the future with their own form in more self-resisting ways that recall the tensions of awkward poetics.[115]

5

The Virtual Anne Frank

> Doing things with Anne Frank is okay. Anne Frank is not ours. She
> belongs to everyone.[1]
>
> —Tom Brink

Given the inextricable link between technological developments and popular culture, it should come as no surprise that Annelies Frank's best-selling
diary has been converted into a number of digital applications and VR tours.
In our interview in 2016 with the head of publications and presentations
at the Anne Frank House, Tom Brink emphasized that the institution
"cannot control" technological versions of the famous diarist, unless they
include Holocaust denial.[2] In the same year, Danny Abrahms was working
with CGO Studios on a VR film in which the viewer can mingle with the
annex's inhabitants: when we interviewed him in Los Angeles, he stressed
that independent technology companies are "the ones starting this new line
of Holocaust memory," and that the latter would quickly "balloon."[3] This
"new line" has so far been distinctly reverent: the 3D Secret Annex Online
and Abrahms's VR film are pedagogical in thrust; Abrahms, for example,
eulogized the possibilities for virtual reality in the History classroom. In this
sense, the film and Secret Annex Online adhere to the pedagogical turn in
the fifth and final era of Holocaust witnessing that we discussed in relation to
the Dimensions in Testimony project. However, such technological advances
in relation to Anne Frank's diary will not be without their critics. Ensuing
disapproval will be bound up with former detractors from her iconicity as
"the most well-known victim of the Shoah," as well as the "childization" of
the Holocaust that we explored in relation to Dimensions in Testimony.[4]
Abrahms's and the Anne Frank House's investment in VR films will have
to negotiate Hannah Arendt's criticism that—following the success of the
Broadway play and Hollywood film—the admiration for Anne Frank has become a "cheap sentimentality at the expense of great catastrophe."[5]

Virtual Holocaust Memory. Matthew Boswell and Antony Rowland, Oxford University Press. © Oxford University Press
2023. DOI: 10.1093/oso/9780197645390.003.0006

These complaints will include the fact that her testimony is singled out as palatable because it predates the unrecorded details of her final experiences: as we noted in Chapter 2, Eva Schloss could not forget that her posthumous stepsister wrote the more redemptive passages in her diary "before she experienced Auschwitz and Belsen."[6] In addition, the development of digital representations of her story will not be able to circumvent the national contexts of Holocaust memory that we have explored throughout this book. Any focus on the diary occludes other testimonies in the Netherlands, such as Marga Minco's *Bitter Herbs* (1957). Its predominance also obscures the sixteen thousand Jewish inhabitants who hid and survived during the war, and the memory of Hannie Schaft, one of The Netherlands' most heroic resistance fighters. Potentially the most damning riposte to these technological developments will be that the memory of Anne Frank has always been vouchsafed with substantial financial backing. As we discussed in Chapter 1, the first twelve recordings of the Dimensions in Testimony project cost six million dollars. The critic does not have to endorse the work of Norman Finkelstein in its entirety to note that the Anne Frank Foundation has benefited from, for example, Otto Frank's lawyer posting "scores of letters to wealthy Americans who might be interested in making donations."[7] The digital and virtual memory of the Holocaust, it might be adduced, follows the money. Yet Primo Levi rebutted such criticisms surrounding Anne Frank's iconicity when he argued that the focus on and investment in one individual was perhaps inevitable, given the impossibility of anyone coming to terms with thousands of Holocaust testimonies.[8] Moreover, as we noted in relation to Dimensions in Testimony, these applications may be well funded, but they are not intended to make a profit. Indeed, given the pace of new developments in digital technology, it may well be that Dimensions in Testimony and the VR films about Anne Frank will be regarded in the future as costly failures, despite their cultural importance to the fifth era of Holocaust witnessing.

As we have argued throughout this book, these "new lines" of Holocaust memory tend to obscure the self-reflection of awkward poetics. In the introduction, we discussed the gulf between vexed aesthetics and the comment by Chris Milk, one of the VR sector's leading entrepreneurs, that virtual reality is the "ultimate empathy machine."[9] What, therefore, are the dangers of overidentification in relation to VR representations of Anne Frank's diary? If, as we emphasized at the beginning of this book, the experiences of the survivors should not be manipulated to service the identity politics of the present, then surely this admonition should be intensified in relation to the testimony of those such as Anne Frank who did not survive the Holocaust. In 2004, Robert Eaglestone argued that the genre of testimony innately resists identification, yet as we have outlined in the previous chapters, the emphasis in new technological versions of Holocaust memory today is, in contrast, on empathy, understanding, and the enriching rather than testimonial dissonance.[10] The digital "turn" in Holocaust studies has resulted in a focus on connectivity rather than the aporias of trauma, and the examples of digital technology in this chapter are no exception. Nevertheless, as with Dimensions in Testimony, we do not consider the technologies surrounding the memory of Anne Frank to be "cold," fulfilling Jean Baudrillard's warnings in the 1980s about a simulated nostalgia that endlessly accumulates.[11] We shall not argue, for example, that The Secret Annex Online is a simulacrum that conflates different time periods and narratives into a *potpourri* of digital entrancement. Central to our defense of digital memory in this chapter is the phenomenon we term "palimpsestic" testimony, in which digitized documents, photographs, and newsreel can be integrated into applications. This example of connectivity presents the metatexts that have always been so important to testimonial accounts *alongside* the original testimony. This "layered" digital space forms one of the most productive new approaches to testimonial narratives over the last fifteen years. Nonetheless, we are also attentive in this chapter to the moments in the digital applications when the historical and fictional become intertwined. As we have pointed out throughout this book, Charlotte Delbo's concept of "truthfulness" allows for a nuanced discussion of such phenomena. We argue that the applications do not attempt to deceive, but encourage the user to engage imaginatively with the secret annex as it *might* have been.

The Secret Annex Online: A "Realistic Hallucination"?

Launched on April 28, 2010 to mark the fiftieth anniversary of the inauguration of the Anne Frank House, the Secret Annex Online allows users to navigate through an interactive 3D version of the annex.[12] This digital project has been an overwhelming success in terms of user numbers, attracting over two million visitors who spend, on average, seven minutes at the site. As Brink commented in 2016, this time-span is "an eternity in [terms of] internet applications." In the context of the VR films discussed later in this chapter, this digital technology felt a little outdated in the year we first discussed the application with Brink, particularly since Flash Player was no longer supported much at that point; in addition, if accessed via an iPad, the Secret Annex Online required the specific Puffin Web Browser. Yet the "eternity" visitors spent and are still spending in the 3D application indicates the attractions of the formal aspects of digitization: through mouse rotation and clicks or a trackpad, viewers can wander through a re-creation of the annex as it might have looked when the inhabitants were in hiding between 1942 and 1944. As with the iPad application at Belsen, users experience a "non-linear" approach to history: the 3D floor plan allows the visitor to "teleport" easily between different rooms in the main building and annex. Alison Landsberg's focus on the importance of affect to prosthetic memories is pertinent to the application, as the Secret Annex Online functions primarily as a pedagogical tool to inform and inspire those who cannot visit the Anne Frank House in Amsterdam for financial or physical reasons.[13] The site's deployment of "hotspots" and "stories" to entice the user to listen in more depth to diary extracts and metatextual details certainly has the potential to fulfill Landsberg's vision of contemporary modes of historical representation that can "change the way ordinary people understand history and acquire historical knowledge in our distracted age."[14]

Although these digital spaces are distinct from the *unheimlich* representations we have discussed in relation to the "ghostware" of Dimensions in Testimony and the Kristallnacht exhibition in Second Life, the Secret Annex Online still has the potential to unsettle with its overwhelming sense of entrapment.[15] Moving through the digitized space behind the famous bookcase, the user encounters cramped corridors and looming staircases. The feeling of confinement is partly at the expense of cognitive mapping: the 2D map of the annex in a book entitled *Anne Frank House: A Museum with a Story* (2011)—as well as the 1961 scale models in the Anne Frank House itself—still give the viewer a clearer overview than the application of the complex intersecting passages, steep staircases and interlocking doors.[16] However, this confusion is partly the point: Landsberg's "historical knowledge" consists here not only of an accretion of the diary's testimonial information in the warren of rooms, but also in the combination of testimony and affect. The application allows the user to accrue knowledge while sensing the claustrophobia of the secret annex, as in the VR film that we discuss later in this chapter. As with Dimensions in Testimony, the application has the capacity to jolt and disturb through its functional dysfunction, as the new user whirls around the ceilings of annex rooms, unable to pinpoint the hotspots, encountering buffering in certain rooms, and an occasional application crash. As Landsberg writes, such phenomena remind the visitor "that you are not really there, [and] that you are engaging with a representation."[17] Indeed, these "teething" problems for the user actually add to the overall sense of constriction.

Overall, the application attempts through digital affect to make the user identify with the families' plight, following the normative emphasis on connectivity in virtual Holocaust memory that we have explored in the first four chapters. External judging panels were clearly impressed with the site's interweaving of diegetic sound and digitized visuals to create a sense of confinement: the Secret Annex Online has received numerous awards, including the History Online Prize in 2010, and the International Design and Communication Award ("Best App" category)—alongside the Red Dot Award for Communication Design—in 2012. In *Engaging the Past* (2015), Landsberg argues that such digital museums forefront the "power of the virtual" in their ability "to reconstruct spaces that literally do not exist anymore or do not exist as they once did and to translate those temporally lost experiences into the present."[18] Yet if we follow the theories of postmodernism that we discussed in Chapter 1, in which digital culture is often characterized as characterless, depthless, and meaningless, the digital images of rooms in the Secret Annex Online could be critiqued as simulacra, as they present only an illusion of the contemporaneous. The Anne Frank House website claims that the Secret Annex Online was created "using photos of the actual furnished Secret Annex, *as it was then*," but the color photographs were actually taken in 1999, when the annex was temporarily furnished to "illustrate in educational materials how the spaces were used at the time."[19] Allard Bovenberg's color photographs—many of which are reproduced in *Anne Frank House: A Museum with a Story*, and in postcards available in the museum shop—are, in turn, based on Maria Austria's striking black and white photographs taken in 1954. Otto Frank famously insisted that the annex remain unfurnished after the war in order to convey a sense of traumatic absence that is missing from the photographs produced in 1999. Austria's pictures were taken during a fifteen-year hiatus between Otto's return from Auschwitz and the opening of the museum in 1960: the international Berghaus company bought the annex in 1953, and threatened to demolish it to make way for new business premises; this threat was only lifted in 1956.[20] Barbara Mooyart-Doubleday commented on the "shabby" annex in 1951, with its "torn paper on the walls": Austria captures this decaying structure in her photographs three years later, in which, for example, the net curtains in Anne Frank and Fritz Pfeffer's bedroom are soiled with leaking water.

However, Bovenberg's color photographs from 1999 powerfully convey a sense of how the annex *might* have "been then"; for example, with the neatly stacked kitchen utensils in the digitized Room Van Pels Family.[21] The "truthfulness" of the color photographs attempts to engage the user with the history of the annex before the families' arrest and deportation: it is difficult not to think about the resultant deaths when looking at Mooyart-Doubleday's images of absence and decaying rooms. Nevertheless, users potentially encounter Baudrillard's "hallucination" in that "when an object is exactly like another, *it is not exactly like it, it is a bit more exact.*"[22] Color photographs might appear akin to the wartime annex, but some critics will still argue that the still-life constructions create their own hyperreality in their artfully arranged objects. Subtle differences between the Bovenberg and Austria photographs reveal that the former do not depict the house and annex "as it was then," but rearrange items in order to make them "more exact." For example, the reconstruction in 1999 based on Austria's picture of the warehouse has arguably been "sanitized" in a similar way to the Belsen installations (see Fig. 5.1). In the Warehouse front in the Secret Annex Online, an even, cobbled surface replaces the pitted concrete floor, and the overhead wiring is missing. Some details have been altered—the bicycle (now without a lamp) has been moved to its position by the wall rather than behind a cart—and

Figure 5.1 The warehouse front
© Anne Frank House, Amsterdam

some features have been added: the originally empty cart now contains neatly packed boxes.

We would stress, however, that the "truthfulness" of the color photographs lies in their approximation, rather than adherence, to historical detail in order to draw the user into an empathetic encounter with the families' experiences in the annex. As we discussed in the Introduction in relation to Marina Amaral's *Faces of Auschwitz* project (2018–), color photographs appear to affect viewers more than "documentary" black-and-white images:

> I think it humanises [the inmates]. They are no longer just numbers or statistics, but are people like you and me. Colours make us feel more empathetic. They help us to connect with the subject in a deeper, meaningful way. . . . When we see the photos in colour, there's no longer an emotional barrier there. . . . These people are suddenly more relatable; more real, flesh and blood—literally.[23]

Amaral argues that history *appears* more tangible and proximate when the images involve color. A similarly empathetic response to colored historical images also occurred in 2018 in relation to Peter Jackson's acclaimed film *They Shall Not Grow Old*, with recolored footage of life in the trenches during World War One. Of course, this feeling of approximation is in some senses illusory, and is a product of normative responses to formal characteristics rather than historical "truth." Stephen Spielberg famously produced *Schindler's List* (1993) in black and white because he knew that viewers would react to the film as if it were, or approximated to, a documentary, despite fictional elements such as ghetto inmates crossing a Krakow bridge in the wrong direction. Nevertheless, even if affect is partly a product of form, its power should not be underestimated in this fifth era of Holocaust witnessing. Viewers may not be experiencing history "literally," as Amaral claims, yet the colored photographs convey an effective if illusory sense of proximity that black-and-white images can struggle to match.

Users thus encounter an *impression* of history through the color photographs in the Secret Annex Online, "truthful" versions of the past as it might have been that, according to Landsberg, "feel real," rather than exact representations of contemporaneous scenes.[24] Of course, it would be impossible to present history "as it was" in the annex, even in the dollhouse-like structures commissioned by Otto Frank, since the multiple details of life behind the bookcase are beyond exact representation. Taken in its entirety, the application forefronts this impossibility through a disjunctive simultaneity that is nevertheless formally necessary. A mixture of timescales is evident in that the Westerkerk bells are permanently stuck at seven o'clock or one o'clock, depending in which room the user hears them, despite the fact that the rooms contain extracts from the diary that were penned after the bells were taken away to be melted down for the war effort in summer 1943.[25] This conjunction may be historically inaccurate, but through the "truthfulness" of the application, this simultaneity is necessary in order to draw the user into an engagement with diverse and asynchronous aspects of the families' experiences in the annex. Unlike the statement quoted above from the Anne Frank House website about history "as it was then," the *form* of the Secret Annex Online actually foregrounds its "truthfulness": Bovenberg's digitized photographs are deliberately blurred, as if to register the fact that the depicted scenes can only ever approximate to the contemporaneous. In the Room Frank Family, for example, the books have indistinct spines to mask their potential inauthenticity (see Fig. 5.2).[26] As with the Belsen installations, the digital spaces do not concur with Baudrillard's sense of the extermination of history through such images: the viewer encounters a representation (the blurred photographs) based on a representation of the referent (Austria's original photographs).

Nevertheless, when the user enters the digital space outside the house and annex, we are closer to experiencing the simulacrum of Baudrillard's "realistic hallucination." Prinsengracht appears as an anomalous mixture of

Figure 5.2 Room Frank family
© Anne Frank House, Amsterdam

digitized buildings based on the contemporaneous—such as the Keg's tea and coffee sign (no. 265) adjacent to the Anne Frank House—and the contemporary: nine cars (too many for 1942) and a van flank the canal on the opposite bank, one of which looks suspiciously like a 2009 model Citroën (see Fig. 5.3).[27] Superimposed graphics of trees and contemporaneous lampposts line the waterway: these mildly disconcerting additions are matched with a soundtrack of children playing, a passing boat and chirping sparrows. Hilda Hein worries that such "simulation and simulacra" in museums and their digital applications present a "stimulus" that is "fraudulently contrived."[28] As we noted in the introduction, Baudrillard goes further, and argues that such simulacra divest reality of thought, imagination, morality, and critical distance.[29] However, even on the digital Prinsengracht we do not encounter an *unheimlich* "hallucination": whereas the avatar in Second Life is trapped in the threatening space of a virtual Kristallnacht, the diegetic (and diurnal) sound in the Secret Annex Online is comforting rather than discombobulating. Signified referents appertaining to 263 Prinsengracht "as it was" between 1942 and 1944 have not been lost completely—as in Baudrillard's dystopian vision of the referent—but they are certainly confused in this less "truthful" space of digital incongruity.

To contextualize these incongruous digital spaces, however, it must be noted that the manipulation of the contemporaneous does not appertain solely to the Secret Annex Online. "Truthful" expositions and downright fictionalizations of the diary have arisen ever since its publication in 1947. As with Delbo's *Auschwitz and After* (1985), the diary itself contains Anne's

Figure 5.3 The view from 263 Prinsengracht
© Anne Frank House, Amsterdam

embellishments of her own experiences in order to focalize their "truth": she self-consciously attempted to edit her testimony into a more novelistic form in what is now referred to as edition "B" of the text.[30] Similarly, Delbo sometimes deals with the "exactingness and uncertainty" of autobiography by inserting fictional episodes such as when the women inmates wash in a stream in order to convey an intense sense of what happened in Birkenau, even when her memory fails her.[31] As Daniel Schwarz argues, the diary forms an example of provisional testimony in that entries "become tentative formulations, discursive hypotheses, which are modified, undermined, and reformulated."[32] Moreover, pure fiction is sometimes an integral aspect of testimony, as when Primo Levi invents an episode in *The Truce* (1963) in which he meets a German woman in Katowice who wrote a letter to Hitler denouncing his policies. Levi aspires to create a narrative that suits the novelistic structure, and adds a fictional element that allows him to present German civilians as not all bystanders and supplicants.[33] However, the 1955 play and 1959 film version of Anne Frank's diary are particularly culpable in inventing egregious fictional episodes.[34] In relation to the Hollywood film, for example, Louis de Jong notes that "I, as a historian have discovered here and there some slight touches and details which did not correspond with reality."[35] De Jong adds that "sometimes certain dramatic effects are necessary in a work of art, even if they did not occur in reality": these include the lengthy celebration of Hanukkah, so as to end part one of the play (and, effectively, the first part of the film) on an uplifting note, whereas Anne records in her diary entry for December 7, 1942 that "we didn't make much of a fuss with Hannukkah, mainly exchanging a few small gifts and lighting the candles."[36] These fictionalities court danger in terms of their reception: Carol Ann Lee recounts an episode in which an American Jewish woman watching the play in New York "expressed amazement that the characters and events in the play were real."[37] Yet there is no guarantee that a more faithful adaptation of the diary would have elicited a different response. Otto Frank himself was always sanguine about these fictions, to the extent that he allowed the transformation of Fritz Pfeffer in the play and film into a bumbling character who knows little about his Jewish heritage, much to the chagrin of his actual relatives (the actor who played the dentist, Ed Wynn, would later appear in 1964 as the eccentric, flying Uncle Albert in *Mary Poppins*). Such fictional versions of the annex even occur in the critic Bruno Bettelheim's account of the Anne Frank legend, when he castigates Otto for not carrying a gun or butcher's knife, and imagines an alternative (and Tarantinoesque) version of history in which Otto takes out a few members of the Green Police before being arrested.[38] Thus the Secret Annex Online can hardly be criticized as the only post-war version of the diary not to adhere to the reality of the situation "as it was then." Moreover, unlike the blatant fictionalizations of the play and film, the blurred photographs try to convey the "truthfulness" of the families' experience alongside concerns surrounding fictional referents within the form of the digital space itself.

Palimpsestic Memory and Accessibility

The Secret Annex Online is committed to ensure that the diary and the topography of the annex are as accessible as possible to a new generation of online visitors, as the equivalent of previous audiences who flocked to the cinema or theater to watch reenactments of Anne's testimony. As we demonstrated in the last chapter in relation to the 3D installations at Bergen-Belsen, accessibility risks being coterminous with simplification, yet the "palimpsest" of digital elements in some of the application's rooms does suggest a more complex approach to prosthetic memory. The "Bombs fall on Amsterdam" story in the Room Frank family aims at what Otto Dov Kulka terms the "intensity" of history, with its amalgamation of diary extracts (read by Ellie Kendrick) and diegetic sounds of air raids, alongside extracts from two diary entries that unfold on-screen (see Fig. 5.4). Tamsin Grieg's narrative voiceover provides the

Figure 5.4 Bombs fall on Amsterdam
© Anne Frank House, Amsterdam

relevant historical metatext, such as the fact that 175 people were killed in the first bombing Anne refers to in the diary extract, while personal photographs drift across the 3D landscape.[39] It may be sacrilege to argue that the "exclusive content" which Kendrick refers to in an information page on the Secret Annex Online improves upon the original diary, but there is certainly a "flatness" to the diary's description of the air raids that palimpsestic digital space enriches.[40] The flattening tendencies of historical accounts of the Holocaust have long been remarked, as in the work of Saul Friedländer, yet testimony contains this possibility too. Anne's description of anti-aircraft guns in her diary entry of March 10, 1943 that were "booming away until dawn" links with the undemonstrative aspects of witnessing that we discussed in relation to Dimensions of Testimony.[41] Derek Attridge's concept of the singularity of certain cultural artifacts does not appertain to the diary and the interview with Anne's posthumous stepsister: episodes from the diary and the more matter-of-fact extracts from Dimensions in Testimony cannot be read in different, fruitful ways by the same reader on varying occasions.[42] In contrast, Kulka's sense of testimonial "intensity" can be experienced in "Bombs fall on Amsterdam": the interaction of the various digital elements rewards several viewings, and Anne's simple description of the air raid is placed in the metatextual context of the attempted bombing of a Fokker aircraft factory (the bombs missed their targets and fell on a civilian area).[43] Metatexts have always been important to testimony, not in order to "understand" testimonial accounts through definitive historicist readings, but as one means to interpret the autobiographical literature; here, the contextual information enriches the digital constellations of visual, aural, and textual interplay. This digital intertwining is not the equivalent of Max Silverman's account of palimpsestic memory—akin to Michael Rothberg's multidirectional memory— that consists of a "dynamic and open space composed of interconnecting traces of different voices, sites and times"; indeed, transcultural memories are markedly absent from the Secret Annex Online.[44] Instead, the interaction of digital elements in "Bombs fall on Amsterdam" points to the potentialities of virtual Holocaust memory, in which testimonial accounts may proliferate in the public sphere, enriched through the palimpsestic forms of the digital.

Lasting three minutes and forty-one seconds, "Bombs fall on Amsterdam" is one of only five relatively long extracts—along with "A sleep-over in the Secret Annex," "A clandestine radio" (Room Van Pels Family), "The source of courage" (Private Office) and "Love in the secret annex" (Room Peter Van Pels)—out of forty-seven "stories" or "hotspots" in total. With its assemblage of contemporaneous photographs, a floating Bovenberg photograph of the Van Pels's room and Grieg's voiceover, "A sleep-over in the Secret Annex" attempts to cut through the potential "flatness" of the diary—and the application itself—by aligning the viewer with Miep and Jan Gies's sleepless overnight stay in the annex. "Only now," Grieg's voiceover announces, "does she [Miep] fully realise what it means to be in hiding." Even if the user cannot "fully realise" what the families experienced, they are at least jolted momentarily into empathic unsettlement, rather than jumping unreflectively from room to room in order to glean information about the inhabitants' internment.[45] Most of the other forty-seven "stories" and "hotspots" contain diverting but less complex digital interactions than "Bombs fall on Amsterdam" and "A sleep-over in the Secret Annex," such as "A group lunch" in the Room Van Pels Family, that recounts the various eating habits of the annex inhabitants and Bep Voskuijel. These shorter aspects of the application could be critiqued through Landsberg's account of accessibility as convenience, in which "the majority of Americans feel most in touch with the past when they believe they have some kind of immediate, direct access" to history (6), rather than testimonial "intensity." Jumping between the shorter testimonial snippets, the visitor is responding to what Todd Presner termed "associative" relations in a database, rather than "the syntagmatic, or combinatory elements that give rise to narrative."[46] As with the iPad application in Belsen, this is a user-driven rather than didactic experience of history: in short, the application's "stories" rely on the transmutation of the diary into a digital collage. Yet the "Bombs fall on Amsterdam," "A sleep-over in the Secret Annex," "A clandestine radio," "The source of courage" and "Love in the secret annex" hotspots nevertheless demonstrate the potential of palimpsestic testimony to draw the user into an encounter with witness literature alongside enriching and informative metatexts.

Necessarily, there are omissions in these hotspots and the Secret Annex Online as a whole: the latter's twenty-one digitized spaces could not possibly contain the three hundred and forty-one pages of "definitive" text in the edition of the diary edited by Otto Frank and Mirjam Pressler.[47] This compression points to the overall emphasis on empathy, connectivity, and identification in virtual Holocaust memory that we have analyzed in relation to Dimensions in Testimony. As we argued in the introduction, the "truthfulness" of this new form of Holocaust memory lies in the user's responsibility for the coproduction of historical meaning in the digital encounter. Indeed, visitors to the Anne Frank House are requested to "personally envision what happened on this very spot," and potentially find redemptive meaning by devising historical knowledge as a springboard for social activism, as Otto Frank always encouraged with his support for post-war meetings of students at the annex. At the same time, this production of "truthfulness" obviously risks the colonization of memory through overidentification in the name of connectivity and accessibility, or what Landsberg terms "overpresence."[48] In *Engaging the Past*, Landsberg argues that the websites in her chapter on "Virtual History Exhibits" resist this possibility by denying their visitors "a kind of seamless point of identification with individual historical figures or specific perspectives."[49] Digitally trapped in the Secret Annex Online like a latter-day Alice, the precariousness of skewed affect is exacerbated in that the viewer can witness nothing beyond the immediate digitized space: as Landsberg rightly contends, the user engages with a "strangely physical visual experience."[50] As we noted in the last chapter, such distorted prosthetic memories are a danger too for students traversing the Bergen-Belsen memorial armed with iPads: pure fiction rather than "truthfulness" may be the result of such well-intentioned attempts at identification. However, the problems of attempting to create an "affective community" of witnesses to the witness is hardly a problem specific to such digital topographies: the transformation of signs into signifieds while reading testimony has always contained the potential to occlude the referent.[51] The difference here is that the intermixing of digital and prosthetic memories do not yet confront the awkward poetics of testimony. At the start of *None of Us Will Return* (1965), for example, Charlotte Delbo's poem "Oh you who know" debunks the concept of a "deeply felt memory" that can be "acquired by anyone" with its claim that nonsurvivors cannot understand what it means to be starving, or confront your mother's corpse.[52] The prose poem ends with the simple statement that "horror cannot be circumscribed": Delbo's attack on civilians' complacent overwriting of survivors' traumatic memories undercuts Landsberg's assertion that "memories have ceased to belong exclusively to a particular group and instead have become part of a common public domain."[53] Indeed, Landsberg's vision of social memory is reminiscent of Dave Eggers's satirical take on internet companies in his novel *The Circle* (2013), in which individuals are lambasted for daring to hoard any experiences, rather than sharing them immediately with the "common public domain" through blogs and constantly updated posts.[54]

However, the risks of "truthfulness" are preferable to an ignorance of history. Nevertheless, the application—alongside the Anne Frank House and diary itself—could be accused of responding to what Theodor Adorno in "Commitment" terms a "limiting situation," in which "humanity flourishes."[55] "Sometimes," Adorno writes, "this develops into a dismal metaphysic which does its best to work up atrocities into "limiting situations" which it then accepts to the extent that they reveal authenticity."[56] As Victoria Stewart records, such emphasis on positivity allows for the "authenticity" of the diary to be read "in a purely humanistic light as an account of the endurance of the human spirit in a young girl *in extremis*," rather than the fragmented, aporetic "sense of radical uncertainty" or "chronicle of trepidation, turmoil, alarm" that Stewart and Cynthia Ozick encounter in Anne's testimony.[57] Of course, the critiqued humanist responses to the diary partly arise out of the "limiting situation" of Anne's most famous aphorism, that the Broadway play manipulated into a finale, and that many people believe to be the last line of the diary: "I still believe, in spite of everything, that people are truly good at heart."[58] Adorno's more dialectical (and morose) comment that "Even the blossoming tree lies" in the post-Holocaust world "the moment its bloom is seen without the shadow of terror" has more in common with the subsequent sentence in Anne's diary entry for July 15, 1942, which could have been requisitioned to comment on the ruins of the post-war period: "It's utterly impossible for me to build my life on a foundation of chaos, suffering and death."[59] The final diary entry (August 1, 1944) actually ends with the anti-redemptive moment of Anne struggling to assert her identity, and wondering "what I could be if . . . if only there were no other people in the world."[60] Despite such instances of "radical uncertainty," many readers have insisted on "the endurance of the human spirit" in the diary: the original publisher of the translated diary in the UK, Vallentine Mitchell, even suggested titling it "Beauty Out of the Night" or "Blossom in the Night" in 1951.[61] Lawrence Langer laments such "inflations" of Anne Frank into "a figure of mythic proportions" which rely on a story that "cannot be told in terms of heroic dignity, moral courage, and the triumph of the human spirit in adversity."[62]

In this context, the "truthfulness" of the Secret Annex Online lies in its openness to redemptive *and* anti-redemptive instances within, and readings of, the testimony. Through its immersive form, this application does not simply peddle what we discussed in Chapter 2 as "Schindlerized" messages.[63] Indeed, the sense of being trapped in the application's digital space certainly conveys the "limiting situation" of the families' internment in the annex— even if users can, of course, never re-experience it—rather than purely redemptory schemas. Moreover, the dark, disheveled and bare features of the bathroom are particularly effective in communicating a sense of claustrophobia within the "limiting situation." Yet in the "Strawberries, strawberries, strawberries . . ." hotspot in the Office Kitchen the user also experiences the joy of a redemptive moment that Adorno's theory would circumscribe in retrospect, as the families join together to gorge on a sudden abundance of seasonal fruit. The hotspot recounts extracts from the jubilant diary entry for July 8, 1944, when twenty-four crates of strawberries resulted in a frenzy of jam-making in the offices and annex: the voiceover comments that "It's almost as if they've forgotten they're in hiding." As we discussed in relation to Dimensions in Testimony, the user can sense here an intense responsibility for the coming-into-being of testimony as co-creators of an affective and effecting archive. For a moment, the metatextual details of the war fade into the background: in its *heimlich* domesticity, the testimony opens out but also simultaneously denies an alternative counterfactual narrative in which the families survive to enjoy such normative and fleetingly joyous moments of family life. In contrast, "Love in the Secret Annex"—the only "Story" in Room Peter Van Pels—could be regarded as culpable in its humanist focus on the "limiting situation" of Anne's romance with Peter (a major focus of the Hollywood film). Lasting four minutes and forty seconds, this "Story" is the second longest in the application, after "A clandestine radio" in the Room Van Pels Family (05:56): it takes place in the user experience of a haven, the "heart" of the application which seems topographically protected from the rest of the annex, and the intervention of any intruding metatext. Yet the application's switch between the redemptive and anti-redemptive continues even in relation to this romantic hotspot. Grieg's voiceover after Anne's diary entry resists any reliance on the "endurance of the human spirit" through a romance narrative when it notes and ends on the fact that the relationship did not endure. Thus the narrative arc of this "Story" mirrors that of "Strawberries, strawberries, strawberries . . .": the "Story" ends with bathos that works against the "limiting situation," as Anne consumes the glut of strawberries "with a bit of sand."

Moreover, the Anne Frank House and Secret Annex Online do not encourage the visitor to leave with a sense of the *heimlich* and nostalgic readings of the limiting situations recounted in "Love in the Secret Annex" and "Strawberries, strawberries, strawberries . . ."; indeed, these narratives function in this context as allegories of the limits of the diary itself. In the museum, visitors must traverse the exhibition room recounting the fate of the eight inhabitants: in the application, "The outcome" on the same toolbar as "Enter the 3D house" encourages the user to discover "The fate of those in the Secret Annex," including Fritz Pfeffer's death in Neuengamme on December 20, 1944, and Peter Van Pels's death in Mauthausen on May 10, 1945, five days after the camp's liberation.[64] In this sense, and unlike Dimensions in Testimony, the application does not forget the "true" victims of the Holocaust that we discussed in Chapter 2. In addition, these are affective moments in the application that do indeed—as Landsberg argues—call attention to the "artificiality and stylization" of the website, and "thus have the effect of visually reminding users that the experience is virtual and not an actual experience of the past."[65] Whereas Judith Goldstein accuses the majority of responses to the diary as adhering to a "deeply Christian template" in the "form of resurrection through words," Anne's "resurrection" in a digital realm gives space to an alternative, anti-redemptive history that is "complex and convoluted" (16).[66] Of course, this complexity could be addressed further: the Secret Annex Online—like the Belsen iPad application—has the potential to encompass much more metatextual content in the future. Important details not included in the application range from the little-known fact about Otto Frank's deliveries to the Wehrmacht (80 percent of Dutch firms delivered to the German army) to the high percentage (approximately 75 percent) of Jewish citizens in The Netherlands killed during the war due, in part, to the efficiency of Dutch civil servants in registering Jewish and non-Jewish inhabitants.[67] In relation to the latter detail, the Secret Annex Online could be accused of "sanitizing" history—unlike the Dutch Resistance Museum in Amsterdam—in that it avoids discussions of Dutch collaborators and bystanders beyond the disputed identity of the person who might have betrayed the annex inhabitants. However, this omission may be partly due to the circulation of the diary itself: Lee notes that its post-war fame deflected attention from such "implicated" subjects; Anne's testimony also tends (understandably) to focus on German invaders rather than collaboration, as when Anne notes in her entry for June 24, 1942 that "it's not the fault of the Dutch that we Jews are having such a bad time."[68]

Ironically, this absence of Dutch perpetrators in the Secret Annex Online does not—as with Belsen's 3D installations—eschew the possibility of a perpetrator perspective in the application. Deploying the mouse to "explore a space," as the pop-up instructions phrase it, sometimes feels uncomfortably like snooping or spying as the user uncovers the families' intimate details through digital "objects," such as a pink dressing gown in the Room Frank

Family, and pictures we cannot quite make out in the Room Van Pels Family. In the latter, there is an empty cup of tea in the same space, as if the user were witnessing the recent aftermath of the raid; as a bystander, or as a perpetrator in the form of a figured member of the Green Police.[69] In the introduction, we discussed this troubling aspect of VR in relation to its tendency to adopt a bystander position, and Jordan Wolfson's satire on VR empathy in his Holocaust-inflected VR artwork *Real Violence* (2017). As with the clinical and "desaturated" lines of the 3D installation in Belsen, it is as if—as Jennifer Rapson puts it—"promoting landscape as a way of seeing, or at least as a platform for encountering, the Holocaust, risks replicating a perspective which has been linked to the perpetrators; the object of the gaze—including the human subject—is evaluated and classified, deemed other and objectified."[70] Drawing on Zygmunt Bauman's *Modernity and the Holocaust* (1989), Presner similarly worries that the digital algorithm contains the "impulse to quantify, modularize, distantiate, technify, and bureaucratize the subjective individuality of human experience."[71]

Moreover, Presner notes that technological inventions during the war were intertwined with perpetrator activity: IBM developed machine technologies in the early 1940s in order to sort through material for the SS Race Office.[72] Presner's chapter in *Probing the Ethics of Holocaust Culture* (2016) originates in a volume that dwells on the potentially objectifying gaze in Knowles et al.'s *Geographies of the Holocaust* (2014), with, for example, its diagrams of "Crowded," "Orderly" and "Disorderly" death marches—which could be imagined as originating in an army training manual—and the "Terrain of encoded memories," that aggregates "letters from six testimonies," and locates "traumatic incidents according to route path coordinates [revealing] the literal verbal density of memories of the experience."[73] Does the Secret Annex Online similarly entail a "cold" perspective in its "visualizing [of] the geography of experience"?[74] *Geographies of the Holocaust* is acutely aware of this problem, and integrates several reflective sections as the equivalent of awkward poetics, in which the editors argue that "we would not want anyone to read our maps as the totalizing gaze of the perpetrator," and stress that "we appreciate the difficulty of imposing the distance of numerical abstraction upon the visceral, deeply emotional experiences that victims of the Holocaust endured."[75] In contrast, the Secret Annex Online, with its emphasis on empathy and connectivity, understandably does not call attention to the potential "coldness" of its digital attempt to make the structure of the Anne Frank House intelligible and meaningful. However, the self-reflection of awkward poetics does not guarantee that the ensuing literature will avoid the exploitative: the same issue appertains to *Geographies of the Holocaust*, that cannot help, as the editors worry, but "dehumanise the Holocaust somewhat" when "one is accustomed to thinking about concentration camps from the victims' perspective."[76] Then again, "coldness" is not entirely beholden to digital mapping: as we pointed out earlier in relation to historiography—and the same could be said of the academic prose in this chapter—"deep emotional experiences" are often lost when translated into another medium, whether prosaic or digital. The Secret Annex Online may necessarily objectify and classify the inhabitants' lives and possessions, but the redemptive and anti-redemptive hotspots and diary extracts still have the opportunity to cut through and provide a balance to the "totalizing gaze of the perpetrator."

Anne's Amsterdam: Apps and the Digital Metatext

The Secret Annex Online has proved to be a key development in Holocaust museums' engagement with digital technology due to its testimonial resistance to this "totalizing gaze," its deployment of palimpsestic testimony, and its ability to compel internet users' attention for "an eternity."[77] Seven years after its launch, the *Anne's Amsterdam* app (2017) was made available for iPhones (see Fig. 5.5). This app was particularly effective in its juxtaposition between a "real" encounter of the contemporary landscape in Amsterdam and historical images, a contrast that Shimon Attie explored so startlingly in his projections of "a now-lost Jewish past onto otherwise forgetful sites" in Berlin, Dresden, Copenhagen, Cologne and Kraków between 1991 and 1996.[78] As James Young notes in relation to Attie's installations, "Some people claim intuitively to sense the invisible aura of past events in historical sites, as if the molecules of such sites still vibrated with the memory of their past," whereas Attie realizes that

> this presence of the past is apparent only to those already familiar with a site's history or to those who actually carry a visual memory of this site from another, earlier time. For Attie, memory of a site's past does not emanate from within a place but is more likely the projection of the mind's eye onto a given site. Without the historical consciousness of visitors, these sites remain essentially indifferent to their pasts, altogether amnesiac. They "know" only what we know, "remember" only what we remember.[79]

Figure 5.5 The *Anne's Amsterdam* app
© Anne Frank House, Amsterdam

Moving from Attie's *Sites Unseen* projections in the 1990s to the era of the smartphone, *Anne's Amsterdam* encourages the user to—as Young might put it—vicariously "remember" the past through the "projection of the mind's eye" onto the town with the application's photographs and metatext. Images in which contemporaneous black-and-white images blend with present-day color are particularly reminiscent of Attie's projections, even if they cannot possibly recreate the charged juxtapositions of the artist's real-time installations, that "bathed" the sites of a now "invisible Jewish past," and provoked one onlooker in Berlin to complain that his father had "bought the building 'fair and square' from Mister Jacobs in 1938."[80] The "presence of the past" can be conjured in a more discrete form—if not, following Young's critique of the metaphysics of place, encountered—as the visitor wanders around various sites in Amsterdam that hold significance in terms of Anne's biography or the Nazi occupation of the city between 1940 and 1945. Created as a response to Brink's and other museum workers' sense that tourists were focusing too much on the Anne Frank House at the expense of a wider engagement with her relationship to the city, the application attempts to divert the visitor from the tourist center to a variety of sites across the Grachtengordel, Rivierenbuurt, and Plantage areas of Amsterdam.

The testimony encountered in the actual annex risks an overfamiliarity akin to the "flatness" of some of the content in Dimensions in Testimony, when, as we discussed in the Introduction, memory is evoked "too often."[81] However, as Brink recounted when we discussed the app in 2017, the well-intentioned programming of *Anne's Amsterdam* unfortunately has the innate drawback that "butterfly" tourists are unlikely to walk for hours between the various sites of interest. Even with a complex series of taxi rides, the digital tour would take over three hours to complete. Indeed, one diversion to collect the "Prisoners" item on Gerrit van der Veenstraat in Apollobuurt entailed an hour's walk (in total) from the "Skating" item in the Vondelpark.[82] A pamphlet available from the Anne Frank House or Dutch Resistance Museum entitled "Persecution and resistance in Amsterdam" is arguably more successful and user-friendly than the application in its apposition of, for example, the current Dam Square with a photograph of the "Groote Club" massacre on May 7, 1945, in which a celebrating party awaiting its liberators was gunned down by members of the German Kriegsmarine. Rather than being scattered across different districts, as in *Anne's Amsterdam*, the thirty-three "Sights" on the pamphlet's walk between the Anne Frank House and Dutch Resistance Museum take just over an hour to traverse, or fifteen minutes by tram.[83]

Nevertheless, Young's "projection of the mind's eye" (rather than "presence") in *Anne's Amsterdam* can connect powerfully to the past as the user shifts between the present neo-Gothic exterior of the Tuschinski theater on Reuliersbreestraat, and a contemporaneous smartphone image of the cinema on fire. "Tuschinski on Fire" informs the visitor that the theater was attacked by the Dutch Resistance on July 18, 1942, after the building was taken over by the German film company Tobis. In a space dedicated to "projection" since the Jewish owner Abraham Tuschinski built the cinema in 1921, the user can appreciate the disjunction between the surviving, luxurious, and wooden-paneled interior and Tuschinski's arrest for using a non-Jewish neighbor's telephone (he subsequently died in Auschwitz on September 17, 1942). As with Attie's *Sites Unseen*, we cannot "literally" see "what was lost," but can appreciate "that loss itself is part of this neighborhood's history, an invisible yet essential feature of its landscape."[84] *Anne's Amsterdam* explored this "lost" history via three different sections in the application: a "Map" that locates thirty "items" of interest across the city using GPS technology, a "List" of these items with a calculated distance from the user, and a digital "Album" into which the contemporaneous photographs and film extracts, such as the image of the burning Tuschinski, could be automatically pasted when the visitor "picked up" an item. As will already be apparent to aficionados of the *Pokemon Go* app—which enjoyed widespread acclamation during the summer of 2016—there are similarities between the apps in that fans have to entrap Pokemon characters (the equivalent of "items" in *Anne's Amsterdam*) using GPS technology. *Pokemon Go* draws on the same frisson between the digital and "real": Pokemon gamers or users of *Anne's Amsterdam* are similarly told that they are too far from "stops" if they attempt to ensnare a Pikachu or "Sweet Margot" too early.

Such a comparison might suggest that *Anne's Amsterdam* trivializes history, turning it into a mere digital game as part of the "childization" of the Holocaust, but this is far from the case. When a photograph of Margot Frank from 1935 outside a Jewish school was juxtaposed with the current "Stichting Marokkaanse Werkgroep" on Jekerstraat, we experienced a strange yet resonant mixture of connectivity and disjunction (see Fig. 5.6). As with *Anne's Amsterdam* as a whole, at the "Sweet Margot" item we partly, but not entirely, experienced the "flatness" that Daniel Mendelsohn recounts in *The Lost: A Search for Six of Six Million* (2007) when he confronts the Bolechow buildings associated with the murder of his family members in 1942-43:

> Once again, as is so often the case when I've finally stood in front of buildings the physical appearance of which does not—and couldn't possibly—suggest the saturated histories of the events that have occurred within then, I feel a vague disappointment, a sense of flatness. It was difficult for me to connect this stolid little structure in front of me with the many and vivid and terrible stories I had heard about it.[85]

Figure 5.6 Sweet Margot
© Anne Frank House, Amsterdam

In one sense, the app provides an example of the fleeting and fraught moments of digital encounter that we discussed in the introduction, that can appear artificial, uncanny, or incomplete. Yet the app is still able to provide the visitor with vicarious memories of seemingly innocuous buildings that a user unfamiliar with the sites' histories would otherwise pass without hesitation. Virtual Holocaust memory thus has the power to displace the user from themselves, even if momentarily, so that the viewer might learn to inhabit the present world differently. Nevertheless, there are glitches in the technology that resulted in frustration rather than an appreciation of Young's "amnesiac" buildings through secondary witnessing, as with the first VR application which we discuss next in this chapter. When attempting to collect the "items," *Anne's Amsterdam* often reverted to information in the "First Meeting" section of the digital album. Minutes after leaving some of the relevant sites, the information appeared on screen, but this was too late to engender the uncanny frisson between the present-day site and metatextual data experienced elsewhere in the suburbs of Amsterdam, when the app worked seamlessly.

The Virtual Annex

In contrast with *Anne's Amsterdam*, the Secret Annex Online has outlasted many developments in museum technology since its inauguration in 2010. Despite its encouragement of the productive yet uncanny encounters we have outlined above, *Anne's Amsterdam* was rescinded from the App Store after only a couple of years in circulation.[86] Its enabling of a powerful encounter with historical knowledge in Amsterdam's suburbs for only a few dedicated tourists is a reminder, as we pointed out in the Introduction, of the transience, frailty, and fallibility of technological engagements with the Holocaust. However, Brink and his team introduced a far more revolutionary form of technology into the Anne Frank House with their commissioning of a VR film in 2015, which became one of the first of such films to be made available in any museum worldwide in the following year. This film forms part of the first generation of VR films to engage with the Holocaust, including Pinchas Gutter's *The Last Goodbye* (2018), which takes the viewer on a virtual tour of Majdanek. Developed by the company VR Producties, the first incarnation of the Anne Frank VR film in 2016 was only available for disabled visitors to the museum and researchers. After an introduction on a virtual Prinsengracht, the VR film switches to the same entry point as the Secret Annex Online: the room with the famous bookcase and (now blocked) stairs from below. The film then navigates the buildings in the same way as the actual museum tour, moving from the Frank family's room to Peter Van Pels's bedroom. As in the Secret Annex Online, Peter's room forms the central testimonial point of the experience: its space is emphasized in the virtual narrative as the guide moves from this room to the attic, but then returns in order to locate Peter and Otto Frank on the morning of the arrest; the guide then concludes the film after ten minutes' viewing time.[87]

This VR film cannot be critiqued as an instance of Baudrillard's "realistic hallucination" due to its reliance on the actual contours of the museum. Baudrillard's *Simulacra and Simulation* (1981) begins with the metaphor of a map that starts to assume its own "reality" as soon as the signifier becomes an independent entity to the referent. In contrast, eight 3D cameras attempt to create a virtual environment as faithful to the museum as possible: the latter remains "truthful" to history in its displays, information panels and preservation of the damaged post-war rooms, but still does not—as we argued in relation to the Secret Annex Online—represent the "reality" of life in the annex. As opposed to Baudrillard's simulacra that spiral away from "truthfulness" into deceitful fiction, the virtual tour merely differs from the "real" navigation of the Anne Frank house by starting on Prinsengracht rather than the back of the former warehouse. A brief introduction subtly emphasizes the advantages of VR as people walk past sporting woolly hats. Avoiding the queues that still snake around Westerkerk despite the introduction of timed visits, the VR film clearly has its advantages for the distant user, or someone booked in for the VR tour. However, the latter experience necessarily curtails an extended experience of palimpsestic testimony. Due to the audio tours introduced in 2017 after some resistance in the museum hierarchy, the "real" tours also offer visitors a metatextual narrative long before they pass through the famous bookcase. As Brink explained in 2017, research has indicated that users are usually only comfortable with a VR headset for a maximum of ten minutes. Thus the first VR film could not possibly encompass the extended palimpsestic testimony in the Secret Annex Online or the metatextual expansiveness of an audio tour.

Nevertheless, the VR film draws on a shortened version of palimpsestic testimony. Enriching interactions between artifacts and metatexts have resulted in the audio guide's ubiquity in museums, yet the visual aspect of the VR film also allows for pop-up photographs and diagrams to complement the tour in a comparable if necessarily curtailed way to the Secret Annex Online. However, the first VR film appears overly didactic. Rather than the user-driven experiences of the Belsen iPad and Secret Annex Online in which the visitor can freely navigate the digital space, the VR film is beholden to the guide's descriptions of the various rooms, even if the intention is to make the visitor who may be unfamiliar with VR as comfortable as possible. Pop-up metatexts are easily missed—or only fleetingly glimpsed by the user—as the visitor moves around the extensive and impressive 360-degree space; nevertheless, these details indicate the *potential* for palimpsestic testimony in VR applications. The guide's static position at the left or right-hand side of the frame also mitigates against the head movements of the user as they explore the virtual crannies of the museum space provided by the 3D cameras. Headsets provide a much more fluid appreciation of the digital landscape than the skittish responses to mouse rotation in the Secret Annex Online. However, the 3D cameras also produce the formal glitches of shadows of the camera and a glimpse of the amalgamated camera stands as the viewer's gaze moves toward the center of the floor.

As with the iPad tour in Bergen-Belsen, the disadvantages of these particular site-specific films and applications are clear: compared to the millions of users engaging with the Secret Annex Online, this VR film could not be accessed remotely for an Oculus headset. However, the VR team at the Anne Frank House have recognized the potential of more immersive and interactive virtual tours of the museum that can be accessed by millions of visitors. Accordingly, the Secret Annex Online has been developed into a downloadable VR film for personal computers as well as smartphones: it allows remote visitors to interact with hotspots and stories without the limitations of mouse rotation or site-specific access. Due to the expense of digitizing the environment with the same Dutch company that produced the Secret Annex Online, the central annex rooms were created first, with the front rooms (such as the Opekta office) and Prinsengracht added later. In conversation with Brink in 2017, we discussed the new VR film in relation to our argument about the dangers of hyperreality in relation to the Prinsengracht scenes in the Secret Annex Online. Brink agreed that the juxtaposition of contemporary, contemporaneous, and digitized images appears odd in the current film, and explained that the developing VR film would include only "truthful" simulations based on historical photographs.[88] Avoiding the problems of 3D cameras—with the inevitable shadows and "stitching" issues—the new virtual environment has been created using 3D scanners: a "skeleton" diagram of the secret annex is populated with animated objects from the Bovenberg photographs.

As with our critique of the Secret Annex Online earlier in this chapter, Brink's team are aware that these color images are examples of "truthfulness," rather than replications of the contemporaneous. Rather than encourage a virtual hyperreality, Brink is aware of the inaccuracy of certain objects in the 1999 photographs which we have discussed above: these images have been erased or updated for the new VR film. The main difference between this film and Danny Abrahms's VR version of the annex is located in the absence of virtual human figures: in the second VR film of the Anne Frank House, it is not possible to peer over Anne's shoulder to glimpse her reading material or join the other members of the annex at the dinner table. Testimony rather than data remains at the forefront of such VR developments, despite the formal and technological innovations. Whether in the guise of hotspots, stories, or voice recordings, the centrality of Anne's diary ensures resistance to Presner's warnings about the objectifying digital algorithm, with its tendency to "quantify, modularize, distantiate, technify."[89] Such dangers are inherent in the digital "Joods Monument," with its focus on a list of Rotterdam names and genealogical records via interconnected algorithms, at the expense of testimonial narratives.[90] On the other hand, the updated VR film is not merely Milk's "ultimate empathy machine" either.[91] As with the Secret Annex Online and *Anne's Amsterdam*, the film attempts to balance the user's desire for facts with an uncanny sense of encounter in a discombobulating digital space.

In May 2018, this second VR film became available for disabled visitors to the Anne Frank House, and also, for the first time, as a free download for owners of Oculus headsets.[92] In 2017, Force Field Entertainment, an Amsterdam company that specializes in gaming, produced a VR film that allows the viewer to visit an actor playing Rembrandt van Rijn, and interact with his painting of *The Night Watch* (1642), but the updated film follows Otto Frank's restriction that there should be no characters present in any representation of the annex, unlike in Abrams's film.[93] In conversation in 2018, Brink mentioned that the Anne Frank Stichting is not keen on a "hologram" version of Anne Frank as a kind of fictional version of the Dimensions in Testimony project, partly to respect Otto Frank's wishes about an "empty" annex. The 2018 VR film thus constitutes a hybrid of the Secret Annex Online and the first VR film, as the viewer encounters hotspots and fragments from the diary within a digitized version of the annex, instead of a fixed tour with a distracting guide. As with the first version, the film focuses on the key rooms within the annex, and excludes the front offices, warehouse, and Prinsengracht.[94] However, the second version is much more interactive, as the viewer uses the mouse to click on the selected objects and testimony extracts.[95] After a voiceover and photographs offer brief contextualization, the user enters the annex (as in the Secret Annex Online) via the room with the bookcase; the viewer then moves from the Room Frank Family to the attic. Unlike the first version (and the Hollywood film), the new VR film does not focus on Peter Van Pels's room as the "center" of the building, and as a focus for the "limiting situation" of the romance which can occlude other aspects of the secret annex and its aftermath. After just one extract from the diary about the adolescents' relationship, the viewer enters the attic.[96] In this room and elsewhere, the viewer can explore a 360-degree perspective from different viewpoints, although without room scale and positional tracking. For example, in Anne Frank and Fritz Pfeffer's bedroom, the user can explore the 360-degree perspective from the doorway (see Fig. 5.7), the window, and the picture of Rembrandt on the wall. The glitch of the amalgamated camera stands in the first version has also been eradicated. Landsberg's sense in *Engaging the Past* of a "strangely physical visual experience" in the Secret Annex Online is exacerbated in this new version.[97] The left stair wall appears directly in front of the viewer's eyes after the bookcase entrance, which immediately induces a sense of claustrophobia that can be more effectively conveyed by VR. In a particularly successful use of the digital medium, the user focuses on the rear attic window as details of the loft around it begin to be obscured, and the narrative of the betrayal begins. This moment is akin to the Nazi "shadows" in the 2D Anne Frank film at the Museum of Tolerance in Los Angeles, who populate the frame as the Green Police enter the attic. In addition, one detail inscribed in the form of the second VR film creates a

Figure 5.7 Anne Frank and Fritz Pfeffer's bedroom
© Anne Frank House, Amsterdam

sense of movement in the otherwise static rooms, and resists Baudrillard's diatribe against "cold" digital environments.[98] Digitized versions of dust motes float through Anne Frank and Fritz Pfeffer's bedroom and the loft: they contrast with the fixed information and contours of the VR spaces, and link visually with the mouse cursor, which appears as a larger circle of light. These slightly oversized drifts of light could have created an off-putting hyperreal syntax in the film. Instead, the subtle use of lighting in the second VR film contrasts the benign motes and the accompanying enhanced sunlight in these two rooms with the increasingly obscured vision as the tour ends and the narrative of the betrayal begins.

However, as we discussed at the beginning of this chapter in relation to the Secret Annex Online, "truthfulness" is inevitably never far from the VR details that viewers encounter, as with the Bovenberg photographs in the Anne Frank House.[99] In the attic, even the exact position of the potatoes in a food barrel is necessarily a fiction, at the same time as their "truthful" presence registers the testimonial fact of the families' provisions. The second VR film also adds details to the first version that intend to bolster the historical veracity of the digital realm, such as dentists' equipment and binoculars in Fritz Pfeffer and Anne Frank's bedroom. The contemporaneous dentists' apparatus actually features in the 1961 scale models commissioned by Otto Frank, which took their place as centerpieces of the museum tour in 2018.[100] Nevertheless, the equipment's specific details and position in the bedroom can only be as approximate—and possibly as fictional—as the toolbox, preserves and pegs in the loft, and the draped suit and overalls in Peter Van Pels's room. These additional objects focus on connectivity with the user, and create a more welcoming, *heimlich* ambience in the second VR film. For example, with the image of the dining table (see Fig. 5.8), which would not be out of place in a dolls' house, there is no sense—as in the Second Life exhibition we discussed in the previous chapter—that we are entering a potentially disturbing recreation of history. Yet, as in the Secret Annex Online, there are still bookcases with blurry or blanked-out spines in the Frank Family Room and Peter Van Pels's Room, which suggests a parallel wariness toward historical authenticity in the VR film developers' construction of the secret annex. Following Otto Frank's sanguinity toward the infelicities of the Hollywood film, it could be argued that these "truthful" approximations in the second VR film simply do not matter. The most important affect is that users overall do not experience something close to Baudrillard's simulacrum, but an uncanny space conveying a sense of entrapment. Moreover, a metatextual

Figure 5.8 The kitchen table
© Anne Frank House, Amsterdam

assertion of fictionality within the film would be at odds with the immersive experience that the VR film encourages. A self-referential assertion that the film is a form of "truthful" fiction based on historical reality could distract the viewer from an intense engagement with the digitized annex and diary extracts; it could even encourage Holocaust deniers to utilize the technology erroneously to create new myths about the atrocities.

As indicated in Abrahms's comments on his independent tech company that we quoted at the beginning of this chapter, despite this danger of technology falling into the wrong hands, the future of the virtual Anne Frank is clearly one of proliferation. However, Brink and his team's close attention to "truthfulness" within the formal aspects of technology indicate that, in terms of the Anne Frank Stichting, the diary's continuing transformation in the digital era will be sensitively curated. For this organization, VR developments are now as important as the digital, as is suggested by the abandoned smartphone app and redevelopment of the Secret Annex Online. Whether this will continue remains to be seen: annual news items in the UK announcing that "this will be the year of VR" iterate with a suspicious willfulness. Currently, the dizzying pace in which cutting-edge technology becomes an anachronism—between two and seven years in the case of *Anne's Amsterdam* and the comparative longevity of the 3D application—indicates the need for cultural critics to engage with such films and applications before the digital forgets the memory of its own formal development. The Secret Annex Online, *Anne's Amsterdam* and the virtual tours of the Anne Frank House all share an engagement with the palimpsestic form of testimony that we have discussed in this chapter, in which the viewer is able to situate testimonial material in an enriching variety of metatextual scenarios. In the context of the digital memory of Anne Frank, the stories and hotspots from the 3D application were the first items to encourage this interaction, that is now extending to the more immersive and interactive contexts of the VR versions of the Secret Annex Online. As we have emphasized throughout this book, there will always be dangers if this technology focuses on connectivity and empathy at the expense of facilitating more discombobulating experiences in the applications. The most impressive aspect of the technology discussed in this chapter can be summed up as its openness to the "truthfulness" of users' uncanny, uncomfortable and disorientating experiences in the various applications and films. Rather than endorsing J. G. Ballard's understandable need to immerse himself "in the threatening possibilities offered by modern science and technology" and do his best "to swim to the other end of the pool," such movement toward awkward poetics in interactive and palimpsestic testimony should be praised as an alternative to technological dread.[101]

6

The Topography of Terror and Resistance to the Virtual

When visitors enter the Topography of Terror in central Berlin they are confronted with a wealth of analog documentation as if virtual Holocaust memory never existed. Our analysis of this museum in our last chapter functions as a corrective to a reader's potential sense that all museums and memorials across the globe are engaged in the same progressive development of digital and virtual applications. In contrast, we stress that museums and memorials' responses to virtual Holocaust memory are dependent on national and institutional contexts. Confronting the vexed histories of German perpetration, collaboration, culpability, and *Mitläufer* ("fellow travelers"), virtual Holocaust memory finds its limit point. Our final chapter thus functions as a counterpoint to the variety of digital and virtual applications discussed in the previous sections: we emphasize that the sensitive issues surrounding perpetrator memory in Germany—and in Berlin in particular—mitigate against the proliferation of virtual Holocaust memory elsewhere in Europe and the United States. Instead, the Topography of Terror presents an opposition between the digital and the "real" with its resistance to what Andrew Hoskins terms "presentist media."[1] With its small café, absent shop and lack of artefacts, the Topography of Terror (see Fig. 6.1) avoids postmodern museums' "spectacular mise-en-scène and operatic exuberance," as well as the development of on-site digital applications, such as the iPad tour at Bergen-Belsen, and the VR film for disabled visitors at the Anne Frank House.[2] Situated less than a mile away in the center of Berlin, the information center at Peter Eisenman's Memorial to the Murdered Jews of Europe contains extracts of victims' diaries presented through light boxes in the museum's floor, whereas the Topography of Terror eschews such visually arresting ways with which to engage with history.[3]

Virtual Holocaust Memory. Matthew Boswell and Antony Rowland, Oxford University Press. © Oxford University Press 2023. DOI: 10.1093/oso/9780197645390.003.0007

Figure 6.1 The Topography of Terror
Antony Rowland

In the context of the examples of virtual Holocaust memory we have explored throughout this book, this abstemiousness is inextricable from the focus on perpetrators at the site. We noted in our Introduction that virtual memory connotes the possibility of the virtuous, yet digital projections of perpetrators' speeches would risk, for some, a kitsch vulgarity. Curatorial nervousness inevitably surrounds the intertwining of the digital and perpetrator memory. Is it possible to imagine perpetrator equivalents of the holograms in the Dimensions in Testimony project at the same time as a 100-year-old guard stands on trial for assisting in the murder of 3,518 prisoners at the Sachsenhausen camp between 1942 and 1945? Or would the mere existence of such holograms constitute an inherent obscenity, if we follow Claude Lanzmann's critical approach to "understanding" the Holocaust?[4] The "turn" to perpetrators in Holocaust Studies which leads to such questions underlines the importance of an extended account of the Topography of Terror and its resistance to virtual Holocaust memory. In the subsequent discussion, we also illustrate how the site resists other influential trends in the discipline, such as the focus on transcultural memories. Indeed, the Topography of Terror withstands developments in digital memory *and* pre-millennial debates about the limits of representation.[5]

The "Spider in the Web": The Permanent Exhibition Space

Established as an exhibition trench in 1987, the Topography of Terror has been redeveloped to include a documentation center (see Fig. 6.1) and site tour that, unlike Bergen-Belsen, currently eschews any digital content. In our interview with the head of the Memorial Museums Department of the Topography of Terror, Thomas Lutz described the center as the "spider in the web" of other Berlin museums, connecting with the Memorial to the Murdered Jews of Europe, the Jewish Museum Berlin and the Berlin Wall Memorial.[6] Opened in 2010 after sixty-five years of "memory-work," the documentation center contains a history of Nazi perpetrators in a roughly chronological timeline.[7] Its sobriety is partly a response to the proliferation of virtual Holocaust memory. The design team was clearly concerned that digital installations and multi-media presentations—such as the Big Picture Show at the Imperial War Museum North (IWMN)—would risk glorifying perpetrator activity on the site of former Gestapo and SS offices that formed the administrative center of the Nazi regime. Such anxiety would seem to be well founded in terms of Edward Linenthal's response to the United States Holocaust Memorial Museum (USHMM): despite his overwhelmingly positive evaluation, he still frets that "what most captures people's attention may be the dazzling technical expertise with which the experience is communicated rather than the moral traumas of history."[8] As we noted in relation to Dimensions in Testimony, Marianne Hirsch similarly worries that technological prowess risks undermining its content.[9] These concerns point to a conundrum that we have returned to throughout this book: is it possible to include awkward poetics in the digital, so that the technology itself can reflect on these issues? Avoiding such difficulties, the design team at the Topography of Terror chose instead the panels and descriptive text of pre-digital museums, and documents such as "Notice dated November 30, 1934 from Reinhard Heydrich, Head of the Secret State Police, concerning a decree from Prussian Minister President Hermann Göring extending Heinrich Himmler's authority as Inspector of the Secret State Police."

In contrast to museums such as USHMM and the IWMN, the emphasis at the Topography of Terror is on the history conveyed through these bureaucratic texts of perpetrators, rather than digital media and personal memory. Perpetrator testimony is markedly absent in the exhibition space: as Erin McGlothlin laments in relation to contemporary representations of perpetrators more widely, their "subjectivity, motivations, thoughts and desires" have been ignored.[10] Ralph Appelbaum, the exhibition designer at USHMM, worried that raised letters announcing Hitler's speeches in the museum might appear to ennoble his remarks: the same anxiety about perpetrators' testimonial remarks in potential digital and multimedia installations pervades the documentation center in Berlin.[11] However, this conundrum results in an assumption that an eschewal of the digital avoids glorifying perpetrator acts—despite an emphasis on blown-up photographs of suffering in the Topography of Terror—and that extracts from Hitler's speeches would inevitably lead to unseemly identification.[12] The design team was also clearly apprehensive that examples of cultural memory aside from photographic evidence, such as the testimony integrated into the iPad application at Bergen-Belsen, would distract visitors from the overall history lesson. A few small screens in individual units are interspersed between the panels, but these are not presented as vital components of digital memory in the exhibition space. Containing visual items such as digitized footage of the Berghof, their discrete appearance suggests that film should be subordinate to the historical narratives conveyed in the dominating panel sections.[13]

It takes approximately six hours to view and read the material in the permanent exhibition, whereas Lutz commented that "butterfly" visitors spend on average about an hour in the center.[14] This information overload without what might be perceived as digital distractions can be read as a response to the ineffability of atrocity: the capacity of the exhibition certainly resists the easy consumption of perpetrator acts. Whereas Huyssen's postmodern museums risk reifying the past in "operatic exuberance," the Topography of Terror could be said to hearken back to pre-millennial debates about responses to the Holocaust in terms of variegated silences and "vexed" aesthetics.[15] Rather than attempt to further integrate such awkward poetics into the exhibition space, however, the documentation center presents history as, ultimately, something that can be conveyed in abundance, rather than drawing attention to problems of representation, and the muddied waters of historiography.[16] Since several hours are required to ingest all its material, the permanent exhibition certainly encourages the "slow space" for contemplation desired by critics such as Christopher Marshall.[17] Of course, the overwhelming focus on bureaucratic artefacts in the museum is partly due to the availability of perpetrator documents compared to those of former camp inmates in the immediate postwar era. Markedly, the documentation also contrasts with the empty vistas outside Bergen-Belsen that we engaged with in Chapter 4, and which the digital installations and iPad application attempt to counteract. However, in its overwhelming totality, the information signifies impenetrability rather than the ineffable: during our five visits between 2014 and 2019, the number of visitors who began to drift toward the windows after reading a few panels was certainly noteworthy. The documentation center purports to encompass the history of Nazi perpetration, if only the visitor were able to stay long and attentive enough in order to digest the information. Yet in their defense of the digital media employed at USHMM, Jeshajahu Weiberg and Rina Elieli point out bluntly that visitors "do not go [to museums] to read."[18] Rather than present a sense of history as absence and loss through the sparse exhibition space of Libeskind's extension to the Jewish Museum Berlin, history is portrayed at the Topography of Terror as an overwhelming process of non-digital accretion. During this process, details of Nazi bureaucracy such as Heydrich's notice (with its rather lengthy title) inevitably subsume victims' experience: perpetrators' documents "tend to concern the *organization* of genocide rather than providing a sense of what it is like to *experience* genocide."[19]

Paradoxically, the danger is that, through an excess of non-digital information, the documentation center becomes a space for forgetting. Just as Young commented that we expect unremarked traditional memorials to perform the memory work that we are unwilling to do ourselves, the documentation center may become an unreflective memorial to perpetrator acts.[20] Given its central position in Berlin between Potsdamer Platz and Checkpoint Charlie, the Topography of Terror has inevitably become part of what Erving Goffman termed "ceremonial agendas involving long strings of obligatory rites."[21] As Theodor Adorno argues in relation to Paul Valéry's experience of the Louvre, "[f]atigue and barbarism" in the form of a superficial acknowledgment of history and culture can converge when·the visitor comes to a museum merely "in fulfilment of an obligation."[22] Visually arresting displays such as the iPad application in Bergen-Belsen or the light boxes at the Eisenmann information center could perhaps have chafed against these "obligatory rites."[23] Instead, Adorno's sense of the "barbaric" still lingers at the Topography of Terror in the form of a fatiguing history lesson. Awkward poetics could be inserted into the visual displays with self-conscious challenges to the representation of troubling artifacts, but the design team, like Appelbaum at USHMM, decided against perpetrator memorabilia because they did not "want to create an environment where people were being reverent in front of the wrong things."[24] Visitors attracted to such evocative objects might, Appelbaum worried, replicate the contemporaneous allure of Nazi artifacts;

Saul Friedländer referred to these potential "mute yearnings" in the 1980s as leading to a "new discourse" on fascism.[25] Moreover, Lutz was concerned that these icons might create a shrine for neo-Nazis: "There was a fear it could be a fascination for the wrong visitors and that was the reason why you have no artifacts here, no black uniforms."[26] Such anxieties over identification are certainly an aspect of what Jenni Adams describes as the wider "sense of literary and cultural unease which surrounds attempts to conceptualise or depict the Holocaust perpetrator."[27] However, rather than "civic pilgrims" transformed by the interactive lessons that emerge from "imaginative engagement" in virtual Holocaust memory, visitors to the Topography of Terror risk leaving with a pre-Arendtian notion of the perpetrators as monstrously "other."[28] Whereas the Nazi narrator of Jonathan Littell's novel *The Kindly Ones* (2006) is constantly at pains to stress the similarities between himself and the reader, the visitor to the Topography of Terror confronts the Nazis as alien humans. Dominick LaCapra's concept of empathic unsettlement cannot work in this context, as there is no initial identification encouraged with, for example, the violated photograph of a smiling Himmler.

As well as the eschewal of digital memory in favor of historiographical data, awkward poetics are absent in that there is little overt reflexivity in the permanent exhibition. No debates are encouraged between art and history, and no sense is conveyed of how representations of perpetrators have evolved in historiography, art, and culture during the postwar period, although this topic was briefly covered in a temporary exhibition in 2015, entitled "1945 in Postwar German Cinema." This exclusion follows the logic of the original design team at USHMM, who were reluctant to include artwork in case it detracted from the proof of atrocity elsewhere in the museum.[29] There is no possibility of the "truthfulness" of virtual Holocaust memory that we have engaged with throughout this book impinging on the lines of panels. In contrast, the exhibitions at the Ravensbrück Memorial contain a section on postwar representations of female perpetrators, including the character based on Irme Grese (Karin Katte) in the film *Gegen Ende der Nacht* (*"Towards the End of the Night,"* 1998). The only artworks in the permanent exhibition at the Topography of Terror consist of a model of how the site would have appeared during the Nazi period—similar to models of Birkenau at USHMM and the Imperial War Museum—and a colored collage of index cards. Throughout the exhibition, color attempts to distinguish between the "facts" of black-and-white text and photographs, and cultural representations of history, whether excerpts from historians' work, or the (single) surrounding artwork.[30] This distinction produces a rare and thereby powerful moment of reflexivity at the end of the exhibition when the visitor is confronted with an orange panel containing a single photograph of defendants at the second Treblinka trial in 1964.[31] The photograph becomes the equivalent of the orange-colored text boxes of quotations from historians' work: the hanging panel then directs the visitor's eye to the artwork behind, entitled "The Trial Concerning the Reich Security Main Office" (see Fig. 6.2). This image consists of 530 colored index cards appertaining to employees of the RSHA: in 1963, the chief public prosecutor started investigating between three and four hundred former members; only sixteen were put on trial, and only three were sentenced, none of whom served their full terms. Hence the covered faces of the accused in the photograph resonate in the context of the bureaucracy signified by cards of the anonymous, unprosecuted perpetrators in the artwork. This anti-redemptive closure is clearly meant to pique the

Figure 6.2 Photograph of the second Treblinka trial and "The Trial Concerning the Reich Security Main Office."
Antony Rowland

visitor's desire for justice. Following the model of USHMM, the exhibition could have ended with an emphasis on rescuers and resisters; those who could be "regarded as role models for people who find themselves in the position of bystanders."[32] Instead, the exhibition provocatively concludes with panels on those who escaped justice in the early years of the FRG, careerists who denied their Nazi past, and veteran SS meetings.[33] However, the disconcerting emptiness at the end of the permanent exhibition also paradoxically evokes the transition from *die Stunde Null* ("zero hour") after the war to Germany's *Wirtschaftswunder* ("economic miracle"). Out of rubble and the absence of objects reflected at the Topography of Terror arise the postwar saviors of trade, low inflation and rapid industrial growth.

Antipostmodernist Architecture: The Documentation Center

Despite its provocative ending, the overall lack of reflexivity in the permanent exhibition is symptomatic of a post-millennial turn to less spectacular museums in Berlin, which chafes against both the proliferation of virtual Holocaust memory and the self-conscious forms of Libeskind's architecture. Digital media constitute an integral part of postmodern museums such as the Beit Hashoah Museum of Tolerance in Los Angeles, with its multimedia presentations on discrimination and tolerance. Such digital pyrotechnics are currently rejected in the context of Berlin, where museums are responding to the legacy of Libeskind's extension to the Jewish Museum, and the current demand for small-scale museums and memorials that respond to, for example, resisters or forced labor during World War II.[34] Examples of museums responding to wartime resistance include the Silent Heroes' Memorial Centre, and the museum based around Otto Weidt's Workshop for the Blind. Unlike Libeskind's extension, the exterior architecture of these museum buildings is innocuous since they are situated in the midst of the Hackesche Höfe shopping complex. Instead of Libeskind's characteristic "slashes" in aluminum or zinc, the plain white decor inside the Silent Heroes' Memorial Centre—like the documentation center's "functionalist" building—does not call attention to itself. Inside this museum, there are no examples of virtual Holocaust memory: visitors' eyes are drawn to the individual cabinets; with their functional right angles, each cabinet represents an individual member of the resistance. Only a few yards away at the entrance to the Hackesche Höfe, the *Stolpersteine* ("stumbling stones") function as another example of recent low-key memorials in Berlin (see Fig. 6.3). These are the antithesis of spectacular digital applications such as Dimensions in Testimony: forged with industrial material, they can easily be missed as tourists traverse the popular shopping complex. All these Berlin museums and memorials respond to a criticism made of Libeskind's extension that it functions as a site of tourist pilgrimage as much as—if not more than—the exhibits inside, echoing Hirsch's worry about the form of Dimensions of Testimony proving more important than its content. Indeed, Libeskind's concrete "Holocaust tower" in the extension to the Jewish Museum is deliberately devoid of objects: it constitutes an attempt to make the visitor think about the impossibility of assimilating all the information in the exhibitions and reflect on their experience so far in the discombobulating extension. Apart from the ending of its temporary exhibition, the Topography of Terror eschews such reflective moments and encompasses a proliferation of information, as if in deliberate contrast to what some critics regard as vapid and self-congratulatory postmodern architecture.

Figure 6.3 Stolpersteine outside the Hackesche Höfe
Antony Rowland

In the specific context of post-millennial Berlin museums, therefore, cautious responses to virtual Holocaust memory have become intertwined with the legacies of postmodernist architecture. The resistance to the digital at the Topography of Terror is reflected in the architectural design of the documentation center and the antipostmodernist tenor of the entire site. Viewed from the eastern entrance, architectural continuity is evident between the center and the modernist Europahaus in its background; any references to postmodernist architecture are significantly absent (see Fig. 6.4). As opposed to the architectural liveliness of the extension to the Jewish Museum Berlin, the documentation center does not—unlike Libeskind—reject the right angle: it is a functional building, devoid of ornamentation in its pastiche of modernism. Critical regionalism stresses the importance of contextual architecture: the low-level building's resistance to attention and deflection of the viewer's eye to surrounding architecture, such as the neo-classical Martin-Gorpius-Bau, avoids the enshrining of a site where, for example, Gestapo prisoners were massacred on April 23, 1945.[35] In 2006, the announcement of Ursula Wilms' and Heinz Hallmann's winning design for the documentation center "was

Figure 6.4 The Topography of Terror and Europahaus
Antony Rowland

praised for fulfilling its remit without any 'theatricals'—and thus avoiding controversy."[36] Whereas the architect James I. Freed wanted USHMM to "take visitors away from Washington into the "feel" of Nazi architecture," the opposite is true of the relationship between Berlin and the Topography of Terror.[37] Period architecture from the 1930s is eminently visible in the form of the former *Reichsluftfahrtministerium* opposite the site: the center reacts against the latter's monumental limestone and travertine slabs with a "non-commemorative" demureness.[38] A pastiche of Freed's evocative "hard industrial forms" at USHMM would have been possible at the Topography of Terror, but instead the visitor encounters a building that also avoids attention through its semi-transparency: visitors can always see through the center's walls from the inside and exterior.[39] As opposed to the "dark and uncompromising" environment in the original Holocaust Exhibition at the Imperial War Museum, the large windows allow for a light exhibition area that also draws visitors toward the view of Berlin outside.[40] This resistance to melodramatic space was embedded into the development of the site at an early stage. Peter Zumther's critical regionalist reaction against the "operatic exuberance" of postmodern architecture was already evident in the plainness of his original building for the documentation center that was demolished, half-finished, in 2004. The site's topography has encouraged a rationalized timidity in its recent development, which is understandable in the light of its history. Countering Berlin's countermemorials in the 1980s, such as Norbert Radermacher's trip light-beam in Neukölln, which was used to remind passersby of the former site of a KZ-Aussenlager, the site's architecture was never meant to be a "brazen" disruption of the everyday, conceived to "challenge the very premises of [its] being."[41]

This anti-digital and anti-postmodernist abstemiousness responds to the individual needs of the Topography of Terror. Unlike USHMM and Libeskind's extension to the Jewish Museum Berlin—which function as monuments as well as museums—the design team and architects clearly wished to avoid the monumental in case it suggested an enshrining of Nazi ideology at the site and might thereby concretize "evil in an unfortunate way."[42] Such resistance to the monumental operates in a very different way to countermemorials: the latter's disruptive effect on what James Young and Caroline Pearce term the "normalization" of memory contrasts with the documentation center's desire for invisibility.[43] Herbert Muschamp stated that USHMM's exterior "vocabulary" of limestone and brick connects with the neighboring buildings: such connections (and disconnections) appertain to the Topography of Terror too, since the "squashed" rectangle—alongside its resistance to the *Reichsluftfahrtministerium*'s architecture—subtly reflects the shape of the modernist Europahaus, where Nazi personnel used to engage in open-air dances. Operatic, postmodern architecture akin to Frank Gehry's Guggenheim Museum in Bilbao would risk being regarded as an unseemly glorification of the Nazi period on this site. However, a strange architectural logic then ensues that presents digital and postmodernist exuberance as suiting the encasement of victimhood in buildings such as Libeskind's extension, whereas only an understated modernism is appropriate to a landscape of perpetrator crimes.[44]

During the redevelopment of the Topography of Terror, a temporary exhibition gave space to such museological issues. One panel included an extract from *Der Tagesspiegel* (January 26, 2006) which expressed satisfaction that "the site will finally be developed," but also regret that Berlin and Germany are "now satisfied with a worthy, functional building" (see Fig. 6.5). Such reflections on the site continued with the panel's description of the landscape's controversial development. In April 1984, Jürgen Wenzel

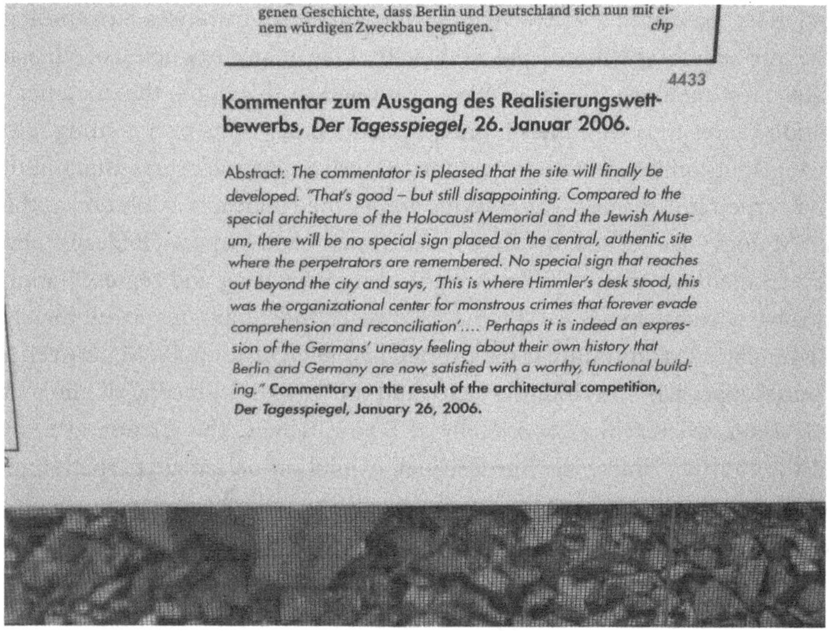

Figure 6.5 Panel extract from the temporary exhibition (2009)
Antony Rowland

and Nikolaus Lang won the first competition to redesign the site: they intended to seal over the area with plates of cast iron, but in December of the same year, the Berlin Senate decided not to go ahead with their plans.[45] In 1993, Peter Zumthor's building won the next competition; Reinhard Rürup, the director of the Topography of Terror at the time, resigned when this redevelopment was abandoned in 2004. In 2006, a senate jury unanimously chose Wilms and Hallmann's new design: the extract from *Der Tagesspiegel* bemoans the "functional" building when contrasted with the "special architecture" of Eisenmann's memorial and Libeskind's extension. Young illustrates that, in Germany, every monument "at every turn, is endlessly scrutinized, explicated, and debated," and that artistic, "ethical, and historical questions occupy design juries to an extent unknown in other countries," yet this metanarrative is now occluded at the Topography of Terror since the closure of the temporary exhibition.[46] This invisible memory contrasts with the Sachsenhausen and Ravensbrück *Gedenkstätte*, which often painstakingly address the vicissitudes of postwar redevelopment.[47] The information center under the Eisenmann memorial similarly ends with a digital console that takes the visitor through the redesigning of the terrain above. Such an instance of digitization could have been included at the Topography of Terror, but most visitors leave instead with no idea of the controversies surrounding the various competitions and architects. Like many examples of virtual Holocaust memory which we have examined in this book, the documentation center thus willfully suppresses the memory of its own coming into being. In its omission of meta-memory, as well as postwar representations of the perpetrator, it seeks—as Hoskins argues the Holocaust exhibition at the IWM does—to "represent a time mostly untouched by post-Holocaust and digital memory, that is, by the weight of remembering and representation that has accumulated since [1945]."[48] However, the exhibitions are ultimately dissimilar: Hoskins outlines the overlap and tension at the IWM between a "purist approach" to exhibition space and the "presentist media" of film and television, whereas the Topography of Terror eschews this friction in favor of the "purist." Unlike the Ravensbrück exhibition on female perpetrators, what the exhibitions do share is a disavowal of popular history in an attempt to "provide a literally 'documentary' past," implying a search for authentic historical memory as the antithesis of digital memory, conceived by proxy as a "debased and [unnecessarily] mediated relation to the past."[49]

In contrast, the site tour at the Topography of Terror embraces the memory work surrounding the landscape. A different form of virtual memory is evident here in that the tour does not contain "trip" projections akin to Norbert Radermacher's countermemorial in Neukölln, but it does encourage visitors to imagine former buildings superimposed on the current landscape. Rather than deploy the augmented reality in the iPad application at Bergen-Belsen, the tourist has to create their own imaginative projections. This process begins with the model of "The Nazi Government Quarter in 1939" near the center's entrance, and its evocation of a psychogeography of contemporary Berlin in terms of absent buildings such as the Reich Chancellery on Voßstrasse. Outside the Topography of Terror center, histories of destroyed buildings are relayed on the *Geländerungang*'s "stations," positioned near the remains of, for example, the outer walls of the Gestapo and SS offices at Wilhelmstrasse 98–101 and ruins of the Prinz-Albrecht-Palais's original colonnade. The history of postwar Berlin is interspersed with contemporaneous photographs: during the 1980s, an "Autodrom" was inaugurated on the site, in which drivers without a license were allowed to roam through the locust trees; the pay booth's concrete foundations have been carefully preserved (see Fig. 6.6). For a time, then, learner drivers were symptomatic

Figure 6.6 The remains of the Autodrom
Antony Rowland

of the forgetting of the entire site of previous Gestapo and SS offices during the early 1980s, before the original Topography of Terror opened in 1987. One fascinating station (no.13) engages with the memory of a former trench. Pearce argues that perpetrator sites "need to strike a balance in ensuring sufficient confrontation with the history of the perpetrators, but in a way that does not . . . overshadow the history of the victims": this "overshadowing" is evident here in that a former air-raid trench was discovered during archaeological digs in 1997 that contained clothes and badges of concentration camp inmates.[50] Curiously, this trench was subsequently filled with earth. In *The Texture of Memory* (1993), Young calls attention to the hundreds that died in the Gestapo-Gelände during the air raids of April and May 1944, including twenty inmates from Sachsenhausen who "had been brought in to clear rubble from the area": the SS "forced them to take cover in an exposed, shallow trench" during the bombing.[51] Information at station thirteen reveals that this could be the same trench that Young refers to: a zigzag in the path—reminiscent of Libeskind's jagged walkways outside the extension to the Jewish Museum Berlin—has been placed adjacent to the former site of the atrocity. Despite the station's reflection on the changing landscape, the trench's (and its contents') disappearance constitutes a disquieting act of forgetting, as if its retention would have provided an unsettling counternarrative that could draw attention away from the site as a " 'spider' in the web" of Berlin memorials, and—as with the Eisenmann memorial—toward a narrative of victimhood.[52]

The Exhibition Trench, Berlin Wall, and Resistance to Transcultural Memory

The visitor's imaginative projection of virtual landscapes onto present-day Berlin is not required at the most powerful moment on the site tour when remains of the Gestapo cellars in the exhibition trench are juxtaposed with a remnant of the Berlin wall. These overlapping signs of oppression are in one sense an example of multidirectional—but not intercultural—memory that harbors the politics of reconciliation. In a post-*Wende* context, remnants of the wall and cellars remind us that "new democracies frequently rely on the same people who were around when the totalitarian regime was in power."[53] This multidirectional appeasement also reflects the *Leitverantwortung* of the SPD-Green government (1998-2005): a coalition treaty (2005) stated the importance of "appropriately considering both dictatorships in Germany," but also to take pride "in post-war achievements, especially unification."[54] However, such comparisons between Berlin in 1945 and 1989 are not always examples of overlapping memory in Michael Rothberg's sense of a dynamic transfer that takes place "between diverse places and times during the act of remembrance."[55] They can be instances of what Young terms the "normalization" of the past, as when Chancellor Helmut Kohl called for a moment's silence to remember the victims of Nazism and Communism at the first parliamentary meeting of a reunified Germany in October 1990.[56]

In addition, a more insidious politics can sometimes be at work in such cases of overlapping memory: Rothberg and Dirk Moses outline these dangers in relation to the specific case of the Palestinian-Israeli conflict.[57] Lutz argues that "We had fewer people who worked for the Gestapo compared to the Stasi": statistical fact presents historical relativity here as a potential route to exculpation.[58] Rather than resulting in the dynamic, interweaving memory narratives that Rothberg primarily analyses in *Multidirectional Memory*, Lutz's comparison of perpetrators cannot help but echo the *Historiker-Streit* in the 1980s over the comparability of the Holocaust. The *Historiker-Streit* consisted of "a remarkable series of debates played out in the German press dealing with the place of the Final Solution in German history," including the contentious issue of whether the plight of East Prussian refugees at the end of World War Two was in any way comparable to the suffering of Holocaust victims.[59] As Daniel Levy and Natan Sznaider argue, *Vergangenheitsbewältigung* ("coming to terms with the past") should not occlude historical specificities: "One must distinguish between the fragile political order of postwar Germany, whose legitimacy was imposed on the Germans from the outside, and the later republic, which was secure in its democracy."[60] Nevertheless, Eric Santner considers the key moment in 1985 when the cardinal of Cologne, Joseph Höffner, contended that Germans "should not, again and again, exhume past guilt and mutually committed injustices, in constant self-torment" (xi). When Santner finished *Stranded Objects* in 1986, there was "still tremendous uncertainty and confusion in contemporary German society about how to approach the tasks of mourning and anamnesis with regard to fascism and the Holocaust" (xi). The extensive documentation at the Topography of Terror in a museum symbolically ensconced at the heat of the German nation indicates that by 2010, this "uncertainty and confusion" in *Vergangenheitsbewältigung* had to some extent been assuaged. Yet when Santner pondered in the mid-1980s the "strategies and procedures by which a cultural identity may be reconstituted in post-Holocaust Germany," he could not have foreseen a digital age in which virtual Holocaust memory would reach its limit point in Germany's current "efforts to master the past" (xi).

This engagement with postwar German history at the Topography of Terror results in an occlusion of wider examples of perpetration, unlike Dimensions in Testimony, which now includes testimonies on the Armenian Genocide, the Nanjing Massacre, the 1994 Genocide Against the Tutsi in Rwanda, and the Guatemalan Genocide. Levy and Sznaider imagine dialectical "memoryscapes" in which "issues of global concern are able to become part and parcel of everyday local experiences and moral life worlds," but the Topography of Terror withstands such fluidity as much as it does the digital.[61] This resistance to transcultural memory can be read in the context of the media furor in 2003 over Erica Steinbach's vision of a center in Berlin that would commemorate all twentieth-century expulsions, from Armenia to the Balkans.[62] Steinbach's response to the ten million ethnic Germans expelled from Eastern Europe after the Potsdam Treaty emphasized German victimhood and obscured "German culpability during the Nazi occupation . . . as the cause of acts of revenge."[63] Such machinations provoked the Polish news magazine *Wprost* into claiming that German suffering was cancelling out Polish recollections of the war in a "zero-sum" clash of memories. The (then) chancellor Gerbhard Schröder insisted that there should not be a refugee center in Berlin in case this signaled that Germany suffered more than neighboring countries. Such are the problems of multidirectional memory in this national context of comparative suffering: the design team avoided all mention of these recent debates in the updated design of the Topography of Terror. Overlapping memories of perpetration have been more productive elsewhere, such as in the Cape Town Holocaust Centre: this museum explicitly juxtaposes the Holocaust with South African history and frames the latter in terms of the consequences of prejudice and racism. For example, if the visitor approaches the opening triangle-shaped panels of the permanent exhibition from one direction, they can read information about the Holocaust; from the other angle, data is offered about South Africa and apartheid. In contrast, the resistance to transcultural memory at the Topography of Terror indicates that the design team felt that Germany still has to work through its own history of perpetration before any attempts can be made at cosmopolitan or virtual memory in relation to the Nazi period. Any other multidirectional approach could have been construed as an evasion of responsibility, and a denial of the singularity of Nazi crimes. However, a "Centre Against Expulsions" was still planned to take over the Deutschlandhaus building in Kreuzberg, only a short walk from the Topography of Terror, situated next to the Europahaus; the former is visible from the site of the former SS canteen. The Gestapo-Gelände's documentation center, and its eschewal of transcultural memory, would thus be placed in proximity to a space that utilizes multidirectional memory in order, controversially, to compare various narratives of European suffering.

Transcultural approaches to culpability are thus as absent as virtual Holocaust memory at the Topography of Terror. Indeed, even though the signs of the Berlin wall and Nazi period openly address perpetration—as the 2005 coalition treaty encouraged—the issue of complicity itself is rarely confronted in the exhibition trench, site tour and documentation center. Rather than leaving visitors with "more questions than they had when they arrived," as USHMM's Kristallnacht exhibition in Second Life encourages, the occlusion of complicity leads to a nostalgic version of history reminiscent of the early postwar period, in which distinctions between "regular Germans" and Nazi "monsters" were useful tools for de-Nazification and reconciliation.[64] Lutz did not refer to culpability or *Mitläufer* in our interview and stressed how the Nazi élite differed from "ordinary" Germans: moreover, he wished to place more emphasis on the biography of Hitler. There are yet no instances of virtual Holocaust memory that engage with the vicissitudes of Hitler's early years. Lutz's "intentionalist" version of history replicates initial postwar historiography that focused on "Hitler's delusional ideas and the small clique of fanatical SS men who put those ideas into action."[65] As Levy and Sznaider sardonically note, such a broad spectrum of German victims were identified early on in the Federal Republic that "one started to wonder who had kept the Nazi regime and its machinery of destruction running."[66] There are a few references to "fellow travelers" in the documentation center, such as a quotation from Ian Kershaw's *Hitler: Profiles in Power* (1991), which refers to "widespread support within the population," and photographs such as the one in which local residents watch a burning synagogue in Ober-Ramstadr, but these are never reflected upon at length amongst the chronological narratives. There is no equivalent moment to one in Second Life's Kristallnacht exhibition in which the user stands by the digitized photograph of broken windows and has to confront their own potential complicity in state oppression. In contrast, after the publication of Christopher Browning's *Ordinary Men: Police Battalion 101 and the Final Solution in Poland* in 1992, historiography has increasingly focused on such fraught issues of *Mitläufer* and complicity.

Unlike the virtual Kristallnacht exhibition, therefore, visitors at the Topography of Terror are not encouraged to confront their own potential complicity in broader structures of implication. Indeed, the bombardment of detail in the permanent exhibition induces the same effect as Daniel Goldhagen's *Hitler's Willing Executioners* (1996): the perpetrators appear irremediably "other" rather than uncannily familiar. However, design teams have to confront the central issue of returning visitors: as Vivian Petraka muses, should spectators ever be positioned as "complicitous bystanders," as in the Second Life exhibition?[67] If visitors are presented as "potential perpetrators of genocide," who, she wonders, would actually come to such a museum? There is something markedly different about confronting your own complicity via a digital or virtual application in the comfort of your own home, as opposed to a tourist site in Berlin. Nevertheless, given that the Gestapo-Gelände housed "'armchair' murderers" in the administrative homeland of the Nazi state, issues of complicity and culpability could be addressed more clearly in the exhibition space. Rothberg's recent work on implication, bystanders, and beneficiaries indicates that this aspect of memory-work is far from over in Holocaust Studies and emphasizes that its critical vocabulary has not yet been fully established. As Rothberg argues in an essay on the South African artist William Kentridge, such subject positions "move us away from overt questions of guilt and innocence and leave us in a more complex and uncertain moral and ethical terrain—a terrain in which many of us live most of the time."[68]

The future intertwining of virtual Holocaust memory and the historiography of complicity offers intriguing future possibilities currently unsuitable for the national specificities of the Topography of Terror. This inefficacy illustrates that we do not wish to construct a simplistic teleology in this book in which pre-millennial debates about representations of the Holocaust simply give way to examples of digital media, such as the development of the holograms at the USC Shoah Foundation. Such a narrative needs to be refined by the demands of particular sites: in this case, our historicist reading of the Topography of Terror explicates its resistance to the digital in the context of anxieties over the representation of perpetrators, the specificities of postwar German history, and the post-millennial development of Berlin's memorial culture. The design team responded with resistance to the possibility of digital pyrotechnics, but the "purist approach" in contrast risks a lack of interaction and fatigue, resulting in visitors drifting away from the panels toward the windows and views of Berlin.[69] Unlike the Kristallnacht exhibition in Second Life, visitors can leave thinking that atrocious history is simply "other" and has nothing to do with their own potential imbrication in oppressive political systems. As Huyssen argues, museums may lead to "possible resurrections, however mediated and contaminated, in the eyes of the beholder," but a danger remains that the Topography of Terror will not prove to be a site for the more productive, "truthful" aspects of virtual Holocaust memory that we have outlined throughout this book. The necessary focus on national history also opposes transcultural memories of the Holocaust and positions the latter as a "decontextualized event."[70] Whereas Levy and Sznaider endorse transcultural memory as "the foundation for global human-rights politics," the documentation center may be regarded as an example of cultural ossification.[71] As opposed to Levy and Sznaider's championing of the "nearness of the faraway," the Topography of Terror illustrates that the politics of national memory in Germany are not so easily circumvented.[72]

Conclusion

> The holograms . . . cannot handle the present; don't ask them what
> they had for breakfast.[1]
>
> —Wulf Kansteiner

In 1911, the first escalators were installed in London at Earls Court station: passengers initially shunned what many considered to be a bizarre and frightening spectacle. Bumper Harris, an enterprising man with a wooden leg, was employed to ride gracefully up and down the moving staircases to emphasize the safety of the unfamiliar machinery. As Andrew Thacker illustrates in relation to such modernist innovations, new technologies "often bring sensations of panic or unease, unnerving our sense of how we affectively relate to a changed environment."[2] Lawrence Langer's expostulations that the holograms are the "craziest thing" and a "gimmick" are symptomatic of such anxious responses, in turn, to instances of twenty-first-century technology.[3] Langer's reaction and Wulf Kansteiner's challenge to the holograms in the epigraph above to ruminate on their breakfast are, in their different ways, symptomatic of the concerns and misunderstandings surrounding the current intertwining of testimony and technology. As a symptom of the latter, a school guide referred to the holograms as a form of artificial intelligence during our visit to New York's Museum of Jewish Heritage in 2018. Yet interactive testimony is not the equivalent of the "hosts" in *Westworld* (2016), in which the robots' curiosity about their origins is triggered by traces of previous programming which is traumatically spliced into the present.[4] The Dimensions in Testimony project can never erase the historical specificity of its recordings: the Holocaust survivors are not required to "handle" the present by becoming embedded in the "social context of the [future] observer."[5]

Virtual Holocaust Memory. Matthew Boswell and Antony Rowland, Oxford University Press. © Oxford University Press 2023. DOI: 10.1093/oso/9780197645390.003.0008

Interactive testimony thus cannot offer something that Dimensions in Testimony never promises: an artificial intelligence that attempts to update itself in response to the vicissitudes of the present, such as a choice of bagels or eggs.[6] Nevertheless, if the visitor actually asks the recordings of Eva Schloss and Pinchas Gutter what they consumed for breakfast, Gutter replies, "porridge; oatmeal. I've not had lunch yet," and Eva responds enthusiastically that she has consumed "two coffees, a pear, bagel—quite a lot more than I'm used to at home." At such times, Dimensions in Testimony plays along with the viewer's potential suspension of disbelief, or any user who mistakenly thinks that they are enjoying a synchronous encounter with a Holocaust survivor. (One spooked visitor asked us worriedly: "Where are they?") At the same time, the recordings obviously do not attempt to fool the viewer into thinking that holograms can eat. Schloss' recording at the Shoah Foundation in Los Angeles contrasts breakfast "at home" with the institution's hospitality: she clearly enjoyed the produce of her Californian hotel. In the context of this implicitly acknowledged historicity, it seems curious that Kansteiner emphasizes that the holograms will date with "small, yet pervasive, markers of historical non-simultaneity" such as their digitized clothes.[7] The USC Shoah Foundation has never claimed that the holograms update themselves or have been programmed to act—like the hosts in *Westworld*—as if they have been seamlessly inserted into the visitors' present. Indeed, the holograms playfully engage with the asynchronous in their responses about breakfast, and their encouragement to calculate their age based on their birthdate and the date of the user's visit. Yet despite the exhibition pamphlet's declaration at the Museum of Jewish Heritage that "virtual conversations" are possible, the visitors' encounter with testimonial details is not that dissimilar to those recounted in the analog testimonies on show elsewhere in the Museum of Jewish Heritage, even if the form of conveying these intimacies is radically different.

The advantages, shortcomings, and uncanny effects of Dimensions in Testimony link to wider debates in memory studies about connectivity, connective memory and what we would term the "digital gothic."[8] Alison Landsberg praises the ability of digital installations such as the Secret Annex Online to enable users to acquire a "deeply felt memory of a past event": her work anticipates the interactive possibilities of other examples of virtual Holocaust memory, such as the VR films set in the Anne Frank House.[9] However, such examples of connective memory are distinct from, but also inextricably part of, the repercussions of connectivity. Alongside many of the contributors to *Digital Memory Studies* (2018), Andrew Hoskins offers a dystopian account of connectivity which is not dissimilar to Jean Baudrillard's apocalyptic vision of the first wave of digital media in the early 1980s. For Hoskins, digital interaction paradoxically results in disconnection: the "smart-portable-machine," for example, "has facilitated a swarm-like insistence in the placement of the machine between the self and the other or event. The act of recording has become more urgent than experiencing that which is being recorded."[10] Gothic discourse permeates Hoskins' ruminations on the end of collective memory: the digital mob struggles to escape its "shadow," hyperconnectivity is a "tyranny," recording "terrorizes" the present, "ensnaring" technology "chills all our futures" and the prospect of eternal digital memory "haunts" us.[11] Hoskins laments that we are now at the mercy of technologies "whose operations, algorithms, ownership and finitude of which we have little understanding."[12] He excoriates the digital "multitude" that arises out of this "compulsive connectivity," and which forms "the basis of a society without memory."[13] At the same time, one of the major concerns of the digital gothic is an overabundance of memory traces and our concomitant inability to control our digital legacies. While little is "seen" through the smartphone, Hoskins argues, "nothing escapes the archive."[14] Amanda Lagerkrist discusses the Web 2.0 Suicide Machine that "provides an automated service for erasure of content and contacts on social media sites."[15] This technology forms a counterpoint to phenomena such as the Superman Memory Crystal at the University of Southampton's Optoelectronics Research Centre, which is expected to hold data for a million years.[16] Connectivity produces an attendant desire for the erasure of what Hoskins terms the "deep glut" of our digital past: as Lagerkrist pithily observes, the Suicide Machine is a symptom of our fear that we "have lost loss itself."[17]

Hoskins and Lagerkrist offer perspicacious rejoinders to any proponent of digital culture who "one-sidedly celebrates the virtues of non-stop connectivity, limitless perpetuation and endless recording."[18] Indeed, Hoskins invites us to see beyond the myth of "digital media democratization," which he argues is resulting in "Society losing sight of itself . . . as it becomes more synchronized with its technologies."[19] For the novelist Will Self, this imbrication is particularly troubling due to a perceived link between the IBM machines working for the SS Race Office in the 1940s and current military hardware:

My view is that we're deluded if we think new technologies come into existence because of clearly defined human objectives—let alone benevolent ones—and it's this that should shape our response to them. No, the history of the 20th century—and now the 21st—is replete with examples of technologies that were developed purely in order to facilitate the killing of people at a distance, of which the internet is only the most egregious example. Our era is also replete with the mental illnesses occasioned by such technologies—sometimes I think our obsession with viewing violent and horrific imagery is some sort of collective post-traumatic stress disorder.[20]

Self's Ballardian response to the digital age forms the apotheosis of the digital gothic: connectivity benefits only perpetrators, so we all verge on madness, glutting on violent imagery in order to cope with our prosthetic facilitation of killing at a distance. Apple connotes *Appel* for an imagination that conceives of all tech companies as perpetrators akin to the omnivorous shark that devours all other forms of life in Dave Eggers' novel *The Circle* (2013).[21] Humans become the equivalent of the ingenious but fallible octopus in Eggers' allegorical tank that try and ultimately fail to hide from such inherently destructive technologies.

Hoskins nevertheless indicates a fissure in the digital gothic when he refers in *Digital Memory Studies* to the "opening up of new ways of finding, sorting, sifting, using, seeing [which] both imprisons and *liberates* active human remembering and forgetting."[22] The overwhelming dystopian vision of this book—which includes Kansteiner's critique of the holograms—needs to be tempered with the more productive elements of virtual Holocaust memory. Currently, the reordering of the past "by and through multiple connectivities of times, actors and events" can be a beneficent as well as a dystopian process.[23] The *Anne's Amsterdam* app (2017), for example, is not symptomatic of Hoskins's sense of a "swarm-like insistence in the placement of the machine between the self and the other": on the contrary, it enables an intense encounter with the presence of absence, as the pedestrian engages with the wartime history of Amsterdam's southern districts.[24] Similarly, the iPad application at Bergen-Belsen does not provide an insurmountable barrier between the technology, user, and experience, or an erasure of the "real"; nor is it an instance of the "institutionalized blockage of the past."[25] On the contrary, the institutionally funded application allows for a richer experience of the present landscape in Bergen-Belsen that might otherwise be understood by "butterfly" visitors as a nature park full of warbling yellowhammers.

Moreover, Dimensions in Testimony does not replicate a perpetrator perspective in an attempt to "quantify, modularize, distantiate, technify, and bureaucratize the subjective individuality of human experience."[26] In the Museum of Jewish Heritage, we experienced instead a new version of testimony in all its affective power and nascent complexity, along with its glitches: a question to Schloss about Amsterdam elicited a response about cabbage soup; an enquiry about Merwedeplein resulted in a short but affecting reply about the concept of love.[27] Kansteiner criticizes the institutional stranglehold on current digital technologies, yet it is precisely institutions such as the USC Shoah Foundation, the Anne Frank House and the Bergen-Belsen museum that are investing in alternatives to Hoskins's vision of the digital gothic. The "post-scarcity digital tsunami" may have "dumped a past of unimaginable scale on to a still unsuspecting present," but aspects of that atrocious past would not be salvageable without the new technologies we have discussed throughout this book.[28] The iPad application at Bergen-Belsen, for example, allows visitors to track the positions of demolished Nazi edifices by deploying Augmented Reality among the pastoral landscape.[29] This application's palimpsestic testimony does not result in the extermination of memory through a "counterfactual impetus"—as Henryk Broder argues in *Digital Memory Studies*—but an intensification of users' engagement with the former camp's topography as they read testimonial accounts and bookmark contemporaneous photographs.[30] Smartphone and iPad apps such as *Tangible Memories* (2018) created by Stand + Stare also allow the user to engage creatively with the landscape and history of former camps such as Bergen-Belsen. The authors of this book deployed *Tangible Memories* at this camp and Neuengamme in a variety of ways, returning with a series of photographs, short films, soundtracks, sound recordings, prose extracts and poems that responded to the minutiae of the topography, details in the exhibitions and the camps' architecture.

In *Digital Memory Studies*, Kansteiner approves of such individual memory work, and, in contrast, decries what he perceives as the generally tentative, uniform, or conservative institutional uses of digital technology. He refers to the "fleet of sterile, homogenous, and uninspiring digital platforms of Holocaust education," and the specific example of the "pious, intergenerational respect" surrounding Dimensions in Testimony.[31] It would be difficult to present the spooked responses to the holograms at the Museum of Jewish Heritage as symptomatic of "sterile" technology. Yet such institutional inflections in Kansteiner's latter comment certainly appertain to the digital film installations at Bergen-Belsen, which strive to offer a detailed, respectful, and "true" version of the former camp as is possible. As we have argued, this trajectory has resulted in a "cold" digital landscape that is as aesthetically neutral as possible, primarily because historians cannot agree whether the barracks were brown or gray. Yet the iPad application at the same site allows visitors to supplement their experience of the landscape with knowledge gleaned from the Augmented Reality. Rather than the application interfering with the visitors' " 'direct visual communication' with the 'real' Bergen-Belsen," empty vistas suddenly become haunted with the details of former guard towers; grass expanses reveal the site of a former kitchen or hospital via photographs, poems, and written testimony.[32] This interactive experience allows the visitor to tailor their visit to their own interests and concerns; yet these can only flourish, of course, among the finite capacities of a pre-programmed device. Nevertheless, this interaction between the visitor, iPad and vista still offers a different experience to the previous "top down" approach of the institution to visitors' understanding of the site. As such, the iPad application actually forms an example of the "more complex communication strategies" that Kansteiner calls for, which "transfer narrative and aesthetic agency from experts to visitors."[33]

Even so, Kansteiner still regrets that in Dimensions in Testimony's interaction between heritage professionals, software developers, schoolchildren, and Holocaust survivors, "the power remains concentrated in the hands of the representatives of the Shoah Foundation."[34] Yet interactive testimony forms a key example of connective memory that could offer a riposte to Hoskins's justified concerns about digital connectivity creating "a society without memory."[35] In one sense, this project responds to "the massive surge of interest" that began in the 1990s "in archiving and publishing survivor testimony in the form of video and oral histories as well as personal memoirs."[36] Understood in this context, new technologies need not be conceived as a radical break in memory studies, but as part of a familiar process of "reformulating, reformatting, recycling, returning and even remembering other media."[37] Nevertheless, after the digital "turn," this activity is now responding to the fact that "few other textual forms will have greater impact on the way we read, receive, search, access, use, and engage with the primary materials of humanities studies than the metadata structures that organize and present that knowledge in digital form."[38] This book thus addresses the increasing epistemological shift in representing the Holocaust primarily through digital technology rather than analog media. The interactive technology of Dimensions in Testimony does not intend to replace the real in an act of postmodernist erasure, simulating reality "without origin," but precisely wishes to facilitate the *activation* of the archive for a new generation of secondary witnesses who may not turn to the Holocaust in the future as the default example of genocide.[39] The Holocaust's "digital shadow" is not part of a gothic scenario in which "the immediate digital potential of recording terrorizes the experience of the present," but one which galvanizes the past in order to facilitate an encounter that, for some, will be fraught, troubling, and curtailed.[40] Yet this experience can also be vital, as the more intensive visitor interactions at the Museum of Jewish Heritage suggested. Moreover, if some users experience Dimensions of Testimony as a discombobulating encounter, then there may be ways in which the interactive technology can turn that affect to its advantage. Rather than trying to erase the distance between the past and present, the "haunting" formal aspects of interactive testimony—typified by the ghostly image on the cover of this book—may actually emphasize that we have a duty to allow the atrocious past to haunt the present. Interactive testimony has the potential to heighten our experience of the archive in the paradoxical world of the digital gothic, in which archives proliferate in an online world of incipient forgetting. Rather than trying to iron out its uncanny formal elements, a more self-conscious version of interactive testimony might choose to emphasize them as an enriching future element of virtual Holocaust memory.

Despite these possibilities, there is a danger that the digital might be replacing poststructuralism as the critical bogeyman in Holocaust studies, as was the case for the latter after the publication of Saul Friedländer's *Probing the Limits of Representation* (1992). As Claudio Fogu, Kansteiner, and Todd Presner argue in the subsequent volume *Probing the Ethics of Holocaust Culture* (2016), the "negative ethical implications of poststructuralism" have "largely played out in the academy," but—as Langer's response to Dimensions in Testimony indicates—the perceived threat of abstract theory may be replaced by traducing accounts of virtual Holocaust memory and its supposed threat to the "real."[41] However, if the forms and (sometimes) self-reflexive concerns of the latter are studied in detail, then literary critics or historians should not regard the advent of the digital as imperiling analog Holocaust memory. Indeed, this book has stressed the fruitful cross-disciplinary dialogue possible between literary studies and virtual Holocaust memory. Our analyses have emphasized that issues that have proven so important to literary texts such as Delbo's *Auschwitz and After* (1995) and its ensuing criticism, such as "truthfulness" and awkward poetics, are also of paramount importance to an understanding of the forms of virtual Holocaust memory. We have argued for the development of more self-conscious poetics into digital memory, as with Delbo's fractured, self-questioning and paratactic testimony.

In contrast, the lack of self-consciousness that Hoskins identifies in relation to connectivity grates not only against pre-millennial trauma theory, but also recent developments in historiography. As the editors of *Probing the Ethics of Holocaust Culture* argue, Saul Friedländer "strives to integrate [a] sense of failure and the corresponding feelings of unease into the very fabric of his historical narratives," an authorial strategy that derives from "a significant, independent tradition of Holocaust studies in philosophy, film, and literary studies that reaches all the way to the end of World War II and calls into question the reliability of method and stability of discipline."[42] Accordingly, in his response to Friedländer's work in this volume, Hayden White proposes that "the techniques of modernism, rather than outdated concepts of realism, might offer the necessary strategies for representing the reality of modernist events."[43] On the one hand, this statement is oddly prescriptive: why should early twentieth-century events be exclusively represented using the techniques of montage, defamiliarization, fragmentation, or dissonance? After all, critics such as Roger Luckhurst and Stef Craps have critiqued the teleology between traumatic events and formal modernisms.[44] Nevertheless, Freidländer's much lauded experiments in historiography, in which narratives interrupt and comment self-reflexively on their own coming into being, have certainly drawn on the techniques of modernism, as White points out. Yet these developments in historiography are still at a nascent stage in digital technologies. This process returns us to the specific etymology of the virtual: it is "that which is not yet but might be (or not), as well as that which might have been. It is the always-present potential" of digital technology.[45] We look forward to future instances of virtual Holocaust memory that call "into question the reliability of [their] method" and "stability" of their incumbent forms.[46] This trajectory is akin to the difference between the famous scene in *Bladerunner* (1982) that we discussed in the Introduction, in which the dying replicant recalls astonishing memories, and a mirror episode at the end of the first season of *Westworld*. In the latter, the host Dolores repeats pre-programmed comments on the path of her "life" as she "dies" in the arms of the ever-attentive Teddy: an audience comprising the park's management and illustrious visitors then claps as the robots freeze, and the moonlit beach is revealed to be a stage. *Bladerunner* and *Westworld* both explore technology's imbrication in exploitative tendencies, but their difference lies in an aesthetics of technology that eulogizes its potential form, and an approach that is more self-conscious about its current limitations.

Awkward poetics would also help to counteract the "coldness" and "flatness" of some examples of virtual Holocaust memory that we have not had space to discuss in this book. The *Auschwitz-Birkenau Virtual Tour* (2014) forms one instance of what Kansteiner might term a "sterile" digital environment.[47] On the one hand, the map provides a fascinating resource for orienting the user through the various topographies of Auschwitz-Birkenau. An initially bewildering mix of temporalities confronts the viewer in different parts of the camp: if the user selects the "Auschwitz II-Birkenau" tour in the Main Menu, they are confronted with the misty image entitled "Auschwitz II—Birkenau: Main Camp Gate" (see Fig. 7.1). In contrast, if they click the arrow in the gates to enter Birkenau, an evocative snowy vista appears. If the user then clicks the next forward arrow to "Camp Unloading Ramp," a sunny landscape at dawn or dusk greets the viewer, emptied of visitors. The user soon adjusts to these temporal dissonances, and the digital map certainly proves to be efficacious in its pedagogical uses. We were able to pinpoint metatextual locations to elucidate the work of writers quickly for lecture audiences: this process proved helpful for students who had not visited the camp, and could place the writings of, for example, Charlotte Delbo or Tadeusz Borowski within the digital application rather than the students' own devised, fictive settings. For example, the digital map is expedient in the context of *Auschwitz and After* (1985) in that it illustrates how, despite

Figure 7.1 Auschwitz-Birkenau Virtual Tour (2014)
© Auschwitz-Birkenau museum

the proximity of Block 25 to the camp's outer edge, Delbo rarely writes about views toward the outside of Birkenau; her emphasis is on the inner experience of the Women's Camp.

However, specific topographies in the camp were also experienced as "cold" digital sites in our experience of the digital map. Delbo's horrific depiction of Block 25 (see Fig. 7.2) in *Auschwitz and After* comprises an inner perdition in which the weakest inmates are taken to die alone alongside piles of corpses, or are corralled into lorries heading for the crematoria. She describes the "haystack of carefully piled corpses"—there is something utterly unnerving in the precision of that adverb—that places the inmates "on the borderline of the bearable."[48] The women spot Alice's wooden leg in the snow, "alive and sentient," and recall that she was "dying alone, not calling anyone."[49] Alongside the horrific testimonial detail, the liminality of the prosthetic that "must have detached itself from the dead Alice" reflects the "borderline" status of the women as they "struggle against letting go."[50] In turn, this liminality points to the traumatic aporia between the previous section of *Auschwitz and After*, "The Same Day," and the subsequent "Alice's Leg" chapter: the former ends with the sentence "The one who took the longest time to die was Alice," but this process is then described only obliquely through the prosthetic.[51] In contrast, the "flatness" of the digital map (see Fig. 7.2) portrays an unreadable site station that registers Block 25's historical veracity, but the user cannot (despite attempting to click the zoom button) get closer to examine the image of the infamous "Death Block."

Figure 7.2 Block 25
© Auschwitz-Birkenau Museum

Unlike the Secret Annex Online, in which extracts from Anne Frank's diary are set alongside contemporaneous photographs and historical information, testimony is here detached from its potential metatexts (and vice versa): the digital map risks showing us everything in Auschwitz-Birkenau, but nothing at the same time.[52] To put it bluntly, the map needs more content: hence our focus on palimpsestic testimony in this book, in which, for example, the historical and cultural metatexts surrounding the diary of Anne Frank intertwine in the Secret Annex Online in order to complement and enrich the user's experience.

Alongside digital maps, videogames form another example of virtual Holocaust memory that we have not had space to engage with in this book. There can be a dubious passivity in the pleasure of killing pantomime Nazis in games such as *Call of Duty: WWII* (2017) and the *Wolfenstein* series (1981–): will videogames ever be able to engage extensively with issues of empathy or vexed aesthetics? Or, put a different way, would such digital games actually ever wish to draw at length on cultural criticism? Or would they be willing to engage with our contention that the virtualization of killing is arguably just a more extreme manifestation of the same logic that led to the creation of the gas chambers, distancing perpetrators from their victims so that they do not see them, ultimately, as human beings? The controversy over perpetrator perspectives in videogames is crystallized in the media coverage surrounding *Cost of Freedom* in 2018. In the initial version of the game set in Auschwitz-Birkenau, players could choose to take the perspective of camp prisoners or the guards: after the ensuing controversy Dimitry Dybin decided to change the game's locale to "Antarctica, or just any snow-covered location."[53] According to the *Mirror*, representatives of The Auschwitz-Birkenau Museum and Memorial attacked the prospective game as "making entertainment out of human suffering." As Kansteiner notes, the denigration of exploitative aesthetics in such responses indicates that discussions about Holocaust impiety now tend to focus on digital games rather than other media such as film: "Transnationally generated arbitrary rules of piety and propriety determine, for instance, that the wildly popular genre of the video game is principally unsuited for the representation of the Shoah."[54]

In relation to videogames, it could be argued that the medium allows the user to immerse themselves, and experience and appreciate different identities in relation to historical events; and, potentially problematically, those of the perpetrator and bystander. Kansteiner claims more broadly that VR and immersion are troublingly rooted in the history of perpetrator politics, since "for several generations, immersion was identical with fascist culture."[55] He argues that submersion in Nazi culture resulted in a horrifyingly destructive form of political consensus. The difficult task for videogames in the future will be to turn to Holocaust perpetrators at the same time as grasping and exposing the games' complicity with perpetrator logic. VR, videogames, and digital memory projects more widely will need to transform the ambivalence of their affect into something that is more ethically and politically self-aware, something that is more troubled and troubling. In this context, Primo Levi's retort comes to mind when he was asked about his own potential for perpetrator behavior: "I do not know, and it does not much interest me to know, whether in my depths there lurks a murderer."[56] Levi was not concerned about any latent "evil" inside his mind: to him, it made no difference to the more patent and important distinctions between the Nazis and their victims. Michael Richardson argues differently in relation to the digital that within everyone, "virtually, resides the potential not only for becoming-tortured but becoming-torturer."[57] Following Levi's response, however, what would we gain by exploring this possibility through virtual Holocaust memory, as opposed to Michael Rothberg's more nuanced concept of implicated subjects? Games designers will need to be acutely sensitive and self-reflexive in their formal responses to this question if we are to reach beyond the pat response that we are all at some level harboring or—in Richardson's Deleuzeian terms—"becoming-to-harbour" perpetrator thoughts.[58] The more interesting question that such designers might explore is: what are the conditions and thought processes that allow individuals *not* to turn into perpetrators?

In the future, will it be possible to integrate such self-critical modes of representation into virtual Holocaust memory as a resistance to uninhibited, commodified, and unreflective connectivity? This book has been in this sense a response to Hoskins's conception of the "restless past" and the risks—addressed in this question—of losing testimony and history among the burgeoning realms of the digital age. These dangers form an integral part of the digital gothic, in which traces of recent historical events proliferate endlessly yet fail to replicate written testimony's formal complexities and affective power. For Hoskins, the central paradox of the digital gothic is that an incipient forgetfulness inheres in its connectivity. We have thus stressed the need to document and analyze the early forms of virtual Holocaust memory before they disappear without trace, such as the first VR film of the Anne Frank House and the taxing *Anne's Amsterdam* app which has now been deleted from the App Store. The "modularity" of virtual Holocaust memory allows for swift obsolescence or edits and updates through flexible software; in contrast, Kansteiner refers to the "dinosaur" of analog Holocaust memory.[59] As we have outlined in this book, such examples of nascent digital memory have been dismissed as crazy gimmicks by critics such as Langer or returned to the familiar binary within which "authentic" (traditional) History triumphs against yet another duplicitous manifestation of memorialization. Yet if placed in a dialectical relationship to the "truthfulness" of ethical memory work from the past, virtual Holocaust memory could prove to be the most successful way in which to respond to Susan Gubar's sense that "the Holocaust is dying."[60] The potential of virtual Holocaust memory will only be realized once the artists and designers of the virtual inscribe self-reflective issues such as aesthetic gratification into digital forms. With *Maus* (1980), Art Spiegelman proved that it is possible to infuse comics with reflexivity and revitalize a popular form that many would have deemed unsuitable for the challenges of Holocaust representation. Virtual Holocaust memory requires its Spiegelman to explore fully the ramifications of its own forms, rather than trying to erase the processes of its own coming into being.

Notes

Epigraph

1. Thomas Frick, "J. G. Ballard, The Art of Fiction No. 85," *The Paris Review* 94, Winter 1984, https://www.theparisreview.org/interviews/2929/j-g-ballard-the-art-of-fiction-no-85-j-g-ballard (accessed August 16, 2018).
2. Charlotte Delbo, *Auschwitz and After*, trans. Rosette C. Lamont (New Haven, CT: Yale University Press, 1995), 1.

Introduction

1. Paul Virilio, *The Administration of Fear*, trans. Ames Hodges (Los Angeles: Semiotext(e), 2012), 35, 33.
2. See Imperial War Museum, "7 Cameras Used to Film War," June 27, 2018, https://www.iwm.org.uk/history/7-cameras-used-to-film-war (accessed June 23, 2020).
3. See Zygmunt Bauman, *Liquid Modernity* (Cambridge: Polity Press, 2000).
4. Wulf Kansteiner, "Genocide Memory, Digital Cultures, and the Aestheticization of Violence," *Memory Studies* 7, no. 4 (2014): 403–408 (403).
5. See Saul Friedländer, ed., *Probing the Limits of Representation: Nazism and the "Final Solution"* (Cambridge, MA: Harvard University Press, 1992); Claudio Fogu, Wulf Kansteiner, and Todd Presner, eds., *Probing the Ethics of Holocaust Culture* (Cambridge, MA: Harvard University Press, 2016).
6. USC Shoah Foundation, "New Dimensions in Testimony," publicity leaflet, January 6, 2016.
7. Marianne Hirsch, "Holocaust Testimony Beyond the Frame," *Los Angeles Review of Books*, May 23, 2020, https://lareviewofbooks.org/article/holocaust-testimony-beyond-the-frame (accessed May 26, 2020).
8. Mitchell's photograph went viral one month after it had been posted on Twitter, thanks to a *Business Insider* article that triggered significant online coverage. However, it soon emerged that the selfie had been taken one year after the death of Mitchell's father, and that the trip to Auschwitz constituted something of a personal pilgrimage for the eighteen-year-old. Mitchell's mother noted that "the two had spent a lot of time studying history together, and the Holocaust was the last thing they covered before his death." With a backstory that complicated the initial media outrage, the controversy ultimately generated a more considered public debate about the appropriateness of taking selfies at sites of mass atrocity, with articles in

publications such as *The Washington Post* drawing on a range of sources, from clinical psychologists to the relatives of Holocaust survivors, in their explorations of a complex phenomenon. Caitlin Dewey, "The Other Side of the Infamous 'Auschwitz Selfie,'" *Washington Post*, July 22, 2014, https://www.washingtonpost.com/news/the-intersect/wp/2014/07/22/the-other-side-of-the-infamous-auschwitz-selfie/?utm_term=.20d35073c979 (accessed December 19, 2018). See also Ruth Margalit's earlier piece, "Should Auschwitz Be a Site for Selfies?," *New Yorker*, June 26, 2014, https://www.newyorker.com/culture/culture-desk/should-auschwitz-be-a-site-for-selfies (accessed December 19, 2018).

9. See https://yolocaust.de/. The Berlin memorial was designed by the architect Peter Eisenman and is located on a 19,000 m^2 site in the center of Berlin, near the Brandenburg Gate and the Reichstag. The undulating site is covered with 2,711 concrete pillars or "stelae" that are arranged in a grid pattern. Punning on the acronym YOLO, standing for "you only live once," Shapira argues that his satirical project was an "exploration of commemorative culture"; yet it was clearly also a condemnation of forms of engagement with the memorial that Shapira judged to be insensitive and inappropriate. The Yolocaust site was taken down once all twelve of its selfie-takers expressed remorse to Shapira and asked for their images to be removed. However, there is nothing about the physical memorial that obviously equates the pillars with the dead bodies of Holocaust victims, in the manner that Shapira's project suggests. The memorial offers an abstract space for historical reflection, rather than a literal symbolic schema or even a scared space for Jewish memory. Eisenman has said that he wanted visitors to behave freely at the site, and a visit to the memorial during daytime is not wholly sombre; visitors experience moments of submersion and darkness, but also relief and light, with children playing between the pillars and families picnicking on its fringes. Indeed, at this memorial, a reassertion of life—which might include taking photographs and posting them on social media—is an important part of the riposte to mass death. See DW, "Play Time at the Holocaust Memorial," May 13, 2005, https://www.dw.com/en/play-time-at-the-holocaust-memorial/a-1582335 (accessed February 20, 2019).

10. Geoffrey Hartman, *The Longest Shadow: In the Aftermath of the Holocaust* (Basingstoke: Palgrave Macmillan, 2002), 12.

11. Sean F. Johnston, *Holograms: A Cultural History* (New York: Oxford University Press, 2015), 160.

12. Dan Chiasson, "'2001: A Space Odyssey': What It Means, and How It Was Made," *New Yorker*, April 16, 2018, https://www.newyorker.com/magazine/2018/04/23/2001-a-space-odyssey-what-it-means-and-how-it-was-made (accessed June 13, 2020).

13. Jean Baudrillard, *Simulacra and Simulation*, trans. Sheila Glaser (Ann Arbor, MI: University of Michigan Press, 1995), 79, 161.

14. Mark Rowlands, *The Philosopher at the End of the Universe: Philosophy Explained Through Science Fiction Films* (New York: Thomas Dunne Books, 2003), 234–235.

15. Jeffrey Shandler's study, *Holocaust Memory in the Digital Age: Survivors' Stories and New Media Practices* (Stanford, CA: Stanford University Press, 2017) offers a

comprehensive account of the ways in which this archive has been brought into the digital age.

16. USC Shoah Foundation, "Preserving the Visual History Archive," https://sfi.usc.edu/vha/preservation (accessed December 5, 2018).

17. USC Shoah Foundation, "Saving Every Testimony," May 28, 2013, https://sfi.usc.edu/news/2013/05/saving-every-testimony (accessed December 5, 2018).

18. Todd Presner, "The Ethics of the Algorithm: Close and Distant Listening to the Shoah Foundation Visual History Archive," in Fogu, Kansteiner and Presner, *Probing*, 175–204 (188).

19. Ibid., 189.

20. USC Shoah Foundation, "First Ever Holocaust Survivor Testimony in Room-scale Virtual Reality to World Premiere at 2017 Tribeca Film Festival," March 13, 2017, https://sfi.usc.edu/news/2017/03/13481-first-ever-holocaust-survivor-testimony-room-scale-virtual-reality-world-premiere (accessed December 6, 2018).

21. Marc Cieslak, "Virtual Reality to Aid Auschwitz War Trials of Concentration Camp Guards," *BBC*, November 20, 2016, https://www.bbc.co.uk/news/technology-38026 007 (accessed December 6, 2018).

22. Philip K. Dick, *Do Androids Dream of Electric Sheep?* (London: Gollancz, 1999), 16.

23. Ibid., 17, 16, 18.

24. Ibid., 24, 59.

25. Chris Milk, "How Virtual Reality Can Create the Ultimate Empathy Machine," March 2015, https://www.ted.com/talks/chris_milk_how_virtual_reality_can_create_the_ultimate_empathy_machine/transcript?language=en (accessed December 6, 2018).

26. USC Shoah Foundation, *The Last Goodbye* press release, "First-ever Holocaust Survivor Testimonial in Room-scale VR, For Archival and Preservation, The Last Goodbye, to World Premiere at Tribeca Film Festival," March 10, 2017, 2–3.

27. USC Shoah Foundation, https://sfi.usc.edu/ (accessed December 6, 2018).

28. United Nations Virtual Reality, http://unvr.sdgactioncampaign.org/vr-films/ (accessed December 6, 2018).

29. Ben Tarnoff, "Empathy—the Latest Gadget Silicon Valley Wants to Sell You," *Guardian*, October 25, 2017, https://www.theguardian.com/technology/2017/oct/25/empathy-virtual-reality-facebook-mark-zuckerberg-puerto-rico> (accessed December 12, 2018).

30. UN Web TV, "70th Anniversary of the Genocide Convention," December 7, 2018, http://webtv.un.org/watch/70th-anniversary-of-the-genocide-convention/597691 9997001 (accessed December 10, 2018).

31. James Dawes, *Evil Men* (Cambridge, MA: Harvard University Press, 2013), 209.

32. Nate Freeman, "A History of Violence: Jordan Wolfson on His Shocking Foray into VR at the Whitney Biennial," *ARTnews*, January 3, 2017, https://www.artnews.com/art-news/artists/a-history-of-violence-jordan-wolfson-on-his-shocking-foray-into-vr-at-the-whitney-biennial-7856/ (accessed December 12, 2018).

33. Michael Rothberg, *The Implicated Subject: Beyond Victims and Perpetrators* (Stanford, CA: Stanford University Press, 2019), 1.

34. Dawes, *Evil*, 210.

35. Carolyn J. Dean, "The Politics of Suffering: from the Survivor-Witness to Humanitarian Witnessing," *Continuum* 31, no. 5 (New York: Routledge, 2017), 628–636 (628).

36. See Victoria Grace Walden, "What Is 'Virtual Holocaust Memory?'" *Memory Studies* 15, no. 4 (2019), OnlineFirst, https://journals.sagepub.com/doi/10.1177/175069801 9888712 (accessed June 12, 2020). In an essay that takes Matthew Boswell's 2015 Arts and Humanities Research Council-funded project "Virtual Holocaust Memory: From Testimony to Holography" as its start point, Walden offers a nuanced answer to this question. Arguing that the word "virtual" is not synonymous with "digital"—a point with which we concur—Walden defines virtual Holocaust memory as an embodied, collaborative form of memory practice that is materialized in both digital and non-digital forms. The very particular experience of Holocaust memory that she identifies can stem from engaging with ruins, photography, and film, as much as with AR apps and digital exhibitions. However, we would argue that contemporary usage means that the word "virtual" has become entangled with digital technologies to such a degree that its meaning will never be reducible to the specific conceptualization of memory that Walden develops by way of Henri Bergson and Gilles Deleuze, whose use of the "virtual" bears no connection with digital technologies for obvious historical reasons. Nonetheless, we share Walden's appreciation of Holocaust memory projects that engage with the past in a critical, self-reflexive fashion.

37. United States Holocaust Memorial Museum, "Introduction to the Holocaust," https://encyclopedia.ushmm.org/content/en/article/introduction-to-the-holocaust (accessed May 1, 2020).

38. Michael Rothberg, *Multidirectional Memory: Remembering the Holocaust in the Age of Decolonization* (Stanford, CA: Stanford University Press, 2009), 3.

39. Ibid., 4.

40. Paul Meincke, "Technology Tells Survivors' Stories at Illinois Holocaust Museum," *Abc7chicago.com*, April 30, 2017, http://abc7chicago.com/education/technology-tells-survivors-stories-at-illinois-holocaust-museum/1938500/ (accessed February 22, 2019).

41. Rothberg, *Multidirectional*, 4.

42. See Alison Landsberg, *Prosthetic Memory: The Transformation of American Remembrance in the Age of Mas Culture* (New York: Columbia University Press, 2004).

43. Steve Goodman and Luciana Parisi, "Machines of Memory," in Susannah Radstone and Bill Schwarz, eds., *Memory: Histories, Theories, Debates* (New York: Fordham University Press, 2010), 343–59 (344).

44. Michel Foucault, "Of Other Spaces: Utopias and Heterotropias," trans. Jay Miskowiec, *Architecture/Mouvement/Continuité* (October 1984): 1–9 (4).

45. Andreas Huyssen, *Present Pasts: Urban Palimpsests and the Politics of Memory* (Stanford, CA: Stanford University Press, 2003), 28.

46. Marc Redfield, *The Rhetoric of Terror: Reflections on 9/11 and the War on Terror* (New York: Fordham University Press, 2009), 2.

47. Ibid., 2.

48. Ibid., 3

49. Ibid., 1.

50. Ibid., 3.

51. Alexander Etkind, "Post-Soviet Hauntology: Cultural Memory of the Soviet Terror," *Constellations* 16, no. 1 (Oxford: Blackwell, 2009), 182–200 (182).

52. Alison Landsberg, *Engaging the Past: Mass Culture and the Production of Historical Knowledge* (New York: Columbia University Press, 2015), 20.

53. Ibid., 3.

54. Dominick LaCapra, *History in Transit: Experience, Identity, Critical Theory* (Ithaca, NY: Cornell University Press, 2004), 125.

55. Ibid., 125.

56. Theodor Adorno, "Cultural Criticism and Society," in *Prisms*, trans. Samuel and Shierry Weber (Cambridge, MA: The MIT Press, 1983), 17–34 (34); Adorno, "Commitment," trans. Francis McDonagh, in Ronald Taylor ed., *Aesthetics and Politics* (London: N.L.B., 1977), 177–195 (188); Antony Rowland, *Holocaust Poetry: Awkward Poetics in the Work of Sylvia Plath, Geoffrey Hill, Tony Harrison and Ted Hughes* (Edinburgh: Edinburgh University Press, 2005).

57. Linda Hutcheon, *A Poetics of Postmodernism: History, Theory, Fiction* (London: Routledge, 1992), 14.

58. Annette Wieviorka, *The Era of the Witness*, trans. Jared Stark (Ithaca, NY: Cornell University Press, 2006).

59. Charlotte Delbo, *Auschwitz and After*, trans. Rosette C. Lamont (New Haven, CT: Yale University Press, 1995), 1. In their essay "The Witness in the Archive: Holocaust Studies/ Memory Studies," Marianne Hirsch and Leo Spitzer explore the different uses and translations of this epigram in Delbo's work.

"Aujourd'hui, je ne suis pas sûre que ce que j'ai écrit soit vrai. Je suis sûre que c'est véridique," writes Charlotte Delbo in the epigram to *Aucun de nous ne reviendra* (*None of Us Will Return*), the first part of her memoir, *Auschwitz et après* (*Auschwitz and After*). It is a phrase she will repeat and use again in another work, *La mémoire et les jours* (*Days and Memory*). But her English translator, Rosette Lamont, translates the sentence differently in the two volumes: "Today, I am not sure that what I wrote is true. I am certain it is truthful" (*None of Us Will Return*), and "This is why I say today that while knowing perfectly well that it corresponds to the facts, I no longer know if it is real" (*Days and Memory*).

Marianne Hirsch and Leo Spitzer, "The Witness in the Archive: Holocaust Studies/ Memory Studies," in Radstone and Schwarz, *Memory*, 390–405 (399).

60. Ibid., 399.

61. Bernard Williams, *Truth and Truthfulness: An Essay in Genealogy* (Princeton, NJ: Princeton University Press, 2002), 20.

62. Baudrillard, *Simulacra*, 3.

63. L. P. Hartley, *The Go-Between* (London: Penguin, 2000), 5.

64. Primo Levi, *The Drowned and the Saved*, trans. Raymond Rosenthal (London: Abacus, 1996), 128.

65. David Walsh, "'They Are No Longer Numbers or Statistics': How Colour Pictures Are Bringing Auschwitz to Life," *Euronews*, January 28, 2020, https://www.euronews.

com/2020/01/28/they-are-no-longer-numbers-or-statistics-how-colour-pictures-are-bringing-auschwitz-to-li# (accessed May 13, 2020).

66. Ibid.

67. Saul Friedländer, "Introduction," in Friedländer, *Probing*, 3.

68. Ibid.

69. Ibid., 17.

70. Andrew Hoskins, "Media, Memory, Metaphor: Remembering and the Connective Turn," "Transcultural Memory" *Parallax* 17, no. 4 (2011): 19–31. See also Andrew Hoskins, "7/7 and Connective Memory: Interactional Trajectories of Remembering in Post-scarcity Culture," *Memory Studies* 4, no. 3 (2011): 269–280.

71. Landsberg, *Engaging*, 18.

72. Ibid., 19.

73. "Doc/Fest Exchange: Digging Deeper into New Dimensions in Testimony," September 14, 2016, https://www.youtube.com/watch?v=ybBkpfV3Ot0> (accessed February 22, 2019).

74. Matthew Boswell and Antony Rowland, interview with Danny Abrahms, Los Angeles (November 7, 2016).

75. Wulf Kansteiner, "The Holocaust in the 21st Century: Digital Anxiety, Transnational Cosmopolitanism, and Never Again Genocide Without Memory," in Andrew Hoskins, ed., *Digital Memory Studies: Media Pasts in Transition* (New York: Routledge, 2018), 110–140 (129).

76. At the height of the upsurge in Holocaust consciousness during the mid-1990s, Peter Novick was a vocal critic of those who sought to excavate genocide for uplifting messages, memorably doubting that the Holocaust contained the kind of inspirational "lessons" that might "fit on a bumper sticker." Peter Novick, *The Holocaust in American Life* (New York: Houghton Mifflin Company, 1999), 262.

77. Mariana Mazzucato, "Capitalism's Triple Crisis," *Project Syndicate*, March 30, 2020, https://www.project-syndicate.org/commentary/covid19-crises-of-capitalism-new-state-role-by-mariana-mazzucato-2020-03 (accessed May 15, 2020). Mazzucato notes that capitalism is facing "at least three major crises." In a world beset by global poverty and structural inequality, more could be added to Mazzucato's list.

78. Claims Conference, "New Survey by Claims Conference Finds Significant Lack of Holocaust Knowledge in the United States," http://www.claimscon.org/study/ (accessed December 6, 2018); Richard Allen Greene, "A Shadow Over Europe," *CNN* https://edition.cnn.com/interactive/2018/11/europe/antisemitism-poll-2018-intl/ (accessed December 6, 2018).

79. Christopher R. Browning, "The Suffocation of Democracy," in *The New York Review of Books*, October 25, 2018, https://www.nybooks.com/articles/2018/10/25/suffocation-of-democracy/?fbclid=IwAR1-N6xHBCenqxOUBrNPLd4OlyKM38QkCmJWr pU5KnIv-CiP-QoHsKNGoyQ (accessed January 15, 2019).

80. Timothy Snyder, *Black Earth: The Holocaust as History and Warning* (New York: Tim Duggan Books, 2015).

81. Timothy Snyder, "The American Abyss," in *The New York Times Magazine*, January 9, 2021, https://www.nytimes.com/2021/01/09/magazine/trump-coup.html (accessed January 22, 2021).

82. Ibid.

83. Ibid. Snyder also identifies key areas where Trump fell short of outright fascism. These include his lack of a clear ideology (beyond his own personal self-interest), his alienation of the military leadership, and the "small and ludicrous" nature of his secret police.

84. Ibid.

85. See Jonathan Dunnage, "Editorial: Perpetrator Memory and Memories about Perpetrators," *Memory Studies* 3, no. 22 (2010): 91–94; Richard Crownshaw, "Perpetrator Fictions and Transcultural Memory," *Parallax* 17, no. 4 (2011): 75–89; Jenni Adams and Sue Vice, *Representing Perpetrators in Holocaust Literature and Film* (London: Vallentine Mitchell, 2013).

86. Claude Lanzmann, "Hier ist kein Warum," in Stuart Liebman, ed., *Claude Lanzmann's Shoah: Key Essays* (Oxford: Oxford University Press, 2007), 51–52 (51).

87. Christopher R. Browning, *Ordinary Men: Reserve Police Battalion 101 and the Final Solution in Poland* (London: Penguin, 2001), xviii.

88. Gillian Rose, *Mourning Becomes the Law: Philosophy and Representation* (Cambridge: Cambridge University Press, 1997), 46.

89. Ibid., 54.

90. Matthew Boswell, *Holocaust Impiety in Literature, Popular Music and Film* (Basingstoke: Palgrave Macmillan, 2012).

91. Zygmunt Bauman, *Modernity and the Holocaust* (Cambridge: Polity Press, 2000), 9. See Edwin Black, *IBM and the Holocaust: The Strategic Alliance Between Nazi Germany and America's Most Powerful Corporation* (Washington, D.C.: Dialog Press, 2009).

92. USC Institute for Creative Technologies, "Bravemind: Virtual Reality Exposure Therapy," http://ict.usc.edu/prototypes/pts/ (accessed March 1, 2019).

Chapter 1

1. The story of Schloss's Dimensions in Testimony interview is the subject of a short film which featured in *The New York Times* Op-Docs series. See Davina Pardo, "116 Cameras," *The New York Times*, September 19, 2017, https://www.nytimes.com/2017/09/19/opinion/the-remembering-machine.html (accessed February 2, 2018).

2. We use the terms "interactive testimony" and "interactive video testimony" rather than "interactive biography" (the USC Shoah Foundation's preferred term), as they better capture the scope of survivor interviews that go far beyond the autobiographical narration of an individual life story. We use Dimensions in Testimony rather than the original New Dimensions in Testimony as the project name, though confess to preferring the confidence and semantic clarity of the latter.

3. USC Shoah Foundation, "Dimensions in Testimony," https://sfi.usc.edu/dit (accessed July 5, 2019).

4. By July 2019, Dimensions in Testimony had been placed on permanent display at Holocaust Museum Houston and CANDLES Holocaust Museum and Education Center in Indiana. The Mandarin-language interactive testimony of Xia Shuqin went on permanent display at the Nanjing Massacre Memorial Hall in China in December 2017 to mark the 80th anniversary of the Nanjing Massacre.

5. Geoffrey Hartman, *The Longest Shadow: In the Aftermath of the Holocaust* (Basingstoke: Palgrave Macmillan, 2002), 143.

6. Ibid., 143.

7. Cofounded by Dr Stephen Smith before he became Executive Director of the USC Shoah Foundation, the National Holocaust Centre and Museum has embraced digital technology through projects such as the Virtual Journey, which will engage schoolchildren with a story about the Kindertransport through a digital experience that can be accessed in the classroom. Whilst the Forever Project uses similar technologies to Dimensions in Testimony, the survivor testimonies were not recorded in 360-degrees, meaning that the interactive recordings cannot be projected as three-dimensional holograms that you can walk around and view from any angle. Instead, a three-dimensional effect is created when viewers watch the Forever Project interviews on a screen using special glasses.

8. Thomas McMullan, "The Virtual Holocaust Survivor: How History Gained New Dimensions," *The Guardian*, June 18, 2016, https://www.theguardian.com/technol ogy/2016/jun/18/holocaust-survivor-hologram-pinchas-gutter-new-dimensions-history (accessed June 20, 2016).

9. McMullan, "The Virtual."

10. Primo Levi, *The Drowned and the Saved*, trans. Raymond Rosenthal (London: Abacus, 1996), 11–12.

11. Karen A. Kim, "New Dimensions in Testimony: Findings from the Student Pilots," August 2015, iii.

12. USC Shoah Foundation, "New Dimensions in Testimony," publicity leaflet, January 6, 2016.

13. UN Web TV, "70th Anniversary of the Genocide Convention," December 7, 2018, http://webtv.un.org/watch/70th-anniversary-of-the-genocide-convention/597691 9997001 (accessed December 10, 2018).

14. Jennifer Billock, "12 Must-See Fall Exhibits Around the World," *Smithsonian.com*, September 14, 2017, https://www.smithsonianmag.com/travel/12-must-see-fall-exhibits-180964834/ (accessed July 17, 2018).

15. USC Shoah Foundation, "New Dimensions in Testimony," publicity leaflet, January 6, 2016.

16. USC Shoah Foundation, "Dimensions in Testimony," https://sfi.usc.edu/collections/holocaust/ndt (accessed November 28, 2018).

17. Britta Lokting, "Meet the World's First 3-D Interactive Holocaust Survivor," *The Forward*, November 24, 2015, http://forward.com/culture/324989/meet-the-worlds-first-3-d-interactive-holocaust-survivor/ (accessed January 22, 2016) .

18. Ibid.

19. Lokting, "Meet," *Forward*. This sweeping, apocalyptic mistrust of technology also marks Langer's landmark study of the Fortunoff Video Archive, *Holocaust Testimonies* (1991), in which he worries that testimonies are in part "doomed . . . by the vicissitudes of technology." In his opening acknowledgements, Langer confesses that his son even had to go to great lengths to persuade him to make use of a new word processor he had bought him as a gift. Lawrence L. Langer, *Holocaust Testimonies: The Ruins of Memory* (New Haven, CT: Yale University Press, 1991), xi and xix.

20. Marianne Hirsch, "Holocaust Testimony Beyond the Frame," *Los Angeles Review of Books*, May 23, 2020, https://lareviewofbooks.org/article/holocaust-testimony-beyond-the-frame (accessed May 26, 2020).

21. Ibid.

22. Ibid.

23. Hartman, *Longest*, 7.

24. Andreas Huyssen, *Present Pasts: Urban Palimpsests and the Politics of Memory* (Stanford, CA: Stanford University Press, 2003), 28.

25. Thomas Frick, "J. G. Ballard, The Art of Fiction No. 85," *The Paris Review* 94, Winter 1984, https://www.theparisreview.org/interviews/2929/j-g-ballard-the-art-of-fiction-no-85-j-g-ballard (accessed August 16, 2018).

26. USC Shoah Foundation, "New Dimensions in Testimony," publicity leaflet, January 6, 2016.

27. USC Shoah Foundation, "New Dimensions in Testimony on NPR," December 20, 2017, https://sfi.usc.edu/news/2017/12/20656-new-dimensions-testimony-npr (accessed July 18, 2018).

28. Ibid.

29. During the pilot at the USHMM in 2016, a member of staff noted that they would not have wanted to use a three-dimensional version even if it had been available, as they did not want the technology to be foregrounded so overtly. More in keeping with the changing technological habits of contemporary society, the two-dimensional version worked because people of all ages have become increasingly comfortable with screen-based interactions, such as Skype and Zoom conversations. The high costs of the bespoke spaces and technologies required to project a fully three-dimensional version may also have been prohibitive.

30. See, for example, Illinois Holocaust Museum & Education Center, "Holocaust Survivors Tell Their Stories Through Interactive 3D Holograms," https://www.youtube.com/watch?v=BbjskSGiqWI&feature=emb_logo (accessed May 23, 2020).

31. Digital Trends, "New Dimensions in Testimony Preserves Holocaust Survivors [*sic*] Stories as Holograms," https://www.youtube.com/watch?v=w83pe-0noUU (accessed August 3, 2018).

32. Sean F. Johnston, *Holograms: A Cultural History* (New York: Oxford University Press, 2015), 202.

33. Ibid., 222.

34. Ibid., 223.

35. This historical reference is made even more explicit in recent sequels and spin-offs. In *Star Wars: Episode VII—The Force Awakens* (2015), for example, rows of storm troopers stand on a vast rollcall square and give the Hitler salute at the climax of a speech by the megalomaniac leader of the First Order. With echoes of the "final solution," in *Star Wars: Episode IX—The Rise of Skywalker* (2019), Emperor Palpatine unveils a fleet of Star Destroyers called the Final Order which are each equipped with weaponry designed to annihilate planets. Similarly, a short scene in *Rogue One: A Star Wars Story* (2016) is set in an "imperial labour camp" called Wobani.

36. Johnston, *Holograms*, 195. Holograms with a flickering, bluish appearance have become a hallmark of the *Star Wars* films, featuring throughout the original trilogy and in the more recent prequels and spin-offs. These include *Rogue One*, in which the protagonist, Jyn Erso, retrieves a holographic message from her father, the scientist Galen Erso, with echoes of Leia's original message. In Erso's message, he tells his daughter how to locate a flaw that he has deliberately built into the Death Star. *Rogue One* is also notable for its use of computer-generated versions of Leia (originally played by Carrie Fisher, who died in 2016) and Grand Moff Tarkin (the commander of the Death Star, originally played by Peter Cushing, who died in 1994). The computer-generated versions of characters as they appeared in *Star Wars: Episode IV—A New Hope* in 1977 feature alongside new characters played by living actors to make a visually coherent prequel to the earlier film.

37. Bill Slavicsek, *A Guide to the Star Wars Universe* (New York: Ballantine Books, 1994), 47.

38. The only word spoken by the digital recreation of Leia in *Rogue One*, which is also the film's closing line, is "hope."

39. Johnston, *Holograms*, 213.

40. Jean Baudrillard, *The Intelligence of Evil or the Lucidity Pact*, trans. Chris Turner (Oxford: Berg, 2004), 17–19.

41. Jean Baudrillard, *Simulacrum and Simulation*, trans. Seila Faria Glaser (Ann Arbor, MI: The University of Michigan Press, 1994), 108.

42. Ibid., 108.

43. Claudio Fogu, Wulf Kansteiner, and Todd Presner, eds., *Probing the Ethics of Holocaust Culture* (Cambridge, MA: Harvard University Press, 2016), 2.

44. Hartman, *Longest*, 142.

45. Shoshana Felman and Dori Laub, *Testimony: Crises of Witnessing in Literature, Psychoanalysis and History* (Abingdon: Routledge, 1992), 60.

46. Charlotte Delbo, *Auschwitz and After*, trans. Rosette C. Lamont (New Haven, CT: Yale University Press, 1995), 1.

47. Friedrich Nietzsche, *Beyond Good and Evil: Prelude to a Philosophy of the Future*, trans. R. J. Hollingdale (Harmondsworth: Penguin, 1990 [1886]), 33.

48. Robert Eaglestone, *The Holocaust and the Postmodern* (Oxford: Oxford University Press, 2004), 7.

49. Vivian M. Patraka, *Spectacular Suffering: Theatre, Fascism and the Holocaust* (Bloomington, IN: Indiana University Press, 1999), 6.

50. Ibid., 121.

51. Ibid., 6–7.

52. Saul Friedländer, "Introduction," in Saul Friedländer, ed., *Probing the Limits of Representation: Nazism and the "Final Solution"* (Cambridge, MA: Harvard University Press, 1992), 17.

Chapter 2

1. Peter Novick, *The Holocaust in American Life* (New York, NY: Houghton Mifflin, 1999), 146, 6.

2. Edward T. Linenthal, *Preserving Memory: The Struggle to Create America's Holocaust Museum* (New York, NY: Columbia University Press, 2001), 44–45, 255.

3. Ibid., 44–45.

4. Ibid., 65.

5. Novick, *Holocaust*, 235.

6. Vivian M. Patraka, *Spectacular Suffering: Theatre, Fascism and the Holocaust* (Bloomington, IN: Indiana University Press, 1999), 112.

7. Linenthal, *Preserving*, xiii.

8. Patraka, *Spectacular*, 128–129.

9. For a comprehensive overview of the political backdrop to Carter's decision and the formation of the commission, see Linenthal, *Preserving*, 17–56.

10. Novick, *Holocaust*, 201.

11. Ibid., 199.

12. USC Shoah Foundation, "New Dimensions in Testimony," USHMM flyer, 2016.

13. Thomas McMullan, "The Virtual Holocaust Survivor: How History Gained New Dimensions," *The Guardian*, June 18, 2016, https://www.theguardian.com/technology/2016/jun/18/holocaust-survivor-hologram-pinchas-gutter-new-dimensions-history (accessed June 20, 2016).

14. Wulf Kansteiner, "Genocide Memory, Digital Cultures, and the Aestheticization of Violence," *Memory Studies* 7, no. 4, (2014): 403–408 (404).

15. Jeffrey Shandler, *Holocaust Memory in the Digital Age: Survivors' Stories and New Media Practices* (Stanford, CA: Stanford University Press, 2017), 172.

16. Hartman, *Longest*, 142.

17. Walter Benjamin, "The Work of Art in the Age of Mechanical Reproduction," *Illuminations*, trans. Harry Zohn (New York: Schocken Books, 2007), 221.

18. National Holocaust Centre and Museum, "The Forever Project," https://vimeo.com/169833468 (accessed November 8, 2017).

19. Novick, *Holocaust*, 11.

20. Carolyn J. Dean, "The Politics of Suffering: From the Survivor-witness to Humanitarian Witnessing," *Continuum* 31, no. 5 (2017), 628–636 (631).

21. Ibid., 631. Roger Luckhurst notes that survivors came to hold a similarly elevated moral status in the work of historians such as Robert Jay Lifton in the 1970s:

> The survivor is explicitly regarded as a prophet or visionary because they have touched death, "crossed over to the other side and returned" and can "now claim an exclusive knowledge of all matters related to death and holocaust." This echoes a long psychoanalytic tradition of believing traumatic experience gifts the patient heightened, even supernatural powers . . . and the value existentialism gave to the "limit situation," where only extremity truly confirmed being-in-the-world.
>
> Roger Luckhurst, *The Trauma Question* (New York: Routledge, 2008), 64.

22. Dean, "Politics," 631–632.
23. Zygmunt Bauman, *Mortality, Immortality and Other Life Strategies* (Stanford, CA: Stanford University Press, 1992).
24. Ibid., 7.
25. Dominic LaCapra, *History in Transit: Experience, Identity, Critical Theory* (Ithaca, NY: Cornell University Press, 2004), 122. It should be noted that LaCapra here uses the term "negative sacralization" somewhat differently, referring to the ways in which critics tend to fetishize trauma as a negative form of sublime knowledge about the Holocaust.
26. Felman and Laub, *Testimony*, 72.
27. Bernard Williams, *Truth and Truthfulness: An Essay in Genealogy* (Princeton, NJ: Princeton University Press, 2002), 11.
28. These spaces of memory are of course not discrete; the complex relationships between them are structured through other places and memories which, in turn, significantly shape how a survivor's Holocaust experiences are remembered.
29. Primo Levi, *If This Is a Man* and *The Truce*, trans. Stuart Woolf (London: Abacus, 1996 [1958]), 17.
30. Marc Chevrie and Hervé Le Roux, "Site and Speech: An Interview with Claude Lanzmann about *Shoah*," in Stuart Liebman, ed., *Claude Lanzmann's Shoah: Key Essays* (Oxford: Oxford University Press, 2007), 44.
31. Felman and Laub, *Testimony*, 232.
32. Shoshana Felman, "Theaters of Justice: Arendt in Jerusalem, the Eichmann Trial, and the Redefinition of Legal Meaning in the Wake of the Holocaust," *Critical Inquiry* 27, no. 2 (Winter, 2001): 493.
33. Felman, "Theaters," 503.
34. Kansteiner, "Genocide Memory," 404.
35. Giorgio Agamben, *Remnants of Auschwitz*, trans. Daniel Heller-Rosen (New York: Zine Books, 1999), 14.
36. Lokting, "Meet," *Forward*.
37. Marianne Hirsch, "Holocaust Testimony Beyond the Frame," *Los Angeles Review of Books*, May 23, 2020, https://lareviewofbooks.org/article/holocaust-testimony-beyond-the-frame (accessed May 26, 2020)
38. Peter Buse and Andrew Stott, eds., *Ghosts: Deconstruction, Psychoanalysis, History* (Basingstoke: Palgrave Macmillan, 1999), 10.
39. Novick, *Holocaust*, 268.
40. Ibid., 268.

41. Alexander Etkind, "Post-Soviet Hauntology: Cultural Memory of the Soviet Terror," *Constellations* 16, no. 1 (Oxford: Blackwell, 2009): 182–200, (182).

42. Etkind, "Post-Soviet Hauntology," 195.

43. Jacques Derrida, *Specters of Marx: The State of the Debt, the Work of Mourning and the New International*, trans. Peggy Kamuf (Abingdon: Routledge, 1994), 6.

44. Ibid., 11. Derrida ends his treatise with a repetition of this motif, asking:

> Can one, in order to question it, address oneself to a ghost? To whom? To him? To *it*, as Marcellus says once again and so prudently? "Thou art a Scholler; speake to *it* Horatio. . . . Question *it*."
>
> The question deserves perhaps to be put the other way: Could one *address oneself in general* if already some ghost did not come back? If he loves justice at least, the "scholar" of the future, the "intellectual" of tomorrow should learn it and from the ghost. He should learn to live by learning not how to make conversation with the ghost but how to talk with him, with her, how to let them speak or how to give them back speech, even if it is in oneself, in the other, in the other in oneself: they are always *there*, specters, even if they do not exist, even if they are no longer, even if they are not yet (175–176).

45. Ibid., 156. Here Derrida's dehumanization of the specter overlooks the fact that the ghost is aware of his (or its) ghostly condition, as he tells Hamlet: "I am thy father's spirit, / Doomed for a certain term to walk the night, / And for the day confined to fast in fires" (1.5.9–11).

46. Ibid., 6.

47. McMullan, "The Virtual."

48. Levi's poem imagines the dead of "the Marne, of Montecassino, / Treblinka, Dresden and Hiroshima" waiting "outside in the cold" as politicians conduct an obscure negotiation. The poem ends:

> Sit down and bargain
> Until your tongues are dry.
> If the havoc and the shame continue
> We'll drown you in our putrefaction.

> Primo Levi, "Song of Those Who Died in Vain," *Collected Poems*, trans. Ruth Feldman and Brian Swann (London: Faber and Faber, 1992), 82.

49. Hartman, *Longest*, 7.

50. Ruth Kluger, *Landscapes of Memory: A Holocaust Girlhood Remembered* (London: Bloomsbury, 2003), 90.

51. Derrida, *Specters*, 97.

52. McMullan, "The Virtual."

53. Ibid.

54. James Dawes, *Evil Men* (Cambridge, MA: Harvard University Press, 2013), 214.

55. Emmanuel Levinas, *Otherwise Than Being: Or, Beyond Essence*, trans. Alphonso Lingis (Hague: Nijhoff, 1981), 119.

56. Derrida, *Specters*, 97.

57. Ibid., xix.

Chapter 3

1. In recent years, numerous academic studies have drawn attention to the extensive written and oral testimonies and other cultural acts of witnessing that were produced during and immediately after the war, thereby challenging longstanding assumptions about the "latency period" and post-war forgetting. See, for example, Hasia Diner, *We Remember with Reverence and Love: American Jews and the Myth of Silence after the Holocaust, 1945–1962* (New York: New York University Press, 2009) and Alan Rosen, *The Wonder of Their Voices: The 1946 Holocaust Interviews of David Boder* (New York: Oxford University Press, 2010).

2. Hannah Arendt, *Eichmann in Jerusalem: A Report on the Banality of Evil* (London: Penguin, 1994), 4.

3. Ibid., 6, 5.

4. Shoshana Felman, "Theaters of Justice: Arendt in Jerusalem, the Eichmann Trial, and the Redefinition of Legal Meaning in the Wake of the Holocaust," *Critical Inquiry* 27, no. 2 (Winter, 2001): 201–238.

5. Carolyn J. Dean, "The Politics of Suffering: From the Survivor-witness to Humanitarian Witnessing," *Continuum* 31, no. 5 (2017): 628–36 (629).

6. Felman, "Theaters," 40; Geoffrey Hartman, *The Longest Shadow: In the Aftermath of the Holocaust* (New York: Palgrave Macmillan, 2002), 153.

7. Hartman, *Longest*, 22; Shoshana Felman and Dori Laub, *Testimony: Crises of Witnessing in Literature, Psychoanalysis and History* (New York: Routledge, 1992), 71.

8. Hartman, *Longest*, 22; Felman and Laub, *Testimony*, 61.

9. Marc Chevrie and Hervé Le Roux, "Site and Speech: An Interview with Claude Lanzmann about *Shoah*," trans. Stuart Liebman, in Stuart Liebman, ed., *Shoah: Key Essays* (Oxford: Oxford University Press, 2007), 44–45.

10. Stuart Jeffries, "Claude Lanzmann on why Holocaust documentary *Shoah* still matters," *The Guardian*, June 9, 2011, https://www.theguardian.com/film/2011/jun/09/claude-lanzmann-shoah-holocaust-documentary (accessed August 15, 2018).

11. Eva Schloss and Karen Bartlett, *After Auschwitz: A Story of Heartbreak and Survival by the Stepsister of Anne Frank* (London: Hodder and Stoughton, 2013), 3.

12. Matthew Boswell, "Beyond Autobiography: Hybrid Testimony and the Art of Witness," in *The Future of Testimony: Interdisciplinary Perspectives on Witnessing*, eds. Jane Kilby and Antony Rowland (Oxford: Routledge, 2014), 144–159.

13. A good example of such a text is Dave Eggers's pointedly titled *What Is the What: The Autobiography of Valentino Achak Deng. A Novel* (New York: Vintage Books, 2007). See Boswell, "Beyond Autobiography," for a discussion of how this novel extends our sense of literary witnessing.

14. Eva Schloss and Barbara Powers, *The Promise: The True Story of a Family in the Holocaust* (London: Penguin, 2006), 100.

15. Eva Schloss and Evelyn Julia Kent, *Eva's Story: A Survivor's Tale by the Step-Sister of Anne Frank* (New York: St. Martin's Press, 1988), 61.

16. Schloss and Powers, *The Promise*, 2.

17. Ibid., 143–144.

18. Schloss and Kent, *Eva's Story*, 2.

19. Ibid., 2.

20. Schloss and Bartlett, *After Auschwitz*, 44–46.

21. Ibid., 46.

22. Ibid., 47.

23. Schloss and Kent, *Eva's Story*, 35.

24. Ibid., 66.

25. See USC Shoah Foundation, "Jewish Survivor Eva Schloss Testimony Part 1," https:// www.youtube.com/watch?v=teOGjk2BdHI> from 2:20 (accessed July 28, 2017).

26. Schloss and Bartlett, *After Auschwitz*, 129.

27. Schloss and Kent, *Eva's Story*, 87.

28. Schloss and Bartlett, *After Auschwitz*, 129.

29. Schloss and Kent, *Eva's Story*, 179.

30. Ibid., 199.

31. Zoë Waxman, *Women in the Holocaust: A Feminist History* (New York: Oxford University Press, 2017), 8. See also "Buried Words: Sexuality, Violence and Holocaust Testimonies," a special issue of *Holocaust Studies: A Journal of History and Culture* (2021) that was in part inspired by the publication of *Buried Words: The Diary of Molly Applebaum* (2017) written by the Toronto-based survivor Molly Applebaum. The two-part book presents Applebaum's previously unpublished wartime diary, written whilst she was a teenager living firstly in a Polish ghetto and then in hiding, alongside a memoir she wrote in the 1990s. Waxman's essay, "Buried Words: Reflections on the Diary of Molly Applebaum," for example, sensitively explores Applebaum's matter-of-fact accounts of sexual encounters with the peasant who was hiding her.

32. Paul Meincke, "Technology Tells Survivors' Stories at Illinois Holocaust Museum," *ABC 7 Chicago*, April 30, 2017, https://abc7chicago.com/education/technology-tells-survivors-stories-at-illinois-holocaust-museum/1938500/ (accessed August 16, 2018).

33. The formal requirement for a consistent tone was approached differently in the Forever Project interviews, where the questions were deliberately asked in a nonchronological order to ensure that the survivors did not become too emotionally distressed by answering a prolonged series of questions about specific incidents.

34. Primo Levi, *The Drowned and the Saved*, trans. Raymond Rosenthal (London: Abacus, 1996), 11–12.

35. Primo Levi, *If This Is a Man* and *The Truce*, trans. Stuart Woolf (London: Abacus, 1996), 397.

36. In *Eva's Story* the sentence reads: "I crouched in terror, my heart beating so loudly that I was sure they could hear it" (33). In *The Promise* this is slightly softened to: "When they threw open the bathroom door I expected them to hear the pounding of my heart, but they didn't" (82). Finally, in the more polished *After Auschwitz*, the whole episode is described far more vividly: "My heart was beating so loudly that I was sure the soldiers would hear it as they flung open the bathroom door and I heard them clomping about, gasping for breath and shouting instructions at each other—only

inches from where Mutti was sitting, curled up on the toilet lid, and where I was crouching beside Miss Klompe's lover" (87).

37. Levi, *If This*, 382.

38. Lawrence Langer, *Holocaust Testimonies: The Ruins of Memory* (New Haven, CT: Yale University Press, 1991), 5–9 and 75–87.

39. Meincke, "Technology."

40. In their extended interview for the Forever Project, one survivor discussed traumatic aspects of their Holocaust experiences that they had not made public before. They subsequently asked the National Holocaust Centre and Museum not to release their interactive testimony until after their death. Another participant, Martin Stern, recognized that the extended duration of his interview allowed him to address ambiguities in his Holocaust memories in ways that had not been possible during public talks. At the time of our conversation, Stern was 78 years old. He told us that he had clear memories of being taken to Theresienstadt in a cattle truck with his younger sister when he was 5 years old, and she was 1 year old. During the journey, he saw a corpse lying on the floor with its eyes open. However, he also remembers being crammed tightly into the cattle truck. When giving his testimony in the form of a lecture, Stern has therefore become accustomed to saying that the corpse was standing up, so that his narrative remains coherent. This means that he now has both what he believes to be the authentic memory of seeing the corpse lying down and a "phantom" memory of the corpse standing up: something that he could address and reflect on through the longer duration of the Forever Project interview.

41. The phrase "the nature of the offence" comes from Primo Levi. Stuart Woolf's translation differs slightly: "Then for the first time we became aware that our language lacks words to express this offence, the demolition of a man" (Levi, *If This*, 32). It was also used by Martin Amis as an alternative title for his Holocaust novel, *Time's Arrow* (1991).

42. Schloss and Powers, *The Promise*, 1.

43. Ibid., 86–87.

44. Ibid., 87.

45. Todd Presner, "The Ethics of the Algorithm: Close and Distant Listening to the Shoah Foundation Visual History Archive," in Claudio Fogu, Wulf Kansteiner, and Todd Presner, eds., *Probing the Ethics of Holocaust Culture* (Cambridge, MA: Harvard University Press, 1992), 183–184.

46. Langer, *Holocaust*, 21.

47. Hartman, *Longest*, 142.

48. Felman and Laub, *Testimony*, 78.

49. USC Shoah Foundation, "Pioneering 'New Dimensions in Testimony' Interviewee Passes Away at 85," *Institute News*, April 13, 2018, https://sfi.usc.edu/news/2018/04/21826 pioneering new dimensions-testimony-interviewee-passes-away-85 (accessed August 16, 2018).

50. Levi, *Drowned*, 65.

51. Noah Shenker, *Reframing Holocaust Testimony* (Bloomington, IN: Indiana University Press, 2015), 112.

52. Ibid., 149.
53. Norman Finkelstein, *The Holocaust Industry: Reflections on the Exploitation of Jewish Suffering* (New York: Verso, 2014 [2000]).
54. See "Doc/Fest Exchange: Digging Deeper into New Dimensions in Testimony," https://www.youtube.com/watch?v=ybBkpfV3Ot0 from 15:00 (accessed August 16, 2018). *Schindler's List* was a relatively unsuccessful film for Spielberg in purely financial terms, with a lifetime gross of $96 million making it only his seventeenth highest earner. http://www.boxofficemojo.com/people/chart/?id=stevenspielberg.htm (accessed June 3, 2016).
55. According to the USC Shoah Foundation website, "funding for New Dimensions in Testimony was provided in part by Pears Foundation, Louis. F. Smith, Melinda Goldrich and Andrea Cayton/ Goldrich Family Foundation in honor of Jona Goldrich, and Illinois Holocaust Museum and Education Center." See USC Shoah Foundation, https://sfi.usc.edu/collections/holocaust/ndt (accessed March 26, 2018).
56. Kertzer, "Don't," 129.
57. Karen A. Kim, "New Dimensions in Testimony: Findings from Student Pilots" (August 2015), 2.
58. Ibid, i–iii. It will be particularly interesting to see whether future evaluations of the project substantiate the Foundation's view that testimony provides "lessons for humanity," which is to say that the lessons it imparts are universal and of relevance to diverse societies around the world. As the project evolves, it will be important to consider how audiences from different backgrounds respond, in order to establish whether it is playing to certain social, economic, and cultural norms. The Foundation's commitment to taking such questions seriously is reflected in the decision to record the testimony of Xia Shuqin, a child survivor of the Nanjing Massacre, in Mandarin, during the first round of Dimensions in Testimony interviews. This testimony is now on permanent display at the Nanjing Massacre Memorial Hall in Nanjing, China.
59. Shenker, *Reframing*, 12.
60. Ibid., 128–129.
61. Here Schindler's sanctification coincides with the film's overt politicization, with the camera cutting to a Soviet soldier on horseback, who informs Stern and his fellow liberated prisoners that it would be unsafe to head either East or West. The straight line connecting the Holocaust with the creation of the nation-state of Israel is emphasized through subtitles informing us that Schindler was declared a righteous person by the council of Yad Vashem in 1958 and invited to plant a tree in the Avenue of the Righteous.
62. Henry Greenspan, "Movement and Memory: An Email Exchange with Henry Greenspan and Tim Cole, Part 1," *OUP Blog*, January 22, 2016, https://blog.oup.com/2016/01/hank-greenspan-tim-cole-part-1/ (accessed July 31, 2018).
63. Jean Améry, *At the Mind's Limits: Contemplations by a Survivor on Auschwitz and its Realities*, trans. Sidney Rosenfeld and Stella P. Rosenfeld (London: Granta, 1999), 62–81.
64. Shenker, *Reframing*, 135.

65. Similar institutional preferences shape the Forever Project. The National Holocaust Centre and Museum was particularly mindful of the need to make connections between the survivor testimonies and the Centre's education program. The Centre hosts visits by students studying a range of topics, including history, literature, and religious education, and the project team selected survivors from the Centre's "pool" of speakers whom they knew had experiences and views that spoke to these subjects.

66. Levi, *Drowned*, 63.

67. On December 3, 2018, the USC Shoah Foundation announced that two new interactive biographies of Russian-speaking Jews from the former Soviet Union would be created, thanks to a partnership with the Genesis Philanthropy Group, which supports the preservation of Jewish culture, heritage, and values amongst Russian-speaking Jewish communities around the world. A Holocaust survivor and a Red Army veteran will be identified to take part in the Russian language initiative, ensuring that experiences of Jewish resistance and suffering in the former territories of the Soviet Union are added to this expanding archive. See USC Shoah Foundation, "Survivors and Soldiers: Revolutionary Technology Preserves Living Testimony of Soviet Jewish Experience of Holocaust and WWII," December 3, 2018, https://sfi.usc.edu/news/2018/12/23621-survivors-and-soldiers-revolutionary-technology-preserves-living-testimony-soviet (accessed December 5, 2018).

68. This is not a criticism of the film, but rather an observation about an unintended consequence of its enduring popularity. As Spielberg himself noted in an interview to mark the twenty-fifth anniversary cinematic rerelease of *Schindler's List*, he has arguably done more than anyone to ensure that thousands of survivor voices are heard through the creation of the Visual History Archive. Recalling a formative childhood experience when a Hungarian Holocaust survivor taught him to count by using the Auschwitz tattoo on his forearm, Spielberg reflects: "This is something that I think, in a way, somehow led me to want to tell a story of the Shoah. Not *the* story of the Shoah, because there are millions of stories of the Shoah. Six million of them we'll never hear. But there were hundreds of thousands more, which is why I started the Shoah Foundation to collect these testimonies." USC Shoah Foundation, "Steven Spielberg Discusses Lessons he Hopes Students Will Take Away from Rerelease of *Schindler's List*," November 30, 2018, https://sfi.usc.edu/news/2018/11/23591-steven-spielberg-discusses-lessons-he-hopes-students-will-take-away-rerelease- (accessed December 6, 2018).

69. Giorgio Agamben, *Remnants of Auschwitz*, trans. Daniel Heller-Rosen (New York: Zine Books, 1999), 13.

70. Levi, *Drowned*, 62–63.

71. Ibid., 63.

72. Ibid., 64.

73. Ibid., 64.

74. Améry, *At the Mind's*, 9.

75. Levi, *If This*, 96.

76. Agamben, *Remnants*, 81.

77. Jáchym Topol, *The Devil's Workshop*, trans. Alex Zucker (London: Portobello Books, 2013), 134.

78. Ibid., 135.

79. Christine Goelz, "Through a Chilly Land—Between First-Person Shoot-Em-Up and Tourist Blockbuster: Jáchym Topol's Fictional Statement on the Possibility of Immersive Remembrance," in *Digital Icons: Studies in Russian, Eurasian and Central European New Media*, No. 6 (2011), 63–79.

80. Topol, *Devil's*, 127, 129.

81. Ibid., 134.

82. See Adriana Cavarero, *Horrorism: Naming Contemporary Violence*, trans. William McCuaig (New York, NY: Columbia University Press, 2008).

83. See Saul Friedländer, ed., *Probing the Limits of Representation: Nazism and the "Final Solution"* (Cambridge, MA: Harvard University Press, 1992).

Chapter 4

1. Edward T. Linenthal, *Preserving Memory: The Struggle to Create America's Holocaust Museum* (New York: Columbia University Press, 2001 [1995]), 30–31.

2. Caroline Pearce, *Contemporary Germany and the Nazi Legacy: Remembrance, Politics and the Dialectic of Normality* (London: Palgrave, 2007), 2.

3. Pearce, *Contemporary Germany and the Nazi Legacy*, 2.

4. John Urry, "How Societies Remember the Past," in S. Macdonald and G. Fyfe, eds., *Theorizing Museums: Representing Identity and Diversity in a Changing World* (Oxford: Blackwell, 1996), 45–68 (63). Victoria Grace Walden discusses the digital films and applications at Bergen-Belsen in *Cinematic Intermedialities and Contemporary Holocaust Memory* (London: Palgrave Macmillan, 2019), 207–209.

5. Andreas Huyssen, *Twilight Memories: Making Time in a Culture of Amnesia* (London: Routledge, 1995), 18.

6. Huyssen, *Twilight Memories*, 14; Andrew Hoskins, "Signs of the Holocaust: Exhibiting Memory in a Mediated Age," *Media, Culture and Society* 25, no. 7 (2003): 7–22 (20).

7. Hoskins, "Signs of the Holocaust," 20.

8. Huyssen, *Twilight Memories*, 32.

9. Daniel Levy and Natan Sznaider, *The Holocaust and Memory in the Global Age*, trans. Assenka Sznaider (Philadelphia, PA: Temple University Press, 2006), 2, 4; Alison Landsberg, *Prosthetic Memory: The Transformation of American Remembrance in the Age of Mass Culture* (New York: Columbia University Press, 2004), 145.

10. Theodor Adorno, *Aesthetic Theory*, eds. Gretel Adorno and Rolf Tiedemann, trans. Robert Hullot-Kentor (London: The Athlone Press, 1997 [1970]), 247. Whereas the "political effect even of so-called committed art is highly uncertain" (232), "the sententious vehemence with which [Brecht] translates [his] hardly dew-fresh insights into scenic gestures lends his work their tone; the didacticism led him to his dramaturgical innovations, which overthrew the moribund theater [*sic*] of philosophy and

intrigue" (247). As Jenni Adams indicates, "Landsberg's theory depends also on a certain construction of mass culture as a largely positive phenomenon whose ideological biases are not greatly relevant, or are at least vastly overshadowed by its potential to evoke cross-cultural remembering." *The Bloomsbury Companion to Holocaust Literature* (London: Bloomsbury, 2014), 241.

11. These quotations are taken from the website information on the iPad application, www.belsen-project.specs-lab.com/summers-fruits-a-new-app-version (accessed November 24, 2020).

12. Shoshana Felman and Dori Laub, *Testimony: Crises of Witnessing in Literature, Psychoanalysis, and History* (New York: Routledge, 1992), *passim*; Cathy Caruth, ed., *Trauma: Explorations in Memory* (Baltimore, MD: Johns Hopkins University Press, 1995), *passim*.

13. Wiener Library, www.wienerlibrary.co.uk/memoryinadigitalage/ (accessed November 24, 2020). SPECS constitutes a multidisciplinary research center founded in 2005 by the ICREA Research Professor Paul Vershure: part of the Department of Information and Communication Technologies at the University of Pompeu Fabra in Barcelona, SPECS became a member of the Centre for Neuro-Robotics and Autonomous Systems (N-RAS) in 2012, a new research group coordinated by Verschure. Thus contributors to the wider project based at Bergen-Belsen have included historians, scientists, and technicians from multiple disciplines, as well as survivors of the camp. This multidisciplinary collaboration thus constitutes an admirable attempt to resolve the disconnection between digital technology and traditional memorialization techniques. Billib recounted how the technicians would work onsite developing the technology alongside historians and museum workers. However, the multidisciplinary acumen does not extend to experts in memory studies, which is partly why these questions of identification and "useless knowledge" have not yet been addressed in these virtual applications and installations. In contrast, James Young writes about his involvement in the development of the Eisenmann memorial in Berlin, and the 9/11 memorial at Ground Zero in *At Memory's Edge* (New Haven, CT: Yale University Press, 2000), 184–223 and in Rick Crownshaw, Jane Kilby, and Antony Rowland, eds., *The Future of Memory* (New York: Berghahn, 2010), 77–92. The relative success of these memorials suggests that experts in memory studies have something tangible to offer in the development of virtual technologies in relation to memorialization.

14. Belsen Project, www.belsen-project.specs-lab.com/summer-fruits-a-new-app-version (accessed November 24, 2020).

15. Belsen Project, http://www.belsen-project.specs-lab.com/tablet-goes-to-class (accessed November 24, 2020).

16. Conversation with Billib at the Bergen-Belsen memorial (June 13, 2016). For the sake of coherence and convenience, the iPad tour does not encompass the Horsten Soviet Prisoner of War Cemetery, which forms part of the *Gedenkstätte* in its entirety, but which is approximately half a kilometer away from the mass graves. However, its omission also indicates the kinds of historical forgetting which are an inherent aspect of such concise tours. Tony Kushner announces that "the history of Belsen as a brutal

and murderous camp for Soviet prisoners of war has only just begun." Jo Reilly, Tony Kushner, David Cesarani, and Colin Richmond, eds., *Belsen in History and Memory* (Portland, OR: Frank Cass Publishers, 1997), 16.

17. Maria Blancas, Syste Wierenga, Kees Ribbens, Carolien Rieffe, Habbo Knoch, Stephanie Billib, and Paul Vershure, "Active Learning in Digital Heritage: Introducing Geo-localisation, VR and AR at Holocaust Historical Sites," in Victoria Grace Walden, ed., *Digital Holocaust Memory, Education and Research* (London: Palgrave Macmillan, 2021), 145–176 (163).

18. Alison Landsberg, *Engaging the Past: Mass Culture and the Production of Historical Knowledge* (New York: Columbia University Press, 2015), 16. Augmented Reality refers to a direct or indirect view of reality (via, for example, television) whose elements are supplemented with computer-generated input such as graphics, sound, or GPS data. This "mediated" reality reflects a real-world environment that is modified by a computer. In contrast, "virtual" reality attempts to replace that environment with a simulation. Augmented reality is a common technique in television: in *War of Words: Soldier-Poets of the Somme*, broadcast by the BBC on July 3, 2016, imposed signs on the contemporary landscape of France point out, for example, how the ruins of a windmill used to operate as a signaling station at High Wood, where Robert Graves was nearly fatally injured. Augmentation is also deployed in more conventional situations, such as in the form of scores on television during a sporting event.

19. Huyssen, *Twilight Memories*, 255; Hoskins, "Signs of the Holocaust," 10.

20. Yehuda Bauer, *The Holocaust in Historical Perspective* (London: Sheldon Press, 1978), 43–44.

21. The Tony Kushner section of "Approaching Belsen: An Introduction," 13. Kushner argues that the liberation footage is bound up with a "popular" mythology which began after 1945 in which "Britain had actually fought the war to end Nazi atrocities and even to save the Jews" (12). Jo Reilly's section writes about the Nazis and British in a single sentence: "the dignity and culture of individuals . . . was stolen from them by the Nazis and, unwittingly again, by the liberator's shell-shocked and limited use of vocabulary and the sensationalist, intrusive newsreel cameras" (22).

22. James Young, *The Texture of Memory: Holocaust Memorials and Meaning* (New Haven, CT: Yale University Press, 1993), 56.

23. Claude Lanzmann, dir., *Shoah* (1985); Michael Bernard-Donals, "Theory and Ethics of Holocaust Representation," in Jenni Adams, ed., *The Bloomsbury Companion to Holocaust Literature* (New York: Bloomsbury, 2014), 103–119 (112).

24. Marianne Hirsch, "Holocaust Testimony Beyond the Frame," *Los Angeles Review of Books*, May 23, 2020, https://lareviewofbooks.org/article/holocaust-testimony-bey ond-the-frame/ (accessed May 26, 2020).

25. The disappearance of the original buildings is partly the fault of British military personnel, who successfully argued for the transformation of the former camp into a landscaped area for commemoration in 1945–1946. Against the wishes of survivors, a smaller area of about 400 m × 800 m around the mass graves was earmarked for cultivation, and the remaining aspects of the camp in other areas, such as guard towers, fences, roads, and the remains of the crematorium, were removed, http://bergen-bel

sen.stiftung-ng.de/en/memorial/grounds-of-former-camp.html (accessed July 13, 2016).

26. Belsen Project, www.belsen-project.specs-lab.com/summer-fruits-a-new-app-version (accessed July 12, 2016).

27. Robert Eaglestone, *The Holocaust and the Postmodern* (Oxford: Oxford University Press, 2004), 15–42.

28. Charlotte Delbo, *Auschwitz and After*, trans. Rosette C. Lamont (New Haven, CT: Yale University Press, 1995), 115–232.

29. Pearce, *Contemporary Germany and the Nazi Legacy*, 6.

30. Belsen Project, www.belsen-project.specs-lab.com/wiener-library-installation (accessed November 24, 2020).

31. Slavoj Žižek, *Violence* (London: Profile Books, 2009), 3, 5.

32. Claude Lanzmann, "The Obscenity of Understanding: An Evening with Claude Lanzmann," in *Trauma: Explorations in Memory*, 200–220. The application is actually (and understandably) more about the inmates than perpetrators: it does not really confront the "ruthless cruelty" of the guards that "gave them a sense of well-being" along with "the bitter sneer of malicious pleasure." Abel J. Herzberg, "Amor Fati. Attachment to Fate: Seven Essays on Bergen-Belsen," trans. Jack Santcross (Amsterdam: Querido's Uitgeverji B.V., 1987), 6, quoted in *Belsen in History and Memory*, 48.

33. The project team are perfectly aware of the limitations of the technology, and are developing the applications. "The tablet app goes to class" article on the SPECS website notes that a class of schoolchildren from Celle took part in a piloting exercise in which they took the tablet "tour," and then offered feedback. The students draw attention to, for example, the color of the buildings, the graphics overall, and the unwieldiness of the iPad. The instructor then comments, "Was there any moment that you'd rather have thrown the thing like a frisbee into the forest?" http://www.belsen-project.specs-lab.com/tablet-goes-to-class (accessed November 24, 2020).

34. However, they would not be appropriate in the contemporary landscape of Bergen-Belsen: whereas the latter has become a nature reserve, Neuengamme was developed on the site of a demolished postwar prison.

35. Walden, *Cinematic Intermedialities*, 207.

36. I am referring here to Delbo's shuttling between "*vrais*" and "*véridique*" at the beginning of *Auschwitz and After* (New Haven, CT: Yale University Press, 1995). For further discussion of this quotation, see Antony Rowland, *Poetry as Testimony* (Abingdon: Routledge, 2014), 72–74.

37. Walden, *Cinematic Intermedialities*, 208.

38. Landsberg, *Engaging the Past*, 10.

39. When we used the iPad application in June 2016, the GPS systems on both iPads soon failed, which meant that the augmented reality did not match the current location, and we could only access the digitized documents in one isolated location. However, two replacement iPads quickly solved this problem. Billib noted that students had previously used the technology to take photographs of the site, or, in one instance, of their feet. Such activity could be critiqued as distracting, or akin to James Friedman's

anti-modernist photographs of the camps as sites for cafes, deliveries, and toys in car parks. See Doral Apel's discussion of Friedman's pictures as opposed to Eric Hartmann's shots of Birkenau's icons in *Memory Effects: The Holocaust and the Art of Secondary Witnessing* (New Brunswick, NJ: Rutgers University Press, 2002), 111–117.

40. Belsen Project, www.belsen-project.specs-lab.com/the-box-installation (accessed November 24, 2020). The "box" was opened at the same time as the sound installation "There, Echoes of Memory," which was located in the passageway between the museum and the entrance to the camp.

41. Belsen Project, www.belsen-project.specs-lab.com/the-box-installation (accessed November 24, 2020).

42. Belsen Project, www.belsen-project.specs-lab.com/the-box-installation (accessed November 24, 2020); Young, *The Texture of Memory*, 60. Young is writing about Dachau in terms of its lack of original artefacts.

43. Belsen Project, www.belsen-project.specs-lab.com/the-box-installation (accessed November 24, 2020).

44. Ibid.

45. Walden, *Cinematic Intermedialities*, 206.

46. Belsen Project, www.belsen-project.specs-lab.com/the-box-installation (accessed November 24, 2020).

47. Huyssen, *Twilight Memories*, 32.

48. Wiener Library, www.wienerlibrary.co.uk/memoryinadigitalage (accessed November 24, 2020).

49. Belsen Project, www.belsen-project.specs-lab.com/wiener-library-installation (accessed November 24, 2020).

50. In "Active Learning in Digital Heritage: Introducing Geo-localisation, VR and AR at Holocaust Historical Sites," Blancas et al. refer to two modes in the tablet application, "Presentation" and "Master": the latter "integrates all information available— including uncertain and contentious elements" (157).

51. Wiener Library, www.wienerlibrary.co.uk/memoryinadigitalage (accessed November 24, 2020). Susan Gubar, *Poetry after Auschwitz: Remembering What One Never Knew* (Bloomington, IN: Indiana University Press, 2003), *passim*.

52. Bergen-Belsen, https://bergen-belsen.stiftung-ng.de/ (accessed July 15, 2016).

53. The website for the Bergen-Belsen memorial reveals that Polish survivors unveiled the wooden cross on the Catholic holiday of All Souls' Day on November 2, 1945, and that the cross has been replaced several times, but still retains its original size and shape, http://bergen-belsen.stiftung-ng.de/en/memorial/grounds-of-former-camp/monuments.html (accessed July 12, 2016). Over the years, the graveyard has proved to be a shifting site: for example, a stone monument with name plaques was installed in the cemetery for Italian military internees in 1950, but it was taken down in 1958 when the bodies were reinterred in Hamburg-Öjendorf.

54. David Cesarani notes that Yossele Rosencraft and Norbert Wollheim "presided over an astounding renaissance of Jewish life in the camp, which became the seed corn for the revival of Jewry in the West German Republic," and that this "astonishing

affirmation of life and the will to overcome the horror of the past is rendered invisible in accounts which end in 1945" (*Belsen in History and Memory*, 19).

55. Hoskins ("Signs of the Holocaust," 10) is referring here to the IWM exhibition. He concludes that to " 'isolate' and display signs of the Holocaust is to attempt to materialize the event, as if all the time passed since has not impacted on what is knowable or understood of this event" (15).

56. Hoskins, "Signs of the Holocaust," 10.

57. Wiener Library, www.wienerlibrary.co.uk/memoryinadigitalage (accessed November 24, 2020).

58. Belsen Project, www.belsen-project.specs-lab.com/the-box-installation (accessed November 24, 2020). Neuengamme has come a long way since Young's description of it in *The Texture of Memory* (in two paragraphs) as a summer camp for international students (59). He does not mention the 1953 memorial that fits perfectly with his wider argument about the generalization of Holocaust victims, which includes, for example, East Germans living under Stalin's regime, in order to fit postwar narratives about victimization.

59. Neuengamme's monuments close to the House of Remembrance also indicate that memorialization is not inherently progressive. In 1953, a seven-meter-high limestone column was erected in a small garden at Neuengamme with the inscription "To the victims/ 1938–1945." A present-day site station critiques this monument as "meagre," and criticizes it as making "no mention of the concentration camp or any other historical facts." The original memorial was then destroyed, and replaced at a site nearby with a taller obelisk that represents the crematorium's chimney. However, compared to the restrained dignity of the 1953 memorial, the newer version comes across as a dull and outsized replacement. In *The Texture of Memory*, James Young criticizes the 1952 memorial at Plötzensee (Berlin) in similar terms to the Neuengamme site station: "By dedicating the memorial to all of Hitler's victims, regardless of nationality, religion, or political convictions, the city defined victims of the Reich in the broadest possible terms, creating a common meaning for the murder of disparate millions" (50). Young is absolutely correct, and yet these early and minimalist postwar memorials deserve to be interpreted and preserved—rather than destroyed, as in the case of the Neuengamme memorial—as the product of particular historical conditions, precisely before the identity politics that James lists began to determine the process of memorialization.

60. Jean Baudrillard, *Simulacra and Simulation*, trans. Sheila Faria Glaser (Ann Arbor, MI: The University of Michigan Press, 1994 [1981]), 49.

61. Ibid., 49.

62. Ibid., 1, 2.

63. Belsen Project, www.belsen-project.specs-lab.com/the-box-installation (accessed November 24, 2020). Dir. Alain Resnais, *Night and Fog* (1955).

64. Tony Kushner's section of "Approaching Belsen: An Introduction," in *Belsen in History and Memory*, 5–16 (5).

65. Reilly, Kushner, Cesarani, and Richmond, *Belsen in History and Memory*, 212, 215.

66. Sarah Kofman, *Smothered Words*, trans. Madeleine Dobie (Evanston, IL: Northwestern University Press, 1998), xv. For a discussion of "seeing" in Delbo's work, see Antony Rowland, *Poetry as Testimony*, 71–72.

67. I am referring here to the "One Day" chapter in *Auschwitz and After* (24–29).

68. Charlotte Delbo, *Convoy to Auschwitz: Women of the French Resistance*, trans. Carol Cosman (Boston: Northeastern University Press, 1997), *passim*.

69. Instead, it focuses on more recent interviews conducted by the Bergen-Belsen memorial, in the form of excerpts such as Michael Gelber's account of the current "nature reserve." Gelber refers to the original camp as the "exact opposite" of this nature reserve. The project team noted that when survivors viewed the first installation, the "spontaneous effect triggered many mentions and was not always desired. In all cases, people were fully respected and could leave the public installation at any time. From these observations came the idea to conduct dedicated, voluntary interviews with survivors, applying the spatial reconstruction and navigation through it as a specific tool to help record important memories of the camp's history, while some of its survivors are still alive. A few of these interviews have been conducted in dedicated sessions outside of the public installation." Belsen Project, www.belsen-project.specs-lab.com/the-box-installation (accessed November 24, 2020). It is no accident that Gelber's testimony is screened first: it established the disjunction between the past and present that the team were keen to establish. His narrative would be read by some historians as a form of "contaminated" testimony, since he interprets his experience through the post-war writing of Elie Wiesel, and yet Gelber's emphatic "*Das war es nicht*" simply and effectively makes the visitor "aware of her/his position in-between present and past."

70. Walden, *Cinematic Intermedialities*, 207.

71. The disquieting music consisting of a low-key synthesizer begs the question: does a digital installation such as this require a soundtrack? Max Richter's synthesizers are central to the aesthetics of Ari Folman's film *Waltz with Bashir* (2008) and provide an apt equivalent to the dream-like recovery of traumatized memory. In a similar way, the slow movement of the cursor in the second installation matches the extradiegetic sound.

72. Landsberg, *Engaging the* Past, 166. Landsberg describes the contours of the exhibition, and its creative process, extensively in *Engaging the Past*, so I shall not repeat that information in this chapter. In "Touching Virtual Trauma: Performative Empathics in Second Life," Bryoni Trezise writes of the "virtual trauma" in the Second Life exhibition that "simulates the presence of a real-life museum that simulates a traumatic history." *Memory Studies* 5, no. 4 (2011): 392–409 (392–393).

73. Landsberg, *Engaging the Past*, 167.

74. Baudrillard, *Simulacra and Simulation*, 105, 49.

75. Saul Friedländer, *Reflections of Nazism: An Essay on Kitsch and Death* (London: HarperCollins, 1984 [1982]), *passim*.

76. Baudrillard, *Simulacra and Simulation*, 44, 107.

77. Ibid., 49.

78. Sigmund Freud, *The Uncanny* (New York: Penguin, 2003 [1909]), xli.

79. Freud, *The Uncanny*, 125, 153.
80. Baudrillard, *Simulacra and Simulation*, 156–157.
81. Freud, *The Uncanny*, 144.
82. Ibid., 125.
83. Ibid., 123.
84. Ibid., 139.
85. Phylis Johnson, *Second Life, Media and the Other Society* (New York: Peter Lang, 2010), xiii.
86. Landsberg, *Engaging the Past*, 170.
87. Ibid., 170.
88. Ibid., 171, 172.
89. Johnson, *Second Life, Media and Other Society*, 18 (my italics).
90. The abstract threat of violence in the exhibition reminds us that Second Life is not a "safe" space: it may have been "created to be a little bit of utopia," but "unfortunately people came in and did exactly what they did to their first life to it" (Johnson, *Second Life, Media and Other Society*, 21). There is now a "dark side of Second Life: seedy alleys spotted with sex pose balls, random shootings on street corners, unsuspecting tourists as prey for vampire lairs, and glimpses of dystopian communities of the future" (216). Thankfully, the exhibition appears to have been free so far from "griefers": Second Life members who are "intentionally hostile to a community" (216).
91. Martin Gilbert, *The Holocaust* (London: HarperCollins, 1987 [1986]), 70.
92. Marianne Hirsch, *The Generation of Postmemory: Writing and Visual Culture after the Holocaust* (New York: Columbia University Press, 2012), 119.
93. Freud, *The Uncanny*, xli. "Noobie" is Second Life parlance for a new user (Johnson, *Second Life*, xiv).
94. Freud, *The Uncanny*, 132. Freud's discussion of the *unheimlich* in relation to supposedly unpatriotic "strangers" in 1909 now appears to contain a back-shadowed prescience: he picks on the phrase, "Ist dir's Heimlich noch in Lande, wo die Fremden deine Wälder roden" ("Are you still at ease in the country, where strangers are uprooting your woods?") (127).
95. Landsberg, *Engaging the Past*, 147. Landsberg endorses a study of the exhibition in which the authors comment that "A cursory reading of the public comment board is more than sufficient to convince anyone that the Holocaust museum succeeded in delivering a kinetic, intellectual, and visceral learning experience for participants" (172).
96. Baudrillard, *Simulacra and Simulation*, 49.
97. Landsberg, *Prosthetic Memory*, 111.
98. Kofman, *Smothered Words*, xv.
99. However, the experience could be utilized by, for example, schoolteachers in order for students to produce their journalistic accounts.
100. Landsberg, *Engaging the Past*, 167.
101. Linenthal, *Preserving Memory*, 104.

102. As Linenthal outlines, the debate over the choice of quotations for USHMM lasted many hours. The central quotation comes from Deuteronomy 4:9 ("Only guard yourself and guard your soul/carefully, lest you forget the things/your eyes saw, and lest these things/depart your heart all the days of your life./And you shall make them known to your children/and to your children's children"). A quotation from Genesis 4:10 ("What have you done? Hark, thy brother's blood cries out to me from the ground!") is followed with Deuteronomy 30:19: "I call heaven and earth to witness me from this day:/I have put before you life and death, blessing and curse./Choose life," which Michael Berenbaum disliked because "it spoke of choice that the victims did not have" (*Preserving Memory*, 98). Wiesel's "For the Living and the dead we must bear witness" appears over the entrance (96), but the museum committee decided against Job 16:18 ("Earth do not cover my blood; Let there be no resting place for my outcry!") because "it did not convey hope" (98).

103. In contrast with USHMM, the Kristallnacht exhibition in Second Life avoids a redemptive ending in the sense of final panels on individual rescuers and resisters, to "be regarded as role models for people who find themselves in the position of bystanders, whereas resisters should be regarded as role models for victimized population groups." Jeshajahu Weinberg and Rina Elieli, *The Holocaust Museum in Washington* (New York: Rizzoli International Publications, Inc., 1995, 55). Weinberg and Elieli go on to argue that "Overwhelming visual predominance of high-tech elements can easily distract from content and draw attention to technological achievement . . . Furthermore, in a Holocaust-related exhibition, the massive use of technical display devices would feel anachronistic and alienating" (63). Yet the audio tour, now an integral and uncontroversial part of the museum experience, is itself "anachronistic" according to their definition. Audio tours are a postwar phenomenon: one of the first museums to experiment with this technology was the Stedelijk museum in Amsterdam (1952).

104. Antony Rowland, interview with Tom Brink, Anne Frank House, Amsterdam (August 15, 2016).

105. Freud, 132. Of course, the confusion of sources would be anathema for any self-respecting journalist. In "Hiding Places," the voices blur without differentiation: the curator comments vaguely that "Susan Warsinger is one of the voices heard in this experience."

106. Belsen Project, www.belsen-project.specs-lab.com/summers-fruits-a-new-app-version (accessed November 24, 2020).

107. Landsberg, *Engaging the Past*, 29.

108. Kofman, *Smothered Words*, xv.

109. Marianne Hirsch writes in *The Generation of Postmemory* of the "cold impersonality of the archive" (249). She argues that digital materials "lack the smells, scale, and tactile materiality not only of the 'actual,' but also of the analogue 'originals'" (241). However, in relation to Kristallnacht, it could be argued instead that there is no particular "actual" or analogue "original" that the exhibition signifies. Moreover, the ability to take in the "smells, scale, and tactile materiality" of Holocaust museums and sites of persecution across the world is the preserve of the well-funded,

cosmopolitan tourist. Digital technology is thus able to respond to the class, and ableist, politics of dark tourism.

110. Adams, *The Bloomsbury Companion to Holocaust Literature*, 309.

111. Linenthal, *Preserving Memory*, xiii.

112. Johnson, *Second Life, Media and Other Society*, 19.

113. Other virtual platforms may need to take up this challenge: Wagner James Au, author of *The Making of Second Life* (2008), argued in 2009 that Second Life "may have run its course, although it has significantly made an impact on how other virtual-world designers are creating their games" (Johnson, *Second Life*, 272). The Blue Mars virtual world appeared more realistic than Second Life in 2010 because its CryEngine graphic package was "a lot better" (274).

114. Landsberg is right in this sense that mass cultural products have the capability "to engage productively and in a more complicated fashion with the past" (*Prosthetic Memory*, 113). The Bergen-Belsen memorial continues to develop too, with an updated indoor installation that was placed at the Garrison extension of the documentation center in 2019, and a desktop/tablet app which was devised for remote use in 2020.

115. Landsberg, *Engaging the Past*, 150. Taking on board the criticisms in this chapter of the various technological approaches, we still concur with Landsberg that popular engagements with the past are not simply "watered-down, oversimplified melodrama" (*Engaging the Past*, 24).

Chapter 5

1. Antony Rowland, interview with Tom Brink, Anne Frank House, Amsterdam (August 15, 2016).

2. Rowland, interview with Tom Brink (August 15, 2016).

3. Matthew Boswell and Antony Rowland, interview with Danny Abrahms, Los Angeles (November 7, 2016).

4. Oren Baruch Stier, *Holocaust Icons: Symbolizing the Shoah in History and Memory* (New Brunswick, NJ: Rutgers University Press, 2015), 100. Tony Kushner claims that the diary "remains the most popular non-fiction work published since 1945" in Martin Evans and Ken Lunn, eds., "'I Want to Go on Living after My Death': The Memory of Anne Frank," in *War and Memory in the Twentieth Century* (Oxford: Berg, 1997), 17.

5. Carol Ann Lee, *The Hidden Life of Otto Frank* (New York: Penguin, 2003 [2002]), 100, 235; Hannah Arendt, letter to the editor, *Midstream* (September 1962), 85–87. The sentimentality that Arendt detects within and surrounding the diary has resulted in its targeting for Holocaust impiety. Shalom Auslander's novel *Hope: A Tragedy* (London: Picador, 2012), for example, imagines Anne Frank surviving the war and ending up writing in the narrator's attic. When he threatens to evict her, he imagines his mother (who imagines herself as a Holocaust survivor) remonstrating: "My

own son . . . ratting out Anne Frank . . . You had to call the police./ What's the matter, you didn't have Dr. Mengele's number? He doesn't make house calls?/ You want Elie Wiesel's address? Maybe you could turn him in, too?" (35–36). Auslander's satire extends to the topography of Sachsenhausen: when the narrator and mother encounter a tour guide, the latter quotes the title of Tadeusz Borowski's famous work: "He clapped his hands to get the group's attention./ This way for the gas, ladies and gentlemen, he said" (207). Auslander's novel takes its cue, of course, from Philip Roth's novel *The Ghost Writer* (London: Jonathan Cape, 1979), in which Anne survives Bergen-Belsen via an army field hospital, moves to America and takes the name "Amy Bellette," not "to disguise her identity—as yet there was no need—but, as she imagined at the time, to forget her life" (125).

6. Eva Schloss and Evelyn Julia Kent, *Eva's Story: A Survivor's Tale by the Step-Sister of Anne Frank* (New York: St. Martin's Press, 1988), 2.

7. Lee, *The Hidden Life of Otto Frank*, 253. Stier bemoans critics who "infantilize" Anne Frank by referring to her as "Anne" (145), but this avoids the issue that by referring to "Frank" it is impossible to distinguish her from the rest of her family.

8. Menno Metselaar and Ruud van der Rol, *The Life of Anne Frank* (London: Macmillan, 2008 [2007]), 207; Primo Levi, *The Drowned and the Saved*, trans. Raymond Rosenthal (London: Abacus, 1988 [1986]), 39. Levi writes that "a single Anne Frank excites more emotion than the myriads who suffered as she did but whose image has remained in the shadows. Perhaps it is necessary that it can be so; if we had to and were able to suffer the sufferings of everyone, we could not live" (39). This necessity is, for Levi, not without critique: he continues that the limits of empathy mean that only "sporadic pity" can be addressed to "the single individual, the *Mitmensch*, the co-man . . . within the reach of our providentially myopic senses" (40).

9. Chris Milk, "How Virtual Reality Can Create the Ultimate Empathy Machine," https://www.ted.com/talks/chris_milk_how_virtual_reality_can_create_the_ultimate_empathy_machine/transcript?language=en (accessed December 6, 2018).

10. Robert Eaglestone, *The Holocaust and the Postmodern* (Oxford: Oxford University Press, 2004).

11. Jean Baudrillard, *Simulacra and Simulation*, trans. Sheila Faria Glasser (Ann Arbor, MI: The University of Michigan Press, 1994 [1981]), 49.

12. AnneFrank.org, http://www.annefrank.org/en/Subsites/Home/Enter-the-3D-house/#/house/start/help/ (accessed June 7, 2017).

13. Alison Landsberg, *Prosthetic Memory: The Transformation of American Remembrance in the Age of Mass Culture* (New York: Columbia University Press, 2004).

14. Alison Landsberg, *Engaging the Past: Mass Culture and the Production of Historical Knowledge* (New York: Columbia University Press, 2015), 16.

15. Alexander Etkind, "Post-Soviet Hauntology: Cultural Memory of the Soviet Terror," in *Constellations* 16, no. 1 (Oxford: Blackwell, 2009): 182–200 (182). In contrast, Victoria Stewart reads the annex (not the Secret Annex Online) as a decidedly Gothic space, "an *unheimlich* house, a house haunted by both the shades of everyday life and by other literary images of hidden chambers and locked rooms." "Anne Frank and the Uncanny," *Paragraph* 24, no. 1 (March 2001): 99–113 (104).

16. *Anne Frank House: A Museum with a Story* (Amsterdam: Anne Frank Stichting, 2013 [2011]), n.p. The 3D scale model in the Secret Annex Online is still less confusing than Anne Frank's description of the various interconnected rooms in her diary entry for July 9, 1942 (23). This model was moved by 2017 to accommodate exhibition developments, and was relocated outside the museum café in 2018.

17. Landsberg, *Engaging the Past*, 159. The "Dreaming of Hollywood" "Story" in Room Anne Frank was inaccessible on January 20, 2016, as was Van Pels's biography on January 25, 2016. On May 17, 2017, the application crashed in Victor Kugler's office.

18. Ibid., 157.

19. AnneFrank.org, http://www.annefrank.org/en/Subsites/Home/More-info/ (my italics; accessed May 30, 2017).

20. Hence Austria's photographs are testament to a moment in history when the annex's future was in no way assured, and the pictures were taken for a differently imagined form of posterity before the museum finally opened in 1960. In "The Anne Frank House: Holland's Memorial Shrine of the Book," James Young notes that Otto Frank's supporters joined forces with the historical society Amstelodamum to block the annex's demolition. Hyman Aaron Enzer and Sandra Solotaroff-Enzer, eds., *Anne Frank: Reflections on her Life and Legacy* (Urbana, IL: University of Illinois Press, 2000), 223–228 (225). The local artist Anton Witsel and his friends even posted a "day and night vigil in front of the house to protect it from the demolition teams" (225).

21. *Anne Frank House: A Museum with a Story* intriguingly contains a few pictures from 1999 of Anne's bedroom by a different photographer, Maarten van de Velde, who—unlike Bovenberg—chose to retain the wallpaper stains in her photographic reconstructions (130–131).

22. Baudrillard, *Simulacra and Simulation*, 107.

23. David Walsh, "'They are No Longer Numbers or Statistics': How Colour Pictures Are Bringing Auschwitz to Life," *Euronews*, January 28, 2020, https://www.euronews.com/2020/01/28/they-are-no-longer-numbers-or-statistics-how-colour-pictures-are-bringing-auschwitz-to-li# (accessed May 13, 2020).

24. Landsberg, *Engaging the Past*, 157. In defense of the Secret Annex Online and Landsberg's thesis, it might be asked: which representations *do* offer faithful representations of contemporaneous scenes? For example, any written account has to inscribe rather than evidence its own veracity. Hayden White and Roland Barthes's engagements with the discourse of history in *The Fiction of Narrative* (2010) and *The Rustle of Language* (1984) demonstrate the difficulty of arguing for any "true" representation in terms of verisimilitude. White returns to this issue in "Historical Truth, Estrangement, and Disbelief" in Claudio Fogu, Wulf Kansteiner, and Todd Presner, eds., *Probing the Ethics of Holocaust Culture* (Cambridge, MA: Harvard University Press, 2016), 53–71. Saul Friedländer responds to White's essay with the familiar critique that White conflates literature and history. For him, the literariness that White detects in *The Years of Extermination* (2007) merely comprises "stylistic accessories" ("On 'Historical Modernism': A Response to Hayden White," 72–78 (73,

75)). However, White does not conflate the two disciplines, but simply points out the "reality effect" in historical discourse, that can never divest itself from literariness. The attacks on White often display a slippage between the terms "literary" and "fiction." To argue that an event is narrativized is not to dismiss it as fictional, whereas Friedländer contends that White is remiss in reading modernist history as "akin to fiction" (76). White actually states that he wishes to "caution against a tendency to confuse all literary writing with fictional writing"; conversely, he wants to counter the category error that assumes that all "poetic utterance" consists of "fictionalization" (63).

25. For example, the Room Frank Family locks the bells at seven o'clock (morning or evening), whereas the Westerkerk tolls at one o'clock in Room Peter Van Pels. In an entry for July 11, 1942, Anne writes that "Father, mother and Margot still can't get used to the chiming of the Westertoren clock, which tells us the time every quarter of an hour. Not me, I liked it from the start; it sounds so reassuring, especially at night" (26). On March 25, 1943, she notes that "the Westertoren bells stopped chiming" (92), and on August 10, 1943 she laments that "our dearly beloved Westertoren bells have been carted off to be melted down for the war, so we have no idea of the exact time, either night or day" (126).

26. Of course, out-of-focus photographs are potentially no less "real" than aesthetically-pleasing ones with sharp lines; our deletion of the former is a matter precisely of form.

27. The pamphlet *Persecution and Resistance in Amsterdam*—which I refer to later in this chapter—notes that cars disappeared from the street during the war due to a lack of fuel.

28. Hilda Hein, "Assuming Responsibility: Lessons from Aesthetics," in Hugh H. Genoways, ed., *Museum Philosophy for the Twenty-First Century* (Lanham, MD: Altamira Press, 2006), 1–9 (3, 6).

29. Jean Baudrillard, *The Intelligence of Evil or the Lucidity Pact*, trans. Chris Turner (New York: Berg, 2004), 17–19. In the updated version of the Secret Annex Online (accessed November 1, 2020), the Prinsengracht 263 section has been pared down and simplified, and includes only contemporaneous photographs of the front of the building and Westerkerk, and some historical information about why the annex was undetected for two years.

30. Melissa Müller, *Anne Frank: The Biography* (London: Bloomsbury, 2013 [1999]), 267.

31. The phrase "the exactingness and uncertainty of confessional autobiography" comes from Derek Attridge's account of J. M. Coetzee's work in *J. M. Coetzee and the Ethics of Reading: Literature in the Event* (Chicago: University of Chicago Press, 2004), xii.

32. Daniel R. Schwarz, *Imagining the Holocaust* (Basingstoke: Palgrave, 2000 [1999]), 104.

33. Primo Levi, *If This Is a Man/The Truce*, trans. Stuart Woolf (London: Abacus Books, 1987 [1958]), 279–281.

34. Dir. George Stevens, *The Diary of Anne Frank* (1959).

35. Lee, *The Hidden Life of Otto Frank*, 248.

36. Anne Frank, *The Diary of a Young Girl*, eds. Otto H. Frank and Mirjam Pressler, trans. Susan Massotty (New York: Penguin, 2002 [1947]), 73.

37. Lee, *The Hidden Life of Otto Frank*, 251.

38. Bruno Bettelheim, *Surviving and Other Essays* (London: Thames and Hudson, 1979), 248–249. Bettelheim writes that "the Franks . . . could have provided themselves with some weapons had they wished . . . Had they a gun, Mr. Frank could have shot down at least one or two of the "green police" who came for them . . . Even a butcher knife, which they certainly could have taken with them into hiding, could have been used by them in self-defense" (248–249). He adds that they should have taken a ladder as a precaution, so that they could escape out of a window when required (249).

39. Kendrick played Anne Frank, and Grieg starred as Edith Frank, in the 2009 BBC miniseries *The Diary of Anne Frank*.

40. AnneFrank.org, http://www.annefrank.org/en/Subsites/Home/More-info/ (accessed July 5, 2017). In the updated version of the Secret Annex Online (accessed November 1, 2020), the "hotspots" lead to videos embedded in YouTube.

41. Frank, *The Diary of a Young Girl*, 86.

42. In *Anne Frank: The Book, The Life, The Afterlife* (London: Atlantic Books, 2010 [2009]), Francine Prose disagrees, and argues that each reading "reveals aspects of the work that we may have missed before and allows us to view the book in the light of our own experience, of everything we have learned, remembered, and forgotten since the first time we read it" (89).

43. I do not intend to argue here that "Bombs fall on Amsterdam" achieves the singularity defined by Attridge: several viewings may be required to garner the information, but this does not result in subsequent, varied, and enriching interpretations of the data.

44. Max Silverman, *Palimpsestic Memory: The Holocaust and Colonialism in French and Francophone Fiction and Film* (New York: Berghahn, 2013), 8.

45. In *Engaging the Past*, Landsberg writes of a constant "oscillation" between affective engagement and empathic unsettlement in the user's experience of the Secret Annex Online (157).

46. Fogu et al., *Probing the Ethics of Holocaust Culture*, 193.

47. Kendrick and Grieg's clipped English accents may ensure a wide audience for the Secret Annex Online—but not, as Brink noted in 2016, in the Spanish-speaking world—but they cannot help but grate against the linguistic interchanges between Dutch and German that Anne discusses throughout her diary, and which are absent in the application. Anne's assimilation into Dutch culture is noted in one of her earliest diary entries (June 14, 1942), when she registers the "beautiful" gift of *Dutch Sagas and Legends* (2). In contradistinction to her occasional deployment of German in the diary, as when she uses "*Ausnahmsweise*" ("by way of exception"), "the only word that will do" to describe the inhabitants "getting on well together" in December 1943 (152), she sometimes isolates the annex adults as "Germans"—and implicitly marks herself out as Dutch—by arguing that they do not recognize the difference between discussions and quarrels (128–129). Yet these linguistic and cultural overlaps and tensions are downplayed in the Secret Annex Online, as if an actress with a Dutch accent might alienate English speakers who require "some kind of immediate, direct access" to the events in the annex.

48. Leanne White and Elspeth Frew, eds., *Dark Tourism and Place Identity: Managing and Interpreting Dark Places* (New York: Routledge, 2013), 191; Landsberg, *Engaging the Past*, 153.

49. Landsberg, *Engaging the Past*, 148.

50. Ibid., 162.

51. Geoffrey Hartman, *The Longest Shadow: In the Aftermath of the Holocaust* (Bloomington, IN: Indiana University Press, 1996), 133. Overidentification has been a particular problem in relation to Anne Frank: Ian Buruma argues that she has become "a Jewish Saint Ursula, a Dutch Joan of Arc, a female Christ" (Goldstein, 16).

52. Landsberg, *Prosthetic Memory*, 2; Charlotte Delbo, *Auschwitz and After*, trans. Rosette C. Lamont (New Haven, CT: Yale University Press, 1995), 11.

53. Delbo, *Auschwitz and After*, 11.

54. Dave Eggers, *The Circle* (New York: Alfred A. Knopf, 2013), *passim*.

55. Theodor Adorno, "Commitment," trans. F. MacDonagh, in R. Livingstone, P. Anderson, and F. Mulhern, eds., *Aesthetics and Politics* (London: New Left Books, 1977), 177–195 (189).

56. Ibid., 189.

57. Victoria Stewart, "Anne Frank and the Uncanny," , 101, 112; Judith Goldstein, "Anne Frank: The Redemption Myth," *Partisan Review* 70, no. 1 (Winter 2003): 16–23 (16).

58. Frank, *The Diary of a Young Girl*, 332.

59. Theodor Adorno, *Minima Moralia*, trans. E. F. N. Jephcott (London: Verso, 1978 [1951]), 25; Frank, *The Diary of a Young Girl*, 332. Roth criticizes the humanist focus on Anne's positivity in *The Ghost Writer*: Amy Bellette "was not, after all, the fifteen-year-old who could, while hiding from a holocaust, tell Kitty, *I still believe that people are really good at heart.* Her youthful ideals had suffered no less than she had in the windowless freight car from Westerbork and in the barracks at Auschwitz and on the Belsen heath. She had not come to hate the human race for what it was—what could it be but what it was?—but she did not feel seemly any more singing its praises" (146).

60. Frank, *The Diary of a Young Girl*, 336.

61. Stewart, "Anne Frank and the Uncanny," 112.

62. Lawrence Langer, "The Uses—and Misuses—of a Young Girl's Diary: 'If Anne Frank Could Return from among the Murdered, She Would Be Appalled,'" and "The Americanisation of the Holocaust on Stage and Screen" in *Anne Frank: Reflections on her Life and Legacy*, 203–205 (203), 198–202 (199). As Langer pithily states in the second essay, the limiting situation of the annex has become iconic because—in terms of the inhabitants' internment between 1942 and 1944—"No one dies" (200). In *The End of the Holocaust* (Bloomington, IN: Indiana University Press, 2011), Alvin Rosenfeld concurs with Langer when he writes (twice) about the dangers of "cherishing" Anne Frank, which "dehistoricize[s]" her story into "the eternal verities of 'the human spirit,'" and other such banalities" (103, 108). In contrast with Langer and Rosenfeld's consistent dismissal of "the human spirit," in *Tony Harrison and the Holocaust* (Liverpool: Liverpool University Press, 2001), I argue for a more complex dialectical humanism which agonizes over such "banalities" as lovers' discourse precisely in the wider context of human suffering.

63. Noah Shenker, *Reframing Holocaust Testimony* (Bloomington, IN: Indiana University Press, 2015), 149.

64. AnneFrank.org, http://www.annefrank.org/en/Subsites/Home/The-outcome/ (accessed June 5, 2017). Landsberg notes that Anne was taken away to Bergen-Belsen (*Engaging the Past*, 164), but she was, of course, deported to Auschwitz-Birkenau first along with the rest of her family.

65. Landsberg, *Engaging the Past*, 148.

66. These complexities include the conflicting accounts of Auguste Van Pels's death. "The fate of those in the Secret Annex," http://www.annefrank.org/en/Subsites/ Home/Enter-the-3D-house/#/house/0/hotspot/5481/video/ (accessed June 7, 2017) recounts that she arrived in Belsen in November 1944: "a few months later" she was taken away on a transport with other prisoners and "horrifically murdered" be-tween April 9 and May 8, 1945. In the "Afterword" to Frank and Pressler's version of the diary, it is noted that she went from Belsen to Buchenwald, then to Theresienstadt on April 9, 1945, "and apparently to another concentration camp after that. It is certain that she did not survive, though the date of her death is unknown" (340). In contrast, Müller writes that Auguste was put on a transport to Raguhn in Saxony-Anhalt (a sat-ellite camp of Buchenwald) on February 5, 1945, and was then sent to Theresienstadt, "but presumably did not live to make it there" (324). In the most detailed account of her death amongst these samples, *Anne Frank House: A Museum with a Story* records that she was "murdered by the Nazis in a gruesome manner: by being thrown under a train" in Theresienstadt (210).

67. Lee, *The Hidden Life of Otto Frank*, 63, 64, 76.

68. Michael Rothberg, "Multidirectional Memory and the Implicated Subject: On Sebald and Kentridge," in Liedke Plate and Anneke Smelik, eds., *Performing Memory in Art and Popular Culture* (New York: Routledge, 2013), 39–58.

69. Lee, *The Hidden Life of Otto Frank*, 139; Frank, *The Diary of a Young Girl*, 13. This uneasiness about "snooping" impresses upon the virtual visitor that we are (as in the actual museum), usually looking *into* the secret annex, rather than attempting to un-derstand "how the world looked *from* the hiding place" (James Young, *At Memory's Edge: After-Images of the Holocaust in Contemporary Art and Architecture* (New Haven, CT: Yale University Press, 2000), 83. Hence the "Anne peers outside" hotspot in the Front office room undermines the former perspective as the user listens to her narrative at the net curtains about "slum kids" and two Jewish passers by wearing stars; she feels a kind of "betrayal" when she watches the latter in December 1942. Shimon Attie's *The Neighbour Next Door* installation in December 1995 precisely attempted to draw attention to "how the world looked *from* the hiding place" (83): sixteen-millimeter projectors played footage taken from those in hiding at Prinsengracht 468, 514, and 572. Young argues that "the national image of sheltering was being turned inside-out, the lens turned back on those for whom the 'neighbour next door' had become a more self-aggrandizing image than a reality. The image of the sheltered was now displaced by moving images of what the sheltered saw: Dutch bystanders, collaborators, and Nazis" (85). The Dutch Resistance Museum opens with a film in-stallation about the choices to "*aanpaasen, meeodon, verzetten*" (adjust, collaborate,

resist): Young is a little over-selective in that the inhabitants of the secret annex would also have seen victims—as Anne does in December 1942—helpers, and members of the Dutch resistance, even if he is correct that "the national image of sheltering" can lead to a distortion of history.

70. Belsen Project, https://www.belsen-project.specs-lab.com/the-box-installation (accessed July 14, 2016); Jennifer Rapson, *Topographies of Suffering: Buchenwald, Babi Yar, Lidice* (New York: Berghahn, 2015), 8.

71. Tod Presner, "The Ethics of the Algorithm: Close and Distant Listening in the Shoah Foundation Visual History Archive," in Fogu et al., *Probing the Ethics of Holocaust Culture*, 175–202 (179).

72. Ibid., 179.

73. Anne Kelly Knowles, Tim Cole, and Alberto Giordano, *Geographies of the Holocaust* (Bloomington, IN: Indiana University Press, 2014), 9, 13, 212, 216.

74. *Probing the Ethics of Holocaust Culture*, 208.

75. Knowles et al., *Geographies of the Holocaust*, 9, 13.

76. Ibid., 44.

77. Antony Rowland, interview with Tom Brink (August 2016).

78. Young, *At Memory's Edge*, 64. *Anne's Amsterdam* is also important to consider in the context of the forgetfulness of technological innovation. Unlike many books currently out of print, it is unlikely that such museum apps will ever be recreated: one of the aims of this study is thus to capture such developmental innovations before they are erased from digital memory. One such app is *Anne Frank House* (2016): Brink explained that this was developed primarily so visitors waiting in the long Westermarkt queue would have something to read before entering the museum. For a small fee, *Anne Frank House* provides the user with metatextual information about, for example, "The Holocaust," "Life in the Achterhuis" and "Anne Frank Foundation," with accompanying photographs.

79. Young, *At Memory's Edge*, 62.

80. Ibid., 64, 72. In "Anne Five Years Old," a black and white photograph of Anne with her new watch has been superimposed on a color photograph of Singel 400, the site of the Opekta offices before they moved to Prinsengracht 263.

81. Levi, *The Drowned and the Saved*, 11–12.

82. The former headquarters of the occupation's security services (no. 99) was a girls' school before the war and is now the Gerrit van der Veen College: the annex's inhabitants and helpers were escorted there after the arrest on August 4, 1944. After the war, Euterpestraat was renamed after van Veen, a sculptor and member of the Dutch Resistance who produced 80,000 false identity papers. Van Veen was arrested on May 12, 1944 and executed near Overveen. In the "Skating" item, Anne recounts her delight in receiving a pair of ice skates that can be permanently nailed to a shoe, rather than her previous reliance on temporary skates that had to be screwed into her shoes. The item's metatext outlines Anne's persistence at skating during the winter of 1941–1942.

83. There is now a link on the Secret Annex Online to a website advertising a two-hour walking tour of Merwedeplein and its environs (120 Euros for four people). Anne Frank Walking Tour, https://www.annefrankwalkingtour.com/ (accessed October 28, 2020).

84. Young, *At Memory's Edge*, 73.

85. Daniel Mendelsohn, *The Lost: A Search for Six of Six Million* (London: William Collins, 2013 [2007]), 588. "[C]ouldn't possibly" indicates a different stance from the perceived "presence of the past" that is apparent "only to those already familiar with a site's history" (Young, *At Memory's Edge*, 62). Mendelsohn's six-hundred and sixty-page epic demonstrates an intimate knowledge of the town's topography, and yet he can only "enjoy" this knowledge (588) rather than "reconnect" with the past.

86. In conversation with Brink in August 2018, he relayed that *Anne's Amsterdam* was scrapped primarily due to the poor download figures, but also due to the updates required for the relatively few tourists using the app.

87. Akin to the Secret Annex Online, the advantage of the digital application and virtual film in relation to the attic is that users can gain entry to a space that is barred to "regular" museum visitors due to the unsafe staircase.

88. An argument could be made that the juxtaposition of different timescales in the Prinsengracht scenes contained in the Secret Annex Online actually points to more self-awareness about the danger of a "realistic hallucination" than the proposed VR images based on contemporaneous photographs.

89. Presner, "The Ethics of the Algorithm," 179.

90. JoodsMonument.nl, https://www.joodsmonument.nl/ (accessed August 18, 2017).

91. Chris Milk, "How Virtual Reality Can Create the Ultimate Empathy Machine," https://www.ted.com/talks/chris_milk_how_virtual_reality_can_create_the_ultimate_empathy_machine/transcript?language=en (accessed December 6, 2018).

92. 'Anne Frank House VR Trailer', https://www.youtube.com/watch?v=HCFUuyi-lIc (accessed September 8, 2018).

93. VRFocus, https://www.vrfocus.com/2017/09/meet-famous-painter-rembrandt-with-gear-vr/ (accessed August 21, 2018).

94. In a conversation in August 2018, Brink said that the next VR version of the annex would include the Front House due to its importance to the overall narrative.

95. 'Become Anne Frank in Virtual Reality', https://www.youtube.com/watch?v=MzQcvwGh5M4 (accessed September 8, 2018).

96. Adorno, "Commitment," 189.

97. Landsberg, *Engaging the Past*, 162.

98. Baudrillard, *The Intelligence of Evil*, 49.

99. In contrast, there are some of Austria's black and white photographs on display, but these were only on display in the museum café in August 2018. Visitors to this section of the Anne Frank House can still appreciate the dilapidated state of the annex in the early 1950s, but their peripherality in the museum's narrative of events ironically encourages the visitor to think of these as the tawdry aftermath to the "real" color photographs of the annex in the 1940s.

100. The visitor now views these scale models after the new, darkened room that completes the museum tour with different version of the diary on display. The muted lighting has the effect of creating a "hallowed" space for the diaries, rather than the (slightly cramped) space in the previous room, where visitors often walked past the central displays, and so missed an opportunity to view the diary. The new

room also contains brief information on a wall panel about the different versions of the diaries.

101. Thomas Frick, "J. G. Ballard, The Art of Fiction No. 85," *The Paris Review* 94 (Winter 1984), https://www.theparisreview.org/interviews/2929/j-g-ballard-the-art-of-fict ion-no-85-j-g-ballard (accessed August 16, 2018).

Chapter 6

1. Andrew Hoskins, "Signs of the Holocaust: Exhibiting Memory in a Mediated Age," *Media, Culture and Society* 25, no. 7 (2003): 7–22 (10).

2. Andreas Huyssen, *Twilight Memories: Making Time in a Culture of Amnesia* (New York: Routledge, 1995), 18.

3. These light boxes include Jitshok Rudashewski's diary entry from April 6, 1943 about the Vilna ghetto. He was subsequently murdered in the Ponary forest.

4. Claude Lanzmann, "The Obscenity of Understanding: An Evening with Claude Lanzmann," in *Trauma: Explorations in Memory*, ed. Cathy Caruth (Baltimore: Johns Hopkins University Press, 1995), 200–220.

5. In "Signs of the Holocaust," Andrew Hoskins still refers to the Holocaust sublime in 2003 ("How does one even begin to represent or simulate the absolutely unim-aginable?" [9]), whereas such rhetoric is absent from Alison Landsberg's *Prosthetic Memory: The Transformation of American Remembrance in the Age of Mass Culture* (New York: Columbia University Press, 2004) and Daniel Levy and Natan Sznaider's, *The Holocaust and Memory in the Global Age*, trans. Assenka Sznaider (Philadelphia, PA: Temple University Press, 2006).

6. Matthew Boswell, interview with Thomas Lutz (June 2013). Lutz founded the International Committee of Memorial Museums in Remembrance of the Victims of Public Crimes (ICMEMO).

7. Young argues that "In shouldering the memory-work, monuments may relieve viewers of their memory burden." *The Texture of Memory: Holocaust Memorials and Meaning* (New Haven, CT: Yale University Press, 1993), 5.

8. Edward T. Linenthal, *Preserving Memory: The Struggle to Create America's Holocaust Museum* (New York: Columbia University Press, 2001 [1995]), xiii–xiv.

9. Marianne Hirsch, "Holocaust Testimony Beyond the Frame," *Los Angeles Review of Books*, May 23, 2020, https://lareviewofbooks.org/article/holocaust-testimony-bey ond-the-frame (accessed May 26, 2020).

10. Erin McGlothlin, "Theorizing the Perpetrator in Bernhard Schlink's *The Reader* and Martin Amis's *Time's Arrow*," in *After Representation: The Holocaust, Literature, and Culture*, eds. R. Clinton Spargo and Robert M. Ehrenreich (New Brunswick, NJ: Rutgers University Press, 2010), 210–230 (213).

11. Linenthal, *Preserving Memory*, 200.

12. Perhaps the design team was worried that visitors would be taken in by the men-dacity of, for example, extracts from Rudolf Hoess's *Commandant of Auschwitz*

(1956) in his confessional attempt at exculpation, whereas they believed that a photograph constitutes uncomplicated evidence of a crime.

13. In contrast, a temporary exhibition in 2015 entitled "Germany 1945: The Last Months of the War" included a section on "1945 in Postwar German Cinema."

14. An hour would, therefore, not give enough time to read one of the five sections of the center. Indeed, the second, extended section—which begins with an account of Himmler—took this visitor fifty minutes to explore with a thorough, but not comprehensive, engagement with the material. In total, this visit—which did not include reading through all the documentation on bureaucracy—took three hours to complete. Information overload is not particular to the Topography of Terror, of course, and is a common response to museums: the vast material held in the extension of the Jewish Museum in Berlin is, for example, impossible to take in during a single visit. However, the bombardment at the Topography of Terror can be contrasted with the minimalist approach at the more recent, and smaller, Berlin museums, such as the Silent Heroes center. Also, the deluge needs to be read differently in the contexts of vastly different museums and memorials. Whereas the various representations of Jewish culture in Germany appears as a rejoinder to the Final Solution in Libeskind's extension, the information in the Topography of Terror can be read, for example, as an ironic retort in the specific context of the perpetrators' attempts to conceal their crimes.

15. Huyssen, *Twilight Memories*, 18.

16. I am paraphrasing here from Dan Stone, "History, Memory, Testimony," in *The Future of Testimony* (New York: Routledge, 2014), 17–30, in which he refers to testimony and memory troubling the "clear waters of historiography" (19).

17. Christopher R. Marshall, "The Contemporary Museum as Art Gallery," in Suzanne MacLeod, ed., *Reshaping Museum Space: Architecture, Design, Exhibitions* (New York: Routledge, 2005), 174.

18. Jeshajahu Weinberg and Rita Elieli, *The Holocaust Museum in Washington* (New York: Rizzoli International Publications, 1995), 69. Their proclamation is, of course, rather too blunt, as visitors *do* read through the data at the Topography of Terror, if maybe not for six hours.

19. Dan Stone, "History, Memory, Testimony," 25. It could be argued that visitors can encounter representations of this victim "experience" elsewhere in the "spider's web," at the Jewish Museum Berlin or the information center under Eisenmann's memorial.

20. Young, *The Texture of Memory*, 5.

21. Erving Goffman, *Relations in Public: Microstudies of the Public Order* (New York: Basic books, 1971), 63.

22. Theodor Adorno, "Valéry Proust Museum," in *Prisms*, trans. Samuel and Shierry Weber (Cambridge, MA: MIT Press, 1981 [1967]), 173–186 (176).

23. Goffman, *Relations in Public*, 63.

24. Quoted in Linenthal, *Preserving Memory*, 199. Such concerns contrast with the Holocaust Exhibition at the Imperial War Museum, where an SS uniform forms one of the opening exhibits. Against the idea that the western "showcase" museum is inherently stocked with objects, many of which are the results of colonial pillaging,

the permanent exhibition space is symbolic of Berlin at the end of the war, devoid of valuable artifacts.

25. Saul Friedländer, *Reflections of Nazism: An Essay on Kitsch and Death*, trans. Thomas Weyr (New York: Harper & Row, 1984), 19.

26. Lutz will have remembered Hans Haacke's recreation of a Nazi memorial in Graz "in order to remind [Germans] of the site's complicitous past": neo-Nazis then torched the edifice on November 2, 1988 (Young, *The Texture of Memory*, 8). In our interview, Lutz commented that, "Since 1987 I have not seen one attempt from right wing activists who [have used] this [exhibition] for any event. I have seen some groups walk through but they were calm. We had an arson attack, bomb threats but not the other."

27. Jenni Adams, "Introduction," *Holocaust Studies: A Journal of Culture and History— Special Issue: Representing Perpetrators in Holocaust Literature and Film* 17, no. 2–3 (Autumn/Winter 2011): 1–9 (2).

28. My argument differs here from Caroline Pearce's in *Contemporary Germany and the Nazi Legacy: Remembrance, Politics and the Dialectic of Normality* (Basingstoke: Palgrave, 2007). Pearce contends that the panels, in "detailing human values, choices and behaviour in a criminal regime" represent "the potential perpetrator in all of us" (227).

29. Suzanne Bardgett quoted in Hoskins, "Signs of the Holocaust," 14.

30. Exceptions are, of course, the few contemporaneous color photographs and footage (such as Eva Braun's).

31. Taken on October 12, 1964, this photograph is first encountered as a black and white image in the main exhibition.

32. Weinberg and Elieli, *The Holocaust Museum in Washington*, 55.

33. Section five includes a photograph of former Waffen SS men in Karlburg (Lower Bavaria), organized by the "Mutual Aid Society of Former Members of the Waffen SS (HIAG)" (July 27, 1957).

34. I am thinking here of the Documentation Centre on Nazi Forced Labour in Schoeneweide (Berlin).

35. Antony Beevor, *Berlin: The Downfall 1945* (New York: Penguin, 2007 [2002]), 351. Beevor records that only seven prisoners were spared: six were and later liberated by the Russians on May 2 (387). As far as I am aware, there is no record of these events in the Topography of Terror. Beevor later notes that the government in Bonn was "extremely vigilant to prevent any shrine to Nazism and its leader" (431).

36. Pearce, *Contemporary Germany and the Nazi Legacy*, 160.

37. Linenthal, *Preserving Memory*, x.

38. Pearce, *Contemporary Germany and the Nazi Legacy*, 215. Built in 1935–1936 on the orders of Göring, the *Reichsluftfahrtministerium* was designed by Ernst Sagebiel, who also rebuilt Tempelhof. One of the few buildings in the area to survive the Allied bombings, it later became the "House of the Ministries" during the GDR, and then, post-*Wende*, the "Trust Establishment," selling off ex-GDR, state-owned companies.

39. Linenthal, *Preserving Memory*, 88.

40. Hoskins, "Signs of the Holocaust," 16. Windows periodically and automatically open in the center: their noise similarly draws the visitors to the buildings' exterior.

41. Young, *The Texture of Memory*, 27. Viewed again from the eastern entrance, the distant and discrete building appears to be rising from the rubble. The latter functions as an important sign of history at the Topography of Terror: the site, as Young recounts, was mainly "a great weed-choked mountain of rubble" until the 1980s. Although Allied bombing badly damaged the Gestapo and SS buildings, they were still structurally sound: left derelict for a while, the Prinz-Albrecht-Palais was blown up with dynamite in April 1949. As Young notes, even the well-preserved Museum of Ethnology—on one of the corners of the Gestapo-Gelände—was destroyed in 1963, even though it had reopened for a time in the 1950s (84). The landscape then became "a great, gaping wound" in which waves of rubble signified an "absence of memory," and the traumatic circumstances of its coming into being (23, 81). Today, the simulacrum of the manicured rubble remembers forgetting in the form of attempts to erase memories of war in what Daniel Levy and Natan Sznaider describe as "the public, future-orientated stance of the reconstruction phase" of West German history in the 1950s (*The Holocaust and Memory in the Global Age*, 66). Active memory-work concerning the Nazi past was considered a "needless complication in the struggle to win the cold war": Levy and Sznaider argue that the denial of guilt "provided the cultural foundations for Germany to become democratic and, within certain limits, "normalize" itself." As well as remembering forgetting, the signs of rubble subtly evoke the *Trümmerfrauen*, "rubble women" between the age of fifteen and fifty, who—by order of allied forces in 1945—had to stockpile sixty million cubic meters of rubble for rebuilding Berlin. The permanent exhibition ignores the *Trümmerfrauen*, presumably because its inclusion might have temporarily shifted the narrative to German victimhood.

42. Linenthal, *Preserving Memory*, 107.

43. The moment of countermemorials is over, bound up as they were with artistic movements of the 1980s and 1990s, and the incitement to Holocaust memory that is now in evidence in memorials and museums across Berlin and Germany. In this sense, the Topography of Terror counters the countermemorial. For example, virtual memory in the form of Norbert Radermacher's trip light-beam used to remind passersby of the former site of a KZ-Aussenlager, a satellite concentration camp of Sachsenhausen. The beam that bathed "a guilty landscape in Berlin's Neukölln neighbourhood with the inscribed light of its past" has now disappeared (Young, 23), so, arguably, a "facade of innocence" returns to the area (42).

44. Different thinking leads to the display at the IWMN, where the Holocaust exhibition is minimalist, as I discuss in "The Imperial War Museum North: a Twenty-first Century Museum?," in *The Future of Memory*, eds. Rick Crownshaw, Jane Kilby and Antony Rowland (New York, and Oxford: Berghahn, 2010), 51–76.

45. Young, *The Texture of Memory*, 87.

46. Ibid., 20.

47. Ravensbrück sometimes evinces a mania of meta-memory: in one of the exhibitions at the former SS houses, the history of a defunct water pipe is carefully signposted on

a landing. However, the Topography of Terror is not the only perpetrator site that is not open to meta-memory, as unremarked, historic tiles in the Wannsee villa indicate. In contrast, in the film *Lore* (2012), such tiles are presented as symbolic of the kitsch sentimentality of Nazism, with its fetishization of the countryside: the eponymous "heroine" symbolically frees herself from her Nazi past when she smashes a porcelain deer that she has preserved throughout the traumatic narrative of defeat and reconciliation. The Wannsee villa is different to the Topography of Terror, of course, in that it was not reduced to rubble, but the building and gardens appear as a simulacrum of history in that they are fashioned to appear contemporaneous. As with the Topography of Terror, the emphasis is on the permanent exhibition rather than the architecture: the villa does not draw attention, for example, to the restoration of the building after its use for many years as a school hostel.

48. Hoskins, "Signs of the Holocaust," 10.

49. Ibid., 10.

50. Pearce, *Contemporary Germany and the Nazi Legacy*, 212.

51. Young, *The Texture of Memory*, 83.

52. The air-raid shelter may, of course, have been structurally unstable.

53. Levy and Sznaider, *The Holocaust and Memory in the Global Age*, 63.

54. Pearce, *Contemporary Germany and the Nazi Legacy*, 217, 2. Pearce adopts the term *Leitverantwortung* "to point to a productive response that encourages remembrance and attempts to incorporate the 'lessons' of the past into political education and international policy as well as public initiatives" (2).

55. Michael Rothberg, *Multidirectional Memory: Remembering the Holocaust in an Age of Decolonization* (Stanford, CA: Stanford University Press, 2009), 11.

56. Young, *The Texture of Memory*, 25.

57. Rothberg states that Israel's occupation of Palestine "has produced some of the most obvious—and often invidious—analogizing of the Nazi genocide in relation to political struggle" (311). In "Genocide and the Terror of History," A. Dirk Moses illustrates that "Rather than being the harbinger of a universal human-rights culture," or "tending only in a liberal direction of transcultural understanding," multidirectional memory in this context "contributes towards terroristic political action in the form of pre-emptive strikes and anticipatory self-defence" Rick Crownshaw, ed., *Transcultural Memory* (New York: Routledge, 2014), 96. Moses quotes the Israeli newspaper *Harretz* from 2006: Yair Sheleg contests that "if hesitating to hurt Lebanese civilians in response to attacks on us could send Iran the message that we will hesitate to hurt civilians if Iran strikes us, then we must not be deterred" (101).

58. Boswell, interview with Lutz, 2013.

59. Eric L. Santner, *Stranded Objects: Mourning, Memory, and Film in Postwar Germany* (Ithaca, NY: Cornell University Press, 1990), xi.

60. Levy and Sznaider, *The Holocaust and Memory in the Global Age*, 70.

61. Ibid., 2.

62. Arddun Hedydd Arwyn, "Forging an Identity? Expellee Organisations and Expellee Culture in the Federal Republic of Germany, 1949–2009," MA dissertation for the University of Aberystwyth (2009).

63. Arddun, 29; Levy and Sznaider, *The Holocaust and Memory in the Global Age*, 76. Levy and Szaider note that another two million refugees followed between 1950 and 1988 (76).

64. Kate Connolly, "Nazi Control Room Re-opens as Topography of Terror Museum in Berlin," *The Guardian*, May 6, 2010, https://www.theguardian.com/world/2010/may/06/topography-terror-nazi-museum-berlin (accessed December 15, 2020).

65. *Unwilling Germans?: The Goldhagen Debate*, ed. Robert R. Shandley, trans. Jeremiah Riemer (Minneapolis, MN: University of Minnesota Press, 1998), 31.

66. Levy and Sznaider, *The Holocaust and Memory in the Global Age*, 76.

67. Vivian Petraka, *Spectacular Suffering: Theatre, Fascism, and the Holocaust* (Bloomington, IN: Indiana University Press, 1999), 117.

68. Michael Rothberg, "Multidirectional Memory and the Implicated Subject: On Sebald and Kentridge," in Liedche Plate and Anneke Smelik, eds., *Performing Memory in Art and Popular Culture* (New York: Routledge, 2013), 39–58 (41).

69. Hoskins, "Signs of the Holocaust," 10.

70. Levy and Sznaider, *The Holocaust and Memory in the Global Age*, 5. By "national" history here I mean the Nazi period specifically: no mention is made of the German killing of Herero in Namibia, for example.

71. Levy and Sznaider, *The Holocaust and Memory in the Global Age*, 4. Levy and Sznaider's work typifies the loss of awkward poetics in transcultural approaches to the Holocaust. Prosthetic memories of the event have become "a moral touchstone in an age of uncertainty," but this "touchstone" eschews the politics of complicity, and any sense that engagements with the Holocaust involve confronting—as in Felman and Laub's writing—the limits of representation.

72. Levy and Sznaider, *The Holocaust and Memory in the Global Age*, 27. They criticize Young's focus on national memory because it "does not sufficiently take into account how global *topoi* are inscribed into local and national discourse," but there are no such *topoi* at the Topography of Terror (9).

Conclusion

1. Wulf Kansteiner, "The Holocaust in the 21st Century: Digital Anxiety, Transnational Cosmopolitanism, and Never Again Genocide without Memory," in Andrew Hoskins, ed., *Digital Memory Studies: Media Pasts in Transition* (London: Routledge, 2018), 110–140 (122).

2. Andrew Thacker, *Modernism, Space and the City* (Edinburgh: Edinburgh University Press, 2019), 184.

3. Britta Lokting, "Meet the World's First 3-D Interactive Holocaust Survivor," *The Forward*, November 24, 2015, http://forward.com/culture/324989/meet-the-worlds-first-3-d-interactive-holocaust-survivor/ (accessed January 22, 2016).

4. At one point, the TV program satirizes the glitches in voice recognition technology that we explored in Chapter 1. At the beginning of episode five of the first series ("Contrapasso"), Dr. Robert Ford ruminates on a dog he owned during his childhood,

and turns to a gnarled host. "Never seen a greyhound have you, Bill?" asks Ford. The old gunslinger replies: "seen a few showdowns in my day."

5. Kansteiner, "The Holocaust in the 21st Century," 122.

6. In *Digital Holocaust Memory, Education and Research* (London: Palgrave Macmillan, 2021), Victoria Grace Walden proposes that critics should use the term "mixed reality" for "immersive" and "intra-action" for "interactive" (269). Walden is right to argue that the immersive aspects of VR have been overplayed, and that "absolute immersion seems to exist more in the imaginary than as lived-world experience of image-spaces" (276). However, whilst "mixed reality" offers the advantage of a focus on form rather than user experience, we would still argue that there is a difference between studying a Renaissance frieze, for example, and the potential sensory disturbances, occlusions, and distortions of VR. (Walden's edited book was published just before the current study went into production.)

7. Ibid., 122.

8. Hoskins uses the term "connective memory" in "7/7 and Connective Memory: Interactional Trajectories of Remembering in Post-scarcity Culture," *Memory Studies* 4, no. 3 (2011), https://journals.sagepub.com/doi/10.1177/17506 98011402570 (accessed February 10, 2021).

9. Alison Landsberg, *Prosthetic Memory: The Transformation of American Remembrance in the Age of Mass Culture* (New York: Columbia University Press, 2004), 2. Caveats remain about whether Landsberg is actually describing a form of memory: how can you remember something that you never experienced?

10. Andrew Hoskins, "Memory of the Multitude: the end of collective memory," in *Digital Memory Studies*, 85–109 (101).

11. Ibid., 106, 105, 102, 103, 105.

12. Ibid., 105.

13. Ibid., 105, 104, 105.

14. Ibid., 101.

15. Amanda Lagerkrist, "The Media End: Digital Afterlife Agencies and Techno-existential Closure," in *Digital Memory Studies*, 48–84 (48).

16. Ibid., 48. "Save your memories for Eternity," announces the website that explains the 5D memory crystal: "New technology enables storing data in glass for billions of years." https://www.5dmemorycrystal.com (accessed February 9, 2021).

17. Hoskins, "Memory of the Multitude," 92; Lagerkrist, "The Media End," 55. Joanne Garde-Hansen, Andrew Hoskins, and Anna Reading agree with Lagerkrist in their introduction to *Save As . . . Digital Memories* (Basingstoke: Palgrave, 2009), and argue that "digital technologies might seem to be changing memory by reversing the age-old default of human societies, which is to forget" (1). Nine years later, "might" has become "have" for Hoskins in *Digital Memory Studies*.

18. Lagerkrist, "The Media End," 48.

19. Hoskins, "Memory of the Multitude," 88, 91.

20. Will Self, "Do We Still Need Stories?" *The Guardian*, November 26, 2016, 18.

21. Dave Eggers, *The Circle* (New York: Alfred A. Knopf, 2013). I am referring here to the morning roll call ("*Appel*") in Charlotte Delbo's *Auschwitz and After*, trans. Rosette C. Lamont (New Haven, CT: Yale University Press, 1995), 31.

22. Hoskins, "Introduction," in *Digital Memory Studies*, 1. My italics.
23. Hoskins, "Memory of the Multitude," 87.
24. Ibid., 101.
25. Ibid., 101; Hoskins, "The Restless Past: An introduction to digital memory and media," in *Digital Memory Studies*, 1–24 (8).
26. Todd Presner, "The Ethics of the Algorithm: Close and Distant Listening to the Shoah Foundation Visual History Archive," in Claudio Fogu, Wulf Kansteiner, and Todd Presner, eds., *Probing the Ethics of Holocaust Culture* (Cambridge, MA: Harvard University Press, 2016), 175–202 (179).
27. Although the technology superficially rewards a choice question, recollections of traumatic experiences are closed off to the visitor either by nonrecognizable questions, censorship, or technological glitches. The speech recognition algorithms have problems recognizing some of the key German and Dutch words in relation to Gutter and Schloss's testimony, such as "Kollwitz" and "Theresienstadt," and—a regrettable glitch given that Schloss is the step-daughter of Otto Frank—"Merwedeplein," where the Frank family lived before moving to Prinsengracht 263. Nevertheless, one of the unexpected pleasures of Dimensions in Testimony is the mining of accidental testimonial details through the failures of the speech recognition technology. In a sense, these glitches are effective and affective symbols for human miscommunication.
28. Hoskins, "The Restless Past," in Hoskins, *Digital Memory Studies*, 15.
29. "Post-scarcity" requires some modification, as access to digital culture across the globe is clearly unequal. As Anne Reading and Tanya Notley note in *Digital Memory Studies*, for example, only five per cent of the Sudanese population has access to electricity: "our digital-global memory production, storage and circulation practices may be widening and deepening inequalities in terms of individual and collective memory-making capacities . . . the political economy of digital memory is as unequal as the capitalist economy of which it is a part" ("Globital Memory Capital: Theorizing digital memory economies," 234–249 (237, 239).
30. Quoted in Kansteiner, "The Holocaust in the 21st Century," 124.
31. Ibid., 111, 122.
32. Ibid., 124.
33. Ibid., 118.
34. Ibid., 123.
35. Hoskins, "Memory of the Multitude," 87.
36. Fogu, Kansteiner and Presner, "Introduction," in Fogu et al., *Probing the Ethics of Holocaust Culture*, 22.
37. Garde-Hansen et al., *Save as . . . Digital Memories*, 14.
38. Johanna Drucker, *SpecLab* (Berkeley, CA: University of Chicago Press, 2010), 9.
39. Jean Baudrillard, *Simulacra and Simulation*, trans. Sheila Faria Glaser (Ann Arbor, MI: The University of Michigan Press, 1994 [1981]), 1.
40. Hoskins, *Digital Memory Studies*, 101. In this sense, our study adheres to what the editors of *Probing the Ethics of Holocaust Culture* refer to as "a perceptible shift in scholarly focus from close readings of (written or visual) texts *within* discrete modes of representation, to questions of remediation typical of a growing sensibility to the

operationality of digital technology" (169). However, as we illustrate throughout this book, scholars also need to be attentive to the forms of representation indicative of this remediation: hence the close readings in this book of Dimensions in Testimony, the Bergen-Belsen applications, the Kristallnacht exhibition in Second Life and the technological developments surrounding the Anne Frank House.

41. Fogu, Kansteiner, and Presner, "Introduction," in Fogu et al., *Probing the Ethics of Holocaust Culture*, 22.

42. Ibid., 14.

43. Ibid., 18.

44. Roger Luckhurst, *The Trauma Question* (New York: Routledge, 2008); Stef Craps, *Postcolonial Witnessing: Trauma Out of Bounds* (London: Palgrave McMillan, 2012).

45. Michael Richardson, *Gestures of Testimony: Torture, Trauma, and Affect in Literature* (London: Bloomsbury, 2016), 101.

46. Ibid., 14.

47. Hoskins, *Digital Memory Studies*, 111; "Auschwitz-Birkenau—Virtual Tour," http:// panorama.auschwitz.org/ (accessed February 9, 2021).

48. Delbo, *Auschwitz and After*, 41.

49. Ibid., 41.

50. Ibid., 41.

51. Ibid., 40.

52. I am referring here to Delbo's argument throughout *Auschwitz and After* about the impossibility of "seeing" the Holocaust. I discuss Delbo's account of "seeing" and provisional testimony in *Poetry as Testimony: Witnessing and Memory in Twentieth-century Poems* (New York: Routledge, 2014), 70–78.

53. Mark Morris, " 'Offensive' and 'Disrespectful' Auschwitz Video Game Scrapped after Public Outrage," https://www.mirror.co.uk/news/world-news/offensive-disrespect ful-auschwitz-video-game-13537726 (accessed February 7, 2021).

54. Hoskins, *Digital Memory Studies*, 111.

55. Wolf Kansteiner, "Digital Memory—with and beyond the Holocaust," November 20, 2020, https://digitalholocaustmemory.wordpress.com/2020/11/24/playing-the-holocaust-part-1/ (accessed January 21, 2021).

56. Primo Levi, *The Drowned and the Saved*, trans. Raymond Rosenthal (London: Abacus, 1989 [1988]), 32.

57. Richardson, *Gestures of Testimony*, 108.

58. Kate Marrison, for example, has commented on the hesitation of the designers of *Call of Duty: World War II* (2017) to represent the Holocaust, with video game's avoidance of more well-known death camps, and the interplay between entertainment software and social commentary, https://digitalholocaustmemory.wordpress.com/2020/11/ 24/playing-the-holocaust-part-1/ (accessed January 21, 2021).

59. Hoskins, *Digital Memory Studies*, 115.

60. Susan Gubar, *Poetry after Auschwitz: Remembering What One Never Knew* (Bloomington, IN: Indiana University Press, 2003), 1.

Bibliography

Jenni Adams, Special Issue: "Representing Perpetrators in Holocaust Literature and Film," *Holocaust Studies: A Journal of Culture and History* 17, no. 2: 3 (Autumn/Winter 2011): 1–12.

Jenni Adams and Sue Vice, *Representing Perpetrators in Holocaust Literature and Film* (London: Vallentine Mitchell, 2013).

Theodor Adorno, *Aesthetic Theory*, trans. Robert Hullot-Kentor (London: The Athlone Press, 1997 [1970]).

Theodor Adorno, "Cultural Criticism and Society," in *Prisms*, trans. Samuel and Shierry Weber (Cambridge, MA: The MIT Press, 1983 [1967]), 17–34.

Theodor Adorno, "Commitment," in *Aesthetics and Politics*, trans. Francis McDonagh (London: N.L.B., 1977), 177–195.

Theodor Adorno, *Minima Moralia*, trans. E. F. N. Jephcott (London: Verso, 1978 [1951]).

Theodor Adorno, "Valéry Proust Museum," in *Prisms*, trans. Samuel and Shierry Weber (Cambridge, MA: The MIT Press, 1981 [1967]), 173–186.

Giorgio Agamben, *Remnants of Auschwitz*, trans. Daniel Heller-Rosen (New York: Zine Books, 1999).

Jean Améry, *At the Mind's Limits: Contemplations by a Survivor on Auschwitz and its Realities*, trans. Sidney Rosenfeld and Stella P. Rosenfeld (London: Granta, 1999 [1980]).

Doral Apel, *Memory Effects: The Holocaust and the Art of Secondary Witnessing* (New Brunswick, NJ: Rutgers University Press, 2002).

Hannah Arendt, *Eichmann in Jerusalem: A Report on the Banality of Evil* (London: Penguin, 1994 [1963]).

Derek Attridge, *J. M. Coetzee and the Ethics of Reading: Literature in the Event* (Chicago: University of Chicago Press, 2004).

Shalom Auslander, *Hope: A Tragedy* (London: Picador, 2012).

Jean Baudrillard, *Simulacra and Simulation*, trans. Sheila Faria Glaser (Ann Arbor, MI: The University of Michigan Press, 1994 [1981]).

Jean Baudrillard, *The Intelligence of Evil or the Lucidity Pact*, trans. Chris Turner (New York: Berg, 2004).

Yehuda Bauer, *The Holocaust in Historical Perspective* (London: Sheldon Press, 1978).

Zygmunt Bauman, *Liquid Modernity* (Cambridge: Polity Press, 2000 [1999]).

Zygmunt Bauman, *Modernity and the Holocaust* (Cambridge: Polity Press, 2000 [1989]).

Zygmunt Bauman, *Mortality, Immortality and Other Life Strategies* (Stanford, CA: Stanford University Press, 1992).

Antony Beevor, *Berlin: The Downfall 1945* (New York: Penguin, 2007 [2002]).

Walter Benjamin, *Illuminations*, trans. Harry Zohn (New York: Schocken Books, 2007).

Jennifer Billock, "12 Must-See Fall Exhibits Around the World," *Smithsonian.com*, September 14, 2017, https://www.smithsonianmag.com/travel/12-must-see-fall-exhibits-180964834/ (accessed July 17, 2018).

Adriana Cavarero, *Horrorism: Naming Contemporary Violence*, trans. William McCuaig (New York: Columbia University Press, 2008).

Michael Bernard-Donals, "Theory and Ethics of Holocaust Representation," in Jenni Adams, ed., *The Bloomsbury Companion to Holocaust Literature* (New York: Bloomsbury, 2014), 103–119.

Bruno Bettelheim, *Surviving and Other Essays* (London: Thames and Hudson, 1979).

Edwin Black, *IBM and the Holocaust: The Strategic Alliance Between Nazi Germany and America's Most Powerful Corporation* (Washington, DC: Dialog Press, 2009).

Matthew Boswell, "Beyond Autobiography: Hybrid Testimony and the Art of Witness," in Jane Kilby and Antony Rowland, eds., *The Future of Testimony: Interdisciplinary Perspectives on Witnessing* (New York: Routledge, 2014), 144–159.

Matthew Boswell, *Holocaust Impiety in Literature, Popular Music and Film* (Basingstoke: Palgrave Macmillan, 2012).

Christopher R. Browning, *Ordinary Men: Reserve Police Battalion 101 and the Final Solution in Poland* (London: Penguin, 2001).

Christopher R. Browning, "The Suffocation of Democracy," *The New York Review of Books*, October 25, 2018, https://www.nybooks.com/articles/2018/10/25/suffocation-of-democracy/?fbclid=IwAR1-N6xHBCenqxOUBrNPLd4OlyKM38QkCmJWrpU5K nIv-CiP-QoHsKNGoyQ (accessed January 15, 2019).

Peter Buse and Andrew Stott, eds., *Ghosts: Deconstruction, Psychoanalysis, History* (Basingstoke: Palgrave Macmillan, 1999).

Cathy Caruth, ed., *Trauma: Explorations in Memory* (Baltimore, MD: Johns Hopkins University Press, 1995).

Dan Chiasson, "'2001: A Space Odyssey': What It Means, and How It Was Made," *New Yorker*, April 16, 2018, https://www.newyorker.com/magazine/2018/04/23/2001-a-space-odyssey-what-it-means-and-how-it-was-made (accessed June 13, 2020).

Marc Cieslak, "Virtual Reality to Aid Auschwitz War Trials of Concentration Camp Guards," *BBC*, November 20, 2016, https://www.bbc.co.uk/news/technology-38026 007 (accessed December 6, 2018).

Kate Connolly, "Nazi Control Room Re-opens as Topography of Terror Museum in Berlin," *The Guardian*, May 6, 2010, https://www.theguardian.com/world/2010/may/ 06/topography-terror-nazi-museum-berlin (accessed December 15, 2020).

Stef Craps, *Postcolonial Witnessing: Trauma Out of Bounds* (London: Palgrave McMillan, 2012).

Richard Crownshaw, "Perpetrator Fictions and Transcultural Memory," *Parallax* 17, no. 4 (2011): 75–89.

Rick Crownshaw, ed., *Transcultural Memory* (New York: Routledge, 2014).

Rick Crownshaw, Jane Kilby, and Antony Rowland, eds., *The Future of Memory* (New York, NY: Berghahn, 2010).

James Dawes, *Evil Men* (Cambridge, MA: Harvard University Press, 2013).

Carolyn J. Dean, "The Politics of Suffering: From the Survivor-witness to Humanitarian Witnessing," *Continuum* 31, no. 5: 628–636.

Charlotte Delbo, *Auschwitz and After* (New Haven, CT: Yale University Press, 1995).

Charlotte Delbo, *Convoy to Auschwitz: Women of the French Resistance*, trans. Carol Cosman (Boston, MA: Northeastern University Press, 1997).

Jacques Derrida, *Specters of Marx: The State of the Debt, the Work of Mourning and the New International*, trans. Peggy Kamuf (New York: Routledge, 1994).

Caitlin Dewey, "The Other Side of the Infamous 'Auschwitz Selfie,'" *Washington Post*, July 22, 2014, https://www.washingtonpost.com/news/the-intersect/wp/2014/07/22/the-other-side-of-the-infamous-auschwitz-selfie/?utm_term=.20d35073c979 (accessed December 19, 2018).

Philip K. Dick, *Do Androids Dream of Electric Sheep?* (London: Gollancz, 1999 [1968]).

Jonathan Dunnage, "Editorial: Perpetrator Memory and Memories about Perpetrators," in *Memory Studies* 3, no. 2 (2010): 91–94.

Johanna Drucker, *SpecLab* (Berkeley, CA: University of Chicago Press, 2010).

Robert Eaglestone, *The Holocaust and the Postmodern* (Oxford: Oxford University Press, 2004).

Dave Eggers, *The Circle* (New York: Alfred A. Knopf, 2013).

Dave Eggers, *What Is the What: The Autobiography of Valentino Achak Deng. A Novel* (New York: Vintage Books, 2007).

Alexander Etkind, "Post-Soviet Hauntology: Cultural Memory of the Soviet Terror," *Constellations* 16, no. 1 (Oxford: Blackwell, 2009): 182–200.

Shoshana Felman, "Theaters of Justice: Arendt in Jerusalem, the Eichmann Trial, and the Redefinition of Legal Meaning in the Wake of the Holocaust," *Critical Inquiry* 27, no. 2 (Winter, 2001): 201–238.

Shoshana Felman and Dori Laub, *Testimony: Crises of Witnessing in Literature, Psychoanalysis, and History* (New York: Routledge, 1992).

Norman Finkelstein, *The Holocaust Industry: Reflections on the Exploitation of Jewish Suffering* (New York: Verso, 2014 [2000]).

Claudio Fogu, Wulf Kansteiner, and Todd Presner, eds., *Probing the Ethics of Holocaust Culture* (Cambridge, MA: Harvard University Press, 2016).

Anne Frank, *The Diary of a Young Girl*, trans. Susan Massotty (New York, NY: Penguin, 2002 [1947]).

Nate Freeman, "A History of Violence: Jordan Wolfson on His Shocking Foray into VR at the Whitney Biennial," *ARTnews*, January 3, 2017, https://www.artnews.com/art-news/artists/a-history-of-violence-jordan-wolfson-on-his-shocking-foray-into-vr-at-the-whitney-biennial-7856/ (accessed December 12, 2018).

Sigmund Freud, *The Uncanny* (New York: Penguin, 2003 [1909]).

Thomas Frick, "J. G. Ballard, The Art of Fiction No. 85," *The Paris Review* 94 (Winter 1984), https://www.theparisreview.org/interviews/2929/j-g-ballard-the-art-of-fiction-no-85-j-g-ballard (accessed August 16, 2018).

Saul Friedländer, *Reflections of Nazism: An Essay on Kitsch and Death*, trans. Thomas Weyr (New York: Harper & Row, 1984 [1982]).

Saul Friedländer, ed., *Probing the Limits of Representation: Nazism and the "Final Solution"* (Cambridge, MA: Harvard University Press, 1992).

Saul Friedländer, "On 'Historical Modernism': A Response to Hayden White," in Claudio Fogu, Wulf Kansteiner, and Todd Presner, eds., *Probing the Ethics of Holocaust Culture* (Cambridge, MA: Harvard University Press, 2016), 72–78.

Joanne Garde-Hansen, Andrew Hoskins, and Anna Reading, *Save As . . . Digital Memories* (Basingstoke: Palgrave, 2009).

Martin Gilbert, *The Holocaust* (London: HarperCollins, 1987 [1986]).

Christine Goelz, "Through a Chilly Land: Between First-Person Shoot-Em-Up and Tourist Blockbuster—Jáchym Topol's Fictional Statement on the Possibility of Immersive Remembrance," *Digital Icons: Studies in Russian, Eurasian and Central European New Media* 6 (2011): 63–79.

Erving Goffman, *Relations in Public: Microstudies of the Public Order* (New York, NY: Basic Books, 1971).

Steve Goodman and Luciana Parisi, "Machines of Memory," in Susannah Radstone and Bill Schwarz, eds., *Memory: Histories, Theories, Debates* (New York: Fordham University Press, 2010), 343–359.

Henry Greenspan, "Movement and Memory: An Email Exchange with Henry Greenspan and Tim Cole, Part 1," *OUP Blog*, January 22, 2016, https://blog.oup.com/2016/01/hank-greenspan-tim-cole-part-1/ (accessed July 31, 2018).

Susan Gubar, *Poetry after Auschwitz: Remembering What One Never Knew* (Bloomington, IN: Indiana University Press, 2003).

L. P. Hartley, *The Go-Between* (London: Penguin, 2000).

Geoffrey Hartman, *The Longest Shadow: In the Aftermath of the Holocaust* (Bloomington, IN: Indiana University Press, 1996).

Hilda Hein, "Assuming Responsibility: Lessons from Aesthetics," in Hugh H. Genoways, ed., *Museum Philosophy for the Twenty-First Century* (Lanham, MD.: Altamira Press, 2006), 1–9.

Marianne Hirsch, *The Generation of Postmemory: Writing and Visual Culture after the Holocaust* (New York: Columbia University Press, 2012).

Marianne Hirsch, "Holocaust Testimony Beyond the Frame," *Los Angeles Review of Books*, May 23, 2020, https://lareviewofbooks.org/article/holocaust-testimony-beyond-the-frame (accessed May 26, 2020).

Marianne Hirsch and Leo Spitzer, "The Witness in the Archive: Holocaust Studies/Memory Studies," in Susanne Radstone and Daniel Schwarz, eds., *Memory: Histories, Theories, Debates* (New York: Fordham University Press, 2010), 390–405.

Andrew Hoskins, ed., *Digital Memory Studies: Media Pasts in Transition* (New York: Routledge, 2018).

Andrew Hoskins, "Media, Memory, Metaphor: Remembering and the Connective Turn," *Parallax* 17, no. 4 (2011): 19–31.

Andrew Hoskins, "Signs of the Holocaust: Exhibiting Memory in a Mediated Age," *Media, Culture and Society* 25, no. 7 (2003): 7–22.

Andrew Hoskins, "7/7 and Connective Memory: Interactional Trajectories of Remembering in Post-scarcity Culture," *Memory Studies* 4, no. 3 (2011), https://journals.sagepub.com/doi/10.1177/1750698011402570 (accessed February 10, 2021).

Linda Hutcheon, *A Poetics of Postmodernism: History, Theory, Fiction* (New York: Routledge, 1992).

Andreas Huyssen, *Twilight Memories: Making Time in a Culture of Amnesia* (New York: Routledge, 1995).

Andreas Huyssen, *Present Pasts: Urban Palimpsests and the Politics of Memory* (Stanford, CA: Stanford University Press, 2003).

Stuart Jeffries, "Claude Lanzmann on Why Holocaust Documentary *Shoah* Still Matters," *The Guardian*, June 9, 2011, https://www.theguardian.com/film/2011/jun/09/claude-lanzmann-shoah-holocaust-documentary (accessed August 15, 2018).

Phylis Johnson, *Second Life, Media and the Other Society* (New York: Peter Lang, 2010).

Sean F. Johnston, *Holograms: A Cultural History* (New York: Oxford University Press, 2015).

Wulf Kansteiner, "Genocide Memory, Digital Cultures, and the Aestheticization of Violence," *Memory Studies* 7, no. 4 (2014): 403–408.

Wulf Kansteiner, "The Holocaust in the 21st Century: Digital Anxiety, Transnational Cosmopolitanism, and Never Again Genocide without Memory," in Andrew Hoskins, ed., *Digital Memory Studies: Media Pasts in Transition* (New York: Routledge, 2018), 110–140.

Ruth Kluger, *Landscapes of Memory: A Holocaust Girlhood Remembered* (London: Bloomsbury, 2003).

Anne Kelly Knowles, Tim Cole, and Alberto Giordano, *Geographies of the Holocaust* (Bloomington, IN: Indiana University Press, 2014).

Sarah Kofman, *Smothered Words*, trans. Madaleine Dobie (Evanston, IL: Northwestern University Press, 1998).

Dominick LaCapra, *History in Transit: Experience, Identity, Critical Theory* (Ithaca, NY: Cornell University Press, 2004).

Amanda Lagerkrist, "The Media End: Digital Afterlife Agencies and Techno-existential Closure," in *Digital Memory Studies: Media Pasts in Transition* (New York: Routledge, 2018), 48–84.

Alison Landsberg, *Prosthetic Memory: The Transformation of American Remembrance in the Age of Mass Culture* (New York: Columbia University Press, 2004).

Alison Landsberg, *Engaging the Past: Mass Culture and the Production of Historical Knowledge* (New York: Columbia University Press, 2015).

Lawrence L. Langer, *Holocaust Testimonies: The Ruins of Memory* (New Haven, CT: Yale University Press, 1991).

Lawrence Langer, "The Uses—and Misuses—of a Young Girl's Diary: 'If Anne Frank Could Return from among the Murdered, She Would Be Appalled,' and "The Americanisation of the Holocaust on Stage and Screen," in *Anne Frank: Reflections on her Life and Legacy* (Urbana, IL: University of Illinois Press, 2000), 198–202.

Claude Lanzmann, "Hier ist kein Warum", in Stuart Liebman, ed., *Claude Lanzmann's Shoah: Key Essays* (Oxford: Oxford University Press, 2007), 51–52.

Claude Lanzmann, dir., *Shoah* (1985).

Claude Lanzmann, "The Obscenity of Understanding: An Evening with Claude Lanzmann," in Cathy Caruth, ed., *Trauma: Explorations in Memory* (Baltimore, MD: Johns Hopkins University Press, 1995), 200–220.

Carol Ann Lee, *The Hidden Life of Otto Frank* (New York: Penguin, 2003 [2002]).

Primo Levi, *Collected Poems*, trans. Ruth Feldman and Brian Swann (London: Faber and Faber, 1992).

Primo Levi, *The Drowned and the Saved*, trans. Raymond Rosenthal (London: Abacus, 1988 [1986]).

Primo Levi, *If This is a Man/ The Truce*, trans. Stuart Woolf (London: Abacus Books, 1996 [1958]).

Stuart Liebman, ed., *Claude Lanzmann's Shoah: Key Essays* (Oxford: Oxford University Press, 2007).

Edward T. Linenthal, *Preserving Memory: The Struggle to Create America's Holocaust Museum* (New York: Columbia University Press, 2001 [1995]).

Daniel Levy and Natan Sznaider, *The Holocaust and Memory in the Global Age*, trans. Assenka Sznaider (Philadelphia: Temple University Press, 2006).

Britta Lokting, "Meet the World's First 3-D Interactive Holocaust Survivor," *The Forward*, November 24, 2015, http://forward.com/culture/324989/meet-the-worlds-first-3-d-interactive-holocaust-survivor/ (accessed January 22, 2016).

Roger Luckhurst, *The Trauma Question* (New York: Routledge, 2008).

Ruth Margalit, "Should Auschwitz Be a Site for Selfies?" *New Yorker*, June 26, 2014, https://www.newyorker.com/culture/culture-desk/should-auschwitz-be-a-site-for-selfies (accessed December 19, 2018).

Mariana Mazzucato, "Capitalism's Triple Crisis," *Project Syndicate*, March 30, 2020, https://www.project-syndicate.org/commentary/covid19-crises-of-capitalism-new-state-role-by-mariana-mazzucato-2020–03 (accessed May 15, 2020).

Erin McGlothlin, "Theorizing the Perpetrator in Bernhard Schlink's *The Reader* and Martin Amis's *Time's Arrow*," in R. Clinton Spargo and Robert M. Ehrenreich, eds., *After Representation: The Holocaust, Literature, and Culture* (New Brunswick, NJ: Rutgers University Press, 2010), 210–230.

Thomas McMullan, "The Virtual Holocaust Survivor: How History Gained New Dimensions," *The Guardian*, June 18, 2016, https://www.theguardian.com/technology/2016/jun/18/holocaust-survivor-hologram-pinchas-gutter-new-dimensions-history (accessed June 20, 2016).

Paul Meincke, "Technology Tells Survivors' Stories at Illinois Holocaust Museum," *Abc7chicago.com*, April 30, 2017, http://abc7chicago.com/education/technology-tells-survivors-stories-at-illinois-holocaust-museum/1938500/ (accessed February 22, 2019).

Daniel Mendelsohn, *The Lost: A Search for Six of Six Million* (London: William Collins, 2013 [2007]).

Menno Metselaar and Ruud van der Rol, *The Life of Anne Frank* (Oxford: Macmillan, 2008 [2007]).

Chris Milk, "How Virtual Reality Can Create the Ultimate Empathy Machine," March 2015, https://www.ted.com/talks/chris_milk_how_virtual_reality_can_create_the_ultimate_empathy_machine/transcript?language=en (accessed December 6, 2018).

Mark Morris, "'Offensive' and 'Disrespectful' Auschwitz Video Game Scrapped after Public Outrage," November 5, 2018, https://www.mirror.co.uk/news/world-news/offensive-disrespectful-auschwitz-video-game-13537726 (accessed February 7, 2021).

Melissa Müller, *Anne Frank: The Biography* (London: Bloomsbury, 2013 [1999]).

Friedrich Nietzsche, *Beyond Good and Evil: Prelude to a Philosophy of the Future*, trans. R. J. Hollingdale (Harmondsworth: Penguin, 1990 [1886]).

Peter Novick, *The Holocaust in American Life* (New York: Houghton Mifflin Company, 1999).

Davina Pardo, "116 Cameras," *The New York Times*, September 19, 2017, https://www.nytimes.com/2017/09/19/opinion/the-remembering-machine.html (accessed February 2, 2018).

Caroline Pearce, *Contemporary Germany and the Nazi Legacy: Remembrance, Politics and the Dialectic of Normality* (New York: Palgrave, 2007).

Vivian Petraka, *Spectacular Suffering: Theatre, Fascism, and the Holocaust* (Bloomington, IN: Indiana University Press, 1999).

Tod Presner, "The Ethics of the Algorithm: Close and Distant Listening in the Shoah Foundation Visual History Archive," in Claudio Fogu, Wulf Kansteiner, and Todd Presner, eds., *Probing the Ethics of Holocaust Culture* (Cambridge, MA: Harvard University Press, 2016), 175–202.

Francine Prose, *Anne Frank: The Book, The Life, The Afterlife* (London: Atlantic Books, 2010 [2009]).

Jennifer Rapson, *Topographies of Suffering: Buchenwald, Babi Yar, Lidice* (New York: Berghahn, 2015).

Marc Redfield, *The Rhetoric of Terror: Reflections on 9/ 11 and the War on Terror* (New York: Fordham University Press, 2009).

Jo Reilly, Tony Kushner, David Cesarani, and Colin Richmond, eds., *Belsen in History and Memory* (Portland: Frank Cass Publishers, 1997).

Michael Richardson, *Gestures of Testimony: Torture, Trauma, and Affect in Literature* (London: Bloomsbury, 2016).

Gillian Rose, *Mourning Becomes the Law: Philosophy and Representation* (Cambridge: Cambridge University Press, 1997).

Alvin Rosenfeld, *The End of the Holocaust* (Bloomington, IN: Indiana University Press, 2011).

Michael Rothberg, *Multidirectional Memory: Remembering the Holocaust in an Age of Decolonization* (Stanford, CA: Stanford University Press, 2009).

Michael Rothberg, "Multidirectional Memory and the Implicated Subject: On Sebald and Kentridge," in Liedke Plate and Anneke Smelik, eds., *Performing Memory in Art and Popular Culture* (New York: Routledge, 2013), 39–58.

Michael Rothberg, *The Implicated Subject: Beyond Victims and Perpetrators* (Stanford, CA: Stanford University Press, 2019).

Antony Rowland, *Holocaust Poetry: Awkward Poetics in the Work of Sylvia Plath, Geoffrey Hill, Tony Harrison and Ted Hughes* (Edinburgh: Edinburgh University Press, 2005).

Antony Rowland, *Poetry as Testimony: Witnessing and Memory in Twentieth-century Poems* (New York: Routledge, 2014).

Antony Rowland, *Tony Harrison and the Holocaust* (Liverpool: Liverpool University Press, 2001).

Mark Rowlands, *The Philosopher at the End of the Universe: Philosophy Explained Through Science Fiction Films* (New York: Thomas Dunne Books, 2003).

Eva Schloss and Barbara Powers, *The Promise: The True Story of a Family in the Holocaust* (London: Penguin, 2006).

Eva Schloss and Evelyn Julia Kent, *Eva's Story: A Survivor's Tale by the Step-Sister of Anne Frank* (New York, NY: St. Martin's Press, 1988).

Eva Schloss and Karen Bartlett, *After Auschwitz: A Story of Heartbreak and Survival by the Stepsister of Anne Frank* (London: Hodder and Stoughton, 2013).

Daniel R. Schwarz, *Imagining the Holocaust* (Basingstoke: Palgrave, 2000 [1999]).

Will Self, "Do We Still Need Stories?" *The Guardian*, November 26, 2016, 18.

Jeffrey Shandler, *Holocaust Memory in the Digital Age: Survivors" Stories and New Media Practices* (Stanford, CA: Stanford University Press, 2017).

Robert R. Shandley, ed., *Unwilling Germans?: The Goldhagen Debate*, trans. Jeremiah Riemer (Minneapolis, MN: University of Minnesota Press, 1998).

Noah Shenker, *Reframing Holocaust Testimony* (Bloomington, IN: Indiana University Press, 2015).

Max Silverman, *Palimpsestic Memory: The Holocaust and Colonialism in French and Francophone Fiction and Film* (New York: Berghahn, 2013).

Bill Slavicsek, *A Guide to the Star Wars Universe* (New York: Ballantine Books, 1994).

George Stevens, dir., *The Diary of Anne Frank* (1959).

Victoria Stewart, "Anne Frank and the Uncanny," *Paragraph* 24, no. 1 (March 2001): 99–113.

Oren Baruch Stier, *Holocaust Icons: Symbolizing the Shoah in History and Memory* (New Brunswick, NJ: Rutgers University Press, 2015).

Dan Stone, "History, Memory, Testimony," in Jane Kilby and Antony Rowland, eds., *The Future of Testimony* (New York: Routledge, 2014), 17–30.

Timothy Snyder, "The American Abyss," *The New York Times Magazine*, January 9, 2021, https://www.nytimes.com/2021/01/09/magazine/trump-coup.html (accessed January 22, 2021).

Timothy Snyder, *Black Earth: The Holocaust as History and Warning* (New York: Tim Duggan Books, 2015).

Ben Tarnoff, "Empathy: the Latest Gadget Silicon Valley Wants to Sell You," *Guardian*, October 25, 2017, https://www.theguardian.com/technology/2017/oct/25/empathy-virtual-reality-facebook-mark-zuckerberg-puerto-rico (accessed December 12, 2018).

Andrew Thacker, *Modernism, Space and the City* (Edinburgh: Edinburgh University Press, 2019).

Jáchym Topol, *The Devil's Workshop*, trans. Alex Zucker (London: Portobello Books, 2013).

John Urry, "How Societies Remember the Past," in S. Macdonald and G. Fyfe, eds., *Theorizing Museums: Representing Identity and Diversity in a Changing World* (Oxford: Blackwell, 1996), 45–68.

USC Shoah Foundation, "Pioneering 'New Dimensions in Testimony' Interviewee Passes Away at 85," *Institute News*, April 13, 2018, https://sfi.usc.edu/news/2018/04/21826-pioneering-new-dimensions-testimony-interviewee-passes-away-85 (accessed August 16, 2018).

USC Shoah Foundation, "Steven Spielberg Discusses Lessons he Hopes Students Will Take Away from Rerelease of 'Schindler's List,'" November 30, 2018, https://sfi.usc.edu/news/2018/11/23591-steven-spielberg-discusses-lessons-he-hopes-students-will-take-away-rerelease- (accessed December 6, 2018).

USC Shoah Foundation, "Survivors and Soldiers: Revolutionary Technology Preserves Living Testimony of Soviet Jewish Experience of Holocaust and WWII," December 3, 2018, https://sfi.usc.edu/news/2018/12/23621-survivors-and-soldiers-revolutionary-technology-preserves-living-testimony-soviet (accessed December 5, 2018).

Paul Virilio, *The Administration of Fear*, trans. Ames Hodges (Los Angeles: Semiotext(e), 2012).

Victoria Grace Walden, *Cinematic Intermedialities and Contemporary Holocaust Memory* (London: Palgrave Macmillan, 2019).

Victoria Grace Walden, ed., *Digital Holocaust Memory, Education and Research* (London: Palgrave Macmillan, 2021).

Victoria Grace Walden, "What Is 'Virtual Holocaust Memory'?," *Memory Studies* 15, no. 4 (2019), OnlineFirst https://journals.sagepub.com/doi/10.1177/1750698019888712 (accessed June 12, 2020).

David Walsh, "'They Are No Longer Numbers or Statistics': How Colour Pictures Are Bringing Auschwitz to Life," *Euronews*, January 28, 2020, https://www.euronews.com/2020/01/28/they-are-no-longer-numbers-or-statistics-how-colour-pictures-are-bringing-auschwitz-to-li# (accessed May 13, 2020).

Jeshajahu Weinberg and Rina Elieli, *The Holocaust Museum in Washington* (New York: Rizzoli International Publications, Inc., 1995).

Bernard Williams, *Truth and Truthfulness: An Essay in Genealogy* (Princeton, NJ: Princeton University Press, 2002).

Hayden White, "Historical Truth, Estrangement, and Disbelief," in Claudio Fogu, Wulf Kansteiner, and Todd Presner, eds., *Probing the Ethics of Holocaust Culture* (Cambridge, MA: Harvard University Press, 2016), 53–71.

Leanne White and Elspeth Frew, eds., *Dark Tourism and Place Identity: Managing and Interpreting Dark Places* (New York: Routledge, 2013).

James Young, *The Texture of Memory: Holocaust Memorials and Meaning* (New Haven, CT: Yale University Press, 1993).

James Young, *At Memory's Edge* (New Haven, CT: Yale University Press, 2000).

James Young, "The Anne Frank House: Holland's Memorial Shrine of the Book," in Hyman Aaron Enzer and Sandra Solotaroff-Enzer, eds., *Anne Frank: Reflections on her Life and Legacy* (Urbana, IL: University of Illinois Press, 2000), 223–228.

Slavoj Žižek, *Violence* (London: Profile Books, 2009).

Index

For the benefit of digital users, indexed terms that span two pages (e.g., 52–53) may, on occasion, appear on only one of those pages.

Figures are indicated by *f* following the page number

Abrahms, Danny, 26, 151, 176–79, 180–81
accessibility, 161–64, 174–75, 258n.29
Adams, Jenni, 186–87, 233–34n.10
Adorno, Theodor, 17–18, 165–66, 186–87
    Aesthetic Theory, 120–21, 233–34n.10
    "Commitment," 164–65
affective community, 101, 103–4, 163–64
Agamben, Giorgio, 112, 113–14
AI. *See* artificial intelligence
Amaral, Marina, 21–22
    Faces of Auschwitz project, 119, 21, 157
Americanization of Holocaust, 61–63,
    105–6, 114, 115
Améry, Jean, 108, 113–14
Amis, Martin, *Time's Arrow*, 230n.41
Amsterdam, 93, 158–59, 169–75, 205
androids, 4–5, 6, 8–9
Anne Frank Foundation (Anne Frank
    Stichting), 152, 177–79, 180–81
Anne Frank House
    Anne's Amsterdam app and
        tourism, 170–71
    demolition threat, 155–56, 244n.20
    digital technology future, 205–6
    and Anne Frank diary, 23–24
    Holocaust memory culture, 3
    Holocaust memory culture
        institutionalization, 25
    palimpsestic memory and accessibility,
        163–65, 166–67, 168–69
    photographs, 156*f*–61*f*, 178*f*, 179–80,
        180*f*, 250n.99
    Secret Annex Online, 151, 153–61
    VR films/tours, 8, 174–81, 182, 203–
        4, 213–14

*Anne Frank House: A Museum with a
    Story*, 154–56, 244n.21, 248n.66
Anne Frank House app, 249n.78
Anne Frank Stichting (Anne Frank
    Foundation), 152, 177–79, 180–81
Anne's Amsterdam app, 169–75, 170*f*,
    173*f*, 180–81, 205, 213–14, 249n.78,
    250n.86
antipostmodernist architecture, 189–96
antisemitism, 63, 141–42, 145–46
apartheid, 198–99
Apel, Doral, 236–37n.39
Appelbaum, Ralph, 184–85, 186–87
Applebaum, Molly, 229n.31
apps
    Anne Frank House app, 249n.78
    Anne's Amsterdam (see *Anne's
        Amsterdam* app)
    Bergen-Belsen iPad app (*see*
        Bergen-Belsen)
    Holocaust memory culture, 3–4
    Pokemon Go, 171–72
    ·*Tangible Memories*, 205–6
AR. *See* augmented reality
architecture, 189–96
Arendt, Hannah, 83–84, 151, 242–43n.5
Aristotle, 17–18
Armenian Genocide, 6–7, 38–39, 198–99
artificial intelligence (AI), 4–5, 202, 203
Attie, Shimon
    The Neighbour Next Door installation,
        248–49n.69
    Sites Unseen projections, 169–72
Attridge, Derek, 161–62, 245n.31, 246n.43
Au, Wagner James, 242n.113

audio guides/tours, 121–23, 175–76,
   241n.103
augmented reality (AR)
   Bergen-Belsen installations, 134
   Bergen-Belsen iPad app, 23–24, 119–20,
      121–24, 125–29, 149–50, 205–7,
      236–37n.39
   definition, 235n.18
   Holocaust memory culture, 1–2, 3
Auschwitz-Birkenau. *See also* Birkenau
   Auschwitz-Birkenau Virtual Tour, 210–
      12, 210*f*–11*f*
   cross symbol, 133–34
   digital technology future, 210–11, 212
   Dimensions in Testimony, 57–58
   Anne Frank and family, 92, 152, 155–56,
      248n.64
   Holocaust memory culture, 3, 12, 21
   Hołuj's poetry, 133–34
   images, 210*f*, 211*f*
   Levi's "Afterword," 99
   liberation footage, 132–33
   Meed on tourism and visitors, 119–20
   poetry after, 17–18
   recolored images, 21
   Schloss family, 87–88, 89–91, 92
   Eva Schloss testimony, 36–37, 90–91,
      93–95, 96, 100–1
   social media, 3–4
   tattoos, 248n.68
   Tuschinski death, 171–72
   videogames, 212
   VR model and trial, 8
Auslander, Shalom, *Hope: a Tragedy*,
   242–43n.5
Austria, Maria, 155–58, 244n.20, 250n.99
Autodrom, 194–96, 195*f*
awkward poetics
   digital and prosthetic memory, 163–64
   digital technology overview and future,
      208–9, 210–11
   palimpsestic testimony, 180–81
   perpetrator perspective, 168–69
   poetics of virtual Holocaust
      memory, 17–18
   Topography of Terror, 184, 185–89
   transcultural approaches, 256n.71
   virtual Anne Frank, 152–53, 168–69

   virtual landscapes and digital
      installations, 121, 128–29, 138–
      39, 149–50

Ballard, J. G., v, 50–51, 180–81
Barthes, Roland, 244–45n.24
Bartlett, Karen, 89–90
Baudrillard, Jean
   cold media, 137, 140–41, 152–
      53, 177–79
   on digital media, 203–4
   digital memory and
      forgetfulness, 145–46
   extermination of memory, 124,
      137, 157–58
   on holograms, 56–57
   hyperreal, 4–5, 56
   "realistic hallucination," 156–57, 158–
      59, 175
   simulacra, 137, 138–39, 140–41, 158–
      59, 175, 179–80
   on simulation, 20, 58–59
Bauer, Yehuda, 124
Bauman, Zygmunt, 1–2, 30–31, 68, 167–68
Beevor, Anthony, 253n.35
Beit Hashoah Museum of Tolerance, Los
      Angeles, 177–79, 189–90
Belsen. *See also* Bergen-Belsen
   Anne Frank and family, 92, 152
   Hugh Le Druillenec on, 137–38
   installations, 156–58, 167–68
   iPad app, 124, 153–54
   liberation of, 123–24, 134–35
   Auguste Van Pels, 248n.66
Ben-Gurion, David, 83–84
Benjamin, Walter, 66
Berenbaum, Michael, 61–62, 241n.102
Bergen-Belsen. *See also* Belsen
   accessibility, 161–62
   "box" installation, 129–31, 130*f*,
      237n.40
   development of memorial, 242n.114
   digital installations and the
      reconstruction of Bergen-Belsen,
      120–21, 129–39, 141–42, 149–
      50, 206–7
   digital technology overview and
      future, 205–7

extermination of memory, 121–29
Anne Frank and family, 92, 133–34, 152, 248n.64
"Here—Bergen-Belsen, Space of Memory" installation, 129–31, 139–40
Holocaust memory culture, 3
images, 122*f*, 127*f*
institutionalization of Holocaust memory culture, 25
iPad application, 23–24, 28–29, 119–29, 146–47, 163–64, 184–87, 194–96, 205–7, 234–35n.16
liberation of, 1–2, 123–24, 131–32, 134–35
loss of original buildings, 235–36n.25
nature reserve, 119–20, 236n.34, 239n.69
Polish wooden cross, 133–34, 237n.53
"There, Echoes of Memory" sound installation, 237n.40
virtual landscapes, 119–21
visitor numbers, 119–20
Wiener Library "virtual panorama," 131–35, 131*f*, 135*f*
Bergson, Henri, 14–15, 218n.36
Berlin
    artifacts, 252–53n.24
    Attie installation, 169
    countermemorials, 191–92
    German unification, 196–97
    memorial culture, 200–1
    memorials, 189–90, 194–96
    museums, 189–92
    Topography of Terror, 182, 189–92, 193–94, 196–97, 200–1
Berlin Wall, 126–27, 184, 196–97, 199–200
Bettelheim, Bruno, 159–61, 246n.38
Big Picture Show, IWMN, 184
Billib, Stephanie, 121–23, 134–35, 234n.13, 236–37n.39
Birkenau. *See also* Auschwitz-Birkenau
    Auschwitz-Birkenau Virtual Tour, 210–11
    Delbo on, 124–25, 128–29, 138–39, 159–61, 210–12
    Hartmann photographs, 236–37n.39
    museum models, 134, 187–89

Eva Schloss on, 90–91, 93
black-and-white images, 157, 187–89
Blade Runner (film), 4–6, 14, 209–10
Blade Runner 2049 (film), 4–5
Blancas, Maria, 237n.50
Bloomfield, Sara, 61–62
Blue Mars, 242n.113
The Book Thief (book and film), 106
Borowski, Tadeusz, 210–11, 242–43n.5
Boswell, Matthew, 30, 89–90, 218n.36
Bovenberg, Allard, 155–56, 157–58, 162–63, 176, 179–80
The Boy in the Striped Pyjamas (book and film), 106
Braun, Eva, 253n.30
Bravemind: Virtual Reality Exposure Therapy, 31, 32
Brecht, Bertolt, 120–21, 233–34n.10
Bright White, 40
Brink, Tom, 147–48, 151, 153–54, 170–71, 174–75, 176–79, 180–81
Broder, Henryk, 205–6
Browning, Christopher, 27–28
    Ordinary Men, 29–30, 199–200
Brunstein, Esther, 137–38
Buchenwald concentration camp, 248n.66
Buruma, Ian, 247n.51
Butler, Judith, 58–59
"butterfly" tourists/visitors, 171, 185–86, 205
bystander perspective, 10–11, 143–46, 167–68, 200, 212–13

Call of Duty: World War II (videogame), 29, 212, 255n.58
camps, liberation of, 1–2, 131–33, 134–35, 235n.21
CANDLES Holocaust Museum and Education Center, Indiana, 222n.4
Cape Town Holocaust Centre, 198–99
capitalism, 27–28
Carson, Rachel, *Silent Spring*, 4
Carter, Jimmy, 63, 225n.9
Caruth, Cathy, 121
Cavarero, Adriana, 115
CEEDS (Collective Experience of Empathic Data Systems), 131–32
Cesarini, David, 237–38n.54

Chelmno extermination camp, 124
Chernobyl VR Project (VR film), 8
childization of Holocaust, 106, 108, 115–16, 120–21, 124–25, 138–39, 151, 172
children, 41–43, 61–62, 65, 93, 113–14, 138–39
Clarke, Arthur C., "The Sentinel," 4
Clinton, Bill, 63
Clouds Over Sidra (VR film), 8
Coetzee, J. M., 245n.31
cold media/representation, 137, 140–41, 152–53, 168–69, 177–79, 206–7, 210–12
collective memory, 75–76
color photographs, 21, 22, 155–58
comic books, 213–14
The Communist Manifesto, 75–76
complicity, 199–201
computer games. *See* videogames
computer memory, 13–14
concentration camps, 1–2, 62, 131–33, 134–35, 194–96, 235n.21
connective memory
    and digital gothic, 203–4
    Dimensions in Testimony, 93, 103–4
    ghostware, 73–74, 79–80
    Hoskins on, 257n.8
    interactive testimony future, 207–8
    limits of, 21–25
    performing truthfulness, 59–60
    remembering "the drowned," 111–12, 115–16
    spatiotemporalities, 72
connectivity
    connective memory and digital gothic, 203–154, 205
    digital technology future, 207–8, 209–10, 213–14
    virtual Anne Frank, 152–53, 163–64, 180–81
    virtual landscapes, 138–39, 149–50
Conscience Display, 37, 63–64
cosmopolitan memory, 27–28
Cost of Freedom (videogame), 212
countermemorials, 191–92, 194–96, 254n.43
Covid-19 pandemic, 27–28, 73–74
Craps, Stef, 209–10

cross symbols, 133–34, 237n.53
culpability (*Mitläufer*), 199–200

Dachau concentration camp, 62, 237n.42
Dante, 137–38
dark tourism, 241–42n.109
Dawes, James, 11, 81
    Evil Men, 10
Dean, Carolyn J., 11, 67–68, 83–84
death, 68, 75–76, 78–79, 82, 113–14, 137–38
deep memory, 19, 98, 99–100, 101–2, 103–4, 111–12
de Jong, Louis, 159–61
Delbo, Charlotte
    Auschwitz and After trilogy, v, 18–19, 57–58, 124–25, 128–29, 138–39, 159–61, 208–9, 210–12
    Auschwitz-Birkenau Virtual Tour, 210–11
    Convoy to Auschwitz, 138–39
    Days and Memory, 219n.59
    None of Us Will Return, 18–19, 57–59, 163–64, 219n.59
    "Oh you who know," 163–64
    truthfulness, 19, 21, 57–59, 69, 70–71, 92, 95–96, 138–39, 149–50, 152–53
    virtual Holocaust memory writers, 12
    virtual landscapes, 121
Deleuze, Gilles, 14–15, 218n.36
De-Nur, Yehiel, 83–84
Derrida, Jacques, 73–77, 78–80, 81–82, 103–4, 113–14, 124
    Specters of Marx, 15–16, 75–77, 78–79, 82
The Diary of Anne Frank (BBC TV miniseries), 246n.39
Dick, Philip K., 52–53
    Do Androids Dream of Electric Sheep?, 4–5, 8–9
digital gothic, 203–4, 205–6, 207–8, 213–14
digital memory, 2–3, 17, 145–46, 193–94, 203–4, 213–14
Digital Memory Studies (Hoskins), 203–4, 205–7
digital technology
    Holocaust memory culture, 2, 3–4
    overview and future, 205–10, 213–14
    terminology, 14

videogames and virtual
memory, 212–13
digital turn, 152–53, 207–8
Dimbleby, Richard, 129–32, 134–35
Dimensions in Testimony
costs, 105–6, 152, 231n.55
cracks in the light stage, 99–104
cultural life of Holocaust holograms,
49–56, 183
development of, 7
digital technology future, 202–4, 205–8
entering Dimensions in
Testimony, 35–60
ghostware, 73–74, 77–78, 79–80
Hirsch on, 124, 189–90
Holocaust memory culture, 2, 3, 6–
7, 9–11
influence of *Schindler's List*, 104–6, 107,
108, 109–11
institutionalization of Holocaust
memory culture, 26
last act of Holocaust witnessing, 35–40
limits of connective memory, 23–25
media and public responses, 49
Nanjing Massacre testimony, 37,
231n.58
New Dimensions in Testimony name,
41–43, 51, 221n.2
other genocides, 198–99
performative methodologies, 85–88
performing truthfulness, 56–60
perpetrators and impiety, 31, 32
photographs, 36*f*, 42*f*, 80*f*, 87*f*
powers of the metatext, 62, 63–64, 65–
66, 69
remembering "the drowned," 111–12
Eva Schloss's interview, 88–98, 99, 107–
8, 109–10
and Second Life Kristallnacht
exhibition, 143–46
speech recognition technology, 253n.27
stereotyped memory, 96–99
testimony periodization, 40
testimony's spatiotemporalities, 69–71
traumatic syntax of virtual
conversations, 41–48
virtual Holocaust memory terminology,
13, 16, 17

virtual landscapes, 121–23, 124
disabled visitors, 174–75, 177–79, 182
distanced realism, 22, 23–24, 59–60
Do Androids Dream of Electric Sheep?
(Dick), 4–5, 8–9
documentary, 21–22, 71, 84–85, 157
Documentation Centre on Nazi Forced Labour
in Schoeneweide (Berlin), 253n.34
Dutch Resistance Museum, Amsterdam,
166–67, 171, 248–49n.69
Dybin, Dimitry, 212

Eaglestone, Robert, 58, 124–25, 128–
29, 152–53
educational programs, 26, 27–28, 105–6,
109–10, 112, 125–26
Eggers, Dave
The Circle, 163–64, 205
What Is the What, 228n.13
Eichmann Trial, 38, 67–68, 72, 83–85
Eisenman, Peter, 182, 193–94, 216n.9
Eisenman memorial. *See* Memorial to the
Murdered Jews of Europe
Elieli, Rina, 185–86, 241n.103
Elster, Aaron, 74*f*, 103–4
empathic unsettlement, 16, 17, 137–38,
148–49, 162–63, 186–87, 246n.45
empathy
Dimensions in Testimony, 106
limits of connective memory, 22–23, 24
videogames and virtual memory, 212
virtual Anne Frank, 152–53, 180–81
virtual Holocaust memory and
terminology, 12, 14, 16, 17
VR as "ultimate empathy machine," 8–
11, 16, 152–53, 176–77
escalators, 202
eternity narrative, 66, 68, 69, 115–16
Etkind, Alexander, 15–16, 75–76
eugenics, 20–21, 141–42
Europahaus, Berlin, 191–93, 191*f*, 198–99
exposure therapy, 31
extermination of memory, 124, 137, 145–
46, 205–6
eyewitness accounts, 32, 40, 57, 83–84,
128–29, 138–39, 146–47

Faces of Auschwitz project, 119, 21, 157

fake news, 27–28
Falstad, Norway, 132–33
fascism, 27–28, 186–87, 197–98, 212–13
Fassin, Didier, 11
Felman, Shoshana, 18, 71–72, 83–84, 121,
    256n.71
female perpetrators, 187–89, 193–94
fiction, and history, 244–45n.24
filmed testimony, 69–70, 73
films. See also *Blade Runner*; *Schindler's List*;
    Star Wars films; *2001: A Space Odyssey*
    Baudrillard and Friedländer on, 140–41
    for children and young adults, 106
    Anne Frank Hollywood film, 159–61,
        165–66, 177–80
    Anne Frank Museum of Tolerance
        film, 177–79
    Anne Frank VR films, 26, 174–81
    Holocaust memory culture, 1–2, 4–5
    Landsberg on, 128–29
    Nazi atrocities, 137–38
    science fiction, 4–5, 6
    videogames and virtual memory, 212
Fink, Ida, 21–22
Finkelstein, Norman, 105–6, 152
"flatness," 126–27, 132–33, 161–63, 171,
    172, 210–12
Fogu, Claude, 56–57, 208–9
Folman, Ari, *Waltz with Bashir*, 239n.71
Forever Project
    consistent tone, 229n.33
    development of, 40
    images, 66*f*, 67*f*
    interviewees, 110–11, 112, 230n.40
    metatext and eternity narrative, 65–67
    National Holocaust Centre education
        program, 232n.65
    technology choice, 50, 222n.7
    testimony's spatiotemporalities, 69, 70
forgetfulness, 115–16, 137, 140–41, 145–
    46, 169, 213–14, 249n.78
Fortunoff Video Archive for Holocaust
    Testimonies, Yale, 38–39, 50, 70–71,
    84–85, 223n.19
Foucault, Michel, 14, 16
Frank, Anne
    Anne's Amsterdam app and digital
        metatext, 169–74
    Auschwitz-Birkenau, 92, 152
    Belsen, 92, 133–34, 152, 248n.64
    diary, 23–24, 91, 92, 109–10, 151–52,
        154–55, 157–58, 159–67, 176–
        81, 211–12
    and Eva Schloss, 36–37, 41–43, 45–46,
        88–90, 91–92, 96, 109–10, 152
    Hollywood film, 159–61, 165–
        66, 177–80
    Levi on, 243n.8
    Museum of Tolerance film, 177–79
    overidentification, 247n.51
    photographs, 155–56, 249n.80
    play of diary, 159–61, 164–65
    Secret Annex Online, 23–24,
        151, 211–12
    the virtual Anne Frank, 151–81
    VR films, 8, 26, 174–81
Frank, Margot, 133–34, 172
Frank, Otto
    Anne Frank diary and adaptations,
        159–61, 163–64, 179–80
    Anne Frank Foundation, 152
    Anne Frank House, 155–56, 157–58,
        163–64, 177–80
    Auschwitz, 155–56
    Eva Schloss testimony, 36–37, 89–90,
        109–10, 258n.27
    VR films, 174–75, 177–79
    Wehrmacht deliveries, 166–67
Freed, James I., 147–48, 191–92
Freud, Sigmund, 73, 141–43, 240n.94
Friedländer, Saul
    distanced realism, 22, 59–60
    on films and television, 140–41
    on flatness, 161–62
    limits of connective memory, 21–23, 59–60
    Nazi artifacts and fascism, 186–87
    *Probing the Limits of Representation:
        Nazism and the "Final Solution,"* 1–2,
        21–22, 56–57, 140–41, 208–9
    the unsayable, 93, 112, 115–16
    and White, 209–10, 244–45n.24
Friedman, James, 236–37n.39
Fritzshall, Fritzie, 13, 95–96, 99–100
Full Spectrum Warrior (videogame), 31

Gabor, Dennis, 52

gaming, and gamification, 28–29, 30–32, 114, 171–72, 212–13
Garde-Hansen, Joanne, 257n.17
Gedenkstätte (memorials), 119–20, 126, 129–31, 132–33, 193–94, 234–35n.16
Gegen Ende der Nacht (*"Towards the End of the Night"*) (film), 187–89
Gehry, Frank, 192–93
Gelber, Michael, 239n.69
genocide
    childization of Holocaust, 108
    Dimensions in Testimony narratives, 54–55, 106, 198–99, 207–8
    Holocaust memory institutionalization, 27–28
    limits of connective memory, 21–22, 25
    perpetrators and impiety, 29, 30–31
    terminology, 12
    Topography of Terror, 185–86, 200
    United States Holocaust Memorial Museum, 62
    Visual History Archive, 6–7, 38–39
Genocide Against the Tutsi in Rwanda, 6–7, 38–39, 198–99
Genocide Convention, 27–28, 45–46
Geographies of the Holocaust (Knowles et al.), 168–69
geolocalization, 23–24, 119–20, 121–23
Germany
    economic miracle, 187–89
    national history, 256n.70
    national memory, 119–20, 124–25, 200–1
    reconstruction phase, 254n.41
    survivor testimony types, 110
    Topography of Terror, 187–89, 193–94, 196–99, 200–1
    unification, 196–97
Gerrit van der Veen College, 249n.82
Gestapo, 184, 194–99
Gestapo-Gelände (Gestapo terrain), 194–96, 198–99, 200, 254n.41
ghosting the museum, 61–82
    ghostware, 73–82
    powers of the metatext, 61–69
    testimony's spatiotemporalities, 69–73
ghosts, 75–77, 78–79, 81–82

ghostware, 15–16, 59–60, 73–82, 111–12, 113–14, 153–54
Gies, Jan, 162–63
Gies, Miep, 162–63
Global Kids, 139–40
Goelz, Christian, 114
Goffman, Erving, 186–87
Goldhagen, Daniel, *Hitler's Willing Executioners*, 200
Goldstein, Judith, 166–67
Goodman, Steve, 13–14
gothic, 203–4. *See also* digital gothic
GPS technology (global positioning system), 171–72, 236–37n.39
graves, 83–84, 119–20, 123–24, 234–35n.16, 235–36n.25
Graves, Robert, 235n.18
Graz memorial, 253n.26
Greenspan, Henry, 107
Grese, Irme, 187–89
Grieg, Tamsin, 161–63, 165–66, 246n.39, 246n.47
"Groote Club" massacre, 171
Ground Zero, 9/11 memorial, 234n.13
Guatemalan Genocide, 6–7, 198–99
Gubar, Susan, 132–33
Guggenheim Museum, Bilbao, 192–93
Gustman, Sam, 7
Gutter, Pinchas
    Dimensions in Testimony and ghostware, 73, 77–78, 79–80, 81
    Dimensions in Testimony and virtual conversations, 41–43, 45–48
    Dimensions in Testimony interview, 7, 37–38, 40–43, 54–55, 63–64, 97, 99–100, 108, 109–10, 145–46, 203
    Dimensions in Testimony performative methodologies, 85–86, 87–88
    images, 47*f*, 86*f*
    The Last Goodbye (VR film), 7, 174–75
    Museum of Jewish Heritage, 41–43, 97
    Sheffield Doc/Fest, 77–78
    speech recognition technology, 258n.27
    testimony's spatiotemporalities, 69–70
    USHMM installation, 41, 46–47, 63–64
    virtual Gutter, 37–38, 41–43, 45–48, 73, 77–78, 79–80, 81, 97, 109
    VR and empathy, 9–10

Gutter, Sabrina, 47, 54–55

Haacke, Hans, 253n.26
Hackesche Höfe, Berlin, 189–90, 190*f*
Halbwachs, Maurice, 13–14
Hallmann, Heinz, 191–92, 193–94
"hallucinations," 140–41, 156–57, 158–
    59, 175
Hamlet (Shakespeare), 76–77, 81–82
Harris, Bumper, 202
Harris, Sam, 39*f*
Harrison, Tony, 17–18
Hartley, L. P., *The Go-Between*, 20–21
Hartman, Geoffrey, 3–4, 6–7, 18, 38–40,
    50, 57, 83–85, 103
Hartmann, Eric, 236–37n.39
haunting, 15–16, 73–76, 78–79, 81–
    82, 207–8
Hausner, Gideon, 83–84
headsets, 175–76, 177–79
heimlich, 142–43, 165–67, 179–80
Hein, Hilda, 158–59
"Here—Bergen-Belsen, Space of Memory"
    installation, 129–31, 139–40
Herero, 256n.70
Hertzberg, Rabbi Arthur, 63
Heydrich, Reinhard, 184, 185–86
Hill, Geoffrey, 17–18
Himmler, Heinrich, 184, 186–87, 252n.14
Hirsch, Marianne
    on Delbo, 219n.59
    on digital archive, 241–42n.109
    on Dimensions in Testimony, 49–50, 73,
        124, 184, 189–90
    The Generation of Postmemory, 143–45,
        241–42n.109
    on Kristallnacht exhibition, 143–45
    postmemory, 24–25
    on Shoah Foundation, 2–3
    on truthfulness, 19
historical memory, 50, 69–70, 193–94
Historiker-Streit, 197–98
historiography, 132–33, 168–69, 185–86,
    199–200, 209–10, 252n.16
history
    Bergen-Belsen digital
        installations, 132–39
    digital gothic, 213–14

and fiction/literature, 244–45n.24
and memory, 19
Topography of Terror
    exhibition, 184–89
truth and truthfulness, 19, 20, 78
virtual Anne Frank, 153–55, 157–
    58, 161–65
Hitler, Adolf, 27–28, 45–46, 159–61, 184–
    85, 199–200
Hoess, Rudolf, 251–52n.12
Hoffman, E. T. A., "The Sand
    Man," 142–43
Höffner, Joseph, cardinal of
    Cologne, 197–98
Hollywood, 1–2, 52–53, 66, 159–61, 165–
    66, 177–80
Holocaust
    Americanization of, 61–63, 105–6,
        114, 115
    childization of, 106, 108, 115–16, 120–
        21, 124–25, 138–39, 151, 172
    definition, 12
    denial, 56–57, 179–80
    digital technology overview and
        future, 206–10
    education, 106, 112, 125–26, 206–7
    Historiker-Streit debates, 197–98
    knowledge of, 27–28, 62
    limits of connective memory, 21–25
    poetics of virtual Holocaust
        memory, 17–18
    truth and truthfulness, 18–21
    virtual Holocaust memory
        terminology, 12–17
Holocaust (television series), 38, 84–
    85, 140–41
Holocaust memory culture, 1–32
    institutionalization of, 25–28
    limits of connective memory, 21–25
    overview, 1–8
    perpetrators and impiety, 28–32
    poetics of virtual Holocaust
        memory, 17–32
    truth and truthfulness, 18–21
    virtual Holocaust memory
        terminology, 12–17
    VR as "ultimate empathy
        machine," 8–11

Holocaust Museum Houston, 222n.4
Holocaust studies, 1–2, 183, 200, 209–10
Holocaust Survivors Film Project, 84–85
Holocaust witnessing
    era of living Holocaust memory, 2–3,
        6, 15–16
    fifth era, 18–19, 40, 72–73, 85, 105–6,
        119–21, 138–39, 151–52, 157
    periodization of Holocaust testimony,
        18–19, 35–40, 57, 83–84
holograms
    Baudrillard on, 56–57
    Blade Runner 2049, 4–5
    cultural life of Holocaust
        holograms, 49–56
    digital technology future, 206–7
    Dimensions in Testimony, 2, 6–7, 37–
        38, 49–57, 58–60, 103–4, 110–12, 203
    ghostware, 15–16, 72–74, 76–77, 80
    Kansteiner on, 202–3, 205
    Langer on, 202
    limits of connective memory, 25
    performing truthfulness, 56–57, 58–60
    perpetrators, 28–29, 183
    Eva Schloss testimony, 36–37
    Star Wars films, 53–54, 224n.36
    USC Shoah Foundation, 200–1
    virtual Anne Frank, 177–79
Hołuj, Tadeusz, 133–34
Home: Aamir (VR film), 8
Horsten Soviet Prisoner of War Cemetery,
    234–35n.16
Hoskins, Andrew
    connective memory and digital gothic,
        203–4, 205–6, 207–8, 209–10, 213–14
    connective turn, 22
    Holocaust sublime, 257n.5
    on IWM exhibition, 193–94, 238n.55
    presentist media, 123–24, 182, 193–94
    restless past, 213–14
    virtual landscapes, 120–24
humanitarianism, 8, 9–10, 11, 24
human rights, 11, 25, 27–28, 125–26, 145–46
Hungarian survivors, 232n.68
Hutcheon, Linda, 17–18
Huyssen, Andreas, 14–15, 50, 120–21,
        123–24, 129–31, 133–34, 185–
        86, 200–1

hybrid testimony, 89–90
hyperconnectivity, 203–4
hyperreal, 4–5, 56, 156–57, 176

IBM, 4, 30–31, 168–69, 204
identification, 124–25, 148–50, 152–53,
        163–64, 184–85, 186–87
Illinois Holocaust Museum and Education
        Center, 7, 37–38, 39f, 51, 74f
immersive technologies
    Anne Frank VR films, 179–80
    Holocaust memory culture, 1–2, 3, 6,
        8, 9–10
    institutionalization of Holocaust
        memory culture, 26
    interactive memory projects, 31
    limits of connective memory, 22, 24, 25
    mixed reality, 257n.6
    Muselmann figure, 114, 115–16
    new technologies, 1–2
    Shoah Foundation, 7
    truth and truthfulness, 19
    videogames and virtual memory,
        114, 212–13
    virtual Holocaust memory
        terminology, 13, 16
    VR and empathy, 8, 9–10
immortality, 63–64, 65, 66, 67, 68
Imperial War Museum, 132–33, 134,
        187–89, 191–92, 193–94, 238n.55,
        252–53n.24
Imperial War Museum North (IWMN),
        184, 254n.44
institutionalization of Holocaust memory
        culture, 25–28
interactive biography, 2, 45, 221n.2,
        232n.67
interactive technology, 207–8, 257n.6
interactive video testimony
    definitions and terminology, 2, 221n.2
    entering Dimensions in
        Testimony, 35–60
    ghosting the museum, 61–82
    witness in the light stage, 83–116
International Committee of Memorial
        Museums in Remembrance of
        the Victims of Public Crimes
        (ICMEMO), 251n.6

Invisible (VR film), 8
iPad applications
    Bergen-Belsen and extermination of
        memory, 121–29
    Bergen-Belsen app and
        Topography, 184–87
    Bergen-Belsen memorial site, 3, 23–24,
        28–29, 153–54, 163–64, 205–7
    Bergen-Belsen reconstruction and
        digital installations, 129–31, 137–38
    Bergen-Belsen virtual
        landscapes, 119–21
    digital technology overview and
        future, 205–6
    images, 122*f*, 127*f*
    and Second Life Kristallnacht
        exhibition, 146–47, 149–50
    Secret Annex Online, 153–54
iPhones, 169
Ishiguro, Kazuo, *The Remains of the
    Day*, 30
Israel, 8, 107, 197–98, 231n.61, 255n.57
IWitness platform, 7
IWMN. *See* Imperial War Museum North

Jackson, Peter, *They Shall Not Grow Old*, 157
Jasenovac, Croatia, 132–33
Jentsch, Ernst, 141–42
Jewish Museum Berlin, 120–21, 184, 185–
    86, 189–93, 194–96, 252n.14, 252n.19
Jews and Jewish culture, 12, 61–62, 63, 67–
    68, 78–79, 232n.67, 237–38n.54
Johnson, Phylis, 142–43, 149–50
Johnston, Sean F., 4–5, 51–52, 55
"Joods Monument," 176–77

Kansteiner, Wulf
    analog Holocaust memory, 213–14
    Digital Memory Studies, 206–7
    digital technology future, 205–8
    exploitative aesthetics, 212
    historical non-simultaneity, 64
    Holocaust memory culture, 1–2, 26–27
    on holograms, 202–3, 205
    immersion and perpetrator
        politics, 212–13
    in *Probing the Ethics of Holocaust
        Culture*, 56–57, 208–9

spatiotemporalities, 72
sterile digital environment, 210–11
Kendrick, Ellie, 161–62, 246n.39, 246n.47
Kent, Evelyn Julia, 89–90
Kentridge, William, 200
Kershaw, Ian, 199–200
Kindertransport, 222n.7
Klevan, David, 139–40
Kluger, Ruth, "Halloween and a
    Ghost," 78–79
Knoch, Habbo, 131–32
Knowles, Anne Kelly, 168–69
Kohl, Helmut, 196–97
Kor, Eva, 49, 73
Kristallnacht exhibition, Second Life
    ending, 241n.103
    Holocaust memory culture, 3, 12, 20–
        21, 28–29
    images, 140*f*, 142*f*, 144*f*, 146*f*, 148*f*
    questions of complicity, 199–201
    and Secret Annex Online, 158–59
    virtual landscapes, 121, 129, 137
    and virtual memory, 139–50
Kubrick, Stanley, *2001: A Space Odyssey*, 4
Kugler, Victor, 244n.17
Kulka, Otto Dov, 161–62
Kushner, Tony, 123–24, 234–35n.16,
    235n.21, 242n.4
Kwoka, Czesława, 21
KZ-Aussenlager (satellite camps), 191–92,
    254n.43

LaCapra, Dominick, 16, 68–69, 186–87,
    226n.25
Lagerkrist, Amanda, 203–4
Lamont, Rosette, 219n.59
Landsberg, Alison
    Adams on, 233–34n.10
    Bergen-Belsen app and extermination
        of memory, 121–23, 125–26, 128–29
    Bergen-Belsen digital installations,
        134, 138–39
    connective memory and digital
        gothic, 203–4
    Engaging the Past, 139–40, 142–43,
        145–46, 155–56, 163–64, 177–79,
        242n.114, 242n.115, 244–45n.24,
        246n.45

historical knowledge, 128–29,
    134, 154–55
limits of connective memory, 24
overpresence, 163–64
prosthetic memory, 13–14, 146–47,
    153–54, 257n.9
Prosthetic Memory, 242n.114, 251n.5
on Second Life Kristallnacht exhibition,
    139–40, 142–43, 145–50, 239n.72
and Secret Annex Online, 153–56, 157–
    58, 162–64, 166–67, 177–79, 203–4
virtual Holocaust memory
    terminology, 16
virtual landscapes, 120–21
Lang, Berel, 49
Lang, Nikolaus, 193–94
Langer, Lawrence, 49, 50, 55–56, 99,
    101–3, 164–65, 202, 213–14, 223n.19,
    247n.62
Lanzmann, Claude, 28–29, 87–88, 100–1,
    125–26, 183
    Shoah documentary, 21–22, 50, 71,
        86–87, 124
The Last Goodbye (VR film), 7–8,
    9, 174–75
Laub, Dori, 18, 57, 68–69, 71–72, 84–85,
    90, 103–4, 256n.71
Le Druillenec, Hugh, 137–38
Lee, Carol Ann, 159–61, 166–67
Leitverantwortung, 196–97, 255n.54
Leopard, Dan, 73
Lety, Czech Republic, 132–33
Levinas, Emmanuel, 81–82, 101, 103–4
Levi, Primo
    "Afterword," 98–99
    on Anne Frank, 152, 243n.8
    If This Is a Man, 70, 98
    immersion and perpetrator
        politics, 212–13
    "The Memory of the Offence," 97–98
    memoryscapes, 145–46
    nature of the offence, 230n.41
    ocean of pain, 103–4
    remembering "the drowned," 112–14
    "Shemà," 70
    "Song of Those Who Died in Vain," 78–
        79, 227n.48
    stereotyped memory, 44, 97–98

survivor types, 110
The Truce, 98, 159–61
truth and truthfulness, 20–21
Levy, Daniel, 27–28, 120–21, 125–26, 197–
    201, 254n.41, 256n.63
liberation of camps, 1–2, 131–33, 134–35,
    235n.21
Libeskind, Daniel, 120–21, 185–86, 189–
    90, 191–96, 252n.14
Lifton, Robert Jay, 225–26n.21
LightShed, 9
Linden Lab, 139–40
Linenthal, Edward T., 61–62, 184,
    241n.102
literary studies, 208–10, 244–45n.24
Littell, Jonathan, *The Kindly Ones*, 186–87
Lore (film), 254–55n.47
Lucas, George, 53*f*
Luckhurst, Roger, 209–10, 225–26n.21
Lutz, Thomas, 184, 185–87, 197–98, 199–
    200, 251n.6, 253n.26

MachineGames, 29
machine learning, 6–7, 43–45, 48
Maio, Heather, 63–64, 109–10
Majdanek camp, 7, 9–10, 46–47, 54–55,
    69–70, 97, 174–75
maps, 210–12
Marcuse, Herbert, *One-
    Dimensional Man*, 4
Marrison, Kate, 259n.58
Marshall, Christopher, 185–86
Martin-Gropius-Bau, 191–92
mass graves, 83–84, 119–20, 123–24, 234–
    35n.16, 235–36n.25
Maus (Spiegelman), 213–14
Mauthausen concentration camp,
    7, 166–67
Mazzucato, Mariana, 27–28, 220n.77
McGlothlin, Erin, 184–85
McMullan, Thomas, 80–81
meaning, 124–26, 148–49, 163–64
media, 1–2, 64, 120–21, 128–29
Meed, Benjamin, 119–20
memorialization, 123–24, 126–27, 213–14,
    234n.13, 238n.59
memorials, 3, 27–28, 186–87, 189–90,
    200–1, 238n.59, 254n.43

Memorial to the Murdered Jews of Europe, Berlin (Eisenman memorial), 182, 184, 186–87, 193–96, 216n.9, 234n.13, 252n.19
memory. *See also* connective memory
collective memory, 75–76
computer memory, 13–14
deep memory, 19, 98, 99–100, 101–2, 103–4, 111–12
extermination of, 124, 137, 145–46, 205–6
and history, 19
Kristallnacht and virtual memory, 139–50
limits of connective memory, 21–25
meta-memory, 193–94, 254–55n.47
multidirectional memory, 13, 25, 126, 159–62, 196–97, 198–99
national memory, 119–20, 124–25, 200–1, 256n.72
palimpsestic memory and accessibility, 161–69
postmemory, 24–25, 107, 143–45
prosthetic memory, 13–14, 121, 146–47, 153–54, 163–64, 256n.71, 257n.9
stereotyped memory, 44, 48, 96–101, 103–4
testimony's spatiotemporalities, 69–70, 71, 72–73
transcultural memory, 161–62, 183, 198–99, 200–1, 256n.71
transgenerational memory, 24–25
virtual Holocaust memory terminology, 12, 13–16
memory crystal, 203–4, 257n.16
memoryscapes, 120–21, 129, 145–46, 149–50, 198–99
memory studies, 13–14, 121, 124, 207–8, 234n.13
Mendelsohn, Daniel, 172, 250n.85
Mengele, Josef, 36–37, 90–91
meta-memory, 193–94, 254–55n.47
metatexts, 23–24, 61–69, 70–71, 152–53, 161–63, 175, 211–12
military, 31, 147–48, 204
Milk, Chris, 9, 16, 152–53, 176–77
Minco, Marga, *Bitter Herbs*, 152
Minority Report (film), 52–53, 53*f*
mirrors, 14–16

Mitchell, Breanna, 3–4, 215–16n.8
Mitchell, Vallentine, 164–65
Mitläufer (culpability), 199–200
mixed reality, 257n.6
mobile technologies, 3–4, 129
modernism, 192–93, 209–10
monuments, 192–94
Monument to the Murdered Jews of Europe, Berlin, 3–4
Mooyart-Doubleday, Barbara, 155–57
Moses, A. Dirk, 197–98, 259n.57
Müller, Melissa, 248n.66
multidirectional memory, 13, 25, 126, 159–62, 196–97, 198–99
Muschamp, Herbert, 192–93
Muselmann figure, 113–14, 115–16
Museum of Jewish Heritage, New York
Dimensions in Testimony exhibition, 37–38, 41–44, 69–70, 77–78, 92, 94, 97, 202–3, 205–8
The Last Goodbye (VR film), 7
photographs, 42*f*, 47*f*, 80*f*
Eva Schloss testimony, 92, 94–95, 97
Museum of Tolerance, Los Angeles, 177–79, 189–90
museums
in Berlin, 189–92
Holocaust memory culture, 3
Huyssen on, 200–1
institutionalization of Holocaust memory culture, 26, 27–28
Linenthal on, 62
performing truthfulness, 58–59
postmodern museum, 120–21, 123–24, 182, 185–86, 189–90
tours and guides, 121–23
music, 141–42, 239n.71
Muslims, 113–14
My Mother's Wing (VR film), 8

Nanjing Massacre, 6–7, 37, 38–39, 198–99, 231n.58
national history, 256n.70
National Holocaust Centre and Museum, UK, 40, 65–66, 106, 222n.7, 230n.40, 232n.65
national memory, 119–20, 124–25, 200–1, 256n.72

natural language processing, 2, 6–7, 36–
    37, 43, 44, 48, 92, 96–97
Nazism
    Anne's Amsterdam app, 170–71
    architecture, 191–93
    artifacts, 186–87
    Eichmann Trial, 38, 67–68, 72, 83–85
    Holocaust education, 109
    Holocaust knowledge, 27–28
    kitsch sentimentality, 254–55n.47
    Kristallnacht and virtual memory, 140–
        41, 145–46
    liberation of camps, 1–2, 131–33, 134–
        35, 235n.21
    national history, 256n.70
    Nazi trials overview, 18, 83–84
    Nuremberg Trials, 83–84
    perpetrators and impiety, 28–29, 30–31
    Topography of Terror, 184, 185–89,
        191–93, 196–97, 198–200, 254n.41
    Treblinka Trials, 187–89, 188*f*
    videogames and immersion, 212–13
    virtual Holocaust memory
        terminology, 12
negative sacralization, 68–69, 226n.25
neo-Nazism, 186–87, 253n.26
Neuengamme concentration camp, 126–
    27, 128*f*, 136–37, 136*f*, 166–67, 205–
    6, 236n.34, 238n.58, 238n.59
Neukölln countermemorial, 191–93, 194–96
new memory, 123–24
new technology, 50, 205–10, 213–14
Niemoller, Pastor Martin, 147–48
Nietzsche, Friedrich, 58
Night and Fog (film), 23–24, 123–
    24, 137–38
The Night Porter (film), 140–41
The Night Watch (Rembrandt
    painting), 177–79
9/11 (September 11 attacks), 15, 234n.13
nonhuman consciousness, 4–5, 6
Notley, Tanya, 258n.29
Novick, Peter, 61–62, 67–68, 75–76, 220n.76
N-RAS (Centre for Neuro-Robotics and
    Autonomous Systems), 234n.13
Nuremberg Trials, 83–84

Ober-Ramstadr, 199–200

Oculus headsets, 176, 177–79
oral histories, 3–4, 18, 38–39, 43, 57, 66,
    84–85, 105–6, 107
oral testimony, 70–76, 112
Otto Weidt's Workshop for the
    Blind, 189–90
Ozick, Cynthia, 164–65

Palestinian-Israeli conflict, 197–98,
    255n.57
palimpsestic memory and
    accessibility, 161–69
palimpsestic testimony, 23–24, 129–31,
    149–50, 152–53, 175–76, 180–81,
    205–6, 211–12
Parisi, Luciana, 13–14
Patraka, Vivian M., 23–24, 58–60, 62, 200
Pearce, Caroline, 119–20, 192–93, 194–96,
    253n.28, 255n.54
"Pepper's ghost," 51, 52
performativity, 58–60, 69, 78, 83–88
perpetrator perspectives
    Bergen-Belsen installations, 138–39
    Dimensions in Testimony, 205–6
    female perpetrators, 187–89, 193–94
    Kansteiner on, 212–13
    perpetrators and impiety, 28–32
    Second Life Kristallnacht exhibition,
        139–40, 141–42, 143–46
    Secret Annex Online, 167–69
    technological inventions, 168–69
    Topography of Terror, 182–89, 197–98,
        199–200
    videogames and virtual
        memory, 212–13
Persecution and Resistance in Amsterdam
    (pamphlet), 245n.26
Pfeffer, Fritz, 155–56, 159–61, 166–
    67, 177–79
photographs
    Bergen-Belsen iPad app, 129–
        31, 149–50
    color use, 21, 22, 155–58
    historical memory, 50
    Ober-Ramstadr, 199–200
    Second Life Kristallnacht exhibition,
        140–41, 143–45, 199–200
    Topography of Terror, 184–85

photographs (*cont.*)
  truth and truthfulness, 21, 156–61, 176–77
  virtual Anne Frank and Secret Annex Online, 155–58, 159–62, 176–77, 211–12, 244n.20
Plath, Sylvia, 17–18
Plötzensee memorial, Berlin, 238n.59
poetics of virtual Holocaust memory, 17–32
  institutionalization of Holocaust memory culture, 25–28
  limits of connective memory, 21–25
  overview, 17–18
  perpetrators and impiety, 28–32
  truth and truthfulness, 18–21
poetry, 17–18, 133–34
Pokemon Go app, 171–72
postmemory, 24–25, 107, 143–45
postmodern architecture, 189–93
postmodernism, 1–2, 4–5, 56–57, 155–56, 207–8
postmodern museum, 120–21, 123–24, 182, 185–86, 189–90
post-scarcity culture, 205–6, 258n.29
poststructuralism, 73–74, 208–9
Powers, Barbara, 89–92
presentist media, 123–24, 182, 193–94
President's Commission on the Holocaust, 63
Presner, Todd, 56–57, 162–63, 167–69, 176–77, 208–9
Pressler, Mirjam, 163–64, 248n.66
Prinz-Albrecht-Palais, Berlin, 194–96, 254n.41
Probing the Ethics of Holocaust Culture (Fogu et al.), 1–2, 168–69, 208–10, 258–59n.40
Probing the Limits of Representation: Nazism and the "Final Solution" (Friedländer), 1–2, 21–22, 56–57, 140–41, 208–9
Prose, Francine, 246n.42
prosthetic memory, 13–14, 121, 146–47, 153–54, 163–64, 256n.71, 257n.9
Proust, Marcel, 14–15
psychoanalysis, 18, 57–58, 85

Radermacher, Norbert, 191–92, 194–96, 254n.43

Raguhn concentration camp, 248n.66
Rapson, Jennifer, 167–68
Ravensbrück concentration camp, 12, 57–58, 124–25, 128–29, 187–89, 193–94, 254–55n.47
Reading, Anna, 257n.17, 258n.29
reading the virtual
  Topography of Terror and resistance to the virtual, 182–201
  virtual Anne Frank, 151–81
  virtual landscapes, 119–50
real, and virtual, 14–15
realism, 22, 23–24, 209–10
Real Violence (Wolfson artwork), 10–11, 28–29, 30
recoloring images, 21, 22
Redfield, Marc, 15
refugees, 9–10, 198–99, 256n.63
Reich, Walter, 105
Reichsluftfahrtministerium, 191–93, 253n.38
Reilly, Jo, 235n.21
The Remains of the Day (film), 30
Rembrandt van Rijn, *The Night Watch*, 177–79
representation, 21–23, 115–16, 121–23, 185–86, 244–45n.24, 258–59n.40
Resnais, Alain, *Night and Fog*, 23–24, 123–24, 137–38
Return of the Jedi (film), 54
Richardson, Michael, 212–13
Richter, Max, 141–42, 239n.71
Rogue One: A Star Wars Story (film), 224n.35, 224n.36, 224n.38
Rose, Gillian, *Mourning Becomes the Law*, 30
Rosencraft, Yossele, 237–38n.54
Rosenfeld, Alvin, 247n.62
Rothberg, Michael
  bystander complicity, 200
  implicated subject, 10–11, 212–13
  minimalist definition of memory, 13–14
  multidirectional memory, 25, 161–62
  Multidirectional Memory, 13, 197–98
  overlapping memory, 196–98
  Palestinian-Israeli conflict, 197–98, 255n.57
Roth, Philip, *The Ghost Writer*, 242–43n.5, 247n.59

Rousseau, Jean-Jacques, 11
Rowland, Antony, 17–18
Rowlands, Mark, 4–5
Rudashewski, Jitshok, 251n.3
Rudof, Joanne, 49, 50, 51
Rürup, Reinhard, 193–94
Russia, 94–95
Russian-speaking survivors, 110–12, 232n.67
Rwandan Genocide, 6–7, 38–39, 198–99

Sachsenhausen concentration camp, 133–34, 183, 193–96, 242–43n.5, 254n.43
sacralization of survivors, 66–69, 115–16
Sagebiel, Ernst, 253n.38
Santner, Eric, 197–98
Schaft, Hannie, 152
Schindler, Oscar, 231n.61
Schindler's List (film), 6–7, 38–39, 61–62, 66, 68, 104–12, 115–16, 157
Schloss, Erich, 87–88
Schloss, Eva
    After Auschwitz, 89–90, 92–93, 94, 95–96, 229–30n.36
    on death of mother, 102–3
    Dimensions in Testimony interview, 35–38, 40, 86–98, 99–104, 107–8, 109–10, 112, 203, 205–6
    Eva's Story, 89–90, 91–92, 93–94, 95–96, 229–30n.36
    and Anne Frank, 36–37, 41–43, 45–46, 88–90, 91–92, 96, 109–10, 152
    photographs, 36f, 87f
    The Promise: The True Story of a Family in the Holocaust, 89–92, 95–96, 99–101, 229–30n.36
    on sexual abuse, 92–93, 94–96, 112, 138–39
    on sexual topics, 93–96
    speech recognition technology, 258n.27
    stereotyped memory, 96–98, 99
    virtual Schloss, 37–38, 41–43, 45–46, 64, 65, 79–80, 92, 94–95, 97, 108, 109–10, 180–81
Schloss, Heinz, 87–88, 89–90, 91, 93, 101–2
Schröder, Gerhard, 198–99
Schwarz, Daniel, 159–61

science fiction, 4–5, 6, 52–53, 55–56, 113–14
Scott, Ridley, *Blade Runner*, 4–5
Second Life
    images, 140f, 142f, 144f, 146f, 148f
    Kristallnacht exhibition and complicity, 199–201
    Kristallnacht exhibition and virtual memory, 139–50
    Kristallnacht exhibition overview, 3, 20–21, 28–29, 121, 158–59, 199–201
Secret Annex Online
    awards, 155–56
    bystander perspective, 30
    context and development, 153–61, 211–12
    Dutch and German cultures, 246n.47
    images, 156f, 158f, 159f, 161f
    Landsberg on, 203–4
    model, 244n.16
    palimpsestic memory and accessibility, 23–24, 161–69
    virtual Anne Frank overview, 10–11, 151, 152–53, 169
    virtual landscapes, 124–25, 126, 128–31, 133–35, 137–38, 147–48
    VR films and tours, 174–81
Self, Will, 204–5
selfies, 3–4, 215–16n.8, 216n.9
September 11 attacks (9/11), 15, 234n.13
sexual abuse, 92–93, 94–96, 112, 138–39
sexual topics, 93–96
Shakespeare, William, 77–78
    Hamlet, 76–77, 81–82
Shandler, Jeffrey, 64–65
Shapira, Shahak, 3–4
Sheffield Doc/Fest, 26, 37–38, 77–78
Sheleg, Yair, 255n.57
Shenker, Noah, 25, 104–5, 106, 109–10
Shoah, 12, 212, 232n.68
Shoah (documentary), 21–22, 50, 71, 86–87, 124
Shoah Foundation. *See* USC Shoah Foundation
Silent Heroes' Memorial Centre, 189–90, 252n.14
Silicon Valley, 10, 31, 37
Silverman, Kaja, 148–49

Silverman, Max, 161–62
simulacra, 137, 138–39, 140–41, 155–56, 158–59, 175
simulations, 20, 31, 72, 73, 158–59
6x9 (VR film), 8
smartphones, 169, 170–71, 176, 203–4, 205–6
Smith, Stephen, 10, 26, 43, 77–78, 109–10, 222n.7
Snyder, Timothy, *Black Earth*, 27–28, 221n.83
social media, 1–2, 3–4, 27, 203–4, 216n.9
social memory, 163–64
Sonderkommando, 57, 110
sound, 149–50, 155–56, 158–59, 161–62, 239n.71
South Africa, 90, 198–99
Soviet Union, 110, 232n.67
spatiotemporalities, 69–73
SPECS ("Synthetic Perceptive, Emotive and Cognitive Systems"), 121–23, 124, 129–37, 234n.13, 236n.33
spectrality, 15–16, 75–76, 81–82, 225n.5, 227n.44
speech recognition technology, 36–38, 44–45, 256–57n.4, 258n.27
Spiegelman, Art, *Maus*, 213–14
Spielberg, Steven
    and Dimensions in Testimony, 45–46, 104–5
    Minority Report, 52–53, 53f
    Schindler's List, 6–7, 38–39, 104–6, 157, 231n.54, 232n.68
    Survivors of the Shoah Visual History Foundation, 104–5
    USC Shoah Foundation, 52–53, 104–5, 232n.68
    Visual History Archive, 6–7, 38–39, 105, 232n.68
Spitzer, Leo, 19, 219n.59
Srebnik, Simon, 87–88, 124
SS (Schutzstaffel), 168–69, 184, 187–90, 194–96, 198–200, 204, 252–53n.24, 253n.33
Stand + Stare, 205–6
Star Wars films, 53–56, 53f, 54f, 224nn.35–36, 224n.38
Stedelijk museum, Amsterdam, 241n.103

Steinbach, Erica, 198–99
stereotyped memory, 44, 48, 96–101, 103–4
Stern, Martin, 230n.40
Stewart, Victoria, 164–65, 243–44n.15
Stier, Oren Baruch, 243n.7
Stolpersteine ("stumbling stones"), 189–90, 190f
Stone, Dan, 252n.16
Sudan, 258n.29
Suicide Machine, 203–4
Superman (film), 51–52
Superman Memory Crystal, 203–4, 257n.16
survivor memory, 13, 44, 68, 72
survivors
    mortality, 2–3
    sacralization of, 66–69, 115–16
    selection of, 109–11
Survivors of the Shoah Visual History Foundation, 104–5
Survivor Stories Experience, 37–38
survivor testimony. *See also* virtual survivors
    digital connectivity, 207–8
    Dimensions in Testimony, 31, 37–38, 57, 222n.7
    Holocaust memory culture, 7
    Holocaust testimony periodization, 18, 38–40
    Kristallnacht and virtual memory, 145–46
    limits of connective memory, 24–25
    National Holocaust Centre and Museum, 232n.65
    performative construction, 23–24
    performing truthfulness, 56–57
    remembering "the drowned," 112, 113–14
    Eva Schloss testimony, 35–36, 37–38
    truth and truthfulness, 18, 56–57
    USC Shoah Foundation core belief, 109
    virtual Holocaust memory terminology, 16
    Visual History Archive origins, 104–5
Sznaider, Natan, 27–28, 120–21, 125–26, 197–201, 254n.41, 256n.63

tablet apps, 121–23, 124–25, 126–29. *See also* iPad applications

Der Tagesspiegel (newspaper), 193–94
Tangible Memories app, 205–6
technology
    awkward poetics, 184
    connective memory and digital
        gothic, 203–5
    cultural life of Holocaust
        holograms, 50, 51
    digital technology overview and future,
        202, 205–10, 213–14
    Dimensions in Testimony metatext,
        63–64, 65, 69
    and extermination of memory,
        124, 128–29
    Holocaust memory culture, 3–5, 6
    perpetrators and impiety, 30–31
    science fiction, 6
    videogames and virtual memory, 212–13
    virtual Anne Frank overview, 151–53
    virtual landscapes overview, 119–21
television, 1–2, 4–5, 6, 140–41
Tempelhof airport, Berlin, 253n.38
Terdiman, Richard, 13–14
Terminator (film), 141–42
terrorism, 15–16
testimony
    digital technology overview and
        future, 205–9
    Dimensions in Testimony, 7, 31, 35–36,
        37–38, 57, 205–9, 222n.7
    filmed testimony, 69–70, 73
    history and testimony, 133–34
    Holocaust memory culture, 7, 9
    Holocaust testimony periodization,
        18–19, 38–40
    hybrid testimony, 89–90
    Kristallnacht and virtual memory, 145–46
    limits of connective memory, 24–25
    moment of testifying, 69–70
    National Holocaust Centre and
        Museum, 232n.65
    oral testimony, 70–76, 112
    palimpsestic testimony, 23–24, 129–31,
        149–50, 152–53, 175–76, 180–81,
        205–6, 211–12
    performativity, 23–24, 56–57, 83–88
    perpetrators and impiety, 32
    reception of, 69–71
    remembering "the drowned," 112, 113–14
    testimony's spatiotemporalities, 51, 69–73
    truth and truthfulness, 18, 56–57
    USC Shoah Foundation core belief, 109
    virtual Anne Frank, 152–53, 161–62
    virtual Holocaust memory
        terminology, 16
    Visual History Archive origins, 104–5
    written testimony, 69–71, 112, 213–14
Thacker, Andrew, 202
Theresienstadt camp, 230n.40, 248n.66,
    258n.27
They Shall Not Grow Old (film), 157
Topography of Terror, Berlin, 182–201
    documentation center, 184, 189–96
    exhibition trench, Berlin Wall, and
        resistance to transcultural memory,
        196–201
    extermination of memory, 126, 129
    images, 183*f*, 188*f*, 191*f*, 193*f*
    limits of connective memory, 25
    "1945 in Postwar German Cinema"
        exhibition, 187–89
    overview, 182–83
    permanent exhibition space, 184–89
    perpetrators and impiety, 28–29
    truth and truthfulness, 19
    visitor numbers, 119–20
Topol, Jáchym, *The Devil's
    Workshop*, 114–16
tourism, 170–71, 174–75, 189–90, 194–96,
    241–42n.109
trace, 124
transcultural memory, 161–62, 183, 198–
    99, 200–1, 256n.71
transgenerational memory, 24–25
Traum, David, 43, 44
trauma, 15, 16–17, 18, 31, 48, 57, 78–79,
    87–88, 121, 209–10
Treblinka Trials, 187–89, 188*f*
Trezise, Bryony, 239n.72
"The Trial Concerning the Reich Security
    Main Office" (artwork), 187–89, 188*f*
trials
    Eichmann Trial, 38, 67–68, 72, 83–85
    Nazi trials overview, 18, 83–84
    Nuremberg Trials, 83–84
    Treblinka Trials, 187–89, 188*f*

Tribunella, Eric, 106
Trümmerfrauen ("rubble women"),
    254n.41
Trump, Donald, 27–28, 221n.83
truth and truthfulness
    Bergen-Belsen digital
        installations, 134–37
    and Delbo, 69, 92, 95–96, 128–29, 138–
        39, 152–53
    digital technology overview and future,
        208–9, 213–14
    Dimensions in Testimony, 48, 55–56,
        70–71, 92, 95–96
    Forever Project, 67
    limits of connective memory, 21–22
    performing truthfulness, 56–60, 78
    photographs, 21, 156–61, 176–77
    poetics of virtual Holocaust
        memory, 18–21
    post-truth and Trump, 27–28
    Secret Annex Online, 137–38, 156–
        61, 165–66
    Shoah documentary, 71–72
    testimony's spatiotemporalities, 70–73
    Topography of Terror, 187–89
    virtual Anne Frank, 152–53, 163–66,
        175, 176–77, 179–81
    virtual landscapes overview, 120–
        21, 128–29
    Williams on, 69
turbo-capitalism, 1–2, 20–21
Tuschinski theater, Amsterdam, 171–72
2001: A Space Odyssey (film), 4–5, 6

uncanny, 73, 75–76, 81–82, 121, 141–43,
    145–46, 148–50, 179–81
unheimlich, 73, 140–45, 146–49, 153–54,
    158–59, 240n.94
United Nations (UN), 24, 27–28, 45–46
United Nations Virtual Reality (UNVR)
    series, 8, 9, 24
United States Holocaust Memorial
    Museum (USHMM)
    activism and empathy, 11
    Americanization of Holocaust, 106
    America, virtual mythologies, and
        eternity narrative, 61–64
    architecture, 191–93

Birkenau model, 187–89
Dimensions in Testimony pilot
    exhibition, 37–38, 41–43, 46–47, 63–
    64, 66, 223n.29
Hall of Remembrance, 147–48
historiography, 132–33
institutionalization of Holocaust
    memory culture, 25, 27–28
limits of connective memory, 23–24, 25
Linenthal response, 184
original design concerns, 184–89
performing truthfulness, 59–60
quotation choice for, 241n.102
Second Life Kristallnacht exhibition, 3,
    20–21, 28–29, 139–40, 199–200
Topography of Terror and technology,
    184–89, 191–93
virtual Holocaust memory
    terminology, 12
Universal Declaration of Human
    Rights, 27–28
University of Southern California (USC),
    51. *See also* USC Institute for
    Creative Technologies; USC Shoah
    Foundation
the unsayable, 22, 93, 112, 115–16
UNVR. *See* United Nations Virtual Reality
    (UNVR) series
USC Institute for Creative Technologies,
    31, 36f, 37, 86f, 87f
USC Shoah Foundation
    digital technology future, 205–6, 207–8
    Dimensions in Testimony and
        holograms, 49, 51, 52–53, 200–1, 203
    Dimensions in Testimony interviews,
        88–89, 109–10, 203
    Dimensions in Testimony overview,
        2–3, 6–7, 37, 40, 45, 64, 203
    Dimensions in Testimony public
        responses, 49, 51–52
    founding and aims, 104–5, 106, 107,
        108, 109–10, 121
    Hirsch on, 2–3
    Holocaust memory culture, 6–7, 9–
        10, 11
    institutionalization of Holocaust
        memory culture, 25, 27–28
    interactive biography, 2, 45, 221n.2

The Last Goodbye (VR film), 7
limits of connective memory, 24
"New Dimensions in Testimony"
    flyer, 63–64
performing truthfulness, 58–59
Russian-speaking survivors, 232n.67
and Spielberg, 52–53, 104–5, 232n.68
Survivors of the Shoah Visual History
    Foundation, 104–5
technology, 64, 78–79, 203, 205–
    6, 207–8
testimony's spatiotemporalities, 70–71
"Theory of Change," 106, 108
Visual History Archive (VHA), 6–7,
    38–39, 88–89, 106
VR and empathy, 9–10, 11
USHMM. *See* United States Holocaust
    Memorial Museum

Valéry, Paul, 186–87
van de Velde, Maarten, 244n.21
Van Pels, Auguste, 248n.66
Van Pels, Peter, 165–67, 174–75, 177–80
Vergangenheitsbewältigung ("coming to
    terms with the past"), 197–98
Verschure, Paul, 131–32, 234n.13
vexed aesthetics, 121, 152–53, 185–86, 212
VHA. *See* Visual History Archive
victims, and perpetrators, 10–11, 16,
    28–29, 30–31, 32, 67–68, 110–11,
    143–46, 212
video calls, 73–74, 223n.29
videogames, 20–21, 28–29, 30–31, 49, 114,
    212–13, 259n.58
video testimonies, 6–7, 49, 64–65, 68–73.
    See also interactive video testimony
violence, 30–31, 32, 137–38, 204–5, 212
Virilio, Paul, 1–2
virtual (concept/definitions), 12, 14–17,
    20, 209–10, 218n.36
virtual Anne Frank, 151–81
    Anne's Amsterdam app and digital
        metatext, 169–74
    overview, 151–53
    palimpsestic memory and
        accessibility, 161–69
    Secret Annex Online, 153–61
    VR films and tours, 174–81

virtual Holocaust memory
    definitions and terminology, 12–17,
        218n.36
    digital technology overview and
        future, 202–14
    entering Dimensions in
        Testimony, 35–60
    ghosting the museum, 61–82
    institutionalization of Holocaust
        memory culture, 25–28
    limits of connective memory, 21–25
    perpetrators and impiety, 28–32
    poetics of, 17–32
    Topography of Terror and resistance to
        the virtual, 182–201
    truth and truthfulness, 18–21
    virtual Anne Frank, 151–81
    virtual landscapes, 119–50
    witness in the light stage, 83–116
virtual landscapes, 119–50
    digital installations and reconstruction
        of Bergen-Belsen, 129–39
    iPads and the extermination of
        memory, 121–29
    Kristallnacht and virtual
        memory, 139–50
    overview, 119–21
virtual memory, 13–15, 124, 142–43, 152,
    183, 194–96, 198–99, 254n.43
"virtual panorama," Wiener Library,
    London, 131–35, 131*f*, 135*f*, 137
virtual reality (VR)
    Auschwitz-Birkenau VR model trial, 8
    Bergen-Belsen digital installations, 134
    definitions and terminology, 14, 16,
        142–43, 235n.18
    empathy, 8, 9–11, 22, 167–68
    exposure therapy, 31
    headsets, 175–76, 177–79
    Holocaust memory culture, 1–2, 3
    mixed reality, 257n.6
    Second Life Kristallnacht
        exhibition, 142–43
    truth and truthfulness, 20–21
    videogames, 212–13
    VR films, 7–8, 9–10
    VR films and virtual Anne Frank, 8,
        151–53, 174–81, 203–4, 213–14

virtual survivors
  Dimensions in Testimony, 16, 17, 64,
    69–70, 77–78, 79–80, 81–82, 94, 103–
    4, 108, 110–12
  Forever Project, 110–11
  holograms, 58–59
  remembering "the drowned," 113–14
  traumatic syntax of virtual
    conversations, 41–43, 45–46
virtual trauma, 15, 16, 239n.72
virtual worlds, 3, 32, 139–40, 149–50,
  242n.113
visor effect, 81–82
Visual History Archive (VHA)
  Dimensions in Testimony, 43
  founding and aims, 6–7, 18, 38–39
  influence of *Schindler's List*, 104–5,
    106, 107
  Eva Schloss testimony, 88–89, 94, 96–
    97, 103–4
  Shandler on video testimony, 64
  Shenker on, 104–5, 106, 109–10
  and Spielberg, 6–7, 38–39, 105, 232n.68
  video testimonies, 64, 103–4, 108
  written and oral testimonies, 112
voice recognition technology, 36–38, 44–
  45, 256–57n.4, 258n.27
Voskuijel, Bep, 162–63
VR. *See* virtual reality

Waffen SS, 253n.33
Walden, Victoria Grace, 126–31, 137–39,
  218n.36, 233n.4, 257n.6
Waltz with Bashir (film), 239n.71
Wannsee Conference, 12
Wannsee villa, 254–55n.47
War of Words: Soldier-Poets of the Somme
  (television show), 235n.18
"War on Terror," 15
Warsinger, Susan, 241n.105
Waves of Grace (VR film), 38–39
Waxman, Zoe, 95–96, 229n.31
Web 2.0 Suicide Machine, 203–4
Weidt, Otto, 189–90
Weinberg, Jeshajahu, 185–86, 241n.103
Wenzel, Jürgen, 193–94
Westworld (television series), 4–5, 202,
  203, 209–10, 256–57n.4

White, Hayden, 209–10, 244–45n.24
Wiener Library, London, 131–35,
  131*f*, 135*f*
Wiesel, Elie, 45–46, 63, 147–48, 239n.69,
  241n.102
Wieviorka, Annette, 18
Williams, Bernard, 19, 69
Wilms, Ursula, 191–92, 193–94
witnessing. *See* Holocaust witnessing
witness in the light stage, 83–116
  cracks in the light stage, 99–104
  enduring influence of *Schindler's
    List*, 104–11
  Eva Schloss's Dimensions in Testimony
    interview, 88–96
  performative methodologies, 83–88
  remembering "the drowned," 111–16
  stereotyped memory, 96–99
witness statements, 128–29, 138–39
Witsel, Anton, 244n.20
Wolfenstein (videogame series), 29, 212
Wolfson, Jordan, *Real Violence*, 10–11,
  28–29, 30
Wollheim, Norbert, 237–38n.54
women
  Delbo on Women's Camp, 210–12
  female perpetrators, 187–89, 193–94
  women's lives in Holocaust, 95–96
Woolf, Stuart, 230n.41
World Trade Center, 15
Wprost (newspaper), 198–99
written testimony, 69–71, 112, 213–14

Xia Shuqin, 222n.4, 231n.58

Yale University, 84–85, 99
  Fortunoff Video Archive for Holocaust
    Testimonies, 38–39, 50, 70–71, 84–
    85, 223n.19
Yaron, Sophie, 90–91
Yiddish, 83–84
Yolocaust project, 3–4, 216n.9
Yoselewska, Rivka, 83–84
Young, James
  Anne's Amsterdam and projection, 170–
    72, 173–74
  At Memory's Edge, 234n.13, 248–49n.69
  on Attie, 169

Bergen-Belsen memorial site, 123–24
Eisenman memorial, 234n.13
on memorials, 186–87, 238nn.58–
    59, 251n.7
national memory, 256n.72
on Neuengamme camp, 238n.58
normalization of memory, 192–
    93, 196–97
The Texture of Memory, 194–96,
    238nn.58–59, 251n.7
Topography of Terror, 192–97, 254n.41
virtual Anne Frank, 244n.20,
    248–49n.69

Žižek, Slavoj, *Violence*, 125–26
Zumthor, Peter, 191–92, 193–94